The Newark Frontier

HISTORICAL STUDIES OF URBAN AMERICA

*Edited by Lilia Fernández, Timothy J. Gilfoyle, Becky M. Nicolaides,
and Amanda Seligman*

James R. Grossman, editor emeritus

Also in the series:

Additional series titles follow index

The Newark Frontier

Community Action in the Great Society

MARK KRASOVIC

To Doug Doyle —
A mighty voice on the
Newark frontier —
With much gratitude,
Mark Krasovic

The University of Chicago Press
Chicago and London

Mark Krasovic is assistant professor of history and American studies and associate director of the Clement A. Price Institute on Ethnicity, Culture, and the Modem Experience at Rutgers University–Newark.

The University of Chicago Press, Chicago 60637
The University of Chicago Press, Ltd., London
© 2016 by The University of Chicago.
All rights reserved. Published 2016.
Printed in the United States of America

25 24 23 22 21 20 19 18 17 16   1 2 3 4 5

ISBN-13: 978-0-226-35279-4 (cloth)
ISBN-13: 978-0-226-35282-4 (e-book)
DOI: 10.7208/chicago/9780226352824.001.0001

Library of Congress Cataloging-in-Publication Data

Krasovic, Mark, author.
    The Newark frontier : community action in the Great Society / Mark Krasovic.
        pages cm — (Historical studies of urban America)
        Includes bibliographical references and index.
        ISBN 978-0-226-35279-4 (cloth : alk. paper) — ISBN 978-0-226-35282-4 (e-book)   1. Newark (N.J.)—History—20th century.   2. Newark (N.J.)—Social policy.   3. Race riots—New Jersey—Newark.   4. Social action—New Jersey—Newark—History—20th century.   5. Newark (N.J.)—Politics and government—20th century.   6. Liberalism—United States.   7. United States—Social policy.   8. Community activists—New Jersey—Newark.
9. United States—History—1945–   I. Title.   II. Series: Historical studies of urban America.
        F144.N657K73 2016
        974.9'32—dc23

                                                                                2015035008

♾ This paper meets the requirements of ANSI/NISO Z39.48-1992 (Permanence of Paper).

For Louis and Frances Krasovic and Clement A. Price

CONTENTS

INTRODUCTION: PLOTTING THE GREAT SOCIETY
AND THE URBAN CRISIS IN NEWARK

Lyndon Johnson had used the phrase several times before—at a hundred-dollar-a-plate fund-raiser in Chicago, for example, where supporters dined on filet mignon and serenaded the president with a rendition of "Deep in the Heart of Texas" before he left on a tour of poverty areas. He used it again in Atlanta, before a crowd of Georgia legislators and at another fund-raiser in Atlantic City, where he spoke from the same stage at which he would later that year accept his party's nomination for a full term. What exactly it meant, no one could say for sure. It was used too off-handedly, with no specifics and no explanation. It was little more than a placeholder, "a fragment of rhetorical stuffing," as his speechwriter later called it, a phrase in search of a meaning.[1]

In that way, it mirrored the new administration. Burdened by the doubt and suspicion of Kennedy supporters both in and out of the White House, Johnson worked to assure them not only that he shared their ideals but that he could make them a legislative reality. In his first State of the Union speech in January 1964, he committed himself to Kennedy's nascent anti-poverty and civil rights programs. In February, he signed Kennedy's long-proposed tax cut. It had been, by those measures, an exuberant and accomplished few months. But Johnson could claim only partial credit for those successes. The need to distinguish his presidency from the previous one, to at once fulfill Kennedy's promise and go beyond it, weighed on him heavily. He said as much one day in early April 1964, while skinny-dipping in the White House pool with his speechwriter and a close aide. He asked them to craft a vision of his presidency that would define a new national purpose and outline a plan to aggressively pursue it. The deadline, he explained, was May 22, when he would address a crowd of about eighty-five thousand in the University of Michigan football stadium.[2]

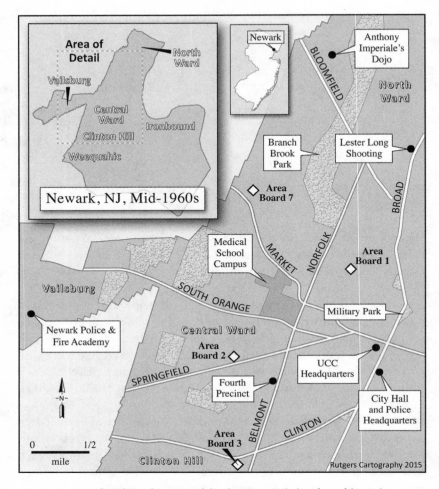

1. Newark in the mid-1960s, with key locations, including four of the city's antipoverty area boards. (Michael Siegel, Rutgers Cartography)

At Ann Arbor, Johnson relaunched his administration and pulled it out of his predecessor's shadow with a repurposed phrase, ceasing its casual use and hanging his presidency firmly on it. After tentatively circling each other for several months, the administration committed itself to "the Great Society," and "the Great Society" became the inescapable byword of the administration. The vision contained therein and offered to Michigan's graduating class—and soon to the rest of the nation—was firmly planted in the historic dilemmas of the moment. Johnson asked Americans what they would do with their hard-won postwar affluence: would they place their riches in the service of their higher aspirations, or would they allow "un-bridled growth" and base commercial desires to trump those ambitions? The Great Society would result if they chose the first path, the merely rich and powerful society if the second.[3]

To get there, though, the nation would have to alleviate the needs of *all* Americans. In this vision, affluence was widespread but not perfectly distributed. The work of building the Great Society, Johnson suggested, should begin where the need was greatest, where the dire costs of run-away growth were clearest. It would begin, he said, in the cities. By that point, a large literature, growing out of an even longer tradition of writing on the possibilities and pitfalls of metropolitan expansion, had established America's inner cities as the capitals of economic contradiction, spaces at the center of dynamic regional conurbations that only rarely shared in their wealth. By the time Lyndon Johnson stepped on the stage in Ann Arbor, Detroit's creeping urban agglomeration on the horizon, there was widespread agreement that we had reached a moment of decision—of crisis—in the cities.[4]

When the president debuted the Great Society that sunny day in May 1964, he staked the future of his administration on what might become of the cities. But he didn't stake it on what his administration could ac-complish alone. On the contrary, he acknowledged that, while there were numerous federal programs targeting the problems that stood in the way of the Great Society—the following year a congressional committee would count thirteen different federal departments and agencies involved in at least forty different urban development programs—"I do not pretend that we have the full answer to those problems." But he did promise one thing: "We are going to assemble the best thought and the broadest knowledge from all over the world to find those answers for America." These best minds would generate the experimentation sorely needed in a nation fac-ing the contradictions of postwar prosperity. Because those contradictions were most evident in the cities, the work would start there, on what the president called "the frontier of imagination and innovation."[5]

From its outset, then, the Great Society sought to address a problem of knowledge production. Despite its expanded postwar activity and its ap-parent success in fostering widespread affluence, the federal bureaucracy did not know how to bring that prosperity to the remaining redoubts of poverty. Newer, fresher knowledge would need to be found and brought into the workings of the state. In Ann Arbor, President Johnson called for a "creative federalism," a new concept of cooperation "between the national capital and the leaders of local communities" to achieve those ends. Most immediately, he announced the formation of various "working groups" to begin that effort.[6]

Seated behind President Johnson on the dais in Michigan Stadium, listening to him lay out his plans, Roger Lowenstein turned to a friend and rolled his eyes. He was among those Americans who were very skeptical of the Texan. As student-body president, it was his duty to recommend a commencement speaker to the university president, and he had really wanted John F. Kennedy there that day. But after the assassination, the invitation had passed to Kennedy's successor.[7]

Skepticism of the man may have been warranted, but the Great Society was much bigger than the president. Launching it via a set of small ad hoc working groups, Johnson yoked the Great Society to a class of administrative tools that would quickly carry its work well beyond the White House, to a greater pool of knowledge, new ways of thinking, and new political desires. In the search for the new knowledge out of which the Great Society would be built, those administrative structures took hold in specific places, where they encountered the particularities of local history and politics. Through such encounters, the state would be stretched in new directions, pulled by the innovation and imagination that Johnson called for but whose consequences he could not foresee. Nowhere was this truer than in Roger Lowenstein's hometown of Newark, New Jersey, where the work of local reformers and activists (Roger's father among them) had laid groundwork that would make Newark the Great Society's greatest laboratory, where its imagination would be stretched to its frontier.

Newark was no stranger to the midcentury depredations then being gathered under the label "urban crisis." It lay at the exact center of what Yale researchers in 1955 described as a six-hundred-mile-long urban agglomeration that stretched from Maine to Virginia.[8] And it was one of the nation's most densely populated cities, 438,000 people crammed into its roughly 23.5 square miles, much of that uninhabited marshes, industrial and port areas, and an airport. With that came a host of urban ills now commonly associated with America's postwar years: an aging housing stock and subsequent slum clearance projects, employment competition in the midst of a dwindling job base, and the growing racial segregation of the inner city.[9]

Residents were not quiescent in the face of such challenges, and they recognized, as President Johnson would more than a decade later, that the very administrative form of government helped shape the possible responses to them. In the mid-1950s, they took advantage of a new state law providing residents the tools to reform their local government. In signing the legislation in 1950, Governor Alfred Driscoll had celebrated the way it kept "government as close to the people as possible."[10] In Newark, where the existing municipal charter had produced a city hall bogged down in patronage and corruption, reformers sought a modernized government, one that would be more responsive to the urban challenges of the moment and to the city's changing population. They believed that administration mattered, that the form government took and the way it interacted with its people were important factors in determining its ability to address postwar ills. And after Newark voters approved a referendum establishing a municipal charter reform commission, Alan Lowenstein—Roger's father and fellow Wolverine—was chosen as its chairman.

Many of Newark's midcentury administrative thinkers were exceptionally attuned to the racial implications of their work, especially as the city's black population grew and spread. Since around World War I and the first mass wave of migration, Newark's black community had been concentrated in the Third Ward, in roughly the geographic center of the city. Yet that geographic density, under the existing municipal charter, did not translate into political representation. So proponents of reform successfully pushed for a

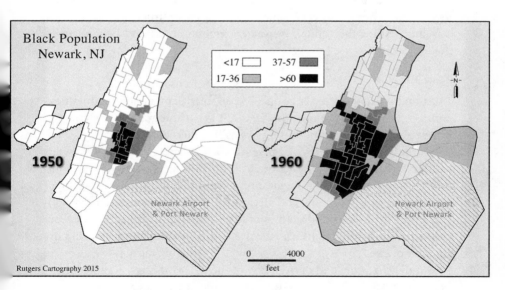

2. Over the course of the 1950s, Newark's black population spread outward from the Central Ward. The consciousness of an imminent black majority would powerfully shape local politics in the 1960s. (Michael Siegel, Rutgers Cartography)

redrawing of voting-ward boundaries to ensure, for the first time, political representation for residents of the expanding black ghetto. Among the benefits of this upturn in black political opportunity was the election of the city's first black councilman in 1954. Another was an intensifying attention to race relations in city hall. In a landmark 1959 report, the Mayor's Commission on Group Relations revealed that, should current demographic trends continue, Newark would soon be a majority-black city.[11] That year, the impending demographic shift was front-page and national news.[12] Four years later, the *New York Times* reported that Newark had "the largest proportional Negro population of any major metropolitan center north of the Mason-Dixon line."[13] In 1965, one new arrival, a native of Richmond, passed through downtown and thought that the only other place he'd seen so many black people was Nairobi.[14]

Though municipal charter reform brought new opportunities for black political power, local outposts of the black freedom struggle continued to battle racial discrimination in both the public and private sectors. And as the consciousness of a black majority grew on either side of Newark's color line, movements to pry open the institutional structures of local government and admit the voices and knowledge of that population accelerated, while movements to secure those structures against such incursions attempted to keep pace. Parties to this struggle sought assistance wherever they could. When the Great Society's administrative structures snaked their way out beyond the capital, Newarkers grabbed hold and bent them to their own desires.

The urban crisis—variously configured as uncontrolled metropolitan expansion, human migrations, the financial and demographic depletion of inner cities, and the political and physical conflicts engendered in particular places by those broad social phenomena—is often traced to the apparent contradictions of postwar American liberalism: how, despite its commitments to integration and widespread economic security, liberalism had produced segregated cities and decimated their economies. Newark appeared the most profound symbol of that failing, an impoverished, deeply divided city where liberalism's promise had gone up in flames during the summer of 1967.[15]

But that's not the end of the story. In the face of those contradictions—made abundantly clear by the black freedom struggle and the "discovery" of poverty amid postwar plenty—Great Society liberalism fostered a critique of the modern liberal state that looked beyond the politics of economic growth and entertained the anxieties growth had produced. While a range of social critics denounced the conventionality and shortsightedness of postwar affluence, Great Society liberalism acknowledged that the state itself had grown similarly staid and inadequate to the challenges of the period. Insisting that the state, in order to address its contradictions, look outside itself for ideas, it cultivated an antibureaucratic and community-oriented ethic that valued experimentation, flexibility, and decenteredness. It sought the guidance of elite experts, to be sure, but it also sought out the knowledge and desires of "the other America," those communities left behind by growth politics. And voices emanating from that "community" would prove the most consequential, as a growing body of work on the Great Society has begun to appreciate.[16]

Much of the drama in this story is produced by the fact that "the community," so broadly rendered in much discourse of the day (community action, community participation, community development, community control), was necessarily and, to an extent, *knowingly* illegible to the state that was calling it into duty.[17] That, after all, was the idea: the administration wanted innovation, *new* ideas, *new* imaginations. It didn't have the answers and didn't know what would come of attempts to find them. Opening up the state to a broad, abstract "community," illegible, full of difference, and, especially in the years of the modern black freedom struggle, dissenting and protestant, was an invitation to conflict. That opening in Newark—a city keyed to its imminent black majority, whether out of desire or fear—became liberalism's leading edge.

More specifically, the drama here is often generated by encounters between official state agents and those communities whose knowledge would be the new stuff of governing. The medium for such encounters was a profusion of decentered administrative forms that reached out beyond the halls of federal power: the ad hoc task forces and working groups that sought new ways of looking at the problems of the postwar years, for example; grant programs that encouraged unique, locally appropriate approaches to locally defined problems; and investigative commissions that constructed knowledge out of an often intractable range of sources. These forms were not entirely new, but they were newly popular. They had exploded in the postwar years, out of a desire to balance new demands on the state with American democratic traditions, to face, in other words, the challenges of the times without succumbing to totalitarianism.[18] Theirs was a model of government well suited to the ironic social style of postwar liberalism rather than its bureaucratic tendencies, to the desire for experimentation rather than purer, unpolluted forms of statism.[19] They grew in sheer numbers during the Johnson years, and more and more of the work of government was accomplished through them.[20]

When such administrative forms arrived in Newark, they provided unprecedented resources, opportunities, and allies to those engaged with its urban crisis and the particular political struggles it engendered. The specific forms that play central roles here—the War on Poverty's Community Action Program (CAP), the executive commissions that investigated Newark's civil disorder, and various congressional hearings on the War on Poverty and violence—gave local activists new operational spaces and new pathways by which they could inject their voices into both local and national politics. For the most part, this was to the benefit of those seeking greater power for Newark's black majority. But one of the ironies of this story is that the community action ethic, as I will call it, and the administrative forms that embodied it also contained opportunities for Newarkers more interested in maintaining the prevailing political order, opportunities most manifest in the politics of local law enforcement.

In addition to the ethic and the administrative structures of the Great Society, then, were the people who populated them and gave them specific meanings and purposes. Newarkers were uncommonly prepared for the Great Society, whether they had an appreciation for the importance of administrative form because they had participated in the recent municipal charter change; because they were concerned about the ills plaguing their city and convinced that local government was impotent or too incompetent to deal with them; because their racial consciousness had reached new heights with the news of the impending black majority and believed the time had come for that majority to exercise its full political power; because they felt threatened by the shifting demographics and sought to secure whatever power they had; or because of some combination of these factors. These were the people—from black power militants to the most conservative upholders of "law and order," and the many, many Newarkers in between—who sought and used the opportunities and resources afforded by Great Society liberalism.[21] With that access, they struggled against the fallout of the larger social forces that liberalism had, at best, left unaddressed and, at worst, fostered.

Ultimately, the conflicts produced by those struggles rendered the experiment unsustainable. The postwar liberal state and its guardians, it turned out, did not have sufficient stores of the improvisatory and pragmatic qualities needed to deal with such an influx of "community." The Great Society's earliest and most vociferous critics, Daniel Patrick Moynihan most prominent among them, decried the local conflicts generated by the Community Action Program. But many others, especially the local people who made use of it, believed protest and conflict were eminently reasonable uses of federal resources and institutional and political change its most desirable outcome.[22]

The Great Society thus proved a brief attempt to rebalance the relationship between the state and "the community," when it became apparent that the former, despite postwar growth, had not done well by the latter. It linked modern American liberalism's commitment to state action and the unprecedented spending permitted by postwar affluence to calls for political empowerment and economic citizenship from some of the nation's most marginalized peoples, whether in the hollows of Appalachia, the reservations of the Great Plains, or the declining cities of the Rust Belt. The agents of that linkage were the decentered administrative structures that spread out from Washington to those places and residents who took hold of them and, in stretching them toward participatory democracy, brought postwar liberalism to its frontier.

The story here plays out on either side of Newark's "riots." One of the reasons those five days in July 1967 have resonated so deeply is that they contained, as some observers quickly recognized, two phases of violence: the initial black rebellion and the state suppression thereof. I find "riots" a useful term worth preserving—though I use it carefully and not exclusively—for several reasons. First, it has the capacity to include both the insurrectionary and reactionary forms of violence. Second, for me it invokes a scholarly tradition that, far from seeing mass violence as politically unmotivated, insists exactly the opposite.[23] Finally, and most important, those five days appear in this book more as narrative than as fact, though fact the violence and its awful toll surely were. In the years afterward—even to today—the riots were used as a particularly powerful political and cultural bludgeon, an immediately usable past that was enlisted in much longer racial-political struggles of which it was surely a part, but not the whole. It's that *use* of the violence that I want to emphasize by calling it a "riot."

Though there are glimpses of events from earlier in the century, the story proper begins in the early 1960s, as community action began to take shape amid small task force and executive committee meetings in the Kennedy administration and came to full legislative fruition under Lyndon Johnson. It then moves quickly to Newark, one of the first cities to file a grant application under the new Community Action Program and arguably the city in which it most quickly reached the heights of national controversy. In

Newark, community action encountered, changed, and was changed by the existing struggles for and against greater black political power, with which it became intimately intertwined. But it also came to town in other forms, including a greater attention among some municipal and police leaders to the relationship between the city's police department and what had taken shape as "the community," a byword that had come to stand in for the coming black majority. That relationship, though never generally warm, had recently taken a turn for the worse, through a series of events that lent more cohesion not only to "the community" but to a nascent alliance between the police department and many white Newarkers facing the reality of their shrinking numbers and looking to the department as their last municipal stronghold. They forged their own brand of community action, a warping of the black community's version, as if in a funhouse mirror.

The riots that occurred in and grew out of this context provided ammunition for all sides in these struggles. But first, their chaos and death and destruction had to be given some order. They had to be made to yield some useful meaning. The problem of doing this is seen most clearly in two investigative commissions established to do just that: to make the violence make sense. The challenge for the liberal government-sponsored commissions considered here was that, if they were to be taken seriously and their investigation and conclusions and recommendations were to have any legitimacy, they would have to hew closely to the ethic of community action. That is, they would have to make sure that they considered a wide array of knowledge and perspectives. This was not only immensely difficult but, in the case of one commission, almost fatal.

For the emerging politics of law and order, this was a problem to be avoided by appearing to take it seriously. When the state Patrolmen's Benevolent Association launched its own investigation and responded harshly to the others, it wore a cloak of commissionness but refused a commitment to community action and, therefore, its epistemological pitfalls. Its report was the most confident yet, and it arrived just as more and more Americans—white Americans especially—were becoming more and more convinced that the politics of community action, as it had played out in Newark especially, had led only to mass disorder and violence. The response was a growing willingness to give law enforcement agencies what they wanted in order to guard the social order, a dialing back of the concern with police-community relations, and an expanded sense of solidarity with the police, as more and more civilians took to the streets in defense of their neighborhoods and what they considered the American way of life.

For two public intellectuals of national stature in the late 1960s, the

Newark riots demonstrated not the dangers of community action but its essential impotence. The state needed neither to be defended nor opened up but to be the target of a revolution. Soon after the violence ended, Tom Hayden, whose articulations of participatory democracy had brought him to Newark and its Community Action Program, left the city to work full-time in the antiwar movement, where he would increasingly dabble in the politics of guerilla violence, convinced that the American rot was so complete that the system might need to be burned down rather than made more accessible. For Nathan Wright Jr., the black Episcopal priest and former Freedom Rider who chaired the organizing committee for the first National Conference on Black Power in Newark, American liberalism could never countenance true black power. So the state needed to be re-made in what he called a politics of black self-empowerment, which would ultimately merge with the rising New Right and its romance with market, rather than participatory, democracy.

While Hayden and Wright left Newark before the close of the decade, their faith in the possibilities of the Great Society shattered, the struggle to pull and stretch its mechanisms toward local desires and goals continued apace. If nothing else, the riots had demonstrated the great inability of the local power structure to maintain order and, once order had been lost, to deal with the situation in a humane way. Among veterans of the city's community action struggles, the goal shifted from opening up that structure to taking it over. The politics of participation yielded to a politics of control, with consequences that continue to shape Newark today.

PART ONE

The Rise of Community Action

ONE

The Construction of Community Action in the Great Society

What sparked President John F. Kennedy's initial interest in American poverty was not a politically powerful constituency of the hardcore poor but some disturbing reading. In the late 1950s and early 1960s, several public intellectuals and journalists—chief among them John Kenneth Galbraith, Leon Keyserling, Michael Harrington, Harry Caudill, and Homer Bigart—rediscovered American poverty and hauled its ugly visage before the American public.[1] Poverty had largely been a partisan Democratic issue—Senator Paul Douglass of Illinois, for example, had repeatedly led the charge for area redevelopment legislation in the 1950s—and Kennedy had made poverty and unemployment a significant theme during his West Virginia primary campaign. But the broader message of the campaign, the one he deployed regardless of where he stumped, was that the Republican Party had done very little to foster national economic growth. Once in office, then, his number one domestic priority was to pass a tax cut and get more capital circulating, a Keynesian ploy promoted most stridently by the head of his Council of Economic Advisors, Walter Heller. Once the tax cut was passed, Kennedy turned to Heller in late 1962 and asked him to investigate the claims about which he had been reading: that postwar conventional wisdom (as Galbraith called it) was beset by gaping holes in our national self-perception, that the golden age of American affluence was in fact run through with stubborn strands of poverty.[2]

Though Kennedy maintained a public optimism that, as he would put it almost a year later, "a rising tide would lift all boats," Heller and other presidential staffers furiously searched for ideas well into the fall of 1963.[3] They established a process that now appears, looking back, a good model of what was to become the Great Society's attention to community action. Their search began in the established halls of power, collecting ideas from the old-line federal departments, but soon reached out beyond them, pulling new actors and new ideas into the process. Eventually, that process spiraled out beyond bureaucratic places and ways of knowing and incorporated ideas from academia, private foundations, and, crucially, local communities of impoverished Americans and brought those ideas back into the administration. In the end, the process itself proved the answer to Kennedy's question about how to deal with the contradictions of growth liberalism. If the solution could not be found in the tide and the state actions that lifted it, maybe the administration had to look beyond the state. The story of how this was done, then, begins with the president, but it soon leaves him behind to follow the administrative routes by which new ideas about how to confront poverty were found and brought into the workings of the state.[4]

During the summer of 1963, the Council of Economic Advisors convened an informal working group of staff from several cabinet departments and executive agencies to consider the problem of poverty, which was, Walter Heller came to believe, even more widespread and intractable than first anticipated. They met every few weeks on Saturdays and discussed both broad diagnostic issues (how is poverty defined? how is it measured?) and specific program proposals. They spoke not only of economics but of politics and race. The results were discouraging. The existing bureaucracy, it turned out, had little imagination. Many of the proposals involved little more than money for existing programs. None conjured as comprehensive and experimental an approach as the problem of poverty demanded. "It was quickly clear," one council staffer later recalled, "that we were getting old categorical program ideas warmed over."[5]

Heller extended the council's search into the fall of 1963 and, with Kennedy's blessing, established a formal task force on poverty. The president's closest advisors were canvassing for program ideas that would take them into the 1964 campaign season, and Heller was determined that a broad antipoverty effort be on their list. The task force issued a formal call for proposals, but the results were no better than the summer's products. "I got back, predictably, garbage," the head of the task force said. "People went into their file drawers and pulled out old programs that they had been floating around or that they had been trying to float before." There were lots of bits and pieces but no overarching theme. Even worse, several departments began to resent this new, annoyingly picky task force and to assert their deeply rooted bureaucratic interests. The Department of Labor insisted on a jobs program, while the Department of Health, Education, and Welfare advocated programs in the fields of health, education, and welfare.[6]

The youthful energy and idealism of Kennedy's closest advisors had been slowed by the tangled bureaucratic morass of the mainline federal agencies. Those in the Bureau of the Budget were particularly disgusted. In the 1930s, Congress had moved the bureau from the Treasury Department to the newly created Executive Office of the President. With the bureau nearby, proponents of the move argued, the administrator in chief would be free of contending bureaucratic interests and would have direct access to the best organization and management research available. It was practically designed to ruffle bureaucratic feathers, and the bureau quickly garnered a reputation as a hotbed of administrative experimentation.[7] When he interviewed for the job with the president-elect, Kennedy's eventual budget director insisted that the bureau was meant to be the strongest arm of the executive with oversight of all other departments and agencies. Under him, he promised, the bureau would be particularly active.[8]

It was a bureau staffer, then, who finally led the task force through the federal bureaucratic tangle and its unoriginal proposals. He knew David Hackett, who had recently led the President's Committee on Juvenile Delinquency. "I knew Hackett and his crew were around and I thought they had some fresh ideas," the bureau staffer recalled. "At least they weren't the ideas coming in from the line agencies." In early November 1963, he asked Hackett to submit a memo outlining his ideas for the administration's proposed antipoverty program.[9]

David Hackett was in his sophomore year at the Milton Academy in Massachusetts when Robert Kennedy entered the class one year ahead of him. Hackett considered himself something of a misfit at the school, more interested in hitting the athletic fields than the books. When John Knowles, who attended Milton rival Philips Exeter, later wrote his novel *A Separate Peace*, he modeled the character Phineas, who "considered authority the necessary evil against which happiness was achieved by reaction," on Hackett.[10] He immediately befriended Kennedy, whom he regarded as a fellow oddball. And when, in the late 1950s, Bobby's older brother ran for president, Hackett worked on the nomination and then the general election campaign. He later commended the campaign's youth and ingenuity: while Senator Lyndon Johnson built his support by rallying his fellow senators, Hackett said, the Kennedy campaign built support state by state and from the ground up. "It proved perhaps the single most interesting thing," he said, "that this group, in effect, was smarter and had better political instincts" than its much older and more experienced competitors. They developed a different system and they won. When President-elect Kennedy named his younger brother attorney general, Hackett agreed to join the Department of Justice as his special assistant.[11]

Before the inauguration, Robert Kennedy asked Hackett to begin studying up on juvenile delinquency. The problem had sparked a national moral panic in the 1950s, and that may have been enough to attract the attention of the soon-to-be attorney general. But Kennedy also knew of the problem from his older sister Eunice, who in the late 1940s, after their father funded the establishment of a delinquency bureau in the Justice Department, became the department's first executive secretary for juvenile delinquency. Then, in the early 1950s, Eunice—who was sometimes called "the conscience of the Kennedy family"—had gone to work at the Federal Penitentiary for Women in Alderson, West Virginia, where she encountered and befriended some of the nation's most notorious criminals, including Tokyo Rose and the queen of Washington, DC's, numbers game.[12] Eunice's younger brother and his old prep-school friend had comparatively little experience with America's down-and-out, but they were eager to get some. "I think that he and I were quite similar in that we'd never been involved with close poverty before," Hackett later said, "and certainly never had been involved up-close with Negroes." In the early months of their work on delinquency and over the next year or so, they traveled around the country to see American poverty firsthand. The experience was eye-opening. They visited poor white mountaineers in Appalachia, Chicanos in East Los Angeles, and black Angelenos in Watts. Kennedy visited schools, playgrounds, and swimming pools in neighborhoods surrounding the capitol building in Washington.[13]

The new attorney general hoped to keep these trips out of the public spotlight, but the press caught up with him in New York in March 1961. He and Hackett took a walk up Manhattan's East Side. The tour had been arranged by a contact at the New York Youth Board, who arranged several meetings between the nation's chief law enforcement officer and members of the Puerto Rican Viceroys and the Italian Redwings, some of them drug addicts and robbery suspects. Kennedy took off his coat and rolled up his sleeves. When he asked the gang members about the problems they faced, some spoke about the lack of jobs and places to play. Others were more reluctant to engage the suspicious tousle-haired white guy with the Brahmin accent. "What do you want to know for?" they demanded. "What are you doing here?" Kennedy responded simply—"I'm interested, I'm the Attorney General"—and they spent over two hours talking.[14]

Whatever the source of Kennedy's interest in juvenile delinquency, it was only that: an interest. There was no method yet, no ideas for how to address the problem. Hackett had been given no specific instructions, so he spent about six months traveling and talking to people, asking everyone he met what they would do if given $30 million to solve the problem of juvenile delinquency. First, he hit up federal agencies, including colleagues in the Justice Department, the FBI, the Bureau of Prisons, and the Department of Health, Education, and Welfare. He later estimated that he found about ten people working on youth and youth programs in the entire federal government, "and what was very striking was the lack of coordination" between any of them. "That was true even within the Justice Department," he said, where "the Bureau of Prisons never talked to the FBI and vice versa." Hackett recommended, therefore, that the administration establish a new cabinet-level committee to address the problem, a body that would coordinate federal efforts rather than leave them scattered in the established departments.[15]

While casting about for ideas, Hackett asked the head of youth affairs at the Ford Foundation if he knew anyone who could get a juvenile delinquency program up and running. The official turned to a recent foundation hire named Richard Boone, and Richard Boone suggested Lloyd Ohlin. Hackett had heard the name before, and on a subsequent visit to New York City he met Boone in a bar to learn more.[16]

Boone had first met Ohlin in the 1950s at the University of Chicago, where Boone had worked on a project tracking felons who were released into the Illinois Selective Service. Upon leaving the university, he worked at the Illinois State Reformatory during the Adlai Stevenson administration, and when one of his Chicago faculty members became the sheriff of Cook County, Boone became a captain in the county juvenile bureau. While there, he served as a consultant to the Chicago YMCA's "detached worker" program, which recruited community residents to work closely with gang members. Boone quickly came to believe that social welfare professionals—especially psychiatric caseworkers—were frauds with little ability to help delinquents. In seeking alternative personnel for the program, he experimented with hiring the gang members themselves. They rose to the task, Boone found, with impressive results, and he decided to toss the professional caseworkers out of the program altogether. Since the predominant approach toward delinquency was at that point psychiatric, the program's initial funding had come from the National Institute of

Mental Health. But after his successful experiment with hiring gang members, Boone poured his new ideas into a funding application that he sent to the Ford Foundation.[17]

While working on the detached worker program, Boone frequently sought Lloyd Ohlin's advice. Ohlin and his Columbia University colleague Richard Cloward had devised a theory that turned conventional thinking about delinquency on its head. They argued that delinquency was the product of a systemic rather than personal pathology and that delinquents, rather than pursuing lives of crime, would take advantage of better (and legal) opportunities if their communities provided them. The individual delinquent, therefore, was not a deviant who needed to adjust (or be adjusted) to the system. Rather, the system was dysfunctional and had to be reformed. Furthermore, rather than unilaterally swooping down with some social science derring-do to rescue the denizens of impoverished neighborhoods, Ohlin and Cloward insisted that residents themselves participate in that reformation.[18]

Ohlin's ideas received their first real tryout on the Lower East Side of Manhattan, in a multiracial neighborhood marked by high unemployment rates and increasing youth crime. In 1958, after a local businessman offered the neighborhood's Henry Street Settlement seed money to begin planning a delinquency program, the esteemed and long-standing social service agency submitted a grant application to the National Institute of Mental Health (NIMH) for a project they called Mobilization for Youth (MFY). The plan was to mobilize existing agencies and saturate the area with social services. But the NIMH rejected this initial proposal and insisted that the project engage more with community organizing (rather than organizing among the local social-service agencies), with local institutions like the schools, and with current social science research.[19]

That is where Ohlin and Cloward came in. The application of their research fulfilled the NIMH's demand for a more modern and scholarly approach. Together, they advocated the organizing of residents to advocate on their own behalf, not by incorporating them into existing power structures—which, after all, did not seem to be doing much for them—but by challenging them directly. While reworking MFY's funding application, Ohlin went to see Saul Alinsky and came away "enormously impressed" with the veteran organizer's vision of social conflict. But because he thought MFY's reliance on federal funds made it unwise to foster such conflict, Ohlin insisted the project pursue a middle course between conflict and cooptation: community participation.[20]

When the NIMH approved the revised grant in 1959, the contrast between the social-service and community-organizing approaches had not been completely worked out in some people's mind, so the two simply existed side by side. The president of the Henry Street Settlement told the *New York Times*, for example, that the project would "emphasize all-out community organization" but that efforts would also be made "to strengthen many of the services now being carried on in the lower East Side community." Other project leaders took care not to perturb existing neighborhood agencies, so they emphasized that MFY would not replace but only supplement them.[21] Nonetheless, MFY generated anxiety and tension among existing social service agencies. A local Catholic priest wondered if his mission's explicitly religious approach to local delinquents—"we tell them frankly that we're interested in their souls"—would clash with MFY's more secular aims. On the other hand, he also wondered if the project's "service saturation" approach wasn't really just a stopgap. "Maybe we should think in terms of a genuine people's movement in the area," he suggested. "A parish cannot successfully operate in a neighborhood like this until its power structure can challenge the other existing power structures—the real estate operators, the housing authority, the police." Perhaps that was the answer to the neighborhood's problems, he concluded, "rather than the manipulation of people by professional social workers."[22]

Hackett later described Ohlin, who was brought onto the newly formed President's Committee on Juvenile Delinquency (PCJD), as "the key architect of both the bill and the philosophy behind the program."[23] The committee's proposed legislation authorizing the distribution of funds for demonstration projects combating delinquency passed Congress in September 1961. Mobilization for Youth was among the first organizations to win a grant the following spring. It proposed a range of antidelinquency work in its effort to transform the local opportunity structure on the Lower East Side: neighborhood service centers, a Boys Adventure Corps, a preschool program, Homework Helpers, and youth cultural centers housed in local coffee shops. But tucked among such proposals was a participatory element that elevated the program beyond the original plan to saturate the area with social services: a "community development program which will seek to organize the unaffiliated to take a greater part in civic affairs."[24]

Soon after MFY received the bundle of grants that would make it perhaps the most studied and influential demonstration project of the decade, the Kennedy administration began work on another idea: a domestic version of its popular Peace Corps. (Once again, it might have been Eunice who planted the seed.) The idea was soon swept up in the stream of New Frontier thinking: it suggested that current service structures were inadequate to the tasks at hand and asked young Americans to selflessly consider what they might do for their country. The president kicked it over to Bobby who, in turn, gave it to David Hackett.[25]

Hackett had recently asked Richard Boone to leave the Ford Foundation, where Boone had been a busy advocate for Mobilization for Youth, and join the PCJD. But within a month of settling in at the Department of Justice, Boone was asked to develop a program for the proposed domestic peace corps.[26] By November 1962, Boone and other Justice staffers had prepared a preliminary report for the president. They recommended providing "visible avenues for service" to Americans wishing to serve their country. The program would be relatively small, about two to five thousand volunteers. They imagined volunteers working in schools, mental hospitals, slum neighborhoods, prisons, migrant-labor camps, and Indian reservations. And, importantly, they suggested that any projects serviced by the volunteers be initiated by local communities and institutions rather than the federal government, just as in the Peace Corps. It was a way, in effect, to help those communities help themselves.[27]

In the middle of November, the president announced the formation of a cabinet-level task force to determine the need for and the viability of such a program. Bobby Kennedy would head the task force, and he, in turn, made Richard Boone a Justice Department representative on it. Boone had been trying to sell the Committee on Juvenile Delinquency on the participation of the poor in local decision making (one PCJD member who later interviewed Boone for a study on the committee wrote in his notes, "Boone becomes a Mau Mau on this issue"), but he redoubled his efforts as a member of the Task Force on the National Service Corps.[28] When the Council of the Southern Mountains, a community development organization headquartered at Berea College in Kentucky, expressed interest in having young volunteers come to Appalachia, Boone warmly greeted their proposal and later visited the area. The following year, when the council began organizing an emergency winter program to help mountaineers cope with colder temperatures, Boone and a local community development expert argued that the mountain residents themselves should be involved not only as receivers of aid but as dispensers of it. "A program based on the traditional concept of charity—giving aid to enable subsistence, but without requiring a commitment by those receiving the aid—will not be complete," they wrote. "And aid based on the concept of charity tends to drive the poor more deeply into dependency." They wanted the federal program to leave a legacy in

Appalachia in the form of a citizenry more active in the work of their communities, especially after federal assistance inevitably disappeared.[29]

In addition to the mountains of Appalachia, whose dire conditions were documented in influential writings by Harry Caudill and Homer Bigart in 1962 and 1963, task force staffers visited migrant-labor camps, inner-city neighborhoods, and Indian reservations, and representatives from these areas sometimes visited Washington to speak to the task force. Boone later said that a common theme ran through their testimony: "Very, very early in the game, they began to hit us, saying, 'For God's sake, quit planning for us. If you really want us involved, then don't play games with us.'"[30] One time, when Bobby Kennedy called representatives from all executive departments to a Saturday-morning meeting, among the representatives of the poor was a group of Native American leaders who, in addition to advocating for local program development, blasted the federal Bureau of Indian Affairs. One in particular made an impassioned speech against the bureaucratic paternalism under which his people had been forced to live, then turned to the attorney general and pointedly asked him what he was going to do about it. Boone felt that this was a turning point for Bobby Kennedy (already primed, no doubt, by his visits to Appalachia, Harlem, and other poor areas), who then became the administration's highest-ranking advocate for opening up federal antipoverty programs to participation from the poor communities they served.[31] The Bureau of Indian Affairs might have been the most egregious example of federal bureaucratic insensitivity— "probably the most ingrown and destructive bureaucratic enclave in the federal establishment," Boone once called it—but it was only one entryway into a much larger world of bureaucratic tyranny and inefficiency, a world that new ideas about community action would seek to pry open.[32]

Over the several years he worked on the delinquency and domestic service corps programs, Hackett had pulled together a close circle of like-minded administrators who met regularly in his office. He called them his "guerillas" for the bureaucratic insurrection they were waging, several of them forming a sort of fifth column in established federal agencies and departments.[33] One of the insurgents—an accomplished social worker whose dissertation on the welfare power structure had concluded that greater political involvement by welfare recipients was needed—felt that delinquency staffers had been encouraged to feel as though they were different from the stuffy and tired federal bureaucrats among whom they worked and whose laziness became a running joke.[34]

At one of the meetings of the guerillas, someone pointed out that they were talking about a lot more than delinquency—that they were, in fact, discussing a broad antipoverty program.[35] So when in the fall of 1963— after Kennedy had done some disturbing reading, after the tax cut had passed, and after the Council of Economic Advisors had given up on finding innovative ideas among existing departments—Hackett heard from his friend at the Bureau of the Budget that the administration was casting about for new ideas on how to fight poverty, he campaigned hard for those generated by his close circle of bureaucratic insurgents.[36]

The idea of community action, in all its antibureaucratic bravado, caught the attention of the White House in ways that proposals from the old-line departments and agencies had not. It suited the administration's penchant for experimentation, its calls for service, and its suspicion of the federal bureaucracy, which the president once reportedly compared to an intractable whale: he tried to grasp it but could never get a firm hold for all the blubber.[37] One senior staffer from the Council of Economic Advisors recalled the heavy influence Hackett and Boone had on the council's thinking. In their search for ideas, he said, "We were bewildered by the complete disarray of the nominal professionals in the field of poverty." They had become convinced that giving money to existing agencies "was not worth a damn." When he met with Hackett and Boone, he said, "I was always sort of swept off my feet." And when Walter Heller himself met with them, he came out of the conversation buzzing about their ideas. Later, after being pulled aside by Robert Kennedy, who "made some very encouraging noises" about community action, his course was set.[38]

By the time Heller, frustrated by the warmed-over conventional wisdom of the federal antipoverty bureaucracy, encountered David Hackett and learned about the work of the executive committees considering juvenile delinquency and a domestic peace corps, the thinking on poverty within those committees had been shaped by numerous encounters between key administration liberals and representatives of the poor: Richard Boone and Chicago gang members, Appalachian mountaineers, and the Native Americans he brought to Washington; Robert Kennedy and the Viceroys and Redwings he met on Manhattan's East Side; the various other people Kennedy and Hackett visited, including their first encounters "up-close with Negroes." The parties to these encounters traveled along the administrative routes—the interagency committees and task forces—established by the need to open the bureaucratic state to fresh ideas. Federal antipoverty policy began to emerge as community action not only because those routes connected Washington with social scientific theories about delinquency and community development (both domestic and international) but also because they extended deep into the other America.[39] The task force experience taught those liberals that local knowledge among the poor and alienated had value. What may have begun as patrician senses of noblesse oblige were soon taken out beyond the personal and made structural. Administrative structures then carried the ethic of community action out into the world, energized it with material resources, and produced unpredictable outcomes. In that process, liberalism was stretched beyond its bureaucratic and paternalistic tendencies toward something more radical.

On the day President Kennedy was assassinated, administration stalwarts found a sticking place for their emerging antipoverty ideas. The interagency task force that had turned up Hackett and Boone and their ideas of community action prepared a statement on the proposed program, and Walter Heller brought it to a meeting with the new president the next day.[40] Heller took detailed notes on their conversation. He told Johnson that, though the program hadn't taken clear shape yet, it had already garnered a lot of support within the administration. The president, Heller wrote, "said we should push ahead full-tilt on this project."[41]

At the beginning of December, Hackett prepared a memo outlining the community action idea. According to Boone, Hackett saw the coming poverty program as a way to fund all the projects that the PCJD could not and to broaden the committee's work beyond the specifics of delinquency to larger structures of poverty.[42] In the December memo, the central values and lessons developed in the crucibles of the PCJD and National Service Corps experiences, among a host of social scientists, federal bureaucrats, and poor Americans, were pithily stated. There were three main points: (1) because the problem of poverty was structural and comprehensive, so too must be the approach to fighting it; (2) this required a shaking up of current bureaucratic structures at both the federal and local levels; and (3) the poor themselves, as a source of competent knowledge concerning their own situation, had to participate in the creation of any program. The way to give these ideas structure, Hackett suggested, would be to create a series of task forces that would study local situations in consultation with the local poor and make legislative recommendations.[43]

Though the proposed series of task forces never materialized, President Johnson did establish a single antipoverty task force shortly after declaring, in his first State of the Union message in January 1964, an "unconditional war on poverty." He asked Peace Corps director Sargent Shriver to lead the effort.

At the end of January, Walter Heller briefed Shriver and his deputy director, Adam Yarmolinsky, on the notion of community action. During a bathroom break, Shriver and Yarmolinsky exchanged their first impressions of the proposed antipoverty effort. Neither was terribly impressed, and they agreed that the program's political prospects were not promising. Community action contained too few fruits for those within the administration who would need to sign off on it. They needed a more diverse package of elements, they thought, if the War on Poverty had any chance of getting off the ground. So Shriver and Yarmolinsky quickly invited a large number of other administrators to attend the task force's first formal meeting, held a couple of days later.[44] Participants included representatives of the PCJD, Labor, and the Bureau of the Budget. Shriver told them that community action could be included in whatever legislative package they proposed, but it couldn't be the whole War on Poverty.[45]

Nonetheless, the architects of community action pushed their case. Richard Boone repeatedly insisted on the participation of the poor in the planning and implementation of local poverty programs. And when Shriver once remarked that Boone had already made his point, Boone responded by saying he would keep bringing it up until it was included in the task force's proposed program. There was some discussion of the extent to which the poor *could* be involved, and the group eventually agreed on a linguistic compromise offered by Boone: the legislation would call for their "maximum *feasible* participation." The phrase was included in the very first draft of the legislation, written just after the task force's first meeting, and it survived all subsequent revisions.[46]

The antibureaucratic thrust of community action had ruffled feathers in the old-line executive departments since the earliest days of Kennedy's PCJD, and those tensions erupted once again in Johnson's antipoverty task force. The specific battle was over whether community action or jobs would take center stage in the legislation. On one side of the battle line stood the veterans of the PCJD (especially Boone, Hackett, and RFK), and on the other were those who wanted community action either decentered (Shriver) or gutted in favor of employment programs (Secretary of Labor Willard Wirtz and his representative on the task force, Daniel Patrick Moynihan). The infighting on the task force was, as one participant recalled, "terribly sharp."[47] Richard Boone later wrote that, in his mind, the community action program was to be *the* antipoverty program, but that other elements, like the Job Corps, were added by advocates who had tried for years to get congressional support for massive youth employment programs.[48] Bobby Kennedy intervened on behalf of community action and reportedly laid down the gauntlet to his frustrated brother-in-law, telling him that if community action was not included in the Economic Opportunity Act, he wouldn't support the legislation and he'd refuse to testify on its behalf to Congress.[49]

In the end, the legislation incorporated both viewpoints. Title I contained its youth employment programs, including the Job Corps, work-training, and work-study programs. Title II established the Community Action Program, which would provide grants to local agencies that developed antipoverty programs with the maximum feasible participation of the poor. But Title II also established an adult basic education program that made grants directly to states and a voluntary assistance program for needy children that worked through local social welfare agencies. Other sections of the legislation provided loans to small businesses and impoverished rural families, provided assistance to migrant farm workers, and established work experience programs through the Department of Health, Education, and Welfare. Of the legislation's other provisions, only VISTA (Volunteers in Service to America), through which the Office of Economic Opportunity (OEO) trained young volunteers and referred them to local social agencies, shared community action's potential for disruption.[50] Hackett, for one, thought this was a betrayal of the work done in the Kennedy administration to reform the federal bureaucracy. Instead of launching a poverty program that would enable and coordinate locally derived efforts, the new OEO now threatened to become just another old-line executive department, jealously running its programs and resources. If JFK had not been killed, Hackett later mused, community action would have been the whole War on Poverty.[51] As it was, it emerged as only one part of it.

By the spring, several community action proponents—including Boone —had been formed into their own small task force within a task force to write the community action section of the legislation. Shriver appointed Jack Conway to head the group. Conway had come from the United Auto Workers (UAW), where, as a sociology graduate student at the University of Chicago, he had been a successful wartime organizer at the Buick plant in Melrose Park. After the war, he became a close assistant to Walter Reuther and acted as the labor leader's liaison with President Kennedy. Conway briefly served in the Housing and Home Finance Agency before leaving, frustrated at the slow pace of political life, to head the UAW's industrial union department in early 1963. In that capacity, he also served as the UAW's representative on the March on Washington organizing commit-

COMMUNITY

the
hometown
fight
in
the
War on
Poverty
☞ a protest
against
apathy
and
disillusion
☞ a commit-
ment
to change

Challenging and creative work in community organization, in education and health programs, in a variety of antipoverty projects is being done in Community Action Programs through-out the country.
If you are graduating from college and looking for work that will test your liberal education, your energy and your concern, write: Community Action Program, Office of Economic Opportunity, Washington, D.C. 20506

3. The intensely local work of community action was promoted as a challenge to those enjoying the fruits of postwar affluence—and perhaps growing apathetic because of them—as seen in this college recruitment poster for the Community Action Program. (National Archives 381-PX-2)

tee, worked to raise bail for those arrested in the Birmingham protests that year, and served on the National Service Corps task force, where he first met David Hackett and Richard Boone.[52]

Walter Reuther was a steadfast supporter of community action. The only criticism he had of the program, as it was emerging in the spring of 1964, was that it didn't do enough. So in April, after a visit with Lyndon Johnson, he announced that the UAW executive board had dedicated $1.1 million to what he called the Citizens' Crusade Against Poverty.[53] CCAP's aim was twofold: to lobby Congress and the public for the antipoverty legislation and to identify and train local community leaders to work in the poverty program. Reuther saw the local community action agencies that would be established by the legislation as the rough equivalent of trade union locals, and Conway recruited UAW labor educators to do the training. In arguing for the creation of CCAP before the UAW's executive board, Reuther said that "what we really have to do is to train people in the poor neighbor-hoods to do in terms of their problems what we did thirty years ago. . . . John Lewis didn't go into a single General Motors plant. . . . The guys in the plants did the job and that is what has got to be done with the poverty neighborhoods."[54]

But while Reuther gave the hard sell, his protégé on the community action task force sent a mixed message about the role of the poor in the program. In meetings and speeches, Conway often declared the centrality of poor people's involvement in the design and implementation of the anti-poverty effort. Three days after Reuther met with President Johnson, testifying on behalf of the legislation to a House committee, Conway promoted the maximum feasible participation of the poor by noting its basis in the "belief that local citizens understand their communities best and that they will seize the initiative and provide sustained, vigorous leadership." But he also popularized the image of a three-legged stool to explain the participation component: community action was a single program supported by city hall, private organizations, and members of the community to be served. He first deployed that image when speaking to a group of visiting mayors.[55]

The tension between Conway's presentations—would the poor lead local antipoverty efforts, or be one equal leg of the stool?—prefigured much of the drama to come as community action was rolled out in specific cities. But that tension had already emerged in the one place that had served as a laboratory for the participatory ethic: the Lower East Side. While anti-poverty officials like Conway stumped for the legislation on Capitol Hill, they had to contend with the drama that broke out when Mobilization for Youth took a social-activist turn and when that turn made it the target of an antiradical backlash. When rioting broke out in New York City that summer, the MFY drama was refracted through it and given higher stakes and greater urgency. The administrative routes along which funds and ideas had traveled to create community action proved equally adept at transmitting local controversies onto the national stage. This was a sign of things to come.

The trouble began in August 1963, at a meeting of the Mobilization for Youth staff. They were called together to discuss the possibility of offering their explicit support to the upcoming March on Washington and of moving beyond what some regarded as a narrow conception of anti-delinquency work. If the goal, following Ohlin and Cloward's theory, was to reform the local power structure and to do that with a heavy dose of resident participation, then, some proposed, maybe it was time to expand their efforts to political organizing. The question before them, according to Cloward, was how to "ride with this groundswell" of the civil rights movement. "The institutional resistances to change, to a redistribution of social and economic resources, to a greater sharing of power with dispossessed groups—these changes do not come about simply because we believe they should or simply because somebody gives us a great deal of money to develop programs to achieve them," he told the meeting. "In the end . . . a broad political thrust—not just a professional one—is needed to bring about basic changes."[56] In response, the staff voted to endorse the march and to launch a voter-registration campaign. Shortly thereafter, the FBI, responding to a request from the Department of Health, Education, and Welfare, initiated a loyalty check of MFY members.[57]

By then, though, MFY had already begun to stir things up on the Lower East Side. Its Visiting Homemakers program, made up of one "indigenous homemaker" from each neighborhood housing project, for example, had taught local women how to stand up for themselves as the central consumers and caregivers in their households. They mapped out reputable stores and health clinics and learned how to confront the local butcher, who regularly sold them bad meat, and how to call the housing authority to demand new kitchen appliances.[58]

As part of its social action work, MFY invited established low-income neighborhood groups to use its facilities and resources. In the process, it formed relationships with local protest movements. At the end of 1963, MFY joined a broad city rent-strike movement and organized local tenant organizations against landlords and city housing agencies.[59] In January, it hosted a three-hour meeting at which a rent-strike coordinating committee was formed by representatives of several Lower East Side neighborhood organizations, including the East Side Tenants Council, the Negro Action Group, the University Settlement Housing Clinic, the Council of Puerto Rican Organizations, and a chapter of the Congress of Racial Equality.[60]

As with housing, so with the local schools: MFY staff members became convinced that the key to reform was to exert pressure on those who controlled the system. One staffer helped organize a group of fifteen Puerto Rican women into what they called Mobilization of Mothers (MOM). In the fall of 1963, MOM rented out a school auditorium and called friends and neighbors to a meeting to discuss the educational needs of their children. They invited a local principal, who came only after complaining that the PTA was really the proper channel for such discussion. When he met the parents in the auditorium, he told them that he'd speak very briefly, since they wouldn't understand him anyway. "Look at how hard it is for me to talk to you," he said. "Imagine how difficult it is then for a teacher to handle a class full of children who can't speak English." The meeting ended in a volley of angry vituperation, and MOM soon organized a petition drive demanding that the principal be fired.[61]

At the end of January 1964, twenty-six school principals on the Lower East Side signed a statement demanding that the city superintendent of schools, the president of the board of education, and MFY's sponsors investigate the group's promotion of a "war against individual schools and their leaders." The principals charged that the head of MFY's action program had turned his workers into "full-time paid agitators and organizers for extremist groups." They deemed these actions "an abuse of the noble purpose for which great sums of federal and municipal money were originally appropriated." Instead of fighting juvenile delinquency, residents organized by MFY were complaining about racial discrimination and the lack of appropriate textbooks.[62]

The chairman of the MFY board voiced his support for the program. He understood that the community action approach was bound to move MFY in unexpected directions. Its staff, he told the *New York Times*, was paid to work with "independent self-directed groups of low-income residents on the Lower East Side. These are groups who know their own minds, who are aware that they and their children have serious problems in education, housing, employment and discrimination generally. Mobilization gives them the staff work they need to voice their concerns effectively."[63] Similarly, members of the local school board districts agreed to hold hearings on the matter but noted that the actions of these parents, rather than marking them as extremist agitators, "may be the normal response of concerned minority group people who simply seek a better education for their children."[64] Undaunted by the controversy, MFY members joined the citywide school boycott, in which nearly half of the city's school children stayed home. Absences on the Lower East Side were said to be particularly heavy, around 80 percent.[65]

As the Economic Opportunity Act made its way through Congress during the summer of 1964, the controversy over MFY heated up even more.

The fatal shooting of a black teenager by police lieutenant Thomas Gilligan on the Upper East Side led to a week of protests, violent confrontations between police and residents, and large-scale looting and vandalism that began in Harlem and spread to Bedford-Stuyvesant in Brooklyn.[66] As the violence subsided on the sixth day, a reporter for the *Times* noted a lingering "air of militancy." He described "a neatly dressed young woman [walking] determinedly along 125th Street," a leaflet with a picture of Lieutenant Gilligan attached to her shirt. The leaflet read: "Wanted for Murder—Gilligan the Cop." Rioting broke out again that night.[67]

A month later, on the morning of August 16, a mayoral aide announced that the city's Department of Investigation was looking into charges that "left-wingers by the score" had infiltrated Mobilization for Youth "and diverted its funds and even its mimeograph machines to disruptive agitation." That night, the mayor and the city council president confirmed the investigation. That councilman was also the coordinator of the city's Poverty Council, which controlled the municipal share of MFY's budget, and he said the council would approve no expenditures to MFY until the charges were proven untrue. The most serious of them, he said, was that a leaflet reading "Wanted for Murder—Gilligan the Cop" had been printed at one of MFY's neighborhood centers.[68]

Winslow Carlton, the chair of MFY's board, flew back from his vacation on Cape Cod to respond to the charges. At a press conference at East Second Street headquarters, he denied that Communists had taken over the organization and said that he'd spoken to David Hackett in the Justice Department and that Hackett knew nothing of any complaints against MFY, let alone a possible FBI investigation. Carlton also denied that their mimeograph machines had been used in connection with the recent rioting but, when pressed, admitted that someone could have entered one of the neighborhood centers at night and turned out the leaflets without his knowing. Later, a spokesman said that the organization's mimeograph machines would have been incapable of producing the type of leaflets ascribed to them and claimed that a local branch of the Progressive Labor Movement had actually printed and distributed the fliers. The next day, an expert printer examined the leaflet and concluded it was printed on an offset press, a piece of equipment MFY did not own.[69]

But the charges and countercharges continued to fly. The FBI revealed that its loyalty check of MFY had turned up fourteen former members of the Communist Party or Communist-front organizations. Upon learning that, Barry Goldwater's vice presidential pick made it an issue in their national campaign, saying that if the Republican ticket was being accused of extremism, it was only fair that the extremism fostered by the opposing party should be publicized.[70]

The timing of the MFY controversy could not have been worse, and officials involved with the creation and shuttling through Congress of the Economic Opportunity Act were reportedly in a panic. The *New York Times* called MFY the "prototype" of the local agencies that would be created by the Community Action Program and reported that its officials regarded the legislation as a mandate to support local rent strikes, school boycotts, and other social action campaigns.[71] The same day the paper ran that story, Sargent Shriver wrote the *Times* a letter stridently denying that MFY was a community action prototype. In fact, he wrote, there couldn't be any prototypes for a program designed to generate countless unique programs, each tailored to the needs of a particular community. He insisted that "local innovation will be the watchword."[72]

Two days after Shriver penned his missive, Lyndon Johnson signed the Economic Opportunity Act into law, and community action became official US policy. Johnson himself seemed to know little about it. Adam Yarmolinsky, the antipoverty task force deputy director, later recalled that he had had a conversation with Bill Moyers, Johnson's special assistant, during which he mentioned that local antipoverty agencies would be receiving grants under the new program. Moyers asked him what he was talking about. Johnson, Moyers said, had been thinking the War on Poverty was like the New Deal's National Youth Administration, which had provided job training and schooling to hundreds of thousands of young Americans.[73]

If the president seemed clueless and potentially alarmed by community action, officials at Mobilization for Youth and the Committee on Juvenile Delinquency had developed a keen understanding of its possibilities and pitfalls. When asked by a reporter whether its programs supporting rent strikes, school boycotts, and MOM protests could be run "without alienating established community leaders," MFY's director said, "It can't be done. These programs involved shifts in power and prestige. If somebody's gaining something, somebody else is giving something up." While others questioned whether such activities should be supported by public funds, one member of the PCJD who had become convinced that the reorganization of local opportunity structures had to be led by the poor themselves said that an important part of the work agencies like MFY could do was to identify "a community's indigenous leadership." He had watched this process on the Lower East Side. The programs supported by the presidential panel need not organize protests or any other direct actions themselves, he said, but should help residents organize themselves around their own wishes and desires. "When you deal in this way with a population that has a lot of pent-up frustration," he admitted shortly after the legislation was signed, "you're bound to have various kinds of explosions that are regarded as unfortunate."[74]

By that time, antipoverty officials had already fanned out across the country to jump-start the War on Poverty in other cities and regions. They met with local community leaders and told them about the grants that would soon be available under the Community Action Program. In July, a small delegation visited Newark, New Jersey, barely twelve miles from the fracas on the Lower East Side.

TWO

Community Action Comes to Newark

At the end of July 1964, a member of Sargent Shriver's antipoverty task-force (and one of David Hackett's former guerillas) visited Newark. The legislation launching President Johnson's proposed War on Poverty had already passed the Senate, and as cities across the country prepared proposals for local community action agencies, some sought the guidance of federal antipoverty officials. In Newark, the proposal was drawn up by the dean of the Rutgers University School of Law, Willard Heckel, and submitted to Mayor Hugh Addonizio at a meeting in the mayor's downtown office attended by Shriver's representative and a small band of civic leaders, "all people certainly of outstanding reputation, whom I believe[d] to be very sincere in their desire to do something worthwhile for the city," Addonizio later recalled. Shriver's man informed the Newarkers that the nascent Office of Economic Opportunity had included their city on a funding priority list and he had come to Newark to help jump-start the process. Addonizio, like many of his colleagues across the nation, was thrilled by the potential financial boon awaiting his city, whose Division of Welfare was barely scraping by on emergency appropriations.[1]

Dean Heckel no doubt shared the mayor's enthusiasm for increased federal aid, but the antipoverty proposal he submitted that day reflected his long-standing interest in municipal reform and civil rights. Over the past decade, he had been intimately involved in several efforts, including the midcentury charter reform movement, to open Newark's political and economic structures to those largely shut out of it, especially the city's burgeoning black population.[2] His antipoverty proposal was based on a joint effort by the city and Rutgers to create a "social renewal" project in Newark, a project designed to think beyond well-entrenched processes of urban renewal, which many deemed too focused on buildings rather than people, as well as beyond existing social welfare agencies, which served more to belittle than empower the people they served.[3] In September 1962, the Rutgers Urban Studies Center chose the neighborhood surrounding South Side High School, an area catching much of the black population overflow from Newark's crowded center and whose population of sixty-five thousand was two-thirds nonwhite, to launch a demonstration project. The South Side Project's board included representatives from city, county, and state government, Rutgers, the Urban League, and the Newark Housing Authority, but they tasked its director with ensuring that all programs "remain as much as possible in the hands of the youths themselves, and not become dominated by the preconceived ideas of outsiders concerning what kinds of programs and rules are best."[4] One city official visited Washington in February 1963 for a two-day meeting with the President's Committee on Juvenile Delinquency and, upon his return, reported that the creation of a local nonprofit corporation would be the best way for the project to win federal grants. He had learned about the Lower East Side's Mobilization for Youth and felt it would be a great model for Newark.[5]

A year later, progress on the project had stalled. Despite the prospect of federal dollars and the impressive amount of work already accomplished, Mayor Addonizio did little to rally support. But the project also ran into opposition from the local Welfare Federation, which accused it of duplicating work it was already doing. Enthusiasm waned, and the project languished.[6] So when the news of a federal Community Action Program reached the city, Dean Heckel recognized an opportunity to revive the project and its goals, not only for the South Side, but for the whole city. At the meeting in the mayor's office that July, the gathered group endorsed Heckel's plan and made it the foundation of the antipoverty effort in Newark.

Community action under the War on Poverty was essentially a grants program, and it is part of the logic of grants that a transfer of funds is also a transfer of power. That transaction took place between the federal Office of Economic Opportunity and, in Newark's case, the United Community Corporation (UCC), the city's officially designated community action agency. In some cities, the local agency was controlled by city hall or existing social welfare agencies. In others, the local agency was largely independent of those power centers. More common was some movement between or hybrid of the two possibilities. In Newark, Mayor Addonizio and other members of his political establishment saw great promise in the funds and jobs that would come through the program and, believing he had nothing to worry about from the people of "outstanding reputation" he met with in his office that day, granted the UCC independent status.

As on Mobilization for Youth's Lower East Side, so in Newark. Community action did not land on a political blank slate, but among multiple existing movements for racial justice and political power, of which Dean Heckel's work was but one small part. Those existing struggles were refracted through community action, which provided them new resources, allies, and directions. An established class of civil rights activists—especially a young generation inspired more by the direct action tactics of the Congress of Racial Equality (CORE) than the comparatively staid work of the National Association for the Advancement of Colored People (NAACP), which for years had served a handful of black Newarkers as the pathway into local machine politics—recognized in community action an opportunity to further their struggle against a city government that was proving remarkably inattentive to the demands of the growing black population. This group of activists formed a large part of the UCC's leadership.

As the program spread out from the UCC's downtown headquarters and into the neighborhoods, however, a third party came into play: the ill-defined "community" called into being by the Community Action Program, those people whose maximum feasible participation was mandated by the Economic Opportunity Act. When it came to programming, Newark's antipoverty agency was certainly active, but its importance went well beyond the jobs it produced or for which it trained people, the educational head start it provided to thousands of preschoolers, the small business loans it provided, or the play streets it blocked off for children in the summer. It opened a space in which poor Newarkers gained a political and cultural self-awareness, where they constructed a potent sense of peoplehood vis-à-vis city government, and where they forged a political vision in which economic disadvantage did not equal political alienation. In several neighborhoods, residents and organizers pushed hard to maintain community action's broad participatory ethic, especially as city officials and their own communities of supporters, who cherished established political structures, began to fight back.

Political wrangling over community action occurred in many cities, of course. But in a city newly attentive to the potentials and shortcomings of municipal administrative form and newly cognizant of an impending black majority, community action's commitments to bureaucratic disruption and local knowledge were pushed to their limits. Community action was embattled from its earliest days, well before, as the story is often told, the Vietnam War diminished its resources. The earliest controversies over its implementation concerned as much the proper definition of "feasible" as they did the proper level of funding. Would that definition be left up to the inhabitants of impoverished areas themselves, to be defined, in effect, by how much they decided to participate? Or would it be determined elsewhere, by city officials, federal administrators, or legislative decree? Events in Newark, which drove much of this discussion, demonstrated that, even if the participatory ethic were gutted legislatively, residents could preserve it at a local level. While officials in Washington began a retreat from community action, Newarkers continued to forge its frontier.

The roots of Dean Heckel's interest in community action stretched back even further than the early-1960s experiments with "social renewal." He had played several roles in the postwar wave of administrative modernization in New Jersey, which began with a state constitutional convention in 1947 and continued through a statewide surge of municipal charter reform. As a young Rutgers law professor he had submitted a monograph on a potential bill of rights to the 1947 convention, in which he not only ruminated broadly on the relationship between state forms and democracy but also specifically recommended that an antidiscrimination clause be included in the new state constitution.[7] Given such expertise, he was chosen six years later to chair the Newark Citizens Committee on Municipal Government.

The committee gathered enough support to organize a formal Newark Charter Commission (this time headed by prominent Newark lawyer Alan Lowenstein, whose son Roger would later invite the president to the university commencement in Ann Arbor).[8] In the commission's subsequent study of alternative government forms, invocations of racial democracy came in the same breath as those of honesty and efficiency.[9] The existing municipal commission had been established just as the numbers of black migrants to Newark exploded during World War I. As the potential voting power of the predominantly black Third Ward—"The Roaring Third," it was called—was about to take off, ward-based elections were abolished. Up into the early 1950s, even as black political protest in Newark grew more and more vigorous, taking on discrimination in Depression-era relief programs and union halls, unfair treatment at local retail outlets, and segregation in public swimming pools and City Hospital, for example, and despite a few electoral successes on the county and state level, black Newarkers' access to city hall was largely limited to patronage positions handed out by city commissioners chosen in citywide voting.[10] Reform proponents, including the Urban League, NAACP, and Congress of Industrial Organizations (CIO), therefore argued that municipal charter reform would provide black Newarkers new opportunities for political representation.[11]

In its final report, the Charter Commission proposed a hybrid system of representation. Under its plan, a city council would consist of nine members, five elected from five new wards (north, south, east, west, and central) and four elected at large. This proposal, the commissioners wrote, would meet six principles "deemed essential to efficient and responsive local government," the sixth of which spoke directly to the democratic demands of an ever-diversifying city. "For the first time in years," the report said, "the principal areas of the city and the important elements of its population will be assured representation."[12] In November, Newark voters approved the new charter plan by a nearly two to one margin, and the first new elections were scheduled for spring 1954.

In the nascent Central Ward—consolidating the old Third and Seventh Wards, along with pieces of several others—the voting was preceded by wrangling between two prospective councilmen, one endorsed by charter reformers and the other Irvine Turner, a Newark native who had twice before run for city commission and lost. Turner had benefited as much as any black Newarker from the older form of government, aligning himself with any commissioner who supported his political and career ambitions. In return, he offered his knack for consolidating the black vote through a mixture of backroom dealing and fiery racial rhetoric. When an early electoral plan proposed expansive ward lines that would have diluted black voting power in the Central Ward, Turner dispatched supporters to the Census Bureau in Washington, where they discovered that the proposal was based on faulty data provided by the city clerk. Turner brought suit against the commission, won a revision to its lines, and assured his victory as Newark's first black councilman.[13]

Once in office, Turner consolidated his power by skillfully trading black votes in the Central Ward to local, county, and state politicians for patronage positions and money. He grew close to the head of the Newark Housing Authority and supported the construction of dense high-rise housing that would, at least potentially, provide him more votes to trade. He attacked slumlords, pushed for fairer sentencing in city courts, and called for increased black presence on the police force, on the bench, and in city services.[14] The political fiefdoms that reigned in Newark under the commission form of government, it seemed, had not been eliminated with charter reform. Rather, they had transmogrified into ward-based systems of political trade with political benefits for Newarkers who had rarely enjoyed them before.

In 1962, black Newarkers swung their votes behind US representative Hugh Addonizio, who was running for mayor without the backing of the county Democratic machine against the city's two-term incumbent. He had garnered Irvine Turner's endorsement by promising, among other things, action on police brutality and an integrated city hall. He coupled that with blatant ethnic appeals to the city's Italian American community, to whom he represented an end of Irish-dominated machine control. Together, Italian American and black residents constituted nearly two-thirds of the city's population, and Addonizio tailored his campaign promises accordingly, lashing out especially at his opponent's record on urban renewal, which had displaced so many black and Italian American residents. To some observers, this was the end of local municipal reform and a return to the blatant racial and ethnic politics of the commission era. But it worked.[15]

To many, Addonizio's victory was a long time coming, but it quickly proved limited. No single city administration could hope to solve the litany of problems that came bundled as "the urban crisis," and Newark's growing black militancy did not fade for the presence of a potential ally behind the mayor's desk. Under Addonizio, city hall became racially integrated like never before, but that hardly appeased all of Newark's civil rights activists.[16] In the summer of 1964, halfway through Addonizio's first term, violent disorders in Harlem, barely twenty miles away, suggested the terrifying cost of failing to address racial concerns and tensions. In response, two black civic leaders, from the Central Ward Democrats and the Labor-Negro Vanguard Conference, a local civil rights group closely allied with the Democratic Party, organized a rally for black voter registration. Two hundred people gathered in the courtyard of the Douglass-Harrison apartments, near the southern edge of the Central Ward. Five speakers addressed the crowd from a sound truck, encouraging them to assert their voting power in the fall. One declared that it was time for a black mayor in Newark. Plainclothes black police officers kept watch, and several local businesses boarded up their windows. But the crowd calmly dispersed after only half an hour, when a thunderstorm rolled in.[17]

Earlier that day, before the storm began and as if in answer to multiple prayers—for help against the urban crisis, for increased black political power—a federal official, one of David Hackett's guerillas, came to Newark to help launch the local avatar of the Community Action Program. He explained that, once the antipoverty legislation went into effect, Newark could expect the new Office of Economic Opportunity to provide 90 percent of its community action funding, so long as the project guaranteed broad-based community participation. Mayor Addonizio spent the afternoon gathering pledges of financial support from the city council and the municipal boards of education and welfare to cover the remaining 10 percent.[18]

With the local share of start-up costs covered, Willard Heckel quickly set about the task of recruiting a new class of antipoverty leadership to sign the UCC's incorporation papers. The group he established contained a mix of government, business, and civic leaders, but the two largest blocks consisted of a group of Addonizio loyalists and a group of activists fresh off recent struggles with the city administration over police brutality and discrimination in the construction trades, struggles that mark the start of the modern civil rights movement in Newark. Most prominent among this latter group was a man named George Richardson.[19]

As a New Jersey state assemblyman representing Newark and other parts of Essex County in the early 1960s, Richardson had risen from Central Ward bartender to a vital position in the local Democratic machine. At one time, he could count among his closest allies county political boss Dennis F. Carey and Congressman Addonizio. So tight was he with the latter that when Addonizio decided to run for mayor of Newark, he tapped Richardson to be one of his campaign managers. As such, he was instrumental in harnessing the voting power of local civil rights organizations and constructing the alliance of liberals, old-line Democrats, and black Newarkers that swept Addonizio into office in 1962. For this, Richardson received a $9,000-a-year position in the new administration.[20]

The honeymoon, however, was short lived. In Richardson's view, black community leaders saw their relationship with Addonizio as a means to an end. Well aware of the political possibilities that inhered in recent black migrations to Newark, they viewed Addonizio's election as a step toward the eventual (and inevitable) election of a predominantly black city administration. Under Addonizio, black supporters and appointees would gain the political education and connections that would help produce future black candidates. But Addonizio, sensing the potential danger, refused many of them jobs in his new administration. Richardson later recalled that that was when black political disenchantment with the Addonizio administration began. Soon after, he became its most visible spokesman. Through a series of confrontations with city hall, he emerged in the mid-1960s as a figurehead of a local campaign for independent black political power, a campaign driven in large part by Addonizio's broken promises.[21]

The first of these confrontations came in early 1963. Local civil rights groups, led by Richardson and the local CORE chapter, agitated for a civilian review board to investigate complaints of police brutality and present recommendations for action to the mayor. Initially supportive of the idea, Addonizio commissioned a team of city officials, including Richardson, to make a study of Philadelphia's review board and report on its applicability to Newark. In the time it took to make the trip and prepare a favorable recommendation, however, the police department got wind of the plan and launched a fervent campaign against it. Addonizio, ignoring the recommendation of the city's Human Rights Commission, reversed course, and the director of the commission resigned in protest. Richardson was soon thereafter fired from his job in city hall.[22]

That summer, as all-white construction crews went to work on a new campus for Barringer High School, Richardson helped found a coalition of civil rights groups—the Newark Coordinating Committee (NCC)—to protest and remedy rampant discrimination in the construction trades. Through July and August, picketers from local chapters of CORE and Americans for Democratic Action, church and labor groups, and local civic associations marched outside the corrugated tin gates of the building site just off Branch Brook Park, carrying signs that read "Negroes Want Jobs" and "Mayor Addonizio: End Job Discrimination or Withdraw Contracts." Richardson walked the picket line, and police intelligence officers snapped photos of him for their records. On the first day of picketing, white workers attempted to break through the demonstrators' human wall, and in the scuffling that followed two picketers were arrested. Richardson accused the police of deploying the "brutal methods" of southern law enforcement.[23]

Alarmed by the prospect of racial violence only a few short months after his inauguration, Addonizio brokered a lengthy series of negotiations between the NCC and the local Building Trades Council that produced an agreement on a new apprenticeship program. But that was only after he buckled under pressure from the construction trades and allowed work to continue at the site—despite objections from the civil rights coalition and a nondiscrimination clause in the building contract—and after he tried to handpick the negotiators on the civil rights side.[24]

Richardson, reportedly in retaliation for his agitation against Addonizio's handling of civil rights issues, was dropped from the county Democratic ticket in 1963. Clearly unwelcome in the county machine, he decided to forge his own alternative political force, centered in Newark, but aimed at local, county, and state offices. Inspired by the Mississippi Freedom Democratic Party, he formed a United Committee for Political Freedom, similar in structure to the coalition that led the protests at Barringer

High School the previous summer. Direct action need not be abandoned, Richardson thought, but neither should electoral organizing be avoided. The new committee, he said, was made up of blacks, whites, and Puerto Ricans who "[had] come to see that if they are going to achieve their goals as far as civil rights is concerned that they must be involved in the political process of our county."[25]

In developing the earliest UCC leadership, Heckel reached out to Richardson, who, along with two other veterans of the construction-trades struggle, signed the incorporation papers.[26] They were filed in August 1964, ten days before President Johnson signed the Economic Opportunity Act. The next month, a fifty-three-member board of trustees was established. Heckel was named the president of the board, and the vice presidents included George Richardson; Kenneth Gibson, a city engineer and close Richardson ally, who saw the UCC as an extension of their civil rights work; Rabbi Jon-

4. After years of working in local Democratic politics, tenant organizing, and youth athletics, Timothy Still—pictured far right in his signature boxing jacket—took over the UCC presidency from Willard Heckel in early 1967. Pictured with Still are Donald Tucker (Area Board 5, future city councilman) and Mary Sanders (Area Board 4), both seated, and Thomas Parks (UCC administrator) and Michael Duffy (UCC deputy director), both standing. (Newark Public Library / *Star-Ledger*)

athan Prinz, who came to understand the UCC's agenda as the transfer of power to the black majority and who was the son of nationally prominent civil rights leader Rabbi Joachim Prinz; and Timothy Still, a former Golden Gloves boxing champ, staunch supporter of Irvine Turner (it was his visit to the US Census Bureau that had assured Turner's election in 1954), and revered local tenant leader. The board included only three elected city officials: the mayor, Councilman Turner, and the city council president.[27]

Among the board's first tasks was to hire an executive director. To that end, Tim Still traveled to Harlem's 135th Street YMCA to visit Cyril Tyson, the acting director of Harlem Youth Opportunities Unlimited (HARYOU), another local community action agency scrambling to join the War on Poverty.[28] The son of West Indian immigrants, Tyson had grown up in New York attending various community meetings with his mother, a seamstress and homemaker and community organizer. Though she herself had little formal education, she headed the parents associations at whatever schools her children attended, organized a neighborhood community league in the Bronx, and helped establish the Forty-First Precinct Community Council in the mid-1940s. She was his inspiration and his model. "My developing notions of community organization had nothing to do with professionality," Tyson later remembered. "It had to do with organizing people around what they perceived their concerns were." After studying sociology at St. Francis College, Tyson became a community organizer with the Two Bridges Neighborhood Council on the Lower East Side, where he worked with gang members and met Richard Cloward. Later, in 1963, he was asked to spearhead a study of Harlem youth for HARYOU, under a planning grant from the President's Committee on Juvenile Delinquency.[29]

At the time of Still's visit, Tyson was fighting to liberate HARYOU from a battle of wills between its founder and guiding light, renowned City College psychologist Kenneth B. Clark, and Harlem congressman Adam Clayton Powell Jr. Tyson's allegiance to Clark, who accused Powell of trying to make HARYOU into an extension of his political machine, was an open secret, but he resisted becoming publicly involved. When the UCC personnel committee assured him that the city administration in Newark fully supported the local community action agency and that there would be no power struggles, Tyson resigned his position at HARYOU and took the job.[30]

UCC officials told Tyson that they particularly liked his reading of the "maximum feasible participation" clause of the Economic Opportunity Act. The final report of his Harlem youth study had emphasized the need for "social action rather than dependence upon mere social services" and, assuming that "effective social action in a community so populous and complex as Harlem requires decentralization," proposed the establishment of local neighborhood boards consisting of residents who would critically study and exert influence on the current service setup. As did many anti-poverty planners in the age of Cloward and Ohlin's thesis, Tyson viewed the War on Poverty as an investment in opportunity for the poor. But to him economic equality arose from political power, not the other way around. Therefore, as he explained to UCC board members at their first meeting, "The way in which you involve people in these services may be more important than the services themselves." Community action had the potential, he said, to bring Newark's poorest into the political mainstream, to democratize the city by enfranchising its most marginalized.[31]

Tyson imported HARYOU's plan for neighborhood "area boards" to Newark. Each would consist of a small staff and a large resident membership, who would elect the board's officers, send representatives to the central UCC board of trustees, and vote in all UCC-wide elections. Each board would craft program proposals out of its residents' unique needs and desires, forward them to the central UCC board, and implement those that were approved and received federal funding. In establishing their constitutions and bylaws, recruiting volunteers and members, and designing and implementing program proposals, each area board would enjoy strict autonomy. And at each stage, from program development to implementation, each would ensure the direct involvement of local residents.

The process of developing local leadership in the War on Poverty, Tyson knew, would take time, but its first fruits were promising. In mid-February 1965, UCC headquarters invited residents in three areas to attend the inaugural meetings of their local boards, each to be hosted by well-known community organizations at the end of the month. Lower Roseville, downtown, and stray sections of the Central Ward would make up Area Board 1, the bulk of the Central Ward made up Area Board 2, and residents of Clinton Hill (the neighborhood targeted by the earlier South Side Project) formed Area Board 3. Over 250 people attended the three meetings, where they established committees to write constitutions and elected temporary officers. Among those elected were a clergyman, two leaders of local tenants' associations, a union representative, and a homeowner and mother of two who was active in a local neighborhood community union project. Tyson told attendees at one meeting that the area boards were designed to "give you a sense of self, and a sense of confidence that you can change the face of Newark." By the end of their first week of existence, the three boards had attracted a thousand members. During the second week, the number doubled.[32]

City officials sensed a stirring. New theories of community action were an affront to the cherished relationship mayors had enjoyed with the federal government since the 1930s. Contrary to the "last hurrah" thesis, which had the federal government replacing local machines as residents' greatest patron, the New Deal had, in many cases, *solidified*, rather than diminished, local urban political structures. The US Conference of Mayors was formed, after all, just weeks before Franklin Roosevelt took office by mayors visiting Washington to lobby for federal loans to their Depression-wracked cities.[33]

Thirty years later, community action's administrative experimentation threatened to rewrite the contract. Federal aid would now skirt city hall on its way to an independent local antipoverty agency. In any city, like Newark, increasingly riven by the politics of race and poverty, there was bound to be conflict over control of the program. Though some federal officials pitched the setup as an efficient way to coordinate antipoverty efforts among residents, politicians, and private concerns, others knew very well its potential to cause conflict among those parties. One Budget Bureau official later recalled that "it was clear there was a democratic, hopefully, political aspect to the CAP agencies and that they might get cross wise with the mayors."[34]

Cyril Tyson's hopes of escaping political squabbles by leaving Harlem for Newark proved naïve. Early in November 1964, two months before his new job began, city council members bitterly debated approving their share of UCC start-up costs. The contributions of other city agencies were dependent on this appropriation, so without it Newark's community action program would sink before leaving port. The council approved the appropriation after some nasty exchanges and a five-minute cooling-off period but added two binding provisions that, if unmet, would freeze the money: the council demanded that all nine councilmen be given seats on the UCC board and that the board consult with them before hiring an executive director. In response, Heckel denounced the council's power play and warned that its action "would bring to a grinding halt the whole work of the corporation."[35] A deal was struck two weeks later: the city council dropped their conditions and, in return, the UCC gave Addonizio and each councilman a seat on the board but granted voting privileges to only the mayor and the two original councilmen.[36]

The immediate crisis fizzled and the UCC got its start-up money, but not before its new director was overwhelmed by a strong sense of foreboding. His first afternoon on the job, wanting to get ahead of any other roadblocks the city administration might erect, Tyson visited Mayor Addonizio at his office in city hall. Their conversation was not openly confrontational—the mayor expressed his satisfaction with Tyson's credentials, though he was skeptical that a qualified Newarker couldn't be found for the directorship and told Tyson that he would keep an eye on him—but Tyson left thinking that Addonizio regarded the city council as an arm of his political machine. At the time, he kept it to himself, but he later wrote that he believed the UCC's early fracas with the city council had really been a fracas with the mayor.[37]

Over the winter of 1964–1965, tensions continued to grow. Several councilmen allied with the mayor opened new attacks on the UCC. Irvine Turner claimed that dissident politicians had "muscled in" on the antipoverty program, while Lee Bernstein and Frank Addonizio (a distant cousin of the mayor) complained that staff salaries were excessive. Soon after, when federal officials cut the UCC's nearly $900,000 first-year budget request to $204,000, several trustees suspected that local politicos had pressured the OEO to do so.[38] Two months later, when investigators from the OEO showed up in Newark, they explained that Mayor Addonizio had accused the UCC of stirring political unrest in the city and they had come at his behest.[39]

These tensions manifested themselves in a war of words and administrative proposals at the UCC's first general membership meeting on May 27, 1965, at West Kinney Junior High School in the Central Ward. The key agenda item was the election of fifteen additional trustees, an attempt by the board to address concerns that it had been stacked with people hostile to city government. Though the UCC's membership now surpassed two thousand people, only about three hundred, including Mayor Addonizio, were on hand to hear Willard Heckel's provocative opening remarks. After touting the UCC's first set of project proposals—two preschool programs, work-training for city welfare recipients, a summer reading program, and a small business development plan—Heckel assured the membership that Newark's community action agency was completely independent. He extolled the War on Poverty as a prelude to "social revolution," the product of which would be "a true grassroots democracy," and predicted that "the power structure of the city will be altered in ways not yet clear."[40]

When Heckel yielded the floor, Mayor Addonizio began his address with social niceties, telling the members how pleased he was with the UCC's progress. Its successes, he contended, were in no small part due to his own steadfast insistence that the program be stridently defended against political interference. Federal legislation had given him the option of controlling the local community action agency, but he, against the advice of many, thought it better to create an antipoverty program independent of city hall.

But now, he said, the tone darkening, we must remember to keep the UCC out of politics. Its proper role was not as a political pressure group but as a central coordinator for existing organizations and programs, an agency that would render the much-needed delivery of social services more efficient. He concluded with a warning: "If the UCC builds itself into a major publicity force and begins to think of itself not as a social agency but as a political counterweight, then, ladies and gentlemen, it will be in trouble. Political force, my friends, always generates counter-force."[41]

Outside the meeting, members of Area Board 3, which called itself the People's Action Group, protested the plans to expand the board. They distributed leaflets that outlined the process by which the slate of nominees had been determined and urged the membership to abstain from voting. "Leave the seats vacant until poor people can be elected," they read. "Please don't vote." Inside, Bessie Smith, cochair of Area Board 3, a homemaker and mother of two and member of the committee that had drawn up the slate of nominees, read a statement that demanded the voting be postponed because those nominees were "not representative of the very poor." The membership, after a lengthy debate, denied Smith's proposal. But they approved a motion to allow the area boards to choose a certain number of trustees in the future and, later, greeted one trustee's assertion that "sometimes too much democracy isn't healthy" with hisses and boos.[42]

In August 1965, Mayor Addonizio announced that he had reached an agreement with UCC officers to expand the board again. This time, they would add an unspecified number of seats for representatives of the poor but would also provide ex officio seats for the mayor, all nine city council members, and the heads of about twenty different city agencies. The agreement would have to be approved by the UCC's current board of trustees and by the full membership, but it promised an easing of tensions by diluting the influence of those the mayor considered enemies of his administration and whose presence on the UCC board had been troubling him for months.[43]

The city council, however, remained obstinate. The day after Addonizio's announcement, its members delayed once again approval of its contribution to the antipoverty program. They claimed the program needed more study. And, as a stunned Rabbi Prinz watched, the council president appointed a special subcommittee to investigate the inner workings of the UCC. The move might have surprised Prinz, but earlier that day Councilman Frank Addonizio had informed the press that such an investigation was forthcoming. An area of primary interest, he said, would be the feasibility of placing the community action agency under the direct control of the mayor and city council.[44] Later that month, before holding a single meeting or hearing a single witness, Councilman Addonizio, who with Lee Bernstein and Irvine Turner would conduct the council's investigation, declared that the UCC would be better off under the control of a "more responsible leadership, not rabble rousers" who used the agency to further their own political careers. Chief among them was George Richardson, who had recently taken leave from the UCC, as per its bylaws, to consider a run for mayor, but the councilman also asserted that "militant left-wing groups" dominated the agency. "The entire UCC program must get a new base of operations," he concluded. The investigation was just getting started, but, he tantalizingly promised, "the revelations we will make will be very startling."[45]

Mayor Addonizio, who often adopted the stance of a levelheaded statesman at pains to transcend the fray, stridently denied any connection between his plan for greater city participation in the antipoverty program and the city council investigation. But he defended the council's right to investigate any organization it funded. If something were amiss, he argued, it deserved a public airing. In his view, "political opportunists" were now threatening the UCC's work and inflaming community tensions. Before the backdrop of the recent racial conflagration in Watts, "these little men," the mayor said, "must be made to understand they are trifling with people's lives and the future of this city."[46]

Three days later, Adam Clayton Powell Jr., who headed the House committee that oversaw the War on Poverty, added to the cloud of suspicion surrounding the UCC. He announced that he would dispatch congressional investigators to probe the antipoverty programs in several cities. Letters of complaint were piling up in his office, he explained, so the investigation would start "where the maximum trouble is brewing." An aide confirmed an imminent visit to Newark.[47]

At the end of the summer, three new area boards were established (the South Ward's Dayton Street neighborhood, the Ironbound, and the eastern half of the North Ward), and the city council began its investigation.[48] In preparation for the subcommittee's first official meeting, its members had requested reams of documents from the UCC: lists of all its programs, its sources and amounts of funding, and all its personnel files.[49] Willard Heckel and Monsignor Joseph Dooling of the North Ward's St. Francis Xavier Church, who represented the UCC at the meeting, lugged the requested records, organized in stacks of color-coded three-ring binders, into the packed hearing room. Two hundred fifty people, most of them UCC partisans, showed up, so many that the balcony had to be opened to accommodate them. They cheered Heckel's opening statement, in which he defended the hiring of Tyson, emphasized the board's desire to include more poor people *and* more city representatives, and declared that the UCC had taken up the task, laid out by President Kennedy in his inaugural address, of reconstructing democracy. They booed and hissed when the city councilmen let loose a barrage of accusatory questions about who controlled hiring and who had purchased the UCC's pricey office furniture. At one point, the crowd grew so restive that Councilman Addonizio threatened to clear the chambers.[50]

The city council investigators could have come straight out of community action's central casting office. They were exactly the recalcitrant, unyielding local politicians that its participatory and experimental ethics sough to disrupt, a local version of the mainline federal departments that had wanted to turn the antipoverty program to their own ends and so dissatisfied those looking for fresh ideas. There was no hidden agenda here; the councilmen's intent was explicit. Bernstein, for one, demanded all of the UCC's applications for employment, claiming that it hired too many outsiders. If the UCC seemed unable to find qualified Newarkers to fill its staffing needs, then perhaps the city council should "consider taking over from the UCC the hiring responsibilities."[51] And at its next meeting, the investigative committee heard testimony about those few UCC programs run by city agencies, such as the Board of Education's summer Head Start program and the Division of Welfare's job training project. The point, committee members said, was that the UCC was not needed. The city itself, through existing agencies, could run the entire program. What's more, according to the city clerk, the current setup might even be unconstitutional, since Article VIII of the New Jersey State Constitution forbids municipalities to give land or money "to or for the use of any society, association or corporation whatever." Therefore, Councilman Addonizio concluded, the city council could not appropriate money for the UCC.[52]

These local conflicts embroiled Newark in a larger national debate surrounding community action. Cyril Tyson suspected that Mayor Addonizio was a covert member of a nationwide mayoral chorus threatening the War on Poverty's cornerstone program. The US Conference of Mayors, its members resentful of all the money bypassing city hall and filling the coffers of independent antipoverty agencies, began complaining to President Johnson and the OEO. At the conference's annual meeting in Saint Louis in the spring of 1965, its members considered a resolution accusing the OEO of failing "to recognize the legal and moral responsibilities of local officials who are accountable to the taxpayers." Some charged community action with "fostering class struggle" and "creating tensions" in their cities. One of the resolution's authors read passages from the OEO's *Community Action Workbook*, which sketched the range of approaches to resident participation being deployed in various cities, including the exertion of the poor's political influence through protest actions. But the mayors traded the resolution for a private consultation with Vice President Hubert Humphrey (former mayor of Minneapolis), whom Lyndon Johnson had designated a special liaison to them on matters of poverty and civil rights. Though the meeting was closed to the press, the executive director of the conference came away much assured. Despite initial misunderstandings about the role of city hall in local antipoverty programs, he said, it was agreed that it was to be "the principal organizer at the local level."[53]

But just as community action promoted solidarity among municipal power structures, signs emerged that it was doing the same for the residents it served in Newark. "The community" was emerging as an entity distinct from, but mutually constitutive of, city hall. Its stirrings could be seen in Bessie Smith and Area Board 3's alternative proposal for expanding the board of trustees, or those UCC proponents who cheered on Willard Heckel and booed the city council investigators. And it was seen late in October 1965, when a young mother named Laura Hayes took the floor at a meeting of the Central Ward's Area Board 2, the city's largest. She explained how she had moved to Newark from North Carolina with her parents and five siblings when they had had enough of sharecropping. The politicians don't know poverty, she said. They could look at it, but that was different from experiencing it firsthand. "I'm tired of politicians using the poor people, making so many promises and such," she said. "If they had done all they said they'd do we wouldn't be here tonight." Now that the poor were organizing in local community action programs, the politicians just needed to give them the funding and get out of the way. "The only thing we need the politicians for is to stand in back of us."[54]

A week later, in the middle of the city council's investigation of the UCC, the *New York Times* reported that the White House's Budget Bureau had advised the OEO that, in its view, "maximum feasible participation" intended for the poor only to *carry out* antipoverty programs, not design them. According to the story, the pressure had come from big-city mayors, led by Richard Daley of Chicago. When asked by the *Times* what he thought of the scoop, Willard Heckel declared that such a move "cuts the whole spirit out of the Economic Opportunity Act." Rabbi Prinz penned an angry letter to the editor in which he wrote that changing the role of the poor "would be a throwback to a well-meaning but archaic concept of social service. It would rob the OEO of its one refreshing and hopeful weapon."[55]

The outcry rattled enough nerves in Washington that the OEO organized a three-day press junket to address the allegations. Vice President Humphrey, who only months before had declared himself the "built-in special agent" for the US Conference of Mayors, denied the *Times'* story. "We don't want Big Daddy out there to tell you what to do," he said. "This is a community action program, not a Washington action program."[56] On the junket's second day, an OEO official singled out Newark's innovative area board structure as a particularly praiseworthy manifestation of maximum feasible participation and noted that other cities had adopted the model. Another hailed the UCC as one of the best-managed agencies in the country, and the OEO's director of community action commended Cyril Tyson directly.[57] Most reassuring was a letter Heckel received from Humphrey at the end of November in which the vice president expressed his full confidence that the War on Poverty would continue with maximum feasible participation intact.[58]

No sooner had the rumors of White House treachery passed than the Newark city council's investigative committee released its final report. For anyone who followed the course of the inquiry, it contained no surprises. Like much of the councilmen's rhetoric during the investigation, it served to bolster the defenses of traditional urban politics against what it called "the hostilities generated by the new bureaucracy in its striving for recognition." It lashed out at Cyril Tyson, whom it accused of using his power to hire friends, pay lavish salaries, and indulge their fancy for luxuries. In short, rather than antipoverty work, which the report defined as job training and employment opportunity, the UCC was concerned primarily with "healthy salaries and material goods, organizational procedures and political action."[59] By pursuing that last item, community action in Newark had further victimized the poor. It had been corrupted by political dissidents more concerned with the "striving and seeking for political power financed with federal funds which can stir up house against house and neighbor against neighbor" than they were with the elimination of poverty. The solution was straightforward: eliminate the UCC and replace it with a nine-member municipal commission consisting of the mayor, four city councilmen, and four nominated by the mayor and approved by the city council.[60]

Days after the report's release, Councilmen Addonizio and Bernstein traveled to Washington to meet with OEO officials and inform them of their intention to seek a city ordinance creating their proposed antipoverty commission. While they were in town, they attended Adam Clayton Powell's press conference announcing the findings of his own investigation. Powell called for an "administrative middle ground" between Chicago's setup, where investigators found "minimum feasible participation of the poor," and Newark's program, which was "so politically pure that it has antagonized all of the city councilmen and ignored the mayor."[61]

In its report, the council investigative committee had warned that the UCC was planning to expand its empire over the rest of the city by organizing its final three area boards in Weequahic, Roseville, and Vailsburg. These areas were the last to be organized because, as the UCC's director of community action explained, they contained less poverty than other neighborhoods, though those living in the small pockets that did exist needed help.[62] For Councilmen Addonizio and Bernstein, especially, the establishment of these new boards "would be laughable, were it not so insulting." This was a sign, their report said, of the ignorance among those outsiders that ran the UCC.[63] Bernstein said that to designate these neighborhoods as "poverty-stricken would be a direct insult to every taxpayer living in those areas."[64]

Indeed, the establishment of area boards in these neighborhoods proved more difficult than elsewhere. First up was the board in Roseville–Forest Hill. Forest Hill was perhaps the wealthiest and certainly one of the whitest areas of Newark. But in its 1959 report, the Mayor's Commission on Group Relations had identified Roseville as one of the main catch basins for the black population that was growing too large for the Central Ward.[65] Yet only about thirty people showed up for the organizing meeting, though the UCC had sent out three thousand invitations. Among those attending, several echoed a concern, first voiced by Councilman Bernstein, that their home values would surely decline should they suddenly find themselves living in an officially designated poverty area. Nonetheless, a majority of those few in attendance ultimately voted to create Area Board 7.[66]

Weequahic, which was identified as another prosperous and mostly white neighborhood in the 1959 report, had grown less so since, as the same demographic pressures that moved black Newarkers north into Roseville also moved them further and further south.[67] Some residents threatened to close their accounts at a local building and loan when they learned it had agreed to host the area board organizing meeting, so UCC officials moved it to a public school. Almost one hundred people showed up and locked horns in what one local newspaper called "two hours of rough-and-tumble debate." One resident argued that Weequahic shouldn't be selfish and take OEO money when other areas of the city needed it more. Others countered that poverty existed even in their more upscale neighborhood, so *not* confronting it would be the selfish act. After rejecting a motion to postpone a vote in order to let tempers cool, residents voted 56 to 35 to form Area Board 9. In voting for a chair, they rejected one of Bernstein's political cronies and installed a well-regarded local clergyman.[68]

Opponents had more success in Vailsburg, which, like Forest Hill, had yet to experience much change in its racial composition. (Both neighborhoods were soon identified as prime targets of Klan recruiting efforts.) It was the preferred address of many municipal officials, including the mayor and the city's police and fire directors.[69] Councilman Addonizio, another Vailsburg resident, had warned that the Federal Housing Authority would refuse to make loans in designated poverty areas, and nervous residents postponed a final decision, pending a fuller survey of local need and opinion. Over the next few weeks, residents signed a petition circulated by Addonizio declaring their opposition to the establishment of an area board, signing under the claim that the board would "reflect on our property values, demean our standard of living and insult our way of life." The Vailsburg Community Council forwarded a unanimous resolution to the mayor and city council opposing the creation of a board. It soon became the only section of the city without an antipoverty area board.[70]

Such neighborhood self-defense, then, stemmed from more than the fear of racial incursion, whether real or imagined. The resistance manifested itself as a showdown between two possible political solidarities. The administrative structure of community action, snaking out from Washington to cities and counties across the country, had come to Newark, where it split into a local network of area boards, which, in turn, spread through much of the city. Residents of the city's most substantial white residential redoubts would not associate themselves with that structure, which had taken on racial and class meanings, as readily as neighbors in other sections did. They wanted to hold on to their home values, but they were also forging a closer solidarity with their local councilmen, Frank Addonizio of the West Ward and Lee Bernstein of the South Ward. As community action's threatened unraveling of the municipal power structure advanced, such solidarities became increasingly important for many white Newarkers.

With their momentum apparently slowing, UCC officials released their response to the city council's investigation shortly before Christmas 1965. At a press conference, Willard Heckel called the investigation "totally irresponsible" and its conclusions "completely unjustified," "reckless," and "untrue," while Rabbi Prinz demanded to know whether the intent of the antipoverty legislation would be carried out or abused in Newark, which he called the "last bastion" of community involvement in the poverty program. Tim Still was blunter still when he took the microphone. It would be "a tragedy and a farce," he said, to let politicians gain control of the antipoverty program.[71]

Though their seventy-seven-page response called the city council's investigation "a rambling excursion into the field of speculation, assumption, inference, and innuendo," it nonetheless carefully disputed its findings point by point. It provided a lengthy case history (including a 1932 decision that allowed the city to pay the Prudential Insurance Company to build housing in the Ironbound) that demonstrated the constitutionality of municipal funding for the UCC; argued that the board of trustees constituted a check on Cyril Tyson's allegedly autocratic reign; and compared UCC salaries to those of similarly experienced city workers and found them comparable. Where Councilmen Addonizio and Bernstein had written the mayor's office out of their story of the UCC's creation, the rebuttal report noted that the antipoverty program had from the beginning enjoyed the blessing and the cooperation of many city officials. In the end, the UCC urged the full city council to reject its investigative committee's recommendations and recommit itself to "a total community-wide effort in which we earnestly seek the cooperation and assistance of the Mayor and the City Council."[72]

Out in the neighborhoods, though, lines were being drawn. Early in January, the members of Area Board 2: Operation We Care gathered to discuss a program proposal recently submitted to the UCC by city hall. The Addonizio administration wanted to institute a program of home rehabilitation for fifteen blocks in the Central Ward. Under the plan, tenants would be provided opportunities to attend educational seminars, and landlords would be provided funds to update their properties. The UCC trustees had twice postponed a vote on the proposal in order to let Area Board 2 members weigh in on it. Many of them no doubt relished the possibility of their decrepit homes being rehabilitated, but there were other issues to consider. Wouldn't this plan, in effect, amount to a tax break for slum landlords? Why should antipoverty money be used to bring their properties up to code? Some residents found the proposal insulting. Wasn't

it the landlords who needed education when it came to housing maintenance? After much debate, area board members gave their conditional
approval to city hall's proposal: if their landlords would guarantee no rent
increase, then they, and the UCC, would send the proposal on to Washington.[73] But when no such guarantee came, the UCC trustees killed the
mayor's plan. It was the first time they rejected *any* proposal. In this case,
community action worked the way it was meant to: residents of the city's
most impoverished neighborhood blocked an antipoverty plan they found
objectionable.[74]

In the South Ward, Councilman Bernstein's political apparatus rallied
from its failed effort to prevent the creation of an area board in Weequahic. The board's first official meeting quickly devolved into what one local paper called "two hours of shouting and a near fight." When the floor
was opened, a portion of the audience erupted. "We don't need a poverty
board!" some shouted. "We want to vote to dis-organize! Call for a vote!"
When one resident demanded that the meeting be saved from such "row-
dies," only the timely intervention of several neighbors prevented fisticuffs.
Over appeals for calm from the UCC's community action director, Councilman Bernstein launched a strident attack on the area board, recycling the
arguments used in the last meeting. Neither the board chair nor the community action director could regain control. Their attempts were shouted
down, and amid the noise they hurried through an adjournment.[75]

While neighborhoods struggled with community action and city officials
fought to gain control of it, Cyril Tyson's old HARYOU mentor came
to Newark and gave a speech before a crowd of nine hundred people at
Temple B'nai Abraham (Rabbi Prinz's temple) in the South Ward on January 11, 1966. Dr. Kenneth Clark had extricated himself from the political
tussling over Harlem's antipoverty program, but the experience had left a
bad taste in his mouth. If such programs truly hoped to reach the poor, he
said, they must engage in "conflict with the existing political apparatus."
If local politicians smile down upon their city's community action agency,
"we can now be reasonably sure it is an irrelevant program." He argued
that the only way to eliminate ghettos was to organize the poor. Without
such organization, the War on Poverty would turn out to be "another set of
cruel political hoaxes perpetrated on the powerless victims of the ghetto."[76]

Soon enough, the UCC membership pushed the conflict further than
even the organization's central leadership had anticipated. While city and
antipoverty officials battled each other, enough members across the city

had acquired a cherished stake in community action that they refused to turn back. In part, for sure, this reflected a commitment to the services the program was developing, sometimes in partnership with city agencies. The Newark Pre-School Council had begun classes in churches and housing project rec rooms the previous summer, and the UCC had approved proposals for a program engineered to serve the needs of the elderly (from the Newark Senior Citizens Commission), two different work-training projects for city youth (from the Blazer Youth Council and the Mount Carmel Guild of the Newark archdiocese), summer education programs for new high school students and illiterate adults (both from Seton Hall University), and a series of small business centers to help local entrepreneurs generate job opportunities for the poor.[77] But it also reflected a growing commitment to the administrative structure of the program and the opportunities and resources it provided out in the neighborhoods, where some residents had already spent nearly a year building their area boards and designing and launching new programs. The two boards that covered the Central Ward had developed flourishing youth programs and one of them (Area Board 2) had actually begun forming antipoverty block associations that stretched the administrative state even further, onto individual streets. Area Board 3 in Clinton Hill had begun submitting proposals to the UCC central office, which in February approved the board's plan for a neighborhood recreation center. More recently organized area boards had developed constitutions and bylaws, elected trustees and officers, and formed committees. Several had proposals in the pipeline.[78] To the thousands of members involved in this work, community action not only provided jobs and services (though those aspects were not unimportant) but also offered a political space in which they developed new leverage to affect their own lives, to confront their urban crisis in their own way. And it was a space they would not readily yield.

UCC officials scheduled an annual membership meeting for February 17, 1966, at Temple B'nai Abraham, five weeks after Kenneth Clark's stirring call to confrontation. The most pressing business was a vote on the UCC's proposal to end the power struggles between the antipoverty program and city hall by adding more city officials *and* more representatives of the poor to the board of trustees. Not all UCC leaders, however, had signed on to the plan. Fearing the proposed expansion would constitute a "stacked deck" for city government, Willie Wright, the chairman of the Central Ward's Area Board 2 and a UCC vice president, took the floor and made a motion to amend it.

Wright epitomized the neighborhood resident who found in community action an opportunity to develop and exercise political muscle. He had studied at Rutgers but continued his education with the UCC. Willard Heckel, who was very close to Wright in the early years of the program, later remembered how Wright intently studied Robert's Rules of Order and engaged in long political discussions. Wright was among those nominated from the floor at the first membership meeting in May 1965 and voted onto the board of trustees.[79] He joined the UCC's bylaws committee, which, in December, had unanimously decided on the current plan to bring peace to the program by expanding the board of trustees.[80] At some point, though, Wright changed his mind.

Under Wright's amendment, area board representation would increase by the same amount, but city representation would grow by only two seats, to a total of seven. Furthermore, those seven seats would be reserved for elected rather than appointed officials: the mayor and six councilmen. "The community will not be losing anything if we cast these [city officials] aside," Wright argued. "If the poor are going to decide their lives, this is the night to do it." Several of his colleagues in the UCC leadership warned against compromising the basis for future relations with city government. But with the backing of the head of the local CORE chapter (additional city trustees would perpetuate a "hold-them-down, keep-them-in-their-places psychology of the plantation"), several members of Clinton Hill's Area Board 3 (the city administration "has helped Newark become the leading center of poverty in the northern states"), and after several hours of at times hostile debate, Wright's proposal carried the day.[81]

Two months later, as the relationship between city hall and the UCC reached new lows, Mayor Addonizio faced his first reelection campaign. His main opponent was former mayor Leo Carlin, whose support of mid-century charter reform and record in office had earned him a reputation for honest administration. Nonetheless, given the powerful coalition of Italian and black Newarkers that had put him in office in 1962, Addonizio was widely expected to win, and win handily.

George Richardson had other plans. Since his break with the county Democratic Party, he had renamed his independent political organization the United Freedom Democratic Party. It now took aim at city hall. Richardson was convinced that by 1970 the black community would have grown to sufficient size and would be sufficiently organized to vote him into office. As an intermediate step, he organized a campaign to challenge Addonizio in 1966. Rather than run himself, however, Richardson asked

Kenneth Gibson, the city engineer and UCC vice president, to be the Freedom Party's candidate. And when the results came in, Gibson's strong performance surprised everyone, especially Mayor Addonizio, who was about six hundred votes shy of a clear majority and was forced into a runoff against Carlin. Gibson had been expected to collect five thousand votes. Instead, he won over sixteen thousand.[82]

That spring, an official OEO publication lauded the fact that, through community action, the poor had found their voice. It called this discovery a "Quiet Revolution in the best traditions of American democracy."[83] But this acclamation—and the seeming victory for maximum feasible participation in Newark—came on the cusp of a new series of attacks on community action at the national level. The efforts of longtime opponents seemed to be paying off. Congress was considering an amendment to the Economic Opportunity Act that would greatly reduce the amount of discretionary funds for the Community Action Program, while earmarking additional money for more politically palatable programs like Head Start and the Neighborhood Youth Corps.[84]

Walter Reuther's Citizens' Crusade against Poverty, originally established to lobby for community action, now rose to its defense. Richard Boone, the War on Poverty architect who had coined the phrase "maximum feasible participation," had since become CCAP's director. When he testified before the Senate on the proposed amendments, Boone asked that they reaffirm the program's participatory mandate, for, as he argued, "A society that has brought freedom to so many can not, in good conscience, deny genuine opportunities to the poor to share in decisions that affect their lives."[85] To demonstrate the popularity and power of that mandate, CCAP scheduled an April "poor people's convention" in Washington.

Sargent Shriver was scheduled to speak on the second day of the gathering and was warned by aides that the crowd, angered by the proposed amendments, might be hostile. After he opened with some dark humor— "I'm not sure whether I was invited here for lunch or as the lunch"— audience members began heckling him. Several approached the stage, called him a liar, and implored others to stop listening. Unita Blackwell, the Mississippi civil rights leader, told him "we are tired of beautiful speeches." Shriver could hardly be heard through the shouting, and when he finished, aides quickly pushed him through a jostling crowd and out of the building. Jack Conway, who had left the OEO around the same time as Boone and returned to work at the UAW, told the *New York Times* that the dissidents were "wrecking the meeting. They have turned on the people who wanted to help them." Boone, though, was a bit more understanding. He said afterward that poor people had come to Washington not to celebrate the OEO's accomplishments but to express their frustrations with the lack of results in their own neighborhoods and the failure to follow through on the promise of maximum feasible participation, which, he thought, had in too many places become "a numbers game between Washington and the local politicians and welfare barons."[86]

In July, the OEO sent a representative to Newark to discuss the impending funding limitations with the UCC's executive committee, who openly worried about the community's response to the news. Willie Wright asked the OEO representative how they could be expected to run a democratic program under such limitations, and the UCC's assistant secretary warned that the result would be a riot. Without appropriate funding, she said, the antipoverty program would just be toying with people: "You are just putting a bad dirty knife in an open sore and turning it around." She recommended the UCC march on the White House.[87]

At the end of September, more than a thousand Newarkers boarded nineteen buses and headed for the nation's capital on a mission codenamed "Operation Concern." They marched along Pennsylvania Avenue four abreast, wielding signs that said "We Need Funds Now!" and "Programs Not Riots!" They crowded into a congressional caucus room, the group so large many had to sit on the floor, to listen to members of their congressional delegation urge them to pressure the opposition Republicans and southern Democrats. They cheered when an OEO official declared that "Newark has one of the finest programs in the nation and we don't intend to let you down."[88] A small delegation of UCC leaders met separately with several other federal officials. Adam Clayton Powell Jr.— who greeted them with "Hello, all you Mau-Maus!"—advised them to tone it down. "We don't have to use violence yet," he told them.[89] In a meeting with Shriver, some delegates (including Mayor Addonizio, who remained honorary president of the UCC) blasted the Johnson administration's increasing commitments to the Vietnam War and to the space program. Shriver expressed total agreement and told them that their demonstration was the most exciting thing that had happened during his tenure as director of the OEO.[90]

Less than a month later, Congress passed its OEO reauthorization. It was a mixed blessing. Amendments mandated that a minimum of one-third of antipoverty boards be composed of representatives of the poor. At the same time, Congress cut discretionary community action funding by

5. Two UCC administrators prepare signs for Operation Concern's trip to Washington, DC. The UCC was a determined defender of the antipoverty program against threats to its funding and participatory ethic. (Newark Public Library / UCC)

nearly a third and earmarked funding increases for more popular portions of the War on Poverty. One anxious federal official told the *New York Times*, "This is really a problem; it's like a whole new ball game."[91]

By early 1967, War on Poverty officials in Washington had themselves come to a more pragmatic position on maximum feasible participation. Increasingly, their vision became broader and more consensual, rather than focusing on the "residents of the areas and members of the groups to be served," as the original legislation had put it. Following the congressional amendments, new OEO guidelines in January proposed that each antipoverty board be divided into equal thirds: one for the poor or their representatives, one for government officials, and one for representatives of private and civic groups, like churches, businesses, labor unions, and social welfare agencies. Where the poor had effectively been shut out of their local antipoverty agencies, the new guidelines opened new opportunities. But in Newark—where the membership, through its steadfast defense of community participation and rejection of increased government interference, its determination to stretch the administrative structure down even to the block level, and its constant appeals to federal officials on behalf of the participatory ethic, had pushed community action to its frontier—the guidelines signaled a retreat.[92]

Cyril Tyson had intended to work in Newark for only one year. The trials and tribulations of establishing the UCC had kept him in the post longer than planned. But in July 1966, he submitted his resignation. In a plaintive letter, he thanked the people of Newark and the UCC, whose "dedication to the philosophy of 'maximum feasible participation' of the impoverished fortified me through many difficult decisions." He wrote that "no words can really express my feeling for an organization which, in its short existence, projected to the City of Newark an integrity of purpose and commitment to the involvement of the poor in all aspects of the democratic process."[93] Tyson left behind a central office, nearly two dozen specific programs ready to be launched the next spring, eight area boards, and a membership of almost ten thousand.[94]

The UCC personnel committee asked William K. Wolfe to replace Tyson. A native of nearby Plainfield, Wolfe had helped establish community action agencies in Westchester County, New York. As he prepared to negotiate a contract with the UCC that November, he provided a glimpse of how he might approach the job in an interview with the *Newark Evening News*. Though he said he had no idea how he might differ from Tyson, his hope was to serve as a "catalytic agent" bringing together diverse forces within Newark. He had already met with Mayor Addonizio and other city officials, but he declined to speculate on how he would get along with them. He did, however, soundly reject the notion that, in order to have an effective antipoverty program, the poor had to be at odds with local politicians.[95]

Portions of the UCC leadership and general membership responded with scorn. In May 1967, barely five months into Wolfe's tenure, the membership voted to suspend him. Spearheading the campaign was the head of a local UCC work-training program, who explained that the UCC staff had "sold out" the poor and (in an ironic echo of the city council investigation's charges) become dominated by out-of-towners. Members applauded when another supporter suggested Wolfe be given thirty days "to move into this town or else pack him up in his little jeep and send him on his way." But the other charge—Wolfe's apparent cozying-up with city hall—was the more salient issue. The Addonizio administration had recently promised the state medical school 150 acres of a predominantly black Central Ward neighborhood for its new campus, and, the dissidents charged, the UCC director had not done enough to oppose it.[96]

THREE

Convergence

In the spring of 1967, Newark police director Dominick Spina ordered two officers from his intelligence division to attend a meeting of local activists at the Black Liberation Center on South Orange Avenue. The meeting was to plan a community response to the city's proposed handover of a Central Ward neighborhood to the state for the construction of a new medical school. The deal—engineered by a partnership among federal, state, and local officials—was the clearest sign yet of the disregard for, if not the outright antipathy toward, Newark's black community among those occupying existing state structures. For those officials, the medical school was an obvious way to combat their urban crisis: the school would provide new educational, employment, and healthcare opportunities for the city, as well as continue its long-standing objectives of slum clearance and urban renewal. For residents and their supporters, this was as complete a repudiation of community action as one could imagine: deals were made without the knowledge, let alone the participation, of members of the community it purported to serve. To them, it represented the potential diminishing of their collective political power and of what capital they had invested in the neighborhood in the form of businesses and homes.

The police intelligence officers were sent to surveil the opposition that had quickly amassed in the Central Ward. The Black Liberation Center occupied an old storefront a couple of blocks from the proposed medical school site, and as the officers entered, they took note of the handbills and posters cluttering its windows: images of Malcolm X, "The Black Panther Is Coming," "Stop the Medical School." Inside, they were unsurprised to find several of the most active local dissidents in attendance. George Richardson and Ken Gibson were there, of course. But the meeting had been organized by a young Student Nonviolent Coordinating Committee

(SNCC) organizer named Phil Hutchings. He had come to Newark from Cleveland early in 1964 and, after working in a variety of community organizations, opened the Black Liberation Center in March 1967. He had invited, among others, his friend Tom Hayden to the meeting. Hayden, the former president of Students for a Democratic Society (SDS), had come to town in 1964 and helped launch the Newark Community Union Project in the Lower Clinton Hill neighborhood. They were joined by Robert Curvin, the former chair of the Newark–Essex County CORE chapter, who, as such, had helped organize a remarkable wave of direct-action protest in the region. These were eminently familiar faces, but another attendee was more of a mystery: a tall black man in a self-styled military uniform, shades, and

6. Though their relationship was sometimes strained, Mayor Hugh Addonizio (left) and Police Director Dominick Spina shared a determination to monitor local dissidents they accused of fomenting trouble in Newark. (Monsignor William Noé Field Archives and Special Collections Center, Seton Hall University)

a beret. He called himself Colonel Hassan and claimed to be the leader of the Blackman's Volunteer Liberation Army.

After the meeting, Spina's officers wrote up a report on what they had seen. It shook the city administration and law enforcement officials. "This marked the first time in the city's history," Spina later said, "where all the political dissidents who didn't like . . . the so-called establishment or the power structure . . . were united." For him, this meeting of "people on the left," as he called them, marked the culmination of a rising temper in the city's black neighborhoods. It signaled not only a new militancy but, more frighteningly, a new unity.[1]

Opposition to the medical school plan was a turning point in the quickening struggle for greater black power in Newark. It marked an unprecedented unity of forces against the city administration and its state and federal partners. Community action was central to the opposition, in the sense that the fight was *against* reigning state structures and processes and *for* the preservation of a denigrated and ignored local community. But the United Community Corporation itself was an integral part of the rising tide of activism that Spina spied. The UCC did not invent community organizing in Newark, and it would not be fair to say that it led the movement. But they did intersect in multiple ways. Many organizations and people already active in Newark when the UCC arrived recognized it as an opportunity to gain new resources, allies, and power, and many of them—including those figures given special attention by the police intelligence officers—plugged into it in one capacity or another, helping shape a program whose vision extended beyond the elimination of poverty to larger notions of political access for the black community. And the UCC and its area boards were similarly opportunistic: when a campaign of value to its constituents got under way—like the fight against the medical school plan—they weighed in, sometimes discursively, but often with material resources. To trace these intersections is to follow the Great Society out onto the streets of Newark, where community action would bear some of its most vital fruits in the form of black power and the anxious response to it.

The Newark Community Union Project was the product of an early discontent among SDS members. After the heady summer days of the organization's national conference at Port Huron, Michigan, in 1962, when the gathered student leaders debated and revised Tom Hayden's draft platform document, members struggled with how to make the document's invocation of "participatory democracy" a lived reality, to fulfill its potential as a call to

action. The daring work of young SNCC activists and their principled decenteredness provided them a model, and the fear of an impending economic
crisis sparked by automation and mass unemployment gave them a cause.
So in 1963, after struggling for months against what Hayden later called an
"intense subculture of discussion," SDS began designing experimental organizing drives aimed at the poor and unemployed. With a contribution from
the United Auto Workers in hand, Hayden proposed a wave of such drives
to the SDS national council that September. The result was the Economic
Research and Action Project (ERAP), which proposed "an interracial movement of the poor, " a movement that would stress "the need for democratic
participation in a society with a publicly-controlled and planned economy"
rather than, presumably, the current oligarchic arrangement.[2]

The Newark project's original goal was to establish a jobs program
in partnership with the National Committee for Full Employment and,
through that, to organize a "union of unemployed to build grass-roots support for political change in Newark." Upon arriving in the Clinton Hill
neighborhood, the ERAPers formed a local committee on full employment, which asserted that "the central socio-economic problem of American society today is unemployment."[3] But if the planners had hoped to organize the white working class around issues of employment, they picked
a bad neighborhood in which to do it. They soon learned that Clinton
Hill actually comprised two very different sections. The Upper Hill was one
of the South Ward's last enclaves of white residents, a mostly middle-class
neighborhood with a strongly liberal bent. And the Lower Hill—where the
project's office was located—was home to an expanding black population,
made up largely of people who had moved there from the overflowing
Central Ward.[4]

One day, sitting in the office writing a letter, Tom Hayden looked up to
see a woman, "strong and tear-choked," walk in the door. Emma Gaskins
explained that a friend of hers, who had recently moved to Newark from
the South, rented an apartment on nearby Clinton Avenue for ninety-five
dollars a month. The payment nearly wrung her welfare checks dry and left
her with little money for other expenses. What's more, the apartment was
dangerous: its back door had gone missing, electrical wires dangled threat-
eningly from the ceiling, and the stench of sewage and dead rats hung
about its rooms. Her friend, however, was fearful of taking on the landlord herself, especially since landlords and municipal housing code officers
were well-known bedfellows. Gaskins wanted to help her friend and had
heard about the project. She had heard they were doing good things in the
neighborhood.[5]

7. As a national figure in the student New Left, Tom Hayden attracted attention
from city officials and the Newark Police, who deemed him a dangerous outside
agitator. Here, in a police surveillance photo, he is singled out among Clinton
Hill residents protesting housing conditions. (New Jersey State Archives)

Scrawny welfare checks. The city inspector's office and housing agency.
Slumlords. Roaches. Rats. ERAP organizers had not anticipated such concerns. As Jennifer Frost has demonstrated, its masculine and producerist
orientation could not survive the innumerable encounters like the one
Hayden had that day. As the earliest organizers—most of whom, beyond
core staff members, were white college students or recent graduates who
came to Newark over a school break—spread out through the community,
picking up new organizers and new members, the residents to whom they
spoke refashioned ERAP's objectives and introduced the white New Left
to a galaxy of issues centered on black women as consumers: as renters of
both public and private housing, as recipients of welfare, as food shop-
pers, and as primary caregivers for their children.[6] Driven by residents'
most pressing concerns, the newly christened Newark Community Union
Project (NCUP, pronounced "n-cup") pioneered a reorientation away from
"jobs or income now" (JOIN) projects and toward what became jokingly
known as "garbage removal or income now" (GROIN) projects, for the

supposedly more quotidian struggles they took on. When it became apparent that Clinton Hill's dangerous traffic intersections, infrequently marked or policed, were the cause of deep concern for parents, the project humorously, but proudly, dubbed itself "the Newark project for jobs, income, freedom and stop signs."[7] This was participatory democracy in action: local residents having the power to determine the form of their own struggle and the shape of their lives. It harmonized well with community action, and, like community action, it would very quickly generate both a larger constituency and a hostile reaction.

On a spring day in 1965, Joyce Wells sat at her kitchen table on Peshine Avenue and worriedly tried to think of her next move. Several weeks earlier, she had had words with her landlord about her apartment's back door, which just barely clung to its hinges. Four days after their shouting match, she received a court summons for nonpayment of rent. When she appeared before the judge, she quickly realized her case had been decided long before she set foot in the courtroom: the judge ordered her to vacate the premises. "I felt like I was lost with no one to turn to," she later wrote. "I began packing my children's clothes, not knowing where I was going or what would happen to my seven children and I."[8]

As Wells sat at her table, two NCUP organizers, tipped off by a friend of hers, knocked on the door. Jesse Allen, a young black man from the neighborhood who had quit his job to become a full-time organizer, and Carol Glassman, a young white woman recently graduated from Smith College, had been knocking on doors like hers for months. Housing problems, they now knew, weighed heavily on the minds of most people they met on their rounds. The project had drawn up and mimeographed a long list of municipal code violations—cracked walls, broken plumbing, bad wiring, rats, roaches—and organizers took the form up and down the blocks and through individual tenements. People generally welcomed them once they explained that they worked for a neighborhood group—you know, the one around the corner whose office has no windows? right across the street from the drug store? where Jack's Barber Shop used to be?—and that they were fighting the landlords who charged exorbitant rates and the city officials who turned a blind eye to them. Once enough residents had studied the form and checked off all the violations that applied to their apartment, organizers took the stack down to the city inspector's office. They were unsigned so no one would be targeted for retribution.[9]

Those collected documents signaled a burgeoning sense of collective interest among poor residents in Lower Clinton Hill. Tenants held meetings, formed block associations, and took direct action. NCUP members presented lists of demands to their landlords, some of whom ignored them and some of whom responded satisfactorily. Where Jesse Allen lived, several residents took photos of their building, pasted them on picket signs, and marched outside the landlord's suburban home. One woman collected a jar of water beetles and, with fellow NCUP members, took them down to the housing inspector's office. And Joyce Wells went down to city hall with Carol Glassman and Jesse Allen and, though the court ruling could not be overturned, won more time to find a new home. Reflecting on what this small victory meant to her, Wells wrote, "NCUP showed me that if we poor people would only pull together and stick together we would have a decent clean neighborhood for our growing children, and better homes to live in."[10]

Many times, though, even minor successes seemed far-fetched given the forces arrayed against them. At the end of NCUP's first summer, Mayor Addonizio visited a tenement building on Clinton Avenue where one of its earliest members, Ida Brown, had begun a rent strike. After surveying the surroundings, he promised Brown he would take action on her behalf. Unconvinced, she continued her strike for several more months and, after leading several trips of NCUP members to city hall to demonstrate, she received an eviction notice. When she and her children moved in with an upstairs neighbor just after Christmas 1964, a city health officer told her they would have to move out, since the now overcrowded apartment constituted a code violation. When Brown refused, a plainclothes policeman broke into the apartment and, according to Brown, hit her and pushed her down the stairs. (The officer claimed he had arrested Brown when she punched him in the mouth.) She was held for seven hours on a $1,000 bond. The municipal judge warned her that should she or any of her comrades threaten the landlord, he would jail them and set their bail even higher.[11]

City government—or at least its health and housing inspection units, judiciary, police department, and mayor's office—had seemingly formed an accord with the Lower Hill's slumlords. Black residents, whose growing presence in Clinton Hill was a clear indication of the city's coming (or perhaps, by this point, already achieved) black majority, wanted safe places to live and tend to their families. In pursuit of this, some of them grasped the opportunity afforded by NCUP's participatory ethic and structure and used them to confront the entrenched city bureaucracy that had effectively shut them out.

Agents of that local bureaucracy, in turn, took aim at NCUP almost from the moment organizers set foot in Newark. In October 1964, NCUP's landlord, citing unnamed pressures, asked the organization to move out. When the group moved its office to a nearby location, its new landlord received repeat visits from city building inspectors, who compiled for him a list of costly required repairs (this at a time when NCUP members' pile of complaints drew little attention from the city). Members reported that their welfare caseworkers warned them away from any affiliation with the group, and others told of local politicians who had visited their landlords to suggest they evict any tenants affiliated with the group. And wherever NCUP went, the police predictably followed. Officers surveilled their demonstrations and took photos of participants. They threatened two organizers with arrest for passing out leaflets at South Side High School. And this all occurred in the context of various other threats and harassments, the sources of which were more shadowy: crank phone calls, vandalism of NCUP's office, warnings of imminent beatings, and bomb threats.[12]

Perhaps the greatest weapon in the city government's arsenal against NCUP was the specter of mass racial violence. Beginning in the summer of 1964, when racial conflagrations in Jersey City, Elizabeth, and Paterson ringed the city without breaching its borders, city boosters had made "peaceful" Newark's defining characteristic. NCUP organizers agitating residents in Clinton Hill seemed to threaten Newark's status as the city that didn't riot. In its very first mass action, NCUP had done something city leaders found unfathomable: they had picketed their local police precinct.[13] By confronting the institution deemed most dedicated to law and order in Newark, they seemed to have declared their hostility toward peace.[14] Later that summer, South Ward councilman Lee Bernstein allegedly circulated fliers calling NCUP a bunch of outsiders, and the head of the city's Human Rights Commission (and a close Bernstein ally) charged in an official commission report that NCUP planned to incite a riot in Newark.[15] The following spring, at a meeting organized by Mayor Addonizio to discuss riot prevention in Newark, Police Director Spina said that, in his mind, there was only one group in Newark that would start and probably enjoy a riot: those outsiders from NCUP.[16]

In February 1965, the local arm of the War on Poverty had established a neighborhood area board in NCUP's backyard. Ever since legislation was signed the previous summer, NCUP had recognized the potential—and the potential pitfalls—of some form of engagement with the federal antipoverty drive.[17] The burgeoning New Left and the liberal insurgents in Washington who helped craft the War on Poverty shared a disdain for bigness. Though the liberals were more likely to invoke problems of administrative inefficiency while the students lamented human alienation, they both recognized the implications for democracy. The Community Action Program, like ERAP, could be seen as a potential fulfillment of the Port Huron Statement's call for a political system "organized to encourage independence in men and provide media for their common participation."[18] If done right, it could be one such medium. Unfortunately, as national ERAP director Rennie Davis wrote in early 1965, around the time Area Board 3 was established in Clinton Hill, most local community action agencies around the country were composed of local power brokers rather than the poor themselves. However, he continued, "refusing to ask for or take federal money should not be a *principle* of the movement. Indeed, we should *demand* it." He called for an "insurgent response" to the War on Poverty that would turn it toward its greatest democratic potential. If an ERAP project found itself in a city where the poverty program was run by many small liberal organizations and where it was somewhat decentralized, it had an opportunity to use the program for its own organizing and political ends. "Newark," Davis wrote, "appears to be this sort of exception."[19]

Despite some deep suspicions and a rancorous internal debate over the compromises that might be required once plugged into a power grid that would connect them so closely to Washington, NCUP members ultimately decided to take a chance on their neighborhood area board.[20] When officials of the United Community Corporation held an organizing meeting for the board in February 1965, NCUP showed up in force. During the meeting, which one local newspaper deemed the longest and liveliest of all the area board meetings to date, residents elected Bessie Smith—a local homeowner and mother of two who had housed several of the young organizers when they first arrived in Newark and who had since become a powerful organizer herself—cochair.[21]

From the beginning, NCUP members made it their mission to ensure that control of the antipoverty program belonged to poor Newarkers. Even before they established themselves as a force in the Clinton Hill area board, members had attended the UCC's first general meeting earlier that February. In the midst of an intense discussion among the UCC trustees concerning political interference in their funding, Tom Hayden rose to ask how they intended to ensure participation of the poor. Told that UCC membership was open to anyone who filled out a card, Hayden pointed out that elections are also open to all citizens but the poor participate much less than other Americans. Another NCUP member, a scar-faced former prizefighter known as Bobo who had recently moved to the Central Ward to organize rent strikes, presented the trustees with the list of housing problems written up for Ida Brown's case and promised to pay the rent if board members would live for a month in his house while he lived in theirs. Taken aback, the board passed the list around like a hot potato until it reached UCC executive director Cyril Tyson, who was more receptive to Bobo's point and agreed to meet with him later.[22]

The crusade to take seriously and make manifest the democratic rhetoric of the War on Poverty consumed NCUP activists, and though it angered some that the Community Action Program had not been structured so that involvement by the poor was unavoidable, they were willing to act within Newark's area board system to force the issue. From their posts on the board's membership committee, for example, Hayden, Jesse Allen, and others agitated for a requirement that the majority of members be poor. Organizers regularly hit the phones and circulated leaflets throughout the Lower Hill, calling residents to meetings in the hope of preventing their neighbors in the more middle-class Upper Hill, no matter how well-intentioned they might be, from gaining a majority. And when the UCC scheduled its first citywide elections for May 1965, NCUP hurriedly signed almost 150 new members, just making the deadline, in order to bolster its voting power. And at that meeting, the one during which Mayor Addonizio warned the antipoverty program away from "empire building," the people on the sidewalk passing out fliers urging fellow members not to vote in UCC elections until poor people were guaranteed seats on the board were all from Area Board 3.[23]

In the neighborhood, NCUP members took advantage of the political space opened by their area board to devise novel organizing campaigns that redefined the issues and methods of the War on Poverty. For the most part, they were left free to do so. Emma Gaskins—the woman who had come to NCUP's office and told Tom Hayden about her friend's housing problems—lived in a building, like many in the Lower Hill, teeming with housing code violations. In the fall of 1965, Gaskins and two other NCUPers took her case directly to the head of the city's Human Rights Commission, who promised an exhaustive inspection of her Peshine Avenue tenement. This time, a city official kept his word, and three days later inspectors compiled a list of over one hundred code violations in that single building. As per official protocol, they sent a copy of the report to the landlord. He, in turn, sent Gaskins an eviction notice.[24]

Emma Gaskins was not only a member of Area Board 3 but one of its trustees. At a board meeting soon after she received the eviction notice, she asked her neighbors to take up her cause and support a building-wide rent strike. One member argued that, since this issue affected the whole community, it was, in his mind, fair game for the area board. Others agreed. Wyla McClain, another NCUP member who lived in the same building as Gaskins, said she had calculated the amount of rent their landlord collected for a building that was, as she said, unsuited for a pig to live in. A rent strike, she said, would hit him hard. When she demanded that all fourteen families in the building withhold their January rent, her neighbors cheered. In the end, the area board voted to support the rent strike. Several members picketed the landlord's home in suburban Millburn with signs calling him a "slumlord" who gave his tenants "rats and roaches for ridiculous rents."[25]

Despite the fervor of the Area Board 3 meeting that launched it, few people joined the picketing and even fewer the rent strike. Gaskins was evicted and her building continued to deteriorate. The fervor had been genuine and palpable—a new force was brewing in the Lower Hill—but its expression, as one observer put it, proved mostly symbolic.[26] But from a broader perspective, their work stands as an instance of local residents availing themselves of the administrative structure that community action had stretched out to them and of the direct action methods of the New Left to pursue their own desire for firmer ownership over their buying (or renting) power. They injected the same issues that had forced a revision of NCUP's original plan into the War on Poverty via its neighborhood outpost in the Lower Hill.[27]

Nearly a year and a half after hitting the suburban sidewalks of Millburn, NCUP and Area Board 3 picketers took to the sidewalks outside the Clinton Hill Meat Market, known locally as "Jack's Store." Their specific target was the system of welfare accounts cheerfully advertised in the front window, under an awning proclaiming the market "Your Southern Store Up North." Indeed, the arrangement was reminiscent of a tenant farm: welfare recipients who bought food on the promise of a future welfare check incurred usurious interest rates, greatly exaggerated prices, and padded bills.[28] On the afternoon of April 1, 1967, about one hundred activists picketed Jack's Store, carrying signs reading, "Don't Buy At the Clinton Hill Meat Market." Police were quick to the scene and, after a series of warnings and a brief scuffle, arrested nineteen protestors for refusing to increase the distance between each picket.[29]

One of those on the picket line was Marion Kidd, an early NCUP member and single mother. For the last two years, she had been the driving force behind a committee of welfare mothers that met at Area Board 3's Badger Avenue offices.[30] The women swapped stories of being ripped off by local store owners and inept welfare administrators and kept their children in line with stern looks and the promise of deferred punishment.[31] Though not reluctant to raise their voices about the injustices they suffered—each summer they joined other welfare organizations in nationwide demonstrations—they did not limit their activism to protest.[32] One of their most important projects turned community action toward proactive consumer politics: they formed a consumer buying club for the welfare mothers of Clinton Hill. In order to give members time to pay off their store accounts, the committee provided them a month's worth of free food if they joined the club. They hit the phones and solicited individuals, churches, and other social organizations for contributions and soon covered the floor of the area board's office with brown paper sacks and cardboard boxes full of food. After that first month, each mother contributed a small fee to get the club started. She then chose the items she wanted from a long checklist, and when enough members had chosen a given item to buy it in bulk, the item was added to the club's collective shopping list.

As they had with the young white organizers who had come to Newark to launch NCUP, these local women now challenged UCC leaders to support the issues and the methods about which they cared most deeply. The UCC provided political space in which poor Newarkers could define their own projects, but the central office maintained an advisory role that sometimes rubbed members of local area boards, struggling to bring their ideas to life, the wrong way. In the wake of the picketing and arrests at the meat market and after having largely ignored the welfare mothers' committee since its founding, UCC headquarters sent Dean Harrison, the acting director of community action, to pay them a visit. When Harrison, who earned $9,000 a year in his professional-class position, arrived in his jacket and tie to share his thoughts on the buying club, he stirred up a small firestorm. He told the committee that the UCC central office would not be able to help them until they had doubled their membership. Only then could they make their club work, and only then would their demands for aid move UCC officials.[33]

The women of NCUP, Area Board 3, and the welfare mothers' committee (many, like Marion Kidd and Wyla McClain, members of all three) pitted their knowledge and methods against official antipoverty knowledge and refused to back down. They had some words for Dean Harrison. Kidd said she'd attended UCC staff meetings to ask for help, but they had never sent any. When Harrison asked how many people she had brought with her, explaining that only hundreds of people would move the UCC, another neighborhood resident angrily insisted that their picketing—and the subsequent closing—of the Clinton Hill Meat Market showed what a small group of people could do. She turned to the gathered mothers: "The UCC sat down on Branford Place! We have a buying club and we're going to do something! Come see us! To hell with them."[34]

Undaunted, the buying club continued apace. After wading through a sea of reluctant wholesalers and comparing the prices of those who agreed to their cash-and-carry plan, committee members visited a cavernous food warehouse where managers in long white smocks guided them through canyons of stacked boxes. Satisfied with their visit, organizers submitted the club's first order the following week. Volunteers loaded the food into the back of a station wagon and brought it to Area Board 3 offices for members to pick up. Marion Kidd admitted that, by that time, all the mothers were exhausted. But, she said, "when I actually seen this happen, it seemed like it was a new thing being born."[35]

Rather than clearing NCUP of suspicion, however, its joining the anti-poverty effort only heightened city officials' anxieties. To them, the convergence at Area Board 3 of New Left direct action, the resources and opportunities afforded by the UCC, and the homegrown desires of Lower Hill residents suggested not the solution to one urban crisis—the overcrowding, decrepit housing conditions, and consumer discrimination that plagued new black neighborhoods like the Lower Hill—but the potential source of another: mass racial violence. If, as the city's Human Rights Commission had concluded, NCUP members were the most likely fomenters of rioting in Newark, police intelligence officers would lock its members in a steady gaze. They could not have been surprised, then, to see one of NCUP's founders at the Black Liberation Center in March 1967, discussing with other city activists plans for opposing the razing of a swath of the Central Ward for a new medical school campus.

By that time, George Richardson, the insurgent Democratic politician and original UCC incorporator, and the members of NCUP knew each other well. He was one of the Addonizio administration's oldest nemeses, and they were one of its newest. But he needed their help. His organization had not managed to generate much support among Newark residents who were not plugged into mainstream liberal or labor organizations. If he hoped to take advantage of their growing numbers, he needed to expand his alliances. So he turned to NCUP. Richardson did not necessarily agree with all

8. In this surveillance photo, George Richardson walks the picket lines at the new Barringer
High School construction site in 1963. Once a political insider, his civil rights activities
marked him as a dissident worth keeping an eye on. (LBJ Library)

its methods, as he later recalled, but its success in developing "a number of
Negro leaders that we might not necessarily construe as leaders . . . people
from the streets, some without high school education but who are basically leaders of their community," was a resource he could not ignore.[36]

As with the prior proposal to work within the War on Poverty, the prospect of joining a political campaign opened new possibilities, but it also

threatened NCUP's antiestablishment ethic. In one of innumerable debates among staff members, one organizer explained that he had come to Newark and joined NCUP because of an intense ingrained prejudice against traditional politics. He thought it pointless to try to change that system. Another largely concurred, noting that Richardson had invited them to join a structure that was already in place and over which, therefore, they would have no power. But others, among them longtime Newark resident Jesse Allen, divined real possibility in the invitation, especially if they could use the campaign to build their movement. It could, in that way, serve NCUP's purposes rather than betray them. In the end, without ever fully resolving their conflicting views on electoral action, staffers voted to join the campaign. In the fall of 1965, three NCUP members ran for state assembly on Richardson's newly dubbed United Freedom Ticket.[37]

A related debate occupied the board of trustees of the United Community Corporation. Richardson, now a candidate for state senate, and his friend and colleague Hilda Hidalgo, running for county freeholder on the United Freedom Ticket, were both UCC trustees. Hidalgo was also its secretary and Richardson one of its vice presidents. The UCC's detractors in city government viewed their candidacies as evidence that the community action agency was indeed more intent on developing an independent power base than fighting poverty. So the trustees, in August 1965, approved a resolution expelling any one of their number who used the UCC for personal political gain and requiring that any trustee running for public office take a leave of absence. Richardson and Hidalgo immediately requested time off.[38]

Thanks to NCUP's deep involvement with Area Board 3 and, now, the United Freedom Ticket, UCC trustees also sought to create regulations governing area boards' political activities. The UCC's executive director, Cyril Tyson, drew up a position paper in which he ruled that no board could "become involved in direct endorsement of any individual candidate, or participate in any partisan activity relative to any political party." The boards could of course continue to lobby government, establish voter registration drives, protest, picket, or otherwise voice an opinion concerning any piece of legislation, he wrote. But if NCUP members wanted to endorse the United Freedom Ticket, they couldn't do it through Area Board 3.[39]

Since Tyson's order did not discourage individual members of NCUP and Area Board 3 from joining the United Freedom Ticket campaign, they added the issues around which they had been organizing in Clinton Hill to those Richardson had tackled elsewhere. They vowed a fight against police brutality, slum landlords, and job discrimination and took to the streets with a mix of old and new tools. As they had many times before, NCUPers canvassed Clinton Hill and the Central Ward with massive numbers of fliers celebrating their candidates. They danced at campaign fundraisers and parties. Jesse Allen and Wyla McClain joined fellow NCUP and Area Board 3 members Melvin Higgins and Anita Warren, two of the tickets' state assembly candidates, to form the Freedom Singers, and they kept the spirit moving at the ticket's independent political convention in October. Others engaged their opponents in noisy sound-truck duels, their cries of "Let's join the fight for freedom! Support the United Freedom Ticket!" clashing with the traditional Democratic chant, "Line A, All the Way!"[40]

Despite the energy NCUP members poured into the campaign, the United Freedom Ticket was buried by a mainline Democratic landslide. A couple of years later, Richardson said that "every thrust that the Negro community attempted to make, they were defeated either by political power . . . [or] by devious means or trickery, but the fact remains [they] were defeated."[41] Nonetheless, he kept his eye on 1970.

The increasingly powerful local CORE chapter also supported the Freedom Ticket in 1965. Like NCUP, this was its first foray into mainstream political endorsement.[42] Its chairman, Fred Means, had earlier that year been elected to the UCC's board of trustees.[43] His predecessor, Robert Curvin, had also served as a trustee, had chaired a UCC committee, and was a friend and frequent ally of NCUP.[44] Like George Richardson, he had attracted the steady attention of the Newark police since 1963, when CORE led the campaign for a police civilian review board and joined the protests over job discrimination at the Barringer High School construction site. "I have never gotten along with him since I met him in 1963 the first time," Dominick Spina once said. "We had an argument and we have been arguing ever since."[45]

Under Curvin's direction, the local CORE chapter rode the high tide of nonviolent direct action to significant victories. In particular, protests at the area offices of several major corporations—including Western Electric, New Jersey Bell Telephone, and Hoffman-LaRouche Pharmaceuticals—produced an array of new minority recruitment programs and hiring practices.[46] Despite such local successes, CORE's national leadership began to push the organization's methods and goals in new directions in the mid-1960s. Direct action against segregation had failed to inspire the growing masses of urban blacks, whose concerns lay elsewhere than with the desegregation of labor markets to which they enjoyed little access in the first place. Direct action, CORE national director James Farmer said, "won us the right to eat hamburgers at lunch counters and is winning us the right to vote, but has not basically affected the lot of the average Negro." In October 1964, Farmer offered plans for a "new direction" in activities: while retaining the direct action tactics they had pioneered, CORE would now add community organizing and electoral activism to its arsenal.[47]

The Newark chapter followed Farmer's lead. Not only did it make its first foray into traditional politics by endorsing George Richardson's United Freedom Ticket, but the chapter declared its intent to capture greater grassroots support by going door to door and making "every person a protestor," as Curvin's successor put it in January 1965.[48] Curvin himself embraced this new direction and became the head of the chapter's Community Organizing Committee that spring.[49] CORE's involvement with the United Community Corporation may have been one aspect of this larger reach for the grassroots. Along with NCUP, CORE was among the strongest defenders of maximum feasible participation. When Councilmen Addonizio and Bernstein issued their report calling for a city takeover of the antipoverty program, the local chairman denounced the councilmen's "ignorance or base motives" and insisted they "accept the political reality that the people of Newark will no longer tolerate the ineffective, paternal handout from City Hall."[50]

In the summer of 1965, however, Newark-Essex CORE gained its greatest strength and publicity—and organized the greatest number of Newarkers—when it spearheaded a renewed wave of protest against police brutality. As the Happy Inn Tavern near the corner of Broadway and Oriental Street in the North Ward closed in the early-morning hours of June 12, its patrons spilled out onto the street. Those who looked saw a patrol car pull to the curb and, suddenly, a black man dash out its backdoor and through the intersection. A police officer exited the car with his sidearm drawn. Moments later, a bullet from his gun hit the fleeing man in the back of the head. Some accounts say he died instantly, others say minutes later.

The account police officials provided to the local newspapers claimed that officers making a routine traffic stop had become the victims of a violent motorist. The suspect, Lester Long, had fled and was shot accidentally by Patrolman Henry Martinez.[51] The press soon learned, however, that the original police report had called the shooting intentional: Martinez had taken aim and pulled the trigger. While reporters and city officials sorted through disparate stories from police officers, the local CORE chapter entered the fray. The day after the shooting, five eyewitnesses (including several patrons of the Happy Inn Tavern and the friend accompanying Long when he was pulled over) provided sworn depositions to Robert Curvin, three other CORE officials, a local attorney, and a court reporter. Horace

Foote, a custodian with the city board of education, said that Long had run right by him, brushed up against his arm, and then dropped to the sidewalk. ("Foote, you almost got that!" someone hollered.) The attorney asked the witnesses if they had seen anything in Long's hand, like a knife or a gun, or if they had heard anyone order him to halt, had seen Martinez stumble, or noticed any blood on either officer. Their answers were consistent: no on all counts.[52]

Armed with these eyewitness accounts, CORE demanded Martinez's immediate suspension. At a rally just yards away from where Lester Long died, Bob Curvin promised a massive demonstration outside police headquarters if it didn't happen.[53] Five days after the shooting, Fred Means met with Mayor Addonizio to impress on him the extent of the community's discontent. The mayor afterward ordered the suspension, but only until the city's Human Rights Commission ruled on the shooting's alleged racial motivations.[54] In the early morning hours of June 22, after an eight-hour closed-door meeting, the commission announced that it had found no evidence that Martinez had acted "other than in the line of duty" or that the shooting had been in any sense racially motivated. Mayor Addonizio accepted their report gladly and announced that, with the issue of race effectively removed and "the threat of riot and bloodshed" diminished, Officer Martinez would now return to active duty in an administrative capacity. But, he warned, this should not be misconstrued as a ruling on the legality of his actions. That judgment awaited a grand jury.[55]

Rather than ensuring civil peace, however, the city's decision making—or more specifically the opacity of that process—inflamed the situation. The Human Rights Commission had apparently accepted police reports of the shooting, despite the discrepancies among them, and ignored the eyewitness testimony gathered by CORE. If municipal institutions could not promise justice in the matter, then those seeking it would have to crack those institutions open. Community organizers and activists responded with calls for citizen participation. In the wake of the Lester Long shooting, this activism took the form of a campaign for a civilian review board.

CORE launched the campaign the day of the Human Rights Commission's announcement. Bob Curvin told an outdoor rally in the heart of Lower Clinton Hill that any refusal on the mayor's part to immediately create a civilian review board would be met with massive demonstrations. "We're going [downtown] to let the man know where the power is," he told a crowd of fifty people. "This is no longer the white man's city."[56] Over the next week, CORE rallies repeatedly emphasized eyewitness testimony: Long was not known to carry a knife, no one heard any orders to halt, no one saw a knife beside his body. If these accounts could not be heard behind closed doors in city hall, they would ring out in the streets. Organizers hired a sound truck and announced upcoming demonstrations throughout several public housing projects and in the neighborhood where Long had been shot.[57]

Curvin and his CORE colleagues were not alone in their efforts. George Richardson, who called the rights commission's finding "a complete farce," demanded the immediate appointment of a group of outstanding citizens to a police advisory board.[58] NCUP called a community meeting—which one organizer deemed "one of the most democratic meetings that we have had . . . in the sense that the people at the meeting really just making the decisions and the conversation being really based on them and what they wanted to do"—to discuss police brutality and to plan their own march. The following weekend, twenty-five NCUPers set off from the Lower Hill on a five-mile march through the South and Central Wards before picketing and leafleting outside city hall. By that time, 125 additional people had joined them, and they all circled the sidewalk chanting, "Is Newark another Mississippi?" They returned the next day to announce that they would join one of CORE's upcoming marches.[59]

After a grand jury dismissed the case against Martinez—since Long had attacked a police officer, the jury reasoned, he was a felon, and felons could be killed while attempting escape—groups of protestors converged on downtown's Military Park for a two-hour rally, the first in a series of demonstrations spearheaded by CORE and designed to put pressure on the mayor as he contemplated the creation of a civilian review board.[60] CORE's efforts to reach Newark's grassroots had paid off: attendance was estimated to be between seven hundred and a thousand. Fred Means opened the rally with an appeal to Newark's booming black population, which had almost certainly become the majority by this date. "Let's wake this Negro giant up," he demanded, as two hundred police officers, many hidden in plainclothes, patrolled the park, "and we could turn this city upside-down!" As applause echoed up Broad Street, Bob Curvin urged the crowd to organize and flex its political muscle. "We've got to try to get more people in the street," he said, "and let the man know where the power in this community is."[61]

Over the next two months, the pressure on the Addonizio administration grew. CORE led a second march on July 20, and this time a substantial list of new cosponsors—including the local chapters of the NAACP and Americans for Democratic Action, several labor locals, the Committee on Religion and Race of the Greater Newark Council of Churches, the Essex County Urban League, and the Episcopal Society for Racial and Cultural

Unity—demonstrated either the widening appeal of CORE's drive or the radicalization of the local civil rights establishment. Newark's middle-class black newspaper endorsed a review board, as did a prominent group of interracial business leaders.[62] George Richardson and his United Freedom Ticket running mate Hilda Hidalgo spoke at CORE's rallies. CORE national chair James Farmer faced down a death threat to march in Newark and tell the crowds that the Civil Rights Act of 1964 had "done little to help Negroes in northern urban areas where housing, jobs, and police brutality are problems. . . . A civilian review board in Newark is CORE's principal aim right now."[63] At the end of July, ten CORE demonstrators—Curvin among them—staged a sit-in outside Mayor Addonizio's office. They were loaded into paddy wagons, driven around the corner to police headquarters, and charged with disorderly conduct and breach of peace.[64]

Mayor Addonizio rejected the immediate creation of a review board and kicked the matter once again to the Human Rights Commission, which held a series of boisterous public meetings on the desirability and efficacy of such boards. Proponents included UCC and NCUP members, Tom Hayden, and George Richardson.[65] After examining 564 pages of testimony and a lengthy closed-door deliberation, the commission's special subcommittee deadlocked and referred the issue to the full commission. On September 7, after more than four hours of further deliberation and a secret ballot vote, the full commission also deadlocked and passed the issue back to Mayor Addonizio, who expressed his commitment to producing a plan that would "draw people together rather than split them apart."[66]

Addonizio's eventual plan—to refer complaints of police brutality and misconduct to the FBI—brought no communal reconciliation.[67] Advocates of a review board assailed the idea. Officials of the county Urban League, the American Civil Liberties Union (ACLU), and the local NAACP chapter all denounced it.[68] Members of the UCC's Area Board 1 met to discuss the plan, and a majority of them urged the board to take an official stand against it.[69] George Richardson called it "just a lot of window dressing," and the local CORE chapter said it was a "public relations gimmick motivated by political expediency."[70]

In October, its disappointment and anger unabated, CORE sponsored a panel discussion on Addonizio's plan, during which Bob Curvin called it "a sham." The crowd heckled and booed the head of the city's Human Rights Commission when he tried to explain the logic of the proposal. The executive director of the state ACLU said the mayor was being foolish if he believed his plan had stifled the city's simmering racial tensions. Indeed, the threat of racial violence, which Addonizio had hoped to check with his attempted compromise, remained very real for those who had worked to open the Newark justice system and its police department to citizen participation. Fred Means, the local CORE head, told the audience of a recent visit he had made to Watts, just after the violence there. It was not so different from Newark, he said, though the police in Los Angeles seemed even worse. Yet, he continued, "if a review board isn't established in Newark there may be trouble. I don't want to see fires in this city."[71]

Given the shared desires and frequent collaborations among those groups and individuals that had emerged as major dissident forces in the city, police director Spina could not have been surprised by his spies' report on the meeting at the Black Liberation Center. Mayor Addonizio had been courting the state medical school since its trustees voted to move out of nearby Jersey City in December 1965. He said Newark would welcome the school "with open arms" and declared his administration willing to make any arrangement that would suit the governor and college trustees. City Hospital, its seventeen floors rising above the Central Ward, he suggested, could be expanded onto adjacent urban renewal land in order to create a "first class medical center to serve the state's largest city."[72]

Newark, of course, had long ceased being the industrial powerhouse it was at the turn of the century. Manufacturing employment dropped precipitously in the 1950s, just as human migrations in and out Newark radically altered the landscape of needed public services. The medical school emerged, in the city administration's vision, as a key component of a postindustrial future, its 1964 master plan for land-use development noting the "additional demands on city health and medical facilities."[73] A large medical school campus in the Central Ward would provide Newark an injection of middle-class, white-collar workers *and* provide services demanded by an increasingly poorer population. Throughout 1966, therefore, the Addonizio administration heavily courted the medical school trustees. Municipal officials took them on tours of City Hospital and adjacent urban renewal land, and they pointed out the city's great need for the first-rate health care the school could provide and the wonderful training opportunities this opened for the school's students.

Nonetheless, in August 1966, the trustees' site advisory committee recommended a more bucolic location in suburban Madison, fifteen miles west of Newark. Faced with the prospect of losing the medical school, the city made a desperate offer: it would provide 185 acres of urban renewal land in the heart of the Central Ward if the medical school decided to move to Newark instead.[74] The promise of land—speedily acquired, cleared, and delivered—was the clincher. In December, medical school trustees chose Newark as the school's new home. But, the board announced, the promised urban renewal land was too irregularly subdivided to be of use to them. For the first phase of campus construction, they demanded a tract southeast of City Hospital that, far from being empty urban renewal land, was a residential neighborhood of predominantly black homeowners and renters. "There's no use trying to kid anybody. I'm disappointed and unhappy," Mayor Addonizio said after meeting with the board. "But this is too important and I'm accepting this responsibility. I'm not going to let this get away from Newark."[75]

Fulfilling such promises was the Newark Housing Authority's expertise. A 1963 study sponsored by Columbia University and the Ford Foundation found that the NHA typically reversed the sequence of events followed by most other urban renewal agencies: instead of locating a blighted area and then attracting developers to it, the NHA found it more expedient to locate the developers first and negotiate an appropriate site with them. With federal funds secured and anxious developers waiting in the wings, the NHA had no trouble securing a blight declaration for the targeted land from the Newark Central Planning Board or the approval of the mayor and city council. The study found that it was "self-evident to Authority officials that the formative stages of a project must be protected from excessive public interference," and it praised the resulting efficiency of its projects. As one anonymous NHA official put it, the authority "own[s] the slums. They can sell any piece of real estate in that area to a redeveloper before it's even acquired. And they don't have to check with anyone before they do it."[76]

So it was with no small amount of shock that Louise Epperson, who lived at 40 Twelfth Avenue in a single-family home she had recently purchased and given a fresh coat of paint and new windows, read a front-page story that claimed the state medical school was moving to Newark and that the city had promised the land she lived on for the campus. She ran inside, picked up the phone, and dialed the numbers of any neighbors she could think of. "Get up and get your paper from the door" she told them. "Did you know that the medical school from Jersey City is about to move to Newark and take our homes?" When some of them did not believe her, she told them to check the paper. "And after you read your paper, today, when you come from church about 4 o'clock everybody meet at my house."[77]

The Committee against Negro and Puerto Rican Removal was the first sign of grassroots opposition to the medical school relocation plan. Epperson explained to a local newspaper that the committee was not opposed to the medical school itself but to the razing of their neighborhood for it, especially since the neighborhood was so close to available urban renewal land. "The Negro has invested a lifetime of hard work in the present and future of this city," she wrote in a press statement. "He has earned the right not to be uprooted to satisfy the political ambitions of a few unscrupulous politicians."[78] At a subsequent meeting of about eighty site residents and concerned citizens at Newark's Longshoremen's Hall, Epperson and others hammered at the threat to the black community's growing political power. The medical school relocation, they argued, was an attempt to break up an increasingly significant black voting bloc. Their demand was straightforward: citizen participation in the planning of the medical school relocation.[79]

In the meantime, committee members took their case directly to city government. About two hundred people (including Epperson, CORE chairman and UCC trustee Fred Means, and NCUP/Area Board 3 staffer Jesse Allen) jammed city council chambers less than two weeks after the committee's founding to protest the administration's most recent tactic. One hundred thirty inspectors from the municipal Department of Health and Welfare had gone door to door to survey the site and gauge public opinion. The city reported that 96 percent of all structures in the area were deteriorated, that 89 percent of the houses were substandard, and that each housing unit in the area was within a half block of a tavern, junkyard, empty lot, burned out building, or other such nuisance. Of the 831 families interviewed, 708 said they were not opposed to the city moving them elsewhere. But, members of the Committee Against Negro and Puerto Rican Removal argued, the survey questionnaires were loaded, a farcical version of citizen participation. It had presented the college relocation as a done deal, so most residents would of course be in favor of the city providing them a new place to live. The city was demonstrating, said a local elementary school teacher, a "total disregard for the uprooting of more than 8,000 families and businesses already experiencing a powerlessness peculiar to Negroes in urban ghettos." Ignoring such concerns, the city council unanimously approved an application for federal funds to survey and plan the site.[80]

Suspicious of the city's survey findings and determined to find out once and for all what local residents really thought about the medical school plan, the United Community Corporation joined the fray. It had already publicly stated its opposition to the city's relocation plan, and several of its members and officials joined the Committee against Removal.[81] The mechanism by which the exorbitant amount of land had been promised was the antithesis of the community action model. In the middle of February, the UCC dispatched a team of canvassers to the medical school site. They spoke to 372 residents, a third of whom lived in the first-phase land guaranteed to be available for construction the following spring, and two-thirds of whom lived in the one hundred acres promised for subsequent phases of construction. In April, Fred Means, now head of the UCC subcommittee on the medical school controversy, presented the survey findings to a meeting of the antipoverty trustees. The results surprised them. Fifty-three percent of respondents favored bringing the school to Newark even if they had to move to accommodate it. While the percentage dropped to 45 percent in the first-phase area, Means conceded that the expected groundswell against the medical school had not occurred. The marketing research center that examined the survey results concluded that "the population appears to be resigned to the necessity of doing what it is told to do." Though some continued to oppose the relocation of the medical school altogether, the trustees ultimately decided to focus on the *process* used by the city administration rather than its ultimate goal. A majority approved a resolution deploring the city's methods and demanding that Addonizio "take the necessary steps to acquaint, inform and involve the people in the decision making processes" for all future projects.[82]

All that stood between the medical school and the Central Ward now was the city's Central Planning Board, which would need to declare the area blighted in order for the project to qualify for federal dollars. The 1963 study of the Newark Housing Authority had determined that such declarations were "routine" and that by the time urban renewal projects had reached the board "the time, energy, and money already expended preclude serious local review."[83] But if city officials had expected a smooth road, the first public blight hearing on May 22, 1967, quickly disabused them. As usual, the Central Planning Board presided over the hearing from the front of city council chambers, city officials presented their case, and members of the general public who had signed slips of paper to be put on the speakers' queue spoke last.[84] But only a few minutes into the hearing, after police ejected "a woman in the second row, wearing a crescent pin," as a local reporter described her, who had pelted board members with three eggs, two UCC officials rose to demand a different format. Instead of allowing members of the public to speak only after the city had presented its case, they argued, the testimony should alternate between proponents and opponents of the medical school plan. The planning board director, Alfred Booker, the board's only black member, agreed to the changes.[85]

That was when Colonel Hassan Jeru-Ahmed made his most widely noted public appearance, though he'd been spotted before. Police intelligence reports said that Hassan had a girlfriend employed by a UCC work-training program but had never actually been seen with a woman. Recently, after a white teacher at the Ironbound's Oliver Street School beat a black fifth-grader, Hassan had joined local antipoverty area board members in a picket line outside the school.[86] At the planning board hearing, dressed in black, with a khaki shirt and red cravat, Hassan demanded to speak first. After calling Booker a "Tom" and "house nigger," he declared that the planning board's racial imbalance rendered it illegal and called the proposed land clearing a "political move to get rid of Negro votes."[87]

For a time after that, the speakers alternated. A municipal official presented the findings of the city's block-by-block survey of the area: three-quarters of the homes and two-thirds of the businesses, he said, were blighted. Harry Wheeler, a local schoolteacher and UCC trustee, wondered whether those statistics mattered when the relocation of the medical school was already a political, if not yet physical, fait accompli. "This meeting is a mere façade to rubber stamp what has been negotiated," he said to raucous cheers. A city housing official then gave a Whiggish history of urban renewal in Newark. Walter Dawkins, head of the UCC work-training program for which Hassan's girlfriend reportedly worked, replied: "You think the Negro is so chained that he won't rise up," when, in fact, "there's a storm coming over the city of Newark and hell and his brother couldn't hold it back." Then the city fire director recommended that "the area be demolished whether a medical school is built or not."[88]

Suddenly, Colonel Hassan stormed the stenographer's desk. It was about 10:30 p.m. He ripped the transcript from the machine and tore it up. The police took him into custody, and several officers escorted him through a sea of people, some watching in silence while others cheered or jeered. They held him outside while their superiors decided what to do. Two city officials and a police captain conferred and, fearing an arrest would only inflame the situation, decided to release Hassan with an order not to return. Ten minutes later, one of Hassan's "soldiers" marched up to the stenographer's desk and smashed the recording machine against the wall, and the hearing fell into chaos. There was "pandemonium. There were jeers, threats, shoutings, foot stompings," Police Director Spina later said. "The insults, the racial threats, the obscenities were atrocious. This was mob action. It was not democracy in action." Amid chants of, "Hell no, we won't go," Booker hastily adjourned the meeting. Hassan hadn't quite put his body upon the gears of the machine, but he stopped it momentarily.[89]

The Central Planning Board scheduled another hearing just two days after the first. But with sixty-five picketers circling outside city hall, officials called it off and rescheduled it for three weeks later. When they learned the news, the picketers demanded a meeting, and a delegation was ushered in to see the city's corporation counsel. Marching up the city hall steps with Colonel Hassan were Jesse Allen of NCUP and Area Board 3; George Richardson of the United Freedom Ticket and the UCC; Walter Dawkins of the UCC's Blazer Training Program; Willie Wright, the chairman of the Central Ward's Area Board 2 and a UCC vice president; Earl Harris, a Republican county freeholder and UCC trustee; and Eulis "Honey" Ward, Central Ward Democratic chairman and UCC trustee. In the meeting, Wright accused the city of postponing the hearing only because the community was "geared to a crescendo" of participation. After angrily storming out, Hassan urged those who had waited on the sidewalk with their picket signs to attend a meeting at the Black Liberation Center.[90]

The outcome of the second and final blight hearing surprised no one. The city council had already unanimously approved a contract promising that the initial acreage would be delivered to the medical school within the year and the additional one hundred acres within eighteen months of any request from the school. At that meeting, Bob Curvin told the city councilmen that the contract constituted a "gross example of racism," and the director of the UCC's Legal Services Project called it illegal, since blight had not yet been officially declared. A UCC aide told the council, "If you build or try to build the medical school there will be violence."[91] Despite such warnings, Mayor Addonizio signed the contract immediately after the city council approved it, the college trustees added their signatures the following day, and the Central Planning Board soon declared the land blighted. The juggernaut, it seemed, was rolling on.

It was in this context that Police Director Spina sent his spies to the meeting at the Black Liberation Center, just doors down from the medical school site. SNCC's Phil Hutchings, who Spina said had established the center and organized the antimedical school meeting there, had spent the previous two years as an organizer with NCUP and Area Board 3 in Clinton Hill. Shortly before establishing the center, he had joined the Central Ward's Area Board 2, been elected one of its representatives to the central UCC board, and been recommended by the UCC personnel committee (chaired by Curvin) for the position of community action director. (UCC director William Wolfe, soon to be suspended, refused the recommendation.) Years later Hutchings said that, in his organizing, he made "practical use of that maximum feasible participation of the poor rhetoric—we didn't use that,

but that was the official rhetoric . . . and we were putting that into practice."
He found in the medical school controversy an opportunity to put that
participatory ethic to work on a large scale. The goal was not to push SNCC
as an organization but to develop locally controlled activist organizations
that would combat powerlessness through racial pride and unity.[92]

As the summer of 1967 approached, the long struggle for black political
power in Newark seemed to converge on the medical school controversy.
It involved multiple organizations with multiple histories, but they came
together under the broad notion that the urban renewal process, born out
of New Deal liberalism and subsequently revised, was undemocratic and
destructive of black communities. Over the previous three years, many of
the protest leaders had found new opportunities for their work and a participatory ethic and structure in the Great Society's Community Action Program. In their use of the program, in holding it to its highest ideals, they
had made it an integral part of an emerging black community consciousness in Newark.

That rising consciousness was captured that summer by Newark's largest
black newspaper. The weekly *New Jersey Afro-American* hit newsstands and
doorsteps every Saturday morning after going to the printer midweek. So it
was without an eye to the violence then engulfing large parts of the Central and South Wards on July 15, 1967, that the paper reported that "new
voices" could be heard in Newark, voices that echoed in the "vast prairies"
of its bulldozed urban renewal areas. The city's physical infrastructure was
indeed in the midst of radical change, the story said, but "one of Newark's
most drastic changes is in the temperament of its citizens who now make
last-ditch stands on issues affecting them as a whole." The wholesale condemnation of large residential areas threatened to scatter the movement's
constituent parts to the winds of housing authority relocation policies. But
for now, in the summer of 1967—at a time and place where the War on
Poverty, the New Left, and a burgeoning black power movement had in-
tersected and become indistinguishable from each other, mobilized thousands of residents, and infected city officials with a fear of the black masses
well before any mass violence ever occurred—the paper declared, "There is
something new in Newark."[93]

FOUR

The Newark Police Department's Great Society

For several decades, the Newark Police Academy occupied an old fire-house in Vailsburg, well beyond both downtown police headquarters and the expanding black population in the city's central wards. It had been established in the mid-1930s by a reform-minded director of public safety, Michael Duffy, who preached the modernization of both police administration and training. In pursuit of the first, he established new motor and radio patrol divisions, which allowed a reduction in the number of precincts from eight to four and saved taxpayers money. In pursuit of the second, he introduced scientific procedures like fingerprinting and detailed crime surveys, including one that counted every one of Newark's bagatelle machines (Duffy especially despised houses of vice). But the "police college" was his crowning achievement.[1]

The academy's devotion to the professional science of policing, however, left little room for training in community relations. A 1943 survey commissioned by Duffy's equally reform-minded successor, though unenthusiastic about the overall state of the department—"costs for police services are excessive, evidence of a high level of accomplishment is lacking"—found the academy's curriculum impressive. It included classes with a social-scientific bent, like police administration and juvenile delinquency; others in cutting-edge police investigation and interview tactics; and a few in jujitsu and personal hygiene. But the closest the curriculum came to community relations training were courses in "practical psychology" and "unethical tactics, force, etc."[2]

Such professional reform, which swept through police departments nationwide in the first half of the century, grew out of a desire to distance police work from politics. Reformers sought to overturn the image of the police department as just one of many corrupt arms of the local machine.

9. J. Edgar Hoover (inset) spoke at the opening of the Newark Police and Fire Academy in 1936. The academy shared his commitment to promoting the science of police work, though critics would later argue that such an approach increased the distance between police officers and the communities they served. © Media General Communications Holdings, LLC. (Newark Public Library / *Newark Evening News*)

They preferred—and often fought for—a more autonomous and efficient administrative structure.[3] Those reformers, seeing close public relations as a potential breeding ground for temptation and corruption, often instructed officers *not* to engage with their constituents unnecessarily. And to the extent that the quest for efficiency and a police science produced more carefully managed deployments of officers—especially in the 1950s when those deployments replaced so many walking beats with patrol cars—the effect was often a greater physical and social distance from the communities served. Another was a resentment, on the part of police officers, of any attempts to close the distance and hold law enforcement more accountable to the needs and desires and political imperatives of the communities they served.[4]

In cities like Newark, where populations grew much blacker than the local police forces, relations between the two were often marked by tension, violence, and mutual distrust. In response, a second wave of police reform sought, through educational and administrative projects, to foster

closer police-community relations, guided by the belief that, as the pioneering academic center in the field put it, "Police are an important *part
of*, not *apart from*, the communities they serve."[5] These efforts grew out of
the experience of World War II, when, amid mass racial violence in several cities, the forging of racial unity on the home front became a wartime
imperative. And they grew slowly during the postwar years, as they were
taken up by a handful of reform-minded big-city police chiefs, elected officials, specialists in the emerging social-scientific field of race relations, and
scholars of public administration.[6] These years stand out for the efforts to
break down the barriers of hostility and suspicion that divided the department from "the community." These efforts ranged from police-community
relations training to administrative reforms that gave community members
unprecedented access to the inner workings of the department, sometimes
as observers of it, sometimes as actual decision makers. Reform efforts were
most often foisted on the department, often by its top leadership and partners from the private and public spheres. In Newark, one of the greatest
experiments was funded by the Johnson administration, which greatly expanded the federal government's role in local law enforcement. This story,
therefore, concerns the politics of community action in terms of specific
public policies, but also the ways—limited, certainly—that notions of community participation and decentralization forced their way into the police
department and formed a new frontier of police reform.

   If these were years of great reform efforts, they were also years of great
reaction, especially in Newark. There were limits beyond which these experiments, in the minds of many in the law enforcement community,
could not go. Increased pressure to pursue improved police-community
relations outside the daily work of law enforcement was less than desirable in a department that remained a largely independent fiefdom after
midcentury charter reform. Efforts to improve those relations were never
popular with the vast majority of officers, and they protested and resisted
in whatever way they could. And when the opening up of the department
was pushed to an extreme—when community activists pushed for civilian
oversight of their work—that vague discontent became a mass movement,
a sort of warped mirror image of community action for white Newarkers
who looked upon the police department as the last city institution over
which they could claim clear ownership.

The Newark Police Department approached the end of the 1950s under the
dark cloud of a public relations disaster. In January 1958, declaring "the

police problem" the "most urgent and crucial challenge of all" in the city's civic life, the *Star-Ledger* began a five-part series on rising crime and the haplessness of local law enforcement. It opened by bemoaning the "dry rot plaguing the department's administration," which was poorly organized, largely apathetic, and undisciplined. For illustration, the paper printed candid photos of on-duty officers at local taverns. "Off his beat," one caption read, "he has one, maybe two." Other officers smoked, dressed slovenly, ran personal errands, and worked second jobs while on duty. Many broke state law by living outside the city. And that was just the first entry in the *Ledger*'s series.[7] Subsequent stories detailed the city's shockingly high crime rates ("It's a tragic panorama of violence and thievery!"); the lack of incentives for officers to improve their performance; the frustrations of local merchants repeatedly burglarized and denied hold-up insurance (accompanied by a photo of a South Ward grocer with the machete he kept behind his counter); and the lengthy response times suffered by crime victims, which inspired residents of one neighborhood to form their own citizen night patrol.[8]

Crime and policing became a central issue in the municipal elections that spring. To its traditional candidate questionnaire, the League of Women Voters added an item asking the mayoral hopefuls what they would do to improve police protection in Newark. Soon after, Alan Lowenstein of the Newark Citizens Committee on Municipal Government, the group whose charter-reform effort earlier that decade had helped reelect Mayor Leo Carlin, told the mayor that the committee would support his reelection only if he promised to appoint a new police administrator. Since charter reform, the department had had two directors, neither of whom had previous law enforcement experience. Now it was time to hire a professional. Once reelected, Carlin nominated Joseph F. Weldon, an assistant chief inspector with twenty-eight years of experience on the force in New York City, who the mayor believed would "bring the desired objective viewpoint to the Police Department." But he also emphasized that his choice of someone from outside Newark should not be taken as an implicit criticism of the local force.[9]

In the wake of Carlin's decision, Newark's two daily papers revisited the issue of local policing. The *Star-Ledger*, nine months after its shocking series, found that the problems with low morale, on-the-job drinking, and incentives, while somewhat ameliorated, still required attention. Some officers continued to hold down two jobs, live outside the city, and, as one local expert complained, wear unsightly argyle socks with their otherwise standard uniforms.[10] The *Evening News* reached similar conclusions in its series, which concluded that Newarkers were getting too little for their $8 million annual investment. The department's cleared-by-arrest percentage barely met "minimum efficiency" standards, for example, and monitoring of its officers was virtually nonexistent. Its inefficiency and lax discipline were summed up in the story of a former city councilman who had been shot in his Weequahic home two years before. A neighbor had spotted the prowler minutes before the shooting and called the police, but no one came. When police operators claimed they had never received a call, the phone company produced the records. "In general," the *Evening News* concluded, "it would appear that there has been a lack of full use of the department's manpower, a reluctance to change the status quo, and a subsequent breakdown in discipline. . . . It would appear that the department's problems can be solved only by an efficient police administrator."[11]

Weldon, Mayor Carlin hoped, would be exactly that solution. Despite the local police unions' opposition to the hiring of an outsider, the city council confirmed Weldon in November.[12] He got to work quickly, like several of his predecessors pursuing efficiency and professionalization through a variety of measures, including the distribution of the latest publications in police science to high-level officers and the continued transfer of neighborhood beat cops to patrol cars.[13] After closely examining a departmental workload study, he decided to redraw precinct lines, make more strategic use of foot patrols (i.e., reduce them), and dramatically increase the number of radio car patrols. "The current practice in leading police departments," he explained, "is to increase the mobility of patrol striking forces by putting as many men as possible in radio cars." In the spring of 1959, an order of thirty-one new cars doubled Newark's fleet.[14] At the end of a decade during which the racial composition of the city was undergoing dramatic change and more and more police officers were breaking the department's residency requirements and joining their former neighbors in the suburbs, Weldon's reforms only widened the distance between the police and the public. The most thorough history of the department concluded that, by the end of the decade, "Newark had become policed by strangers."[15]

While the establishment of an administrative unit dedicated to the task would have to wait until 1957, educational efforts to improve police-community relations multiplied in the postwar years. At the forefront of this national effort was the National Conference of Christians and Jews. In the early 1950s, the conference's regional director in Newark was Daniel Anthony. When he left that position to become the executive director of Newark's newly formed Mayor's Commission on Group Relations, Anthony launched what appears to have been the city's first effort to provide focused training in community relations to its police officers. In 1953, Anthony led eight weekly courses on "Community and Group Relations" to about twenty patrolmen. They listened to a ten-minute lecture and then discussed as a group the problems they encountered in their interactions with the public.[16] In subsequent years, the commission offered four-hour workshops to police recruits, which Anthony himself conceded were woefully inadequate, especially since the recruits tended to laugh at the training.[17]

Anthony's successor at the conference's regional office was a former suburban police officer and president of the state Patrolmen's Benevolent Association named Howard Devaney. In 1961, Devaney organized a Newark Police Institute on Community Relations, cosponsored by the conference and the Newark Police Department. In contrast to Anthony's relatively brief but pioneering run of courses, Devaney's plan was to reach every officer in the department over the course of three years. With the conference's several years' experience at his back, this would be Newark's most concerted effort to date to bring the police closer to the public.

The institute opened on the afternoon of April 21, 1961, at the Newark Police Academy. Devaney explained to the participants, all superior officers, plans for the six weekly meetings—mostly lectures and discussions of assigned reading—that constituted each session of the institute. To start with, the officers would hear a talk on the importance of community relations training in police professionalization. Subsequent topics included "our changing communities" ("population, migration, economic conditions, employment opportunities, housing, etc."), the public image of the police officer, and "Strangers and Neighbors: Understanding Minority Groups."[18] Participants were provided a small set of reading materials, including a pamphlet written by Devaney entitled "Prejudice, Discrimination and Delinquency," which implored "each and every law enforcement officer, whether administrator, supervisor, field officer or beat patrolman to participate in a uniform program . . . for the prevention of a disruption of community relations." If community tensions were left to grow beyond the ability of local agencies to control them, it warned, "the greatest breach of public order," was likely to follow: a riot.[19]

After one year and five more sessions, each with a new cohort of officers, Mayor-elect Addonizio told Devaney in June 1962 that he would support the institute's renewal. The next round was scheduled for the middle of September, which turned out to be around the same time the US Commission on Civil Rights would visit Newark for two days of hearings on racial discrimination.[20]

Devaney was among those asked to testify. After a rather tedious explication of the Institute on Community Relations' first year and explaining that Addonizio had supported its extension, Devaney said that recent efforts to prevent police misconduct, while worthwhile and successful, still left plenty of room for improvement among the department's superior officers, about fifty of whom had mysteriously failed to attend the first round of mandatory training. He believed community relations training had to begin with them, and he recommended establishing a permanent command school for those ranked lieutenant and above. When asked whether the department tended to discriminate against racial minorities, Devaney replied that he thought it possible that individual officers did, but "collectively," he said, "I don't think it's done as a whole."[21]

The next day, Devaney received an angry phone call from Newark's new police director, Dominick Spina, who told him that his statements to the Civil Rights Commission were "unfair and out of line" and that he was thinking of canceling all future sessions of the institute. Spina's appointment came as the fulfillment of Addonizio's campaign promise to replace the "outsider" from New York City with a veteran of the Newark police force. The local police unions and superior officers had all demanded it, and Addonizio publicly pledged to get it done once he took office.[22] Spina, who had actively campaigned for Addonizio without going on leave from the department, had been born and raised in the Italian community of Newark's North Ward and had graduated from its public schools, the University of Newark, and, later, the FBI Academy. A former Congress of Industrial Organizations (CIO) organizer—his arrest for distributing union literature in Jersey City led to the 1939 Supreme Court case *Hague v. CIO*—he had joined the Newark police force after serving in World War II. By the time Addonizio appointed him police director, the list of Spina's organizational affiliations swelled with police unions and professional groups. Rising to the defense of the department came naturally.[23]

Spina's case against Devaney and the institute was soon joined by other police officials. If Newark officers were so poorly trained in community relations, Spina asked, wasn't that an indictment of Devaney's own program? Anthony Giuliano, the president of the local Patrolmen's Benevolent Association (PBA), thought so and called for the classes to be canceled. After all, he explained in a statement, "it was the consensus of opinion" among officers who attended the previous sessions "that they were a waste of time."

Better to turn such training over to members of the department—no outsiders needed—who were better trained in human relations than Devaney.
Devaney would be better off expending his energy in his affluent suburban
hometown, Giuliano concluded, "where Negroes still feel they are living in
the Deep South."[24] Citing the differences between his police director and
Devaney, Mayor Addonizio soon canceled the planned resumption of the
institute. He supported such training in theory and would explore other
options, he explained, but the program run by the National Conference of
Christians and Jews was no longer welcome in Newark.[25]

Though one of the earliest and most moderate efforts to open the Newark Police Department to the changing demographics of its city had foun-
dered on the shoals of departmental pride and autonomy, a new wave of
experiments—both police training programs and community participation
in policing—soon swept over the department. The initial and comparatively innocuous training program devised by a moderate national religious
organization had greatly annoyed officers and their supporters. But new efforts to restructure their systems of accountability and to further their education in community relations would prove infuriating. The give-and-take
of these reform efforts—the push for more democratic policing versus the
safeguarding of the autonomy police departments had won over the course
of several decades—exacerbated the tensions between Newark's emerging
black majority and the law enforcement officers sworn to serve them.

Driving this wave of reform efforts was the painfully slow emergence of
police brutality as a major public issue. It had been around for decades in
Newark's black community but had failed to gain much attention outside
it. Exculpatory reports and findings—including those of the federal Wicker-
sham Commission in the 1930s and the Bureau of Municipal Research in
the 1940s—overshadowed persistent complaints.[26] But things changed in
the 1950s, when the Mayor's Commission on Group Relations gave such
allegations a greater airing. In 1953, a small investigative subcommittee
of the commission met with representatives of the local Urban League, the
NAACP, Americans for Democratic Action, and the community association
of Newark's only integrated public housing project to hear charges of brutality. When a grand jury exonerated an officer named during that meeting, commission members questioned the thoroughness of its hearings.[27]
But they kept at it, and a 1957 report to the commission compiled black
community leaders' denunciations of the police department. "Newark has
one of the most vicious police forces outside of the South," one said, and

another cited a "long and livid history" of brutality in the city. That history included, according to yet another, the officers' penchant for shooting unarmed black Newarkers in the back.[28] And in surveying black and white residents' views on intergroup relations for its landmark 1959 report, the one that pointed to an impending black majority, the commission found that nearly half of black respondents (compared to 8 percent of white residents surveyed) had heard stories of police mistreatment, and a majority of them believed the stories to be true.[29]

Despite this attention, police brutality remained largely a local issue and, at that, one framed in terms of allegations rather than firm findings and conclusions. But the tenor of the discussion changed in the early 1960s, in part because of the intervention of the US Commission on Civil Rights and the Kennedy Justice Department. The year before it came to Newark and listened to Howard Devaney's criticisms of the local police hierarchy, the commission had issued a unanimous report concluding that police brutality was "a serious problem throughout the United States" and that, though "whites are not immune, Negroes feel the brunt of official brutality."[30] The next spring, Attorney General Robert Kennedy proposed to Congress several actions derived from the commission's recommendations, including mandatory fines and imprisonment for officers convicted of brutality and the toughening of legal language, some of it dating back to Reconstruction, to hold police officers to state and federal law.[31]

In Newark, activists seized upon the issue with a greater focus than ever before. Shortly before the commission's visit, eight black community leaders, including Tim Still and George Richardson, sent Police Director Spina a letter urging him to "recognize that mistreatment of minority citizens by the police has existed in the past."[32] When Bob Curvin rallied hundreds of CORE supporters in Washington Park just days before the commission hearings, he included brutality on his list of complaints.[33] And when the commission arrived, it heard detailed accounts of police-brutality cases from a local attorney, accounts that, surprisingly, roiled Spina much less than Howard Devaney's comparatively tepid criticisms of the police hierarchy. The reason may have been that the attorney had confined his notions of remedying the situation to existing structures of law and administration rather than resorting to new forms of training or investigation. He hadn't, in other words, offended the department's cherished autonomy.[34]

The struggle between police administration's defense of that autonomy and movements to open that administration to the community reached new heights in the winter of 1963. Activists latched onto the idea of creating a police advisory board in Newark and, through that new administrative structure, prying open the workings of police oversight. In February, a group of over one hundred people, including several city and police officials, gathered at St. James AME Church in the Central Ward to hear the executive director of the Philadelphia Police Advisory Board describe his experience. He gave a brief history of the board, which had been established in 1958 as the Police *Review* Board, before a suit brought by the local police union forced a few reforms, including a clarifying name change. The director explained that its creation had served all Philadelphians, not just black ones, and that, in fact, all races had since made use of it. Despite what police officers would have you believe, he said, the board sought neither the control of the department nor the destruction of its morale. Rather, it had helped officers as much as the public. The proof was in the numbers of complaints the board heard, which had recently begun to drop for the first time since its founding.[35]

The meeting had been organized by George Richardson and cosponsored by nineteen local organizations, including the Hayes Homes tenants' association (Tim Still), CORE (Bob Curvin), several union locals, church groups, and at least two Puerto Rican organizations. Planned as a one-day conference on the general theme of police-community relations, it ended up being the launch event for a campaign to establish a police *advisory* board in Newark (though opponents insisted on calling it a *review* board). Richardson slammed the police department for continuing to insist that brutality didn't exist. "Law enforcement by fear will no longer work," he said. A petition demanding the creation of a board began circulating. The goal, Richardson explained, would be to gather thirty to forty thousand signatures to persuade the mayor to their cause.[36]

Several weeks of fierce debate followed. Richardson argued that the existing structures of legal governance and oversight were inadequate to the task. Internal police investigations were largely regarded as "white-washes," he told one reporter, and the municipal courts were seen as too cozy with the police. Director Spina, however, believed that board proponents just needed an education. There had been no whitewashing, he insisted. "I know there are many people who believe there is police brutality in Newark. But it's not a police problem, it is a matter of educating people to the true facts." Worse than unnecessary, he continued, such a board would destroy the police force and thereby increase crime. He would ensure, therefore, that Newark police officers could go about their work free from the worry that they might be hauled before a board acting "outside the framework of the police force and the law."[37]

In the midst of these debates, the local police unions emerged as a strong voice in defense of police autonomy and security, which they increasingly presented as a civil right as worthy of defense as any claimed by their opponents. Anthony Giuliano, the president of the local PBA chapter, insisted that Newark risked the same fate as York, Pennsylvania, some hundred miles west of Philadelphia, where a board "almost destroyed the police force" through the familiar formula of declining morale and rising crime. The truth, he claimed, was that there were actually "many more assaults on police officers during a year than there are against criminals."[38] A few days later, after the director of the city's Human Rights Commission came out in support of a board, Giuliano called such boards "un-American," and PBA members marched on city hall. They called for the director's immediate resignation (he refused), and Giuliano accused him of "attempting to meddle in police affairs and hamper a policeman's efforts in carrying out his duties." Newark's other, smaller police union, the Fraternal Order of Police, issued a statement the following day, initiating the new rights-based rhetoric: "With all the talk about civil rights of minority groups it is strange there is no talk about civil rights for a policeman."[39] Over the next month, two other union leaders publicly joined the opposition. The president of the local Superior Officers Association doubted the legality of a board and claimed that "only the habitual criminal violator" would want one, while the president of the New Jersey state PBA argued that a board would "subject the vast majority of law-abiding citizens to the tyranny of a minority": criminals who hid their crimes behind calls for civil rights.[40]

As Mayor Addonizio weighed his options, many others joined the debate: the National Conference of Christians and Jews, the Essex County Urban League, the state ACLU, and various local clergymen in support of a board; the Newark Police Post of the Veterans of Foreign Wars, the Essex County Emerald Society, the chief of Newark police, and the city attorney all opposed.[41] At a press conference on April 6, with Police Director Spina and the city attorney at his side, Addonizio declared himself "unalterably opposed" to the creation of a police advisory board, which, he said, "would serve no useful purpose and could conceivably be a detriment to efficient law enforcement." If instances of police brutality came up, there were already numerous avenues of redress, including the Human Rights Commission, the county prosecutor's office, the state attorney general, and the FBI. However, he continued, a careful review of allegations revealed that only one such charge had been brought to the commission since 1961, and it had proved unfounded.[42]

The police advisory board proposal had put Addonizio in an uncomfortable spot. His election the previous spring had been due in no small part to support from black Newarkers and the city's civil rights establishment. But suddenly, not a year into his administration, those supporters had made a demand that put him at odds with another of his strongest constituencies: the city's police officers. Addonizio had promised them a native Newark police director and, implicitly, an end to what many felt was outside interference in their department. Dominick Spina had been the fulfillment of that promise, and he soon proposed strengthening the department's autonomy and centralizing its control by shutting down all precinct houses and consolidating command and control in a modern police headquarters building at the corner of Jones Street and Fourteenth Avenue in the Central Ward.[43] It never happened, but the new director had made an impression. A close mayoral aide later said that Addonizio always seemed "afraid" of Spina because of his popularity within the department and, by extension, in the largely Italian North Ward, which had also strongly supported Addonizio's election.[44]

The mayor, in short, was caught between growing demands for a more democratic form of police review and ongoing reform efforts to secure the department's sovereignty. The city's most prominent black newspaper editorialized that Addonizio, in rejecting a police advisory board, had effectively given up on ever being reelected: black Newarkers would likely never vote for him again. "His allegiance," the editor wrote, "should be to the populous, not to a group of policemen who feel it is their in-born right to walk the streets tapping innocent citizens on the head with their billies at will."[45]

The *Star-Ledger* reported that George Richardson would lose his $8,300-a-year city job as payback for his agitation. Though Addonizio at first denied such retribution, by the middle of the year Richardson had been replaced by the wife of the head of the local NAACP chapter, which had consistently refused to take a stand on the police board issue.[46] For now, the police had proven themselves a more potent pressure group than the city's civil rights forces. But those forces—and Richardson, in particular—quickly began organizing for their electoral challenge to the Addonizio administration.

As a way to placate those seeking more community input into police work, and demonstrating that police reform and community relations could go hand in hand, even in Newark, even if tensely and awkwardly, Addonizio in his press conference revived a proposal that had been floating around town since early in his term. Howard Devaney, in his testimony to the US

Commission on Civil Rights in September 1962, had recommended the establishment of precinct-based "police-citizens groups" made up of local commanders, clergy, and other community leaders.[47] Spina, who in his angry phone call to Devaney the next day had claimed such precinct councils were *his* idea, proposed them again in March 1963, in the midst of the police advisory board firestorm, at a community meeting in the Central Ward. He told the gathered residents that Newark now topped the national crime list and proposed the creation of citizens' councils in each precinct to help local captains fight the scourge.[48]

When Addonizio announced his unalterable rejection of a police advisory board, he offered the precinct councils as an olive branch to advocates of greater community participation in law enforcement. He said that between twenty-five and fifty citizens would serve on each council. They would be called on not only to improve police-community relations but also to handle accusations of police brutality. (Details on how they would do this were not provided.) During his press conference Addonizio gave his police director credit for the idea and asked him to explain it. Spina said that participants, whose recruitment had already begun, would come from every walk of life and would represent the business, labor, and civic sectors. They would meet once a month with precinct captains and exchange views on community and police problems in order to reduce the mutual ignorance that had plagued their relations. Spina placed the blame squarely on one of his predecessor's most sweeping reforms: the shift from foot to car patrols. As a result, officers had "gained mobility but lost the personal contact," he said. "Nowadays the policeman is just a faceless figure in uniform." That, however, would change once the precinct councils were up and running that summer.[49]

So while a police advisory board would yield too much power, departmental leadership *did* allow a range of reforms and programs that opened—slightly and always on their own terms—the Newark Police Department in unprecedented ways, to involve more people in the work of police training, crime fighting, and observation. These city-led experiments were often weaker versions of the decentralization of police power and training called for by community activists, but they were new formations nonetheless, and they produced unpredictable and complicated results.[50] In addition to the precinct councils, one of the earliest efforts was Spina's effort to enlist youngsters in educating the public about security and policing. These Junior Crime Fighters, as they were known, distributed literature on narcotics and the prevention of auto theft.[51] Spina proudly touted his regular Wednesday-night open-door policy, which he established soon after taking office, "knowing that people in the city, especially small people, are continually frustrated by democratic governmental bureaucracies," as he later recalled. Starting at 7:30 and lasting sometimes until the early morning hours, any citizen was welcome to come speak with him.[52] Over the years, several proposals to enlist taxi drivers in the department's crime-fighting efforts were floated, most often as a mobile neighborhood watch, though it was once proposed they be issued nightsticks.[53] At one point, Spina proposed putting all radio-equipped commercial vehicles to work fighting crime in what he dubbed Operation CALL (Community-at-Large Lookout).[54]

And the department never completely abandoned community relations training. After breaking with the National Conference of Christians and Jews, for example, the city asked the New Jersey State Division of Civil Rights to begin classes in March 1963 on Thursday afternoons at the city's police academy, in the hope that every officer on the force would go through the training within the next three years.[55] In 1965, Spina established a departmental Police Community Relations Bureau, whose sole

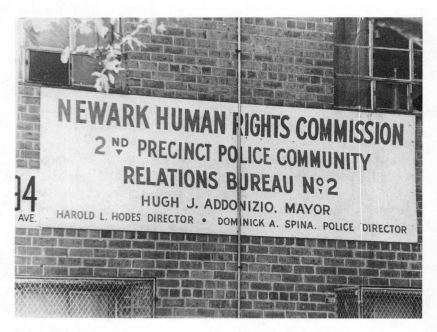

10. City and police officials trumpeted their commitment to improved police-community relations. To many residents, though, it seemed the police department wore such commitments lightly. (Newark City Archives)

task was, as he later put it, "to become friendly with these people in the various social agencies and civil rights movements."[56]

In each case, these programs fostered new encounters between the police and "outsiders," whether Newark residents or those trained in human relations. While none promised a radical restructuring of the police department, they sometimes had unpredictable outcomes. Such was briefly the case with the Citizen Observation Program, begun in 1963 and planned by Spina in partnership with the generally supportive local chapter of the NAACP. Over the objections of his own superior officers, Spina encouraged citizen-observers to visit precinct houses, where they were given free rein to watch the police and to take down badge numbers if they witnessed something objectionable. They were also invited to ride along in patrol cars.[57]

In the early morning of June 12, 1965, the office secretary of the Newark NAACP was riding in a patrol car through the North Ward when it received word of a shooting near the corner of Broadway and Oriental Street. She had been working for weeks to organize the Citizen Observers and, when she failed to reach her target number of participants, volunteered to go herself. When they arrived on the scene, she watched as a crowd formed around the body of a young black man, who died minutes later. In shock, she didn't think to interview any of the witnesses, but she delved into her role as observer. She watched as the police officers calmly tried to corral the crowd for fear their curiosity would soon turn to anger, though the crowd to her seemed more interested in seeing a dead body than anything else. When the local *New Jersey Afro-American* newspaper asked her to recount the experience, she repeated police allegations—that the dead man had attacked them with a knife, fled, and then been shot accidentally when one officer stumbled on a curb. But she did allow herself a moment to editorialize on what she observed. "To me," she wrote, "this was a senseless murder."[58]

Soon, Patrolman Henry Martinez was suspended, CORE began its campaign for a civilian review board (and it was, this time, a *review* board), and the *New Jersey Afro-American* called out "the arrogant stupidity of the police themselves." But Newark police wouldn't let this agitation go unanswered. Officers picketed city hall to demand Martinez's reinstatement and the rejection of a review board. On June 18, less than a week after the shooting, more than 150 off-duty officers, their wives, and their children were joined by 100 civilians bearing placards that read "CORE Runs the City" and "Mayor Yields to Mob Rule," while Martinez's wife carried a sign saying that CORE had suspended her husband. Some officers handcuffed themselves together to symbolize the constraints under which they were now forced to work. Inside, Mayor Addonizio met with local and state PBA officials but refused to end the suspension. When he and Police Director Spina encouraged the crowd to disperse, the crowd shouted them down.[59]

Over the next several days, the number of picketers swelled to over a thousand officers and supporters. They continued to bring their families, and their children made a show of presenting Father's Day gifts to their dads on the line. The head of the New Jersey PBA claimed that every chapter in the state supported the protest, and indeed, many of their officers were in attendance. The New York City PBA brought dozens of its members to Newark on a chartered bus. Despite the mayor's admonition that "a policeman's job [is] to guard picket lines, not walk in them," the condemnation of Martinez's suspension was unanimous across the department's racial and ethnic lines. A spokesman for the Bronze Shields, a fraternity of black officers, objected to the absence of an official hearing before the suspension, though not to CORE's right to demand an investigation, while the presidents of the Jewish Shomrim Society and the Italian Columbians declared their groups in wholehearted endorsement of the protest. In sweltering heat, dripping with sweat, the picketers marched first along city hall steps, then from street corner to street corner, and eventually around the entire block, led by white-gloved pallbearers carrying a casket with a sign that read, "Newark Police Department—Rest in Peace." When the city Human Rights Commission ruled that race had not been a factor in the shooting and Mayor Addonizio lifted Martinez's suspension, the head of the Newark PBA chapter shouted the news from the steps of city hall to raucous cheers. The picketing ended, and the protestors went home.[60]

While the police picketed, a small group of friends had planned their own protest over a couple of beers in a bar in the Down Neck section of the Ironbound. Officer Martinez had been reinstated, but CORE's demand that Mayor Addonizio establish a board of citizens to review charges of police misconduct and make recommendations on disciplinary action was unresolved. Ted Dachowski and his friends took it personally. Dachowski had lived all his life in the neighborhood and he knew Martinez personally. They were card-playing buddies and thinly connected through family—Martinez's brother-in-law was one of Dachowski's cousins, almost twenty of whom lived on the same block. Ted's father tended bar at a watering hole on Market Street, just blocks down from the Third Precinct and around the corner from their home on Fillmore. The bar was popular with off-duty officers, and Ted had spent a lot of time around them as a kid. When he married in 1959, he and his wife moved into a house one block

down from Fillmore on Somme Street. So interconnected were the imperatives of neighborhood and friendship, so central were they to political sen-
timent, that Dachowski's later explanation for opposing the establishment
of a civilian review board was disarmingly simple: "It was a question of: we
can't let them impose their will upon us, and we'll stand up and [oppose
it]. . . . It was just, hey, we believe so strongly in the cops, and we knew the
cops. They were friends of ours, in addition to being law enforcement." So
Dachowski and his friends wrote up a petition opposing the establishment
of a civilian review board in Newark.[61]

They brought their makeshift campaign from tavern to tavern and civic
group to civic group, under a cumbersome but straightforward moniker:
the United Citizens of Newark against a Civilian Review Board. Within
days, donations and phone calls poured in from all over the state. By the
end of June, they had collected nearly sixty thousand signatures. The small
group of drinking buddies had unwittingly sparked a mass movement.

The dissolution of traditional elected and administrative control, the
dispersion of decision making beyond the established halls of power: this
is what community action had been threatening over the previous year in
Newark. And if some segment of Newark's population felt a sense of ownership over police administration—this was, the United Citizens said, *our
police department*"—then this proposed revision of that administration in
the name of civil rights, community participation, and the prevention and
prosecution of police brutality created a real political and cultural problem
for them: political since their connections to the police as important city
power brokers would grow more tenuous, and cultural because these connections so clearly intertwined with senses of self, especially in their racial
and spatial dimensions (white neighborhoods). The United Citizens was
a mirror image of community action as it had taken hold in and helped
shape Newark's black community: rather than crack open a heretofore
closed and hostile institutional structure, it sought to preserve perhaps the
last municipal institution over which they still had clear claim. This was,
in part, one more example of mid-1960s law-and-order politics, but it expanded that politics to the ownership and preservation of local administrative structures at a time when they seemed to be facing an existential challenge from the forces of community action.

The United Citizens issued their first public statement on July 1, after
a meeting attended by, among others, the East Ward city councilman, the
head of the East Ward Young Democrats, and the president of the state
PBA. Their statement was a model of uneasy determination. The group's
purpose was twofold, it explained: they would physically present their peti-

tion to the city administration, and they would publicly demonstrate "in support of our Police Department." The statement forcefully spoke of the protestors' greatest desire: "that the government of the city be kept in the hands of the duly elected officials and that the Police Department be allowed to perform its proper function without any interference from unauthorized groups."[62]

If the United Citizens' goal was conservative, their methods were not, and this is where the uneasiness set in. Two years after the massive March on Washington, several months after the perilous Selma to Montgomery voting rights march, and while the local proponents of a police review board repeatedly took to the streets, the United Citizens of Newark decided to stage a march of their own. Though they went out of their way to avoid serious disruption—scheduling the march for a Thursday, when downtown stores closed early, and insisting they were "not interested in being sensational nor in harassing the City Government"—the organizers still felt the urge to declare their general opposition to "demonstrations of this sort." They accused "various groups" of attempting to "blackmail" the city administration through such means but begrudgingly bowed to their efficacy: "If this is what is needed to impress upon the City Fathers what the feelings of the people are, then this is what we must do." In crossing some imagined methodological and, no doubt, racial line, the United Citizens staked a claim for their own minority status, in a city whose black majority had by then likely arrived. It was inconsistent, the statement continued, for civil rights groups "to make demands on behalf of a minority that represents over 50% of the population." The implication was that such public demonstrations now more properly belonged to white Newarkers.[63]

As CORE demonstrators staged a sit-in outside Mayor Addonizio's office on the evening of July 29, 1965, a crowd organized by the United Citizens gathered in Lincoln Park near the southern end of Broad Street and then began walking north, five abreast, toward Military Park. Ted Dachowski estimated the crowd at six thousand, Police Director Spina at between eight and nine thousand, another city official at only two thousand. But even at the low end, it outnumbered each of CORE's marches by several hundred people. Their placards read: "Support the Finest Policemen in the Nation," "Only Communists Benefit by Police Review Boards," "Handcuffs Are for Criminals, Not Policemen," "Criminal Brutality—Is CORE Concerned?" and "We Also Have Constitutional Rights." They carried scores of American flags. They further distinguished themselves from their opponents by marching silently: there was neither singing nor shouting, only a lone loudspeaker playing patriotic music. When they reached Military Park, Dachowski climbed atop a temporary dais before Gutzon Borglum's *Wars of America* sculpture, while listeners perched themselves atop the monument. "We cannot stand by and see groups demand and demand and demand," he told them. "We are here in support of our Newark Police Department and its officials and never before have so many citizens come forth in such masses as are here tonight." He implored them to bring the fight back to their homes and neighborhoods and to let their politicians know how they felt. He spoke for less than ten minutes and then invited marchers to sign the petitions on tables set up around the park.[64]

Though the United Citizens expunged their struggle of explicitly racial rhetoric, the racial component of the Lester Long shooting—the racial component, in fact, of so many instances of police brutality—proved impossible to suppress. The editor of the city's mainstream black newspaper, *The New Jersey Afro-American*, for example, was not so reticent. Two days after the United Citizens announced themselves publicly, he printed a cartoon lampooning the burgeoning movement on the paper's front page, separated by several columns from photos of Lester Long's funeral. In the cartoon, a grossly rotund white policeman, his uniform marked with the words "Police Benevolent Association," stands over a body splayed out in a pool of blood. In the background, three figures representing civil rights organizations demonstrate in front of city hall with a sign that reads, "Legal Killing Must Stop!" While the policeman rubs tears from his eyes and complains that "they keep picking on poor little me," his other hand forms a pistol that he points at the picketers.[65]

The cartoon slyly poked fun at the white officer's performance of victimhood. In fact, Officer Martinez's defense relied on such a notion: it claimed Lester Long had assaulted his partner and was, therefore, a felon whose attempted escape could legally be stopped with deadly force. Writ large, this notion of victimhood, its whiteness explicit or not, was a powerful idea in a city with a new black majority demanding access to its most guarded institution. Read against the grain, as a police officer might have seen it, the *Afro-American* cartoon implied an unholy alliance between black power demonstrators and the black "criminal" lying dead in the street, between CORE and Lester Long, between those who waved pickets at police officers and those who waved knives. When Mayor Addonizio ordered Officer Martinez's suspension, the whole world seemed upside down, a dystopia in which law held no sway and criminals ran the system. As the president of the state Fraternal Order of Police (and a Newark patrolman) saw it, the city's system of government had turned on its own police force. For everyone else, the law said you were innocent until proven guilty, he said. But that didn't apply to the police. The city administration, he declared, had turned the police department over to CORE. "All police actions and duties must now be cleared through" them, he said, though "as of now they have not taken office."[66]

On September 15—a week after the city's Human Rights Commission had failed to reach a decision on a review board, and the day after a police officer shot another black man in the head while he and his friends fled a traffic stop—Addonizio offered a truce.[67] In a lengthy public statement, he presented what became known as the "Newark Plan," the first of its kind in the nation for handling complaints of police misconduct. From now on, he explained, the mayor's office would refer all such complaints to the FBI, "an agency that all can support," thereby removing the investigation and its findings from local squabbling. The FBI would forward its conclusions to the federal Department of Justice. If officials there substantiated the findings, they would refer them to the US Attorney for prosecution. Such a plan, Addonizio said, guaranteed "a thorough, impartial and speedy investigation under the instrumentality of law and due process, which is the basic and fundamental concept of our democratic system of government."[68]

However, the mayor continued, behind the calls for a civilian review board lurked a more fundamental problem. "The underlying issue is not simply to resolve charges of police brutality," he said, but "to give all of us enough faith in the law to trust and obey it." To that end, he offered a new program to improve police-community relations. The police department, he said, would establish a new code of conduct forbidding officers to abuse any citizen on account of skin color, economic status, or national origin and would assign one superior officer to each precinct to work full time on community relations. The department would extend invitations to various church, parent-teacher, business, and civil rights groups to participate in an expanded police observer program (the same program that had, three months before, brought a local NAACP official to the corner of Broadway and Oriental). In what Addonizio termed "a G.I. Bill for policemen," the city administration would itself fund a professionalization program, providing funds for officers to enroll in college-level courses in police and other social sciences, and it would seek federal funds to provide expert human relations training to all Newark police officers and "selected community leaders."[69]

Mayor Addonizio's timing was fortuitous, for the Johnson administration, in response to national alarm over rising crime rates, which the president called "a malignant enemy in America's midst," had six months earlier announced that the federal government was expanding its role in local law enforcement. It would do so, unsurprisingly, through a grants program. In his March 1965 address to Congress on crime and law enforcement, the president emphasized the need for greater action. But rather than calling for a direct federal role—"our system rejects the concept of a national police force," he said—the president proposed a Law Enforcement Assistance Act to promote, as he explained, "the development and testing of experimental methods of crime control."[70] When the legislation was signed that September, it established the Office of Law Enforcement Assistance as the entity within the Department of Justice responsible for disbursing federal monies to local projects promising innovation in law enforcement.

From its inception, the grant program contained conflicting notions of purpose, conservative legislators seeing in it the (often technological) promise of crime and riot suppression, their more liberal counterparts seeing the potential for the elimination of conditions—poor police-community relations, especially—that caused crime and rioting.[71] The office's first director, appointed the following month, insisted that law enforcement was long overdue for an update and pointed directly to the need to harness new technologies in the service of crime prevention, "something comparable to the innovation in the sciences that preceded the space age."[72] With money from the office, municipal and state police agencies across the country established lines of communication with the FBI's National Crime Information Center in Washington, where fourteen-inch memory disks on two IBM 360s spun and spat out information on wanted persons and stolen property. In New York City, officers at the police department's central records office entered information into two terminals, which then sent the data on to the IBMs in Washington, the two cities thus connected by both the Great Society's funding flows and an early computer network.[73] But many of the office's monetary commitments went not to projects connecting local police officers to the latest technology but rather to the people they served. While those few New York officers planted themselves in front of computer terminals, for example, their colleagues who worked in Spanish-speaking sections of the city flew to sunny Puerto Rico—all expenses paid by the Office of Law Enforcement Assistance—to attend a one-month community relations training program at the Catholic University in Ponce.[74]

It was the Addonizio administration's renewed interest in police-community relations that brought funding to Newark in the summer of 1966, where it was used to launch the Newark Police-Community Relations Training Program. The impetus for the grant came from the mayor himself, for whom it represented a partial fulfillment of the promises he had made when he refused to establish a police review board the previous summer and who, in any case, rarely passed up a federal grant program. Addonizio suggested the current head of the city's Human Rights Commission, James Threatt, as the program's director. (Threatt was hired after Daniel Anthony criticized Addonizio for ignoring the commission and resigned in 1963, and after Anthony's successor authored a highly critical report on human relations in Newark and resigned in 1965.)[75] Threatt later wrote that the program's aim was "to modify attitudes of suspicion and hostility of the citizens toward police and police towards the citizens" and "to allow both police and citizens the opportunity to examine stereotypes and to explode myths about various groups in the community."[76] Among those myths, the grant application explained, was the belief among so many officers that the poor and racial minorities were all criminals and the belief among the poor and minorities that officers were all brutal. Security in Newark would never be had if the police and residents remained so alienated from each other. The goal, therefore, would be that policemen and civilians "learn to perceive each other as people, not as symbols."[77]

The program would achieve these goals by providing individual officers and residents the opportunity to commune outside the stress of everyday encounters in sections of the city with high crime rates and persistent tensions. Organizers focused their efforts on recruiting residents of the Central and South Wards and hired three "neighborhood assistants"—a middle-aged black man with a long rap sheet who was well-known in both community and police circles, a young white psychology graduate student, and a "well-known militant and activist" and former intern with the Community Action Training Program at Rutgers—to round up civilian volunteers.[78] An elite cohort of these volunteers attended leaders training in October 1966, where they met with an expert on small-group dynamics from Scientific Resources, Inc., a consulting and training firm founded by behavioral scientists.[79] At the end of the day, when asked to fill out a questionnaire that gauged their attitudes, to later compare with their attitudes at the program's end, civilian volunteers expressed some skepticism that the training would improve relations with the police. They were nonetheless willing to give it a try.[80]

The police officers attending the training sessions did not come voluntarily. Their superiors selected them according to the extent of their contact with the public and ordered them to participate, the only concession being that all sessions were scheduled during normal working hours so that they were, technically, paid for attending. (Aside from carfare, the civilians received no compensation.) The officers' questionnaires revealed a more hostile attitude toward the program. Ten of the twelve officers attending the initial training sessions bristled at what they deemed a pointless effort to explain themselves to the public and win them over.[81]

From this inauspicious start, James Threatt and his staff organized six months of training activities, using what he called "classical pedagogic techniques": lectures with visual aids, small-group discussion (led by two-person teams—one civilian, one officer—drawn from the initial leaders cohort), field trips (almost all-civilian, since the police trainees were not given time off to attend and so, mostly, didn't), and role-playing exercises. The trainees gathered over coffee and danishes to hear experts expound on a range of topics: Willard Heckel on the Supreme Court and human rights, a topic of great interest to the trainees in the aftermath of the Supreme Court's recent *Escobedo* and *Miranda* decisions; Donald Malafronte on the history of police-community relations in Newark; and a Rutgers psychologist on the relationship of poverty to delinquency and crime. In the question-and-answer period that followed each lecture, officers frequently voiced objections to what they had heard. Many of them balked at one speaker's claim that bad policing had led to many recent urban riots, for example, and vocally opposed another's assertion that police standards of conduct needed to be raised.[82]

But these exchanges were mild compared to what happened when Bayard Rustin lectured on the relationship between civil rights and police-community relations. When Rustin told the trainees that his mother had always told him to avoid two types of people—white women and police— one officer suggested that such a discussion was off topic. In response, a civilian "exploded" at him. "Do you know what it means not to have any beans in the pot when your kids come home?" she asked. An unidentified man in sunglasses asked from the back of the room if there were any connections between Rustin's activities and socialism, and Rustin responded, "My good friend, I *am* a socialist." The session leaders struggled to silence the shouting and laughter that followed. In the small-group discussions, one officer said that, though he had overcome his initial skepticism and had begun to feel that something was being accomplished, after Rustin's appearance he would have nothing more to say.[83]

The final phase of the training program was a role-playing tour of city sites, a sort of performative community action, during which attendees inhabited, for a time, both the spaces and the identities of their classmates. The program's final report noted that police officers were often initially reluctant to join in the performances ("I am not going to make a fool of myself"), even though the scenarios were familiar to them: a spousal argu-ment, a landlord-tenant dispute, "juvenile street lounging," a traffic stop, mass demonstrations, and a street brawl, for example. But when civilian actors took up police roles, the officers grew frustrated and often jumped in to show how they would really perform in such circumstances.[84]

The workshop arranged visits to the Newark Police Academy, City Hos-pital, several antipoverty offices (including a few area boards), and several precinct houses. Not many officers were given time off to attend these field trips, and fewer still were willing to spread the word to their colleagues. But one police sergeant did suggest that police members of the workshop have lunch at a civilian classmate's home, where they could talk to the neighbors and hear their perspectives. The final two sessions of the program, whose grant period ended on June 30, 1967, were organized as role-playing dem-onstrations with two local precinct councils. On June 21, thirty people at-tended the session at the Fifth Precinct in the South Ward. On June 26, the training institute concluded at the Central Ward's Fourth Precinct, where about seventy attendees worked through a scenario in which a woman was robbed in a public housing project and the police were slow to respond.[85]

Barely two weeks later, residents and police would meet at the Fourth Precinct again, this time in a demonstration of how far their relation-ship, despite the halting efforts of the past several years to improve it, still had to go.

INTERLUDE: THE RIOTS

Esta Williams lived across the street from the Fourth Precinct, in the Hayes Homes public housing project. A job as a bookkeeping machine operator in the city tax department paid the bills, but she made a vocation of community activism. By July 1967, Williams was the first vice chairwoman of the Hayes Homes Tenants League, the chairwoman of the Fourth Precinct Council, and an active member of the antipoverty program's Area Board 2.

On the evening of July 12, Williams was at an area board meeting on Clinton Avenue when the telephone rang. It was for her. The caller said that a crowd was gathering at the Fourth Precinct and that she should get there right away. People had seen two officers drag a man into the building, punching and kicking him. Two years before, Williams's husband had gone missing and she found him—bruised, blood in his urine—two days later in a jail cell at the precinct. He spent nine days in the hospital. Nothing ever came of the complaints they filed with the city Human Rights Commission and the county prosecutor's office. So when she received that call, she headed straight for the precinct. There, she met up with several other community activists—including Bob Curvin and Donald Tucker, head of the United Community Corporation's Ironbound area board—and they were allowed in to see the prisoner, whose name, they learned, was John Smith.

Unless otherwise noted, Esta Williams's and Timothy Still's stories are reconstructed, and at times quoted, from GSCCD hearing transcript, October 20, 1967, 100–119; October 13, 1967, 41–48; October 17, 1967, 12–18. Kenneth Melchior's story is reconstructed and quoted from GSCCD hearing transcript, October 31, 1967, 3–41, 57, 63–70, 75–76. Any grammatical or spelling errors in quotations (including the frequent transcription of "disperse" as "disburse" in Melchior's testimony) are in the original.

We went into the cell block and my observation of Mr. Smith at this time, he was in agony from his facial expressions to be a man to be crying. This man was crying. He was complaining of his stomach and his ribs. He said, "I think I have some broken ribs." I didn't do any questioning. I just stood by and listened to others questioning him. He said, "And I have a terrible head-ache. They beat me on my head."

The community leaders urged that Smith be brought to the hospital immediately, and the police relented.

By this time, other antipoverty officials, including UCC president Timothy Still, had arrived. Like Williams, Still lived in the Hayes Homes and was active, as chairman, in its tenants' league. He too had been summoned to the scene by a phone call during an antipoverty meeting. His caller had estimated the crowd at 150 to 200 people.

When we got there the man had been taken out to the radio car. . . . The crowd was merging toward the car, and there is no question in my mind they were going to physically take the man out of the car and take him away from the police. However, one of our fellows on the staff got into the car with him, one of the fellows on the United Community Corporation staff got in. . . . When the crowd seen he was in the car with the man, they let the car go. I could only assume that the man, they were fearful the cops would beat the man or hurt him if they took him.

After getting the story of Smith's arrest from the police inspector on duty, Still went back outside to talk to people.

Some of the women who live in the community homes I have known for many years, women who are not black power advocates, not extremists, just plain, ordinary community people, came and told me that they saw the policeman strike and kick the man as the other policemen drug him into the precinct. These are people that I have known who come to me and would not lie in front of everybody. There was not just one, but a number of people around willing to say this and did say this. . . . This was a warm night and Hayes Project is a big project where 144 families live in each building. This is right across the street from Building 9. This is the area where there is a lot of people. There were scores of people out in the street because it was warm and scores of people saw what happened.

Still and Curvin, who was among the first community leaders on the scene that night, decided to address the crowd. Still pointed out that the police had guns and urged the crowd to go home. He suggested they all gather at city hall the next day to demand a meeting with the mayor and the police director, and make sure nothing like this ever happened again.

> We saw they wasn't going home. Somebody at that point threw some fire bombs. These were fire bombs, gasoline bombs against the precinct. . . . It lit up like day, but because it was brick it just burned out. . . . About fifteen minutes later the cops came rushing out of the precinct with helmets and sticks in their hands.

The police and crowd stared each other down from either side of the street. According to Still, each side hurled racial epithets at the other. The police inspector came out, too, and Still and Curvin convinced him to order his troops back inside. He agreed to give them fifteen minutes to disperse the crowd. They asked for a bullhorn, and Curvin climbed atop a car near the precinct. By this time, the crowd had grown by several hundred. He told them it was obvious that the police had declared war on them, and that they had to get together and do something about police brutality. Still urged them not to wait until the next day, but to march on city hall right then.

> There were quite a few people who didn't get in line, many people were just there observing to see what was going on. They didn't feel they would start. The police came out of the precinct and they began to throw at them. . . . I don't know why they came out, but they came out of the precinct. They had agreed to stay in the precinct for fifteen minutes. . . . It was only about seven or eight minutes from the time we got the line moving. They came out and then people began to throw stones at the policemen. Then the fire broke out in the parking lot [of the Hayes Homes] from an old car that was there for two or three months. It broke out into fire, and from that point on it was sporadic. It never really stopped again.

The next day, Thursday, July 13, Esta Williams attended Smith's court hearing. That afternoon,

> I went to an executive committee meeting of the UCC and I left UCC and I went into the area. When I got into the area where I live the cab could not go into my area because the police had the street so blocked off. I got the cab at

Montgomery and Belmont Avenue and as I was going down the walk, some kid yelling said, "That Smith, that cabbie, he died." To me I knew at this point it was a vicious rumor because I had just left him prior, unless he died in the course of my leaving a meeting and coming into the area. About this time I heard a shot, like a sound in front of the precinct and people started to disperse, going in different directions. I didn't go or in fact I couldn't go up 17th Avenue, so I went around the building through the parking lot area and went into my home. . . .

When I went into my apartment—well, from my bedroom window I can look direct at the Fourth Precinct desk. The cops ran out and they was hollering "Get moving, get moving. Disperse the crowds." . . . The people were running in different directions.

She watched with her ten-year-old son and a friend as a group of eight or nine policemen surrounded a black photographer. They kicked him and beat him with their billy clubs. When they let him up, he staggered near Williams's window. His head turned just enough to provide a glimpse of the blood caked on his face. Her son fainted. "I was just petrified," she later said. "I couldn't move." But she did. She went out to the bloodied photographer, who by that time was being tended by other area residents. The chairman of the city Human Rights Commission walked up and asked if she had seen what happened. When she said she had, he asked if she would be willing to testify about it. She said yes.

Meanwhile, some of the crowd dispersed by the police fled to their homes. Others began the looting.

Kenneth Melchior had been a member of the Newark police force since just after World War II and had attained the rank of inspector in May 1967. As such, he ranked below only the deputy chief, chief, and director of the police department. His duty was to make sure officers followed the proper rules and regulations and, should a situation arise that was beyond officers' capability, to make decisions for them.

On the night of July 12, at about 10:15 p.m., he was on routine car patrol, driving along McCarter Highway, when he received a call over the air to contact the Fourth Precinct. He found a telephone and spoke to the desk sergeant on duty. "He told me that police officers had been assaulted during the process of making an arrest," he later said, "and that there was a small crowd gathering outside of the Fourth Precinct."

11. A photo taken from an upper-story window at the Fourth Precinct on July 13, 1967, captures some of the tension as police officers returned from an effort to disperse the crowd into the Hayes Homes, just across Seventeenth Avenue. (Newark Public Library / *Star-Ledger*)

It was a normal summer evening. There are always during that time a great number of people in and around the area of the Hayes Project on Belmont Avenue. In fact, there is an ice cream place right on the corner that often draws a lot of people there. They were sitting on benches over by the Hayes Homes, children around, adults mixed in. There were quite a few people in the area but not concentrated in any one point or it did not appear their attention was directed to any one point.

Melchior entered the precinct through the back door and saw a small group of people—a few of whom, like Timothy Still and Bob Curvin, he immediately recognized—talking to the desk sergeant. They told him about a man being beat up by his officers, and he asked them to give him a minute to find out what had happened. He located the written incident reports.

I scanned them rapidly to get the gist of what had happened, and in brief they said that these officers had seen a traffic violation, had stopped the driver who had used some obscene and profane language, that they placed the driver under arrest and as a result he became violent, attacked them. It was necessary to subdue him and force him into the patrol car, and they brought him to the precinct station in a patrol car, that upon arrival at the station the man refused to leave the car. They had to use force to get him out of the car and carry him bodily into the police station. . . . I asked the lieutenant whether the prisoner had any visible injuries or had complained of any injuries. He told me that there were no visible injuries, that the prisoner was extremely uncooperative or would not identify himself, was fighting the officers in front of the desk, that he had him put back in the cell. . . . I then asked the lieutenant about the officers and their injuries. They were brought over. They were still behind the desk. They were brought over. I had noticed that Patrolman De Simone had an injury to his lip, a slight laceration and a contusion. . . . I then asked him about the report, referring about the fact that the trousers of both men were torn. I asked them where the trousers were torn. De Simone, his trousers were not torn, but Patrolman Pontrelli showed me his right knee where the trousers were abraded away and there was a slight bruise to the knee.

Melchior turned back to the group of community leaders. They demanded to see the prisoner, and Melchior allowed four of them to enter the cellblock. When they returned, he made arrangements to have Smith transported to the hospital. He was led, still in restraints, out the front door of the precinct and around the corner to a patrol car.

At this time a fairly large group had appeared in and around the precinct and was pressing close in on the car prohibiting it from leaving easily. It had to be maneuvered around. Other police officers from around the building tried to move the crowd away from the car in order for it to leave the scene. . . . I would say the crowd in that area at that time was approximately 250–300. . . . I didn't see anything that would say it was disorderly, but they were pressing in in an inquiring manner to determine what was going on. . . . As soon as the car had cleared the area I instructed the police officers, who were there, to disburse the crowd. . . . It disbursed easily, there was no resistance. . . . It had been disbursed so it was not dense. I won't say that the people had completely left the area. They were back on the Seventeenth Avenue side from the Reverend Hayes Homes area which does have quite a bit of open space.

By that time, community leaders had demanded a meeting with Inspector Melchior, and he gathered them into the precinct assembly room.

Everyone had something to say, and it was hard to get straight stories or provide straight explanations. Melchior tried to direct the conversation through Oliver Lofton, head of the antipoverty program's Legal Services Project. At about 11:40 p.m. someone somewhere else in the precinct building cried out that the kitchen was on fire.

> Immediately everyone left the room. As I left the Assembly Room I turned toward the desk. Lieutenant Price had said a fire bomb had hit, had been thrown from the outside. I started to the outside. At this time Sergeant Popek and several other officers were in the process of going through the door to the Seventeenth Avenue side of the building. As they hit the street they circled the building to determine the extent of injuries. I had ordered Sergeant Popek to set up a line of officers around the building in order to protect it from any other damage and to try to apprehend anybody who would throw any fire bombs or any other missiles at the building at any time.

A fire broke out in the parking lot of the Hayes Homes. The police officers and firemen who responded, Melchior later said, were stoned and driven from the area.

> At this point there was a small group standing in front of the Fourth Precinct talking to me. This was generally what you would refer to as the CORE group consisting of Mr. Walker, Mr. Curvin, Mr. Still, Mr. Wendell and Mr. Lofton. They were asking me to get the policemen off the street so that they could handle the crowd, that they could control the crowd. I told them that it was our duty to protect the people and to see that no one was injured in the area. They kept insisting that the presence of the officers was inflaming the crowd, irritating them, and that if they were withdrawn, this group of people could control and disburse the crowd and prevent any disorder. . . . They kept using the word "control." I answered them at one point the fact that they had not indicated to that point any control over the crowd, any power to disperse or prevent disorders. Even during this conversation an occasional missile would be thrown. . . .
>
> After being out on the sidewalk there about ten minutes at this time I came to the conclusion that we were not going to get anywhere just bickering over this thing; that if they could control and disburse the crowd they would in fact be doing us a favor. I told them that I would give them fifteen minutes to exercise this control and then I would have the police officers out and the police officers would then take such measures as might be necessary to completely disburse the crowd and prevent further disorder. I then ordered the police officers back into the building.

Bob Curvin asked Melchior for a bullhorn. Thinking it would help calm the situation, Melchior ordered a patrolman to retrieve one and watched Curvin cross the street and climb atop a car.

He started to talk to the crowd, haranguing them in a demonstration to pro-test the actions of the police officers. . . . I didn't stay to listen very long. I felt that Mr. Curvin was not living up to what the promise was, to control and disburse the crowd. . . .

I went back into the precinct. I notified the desk to see if they could get hold of Deputy Chief Redden and the director. . . .

It was now approximately twelve-fifteen when a real barrage of all types of missiles hit into the street and against the building. . . . I heard it from the inside. We went out of the building to the front. There was a group of approx-imately eighty or one hundred people lined up four or five abreast marching west on Seventeenth Avenue from the direction of Belmont Avenue. . . . They were in march formation walking along. This barrage of missiles was falling in amongst the group as well as in and against the building. The group, when I first saw them, was in the process of disintegrating, or breaking up.

The crowd mostly fled, Melchior explained, though some residents stood their ground. For the most part, his officers did not try to disperse these people, but they did chase down small groups of youths that were roaming the area.

We kept pulling the officers back to the front of the building. Groups of young teenagers would keep reforming and would throw missiles sporadi-cally. Almost during the entire course of the rest of the evening there were missiles being thrown in and towards the building or towards any group of officers. . . .

Other officers were arriving at the precinct. I think we had a total of ap-proximately fifty. We then formed them up in groups of eight or ten. We had them get what helmets were available in the precinct. They donned these helmets. They obtained nightsticks and they started to patrol in the groups through the Hayes Project area. . . . Missiles would be thrown at them from rooftops. . . . The missiles seemed to be thrown by young teenagers who would rapidly form a group, approach, throw two or three objects, and run at the approach of a police officer. . . . This continued in varying degrees for quite a period of time. The patrol activities of the men soon became effec-tive, and it lessened. Things were quiet and complete order restored at about four o'clock in the morning.

The next day, Thursday, July 13, Melchior came back on duty late in the afternoon. He met with other police officials downtown before heading back to the Fourth Precinct at about 6:45 p.m.

When I got there, there was a small group of people standing on the sidewalk across the street. . . . This group across the street would vary in size as I was at the precinct and as I would look out. Sometimes there were a few more, sometimes a few less. Just about at that time a small picket line started with eight or ten people marching up and down in front of the building. . . . There was no disturbance outside. At one point I had asked the men to go up to the second floor and again give me an estimate of the number of people out there. They told me there were about three hundred in the crowd across the street. The picket line had gradually grew larger, but you couldn't see the number that were involved in it. . . .

About eight o'clock a barrage of missiles, and for lack of a better word to describe the rocks, stones, bottles, pieces of wood, pieces of metal, a barrage hit the front of the building breaking several windows. This was the heaviest concentration of missile throwing that had taken place up to this time. . . . I sent two squads out the back door and the remainder of the men that were in the building out the front door to take whatever action could be possible, and followed them out the front door. . . . As the policemen hit the street everybody was running in all directions. The group of demonstrators that were marching were running. Some of them had been hit by some of these missiles. The police officers came out of the street, ran toward the crowd. The crowd disbursed and ran with few exceptions. They scattered all over the housing project area and up Seventeenth Avenue and out towards Belmont Avenue. . . . During the rest of the course of the night until the action left the Fourth Precinct area groups of thirty to fifty young teenagers would approach in almost military formation, unleash a barrage of missiles and disburse at the approach of the police officers. . . .

Then reports began to come in, began to be told about reports coming in the difficulty was growing on Springfield Avenue. As the perimeter of the building began to quiet down and we had the men more established and the reports were getting worse about Springfield Avenue. Gradually the groups of missile throwers left the vicinity of the Fourth Precinct, and we returned to relative quiet. . . . Relatively speaking it became quiet somewhere around midnight more or less. As I would return to the precinct, I would be informed about more and more disorder further away.

PART TWO

The Commission Response to Rioting

FIVE

The Kerner Commission

Late-night television watchers, some perhaps dozing off near the end of the CBS Thursday Night Movie (*Toys in the Attic*, with Dean Martin and Gene Tierney) or still enjoying NBC's *Dean Martin Summer Show* (hosted that night by Vic Damone), were interrupted by an urgent message from their president. Two weeks before, Newark had exploded. The recent violence in Detroit still smoldered. A grim-faced Lyndon Johnson wanted to take a few minutes of their evening to talk about this recent wave of rioting and about "the deeper questions that it raises for us all." One thing was beyond question, he said: rioting was a crime, not a civil rights protest, and the perpetrators should be captured and punished.[1]

However, Johnson continued, we could not stop there, could not settle "for order that's imposed by the muzzle of a gun." A better solution was at hand: "an attack—mounted at every level—upon the conditions that breed despair and breed violence." Everyone, Johnson insisted, was familiar with these conditions: "ignorance, discrimination, slums, poverty, disease, not enough jobs." Since he'd been president, the nation had launched a historic legislative assault on those conditions in an effort to forge the Great Society. Yet some had recently come to believe that this effort—"this beginning," Johnson called it—was too much and had begun to turn against it, slashing funding and rejecting further legislation. They believed that the nation could not afford to hire more teachers in the poorest inner cities, to secure housing for those without it, or to provide literacy programs for those who could not read or write. Theirs, the president said, "is a strange system of bookkeeping."

Johnson's late-night wake-up call contained an unmistakable sense of loss. From his vantage point, the national will had flagged. So he asked television viewers to search their hearts, to look at themselves, to look around them. If they did so not out of hatred and fear and "angry reaction," but with honest self-reflection, they would see that most Americans—"Negro and white"—desired the same things: safety and harmony and the opportunity to lead decent and productive lives. He called on white Americans— for surely they were the ones, in the president's estimation, most likely to overlook shared interracial desires and to respond with hatred and fear and anger—to push immediate reactions aside and to remember, as he pointed out, that responsible black Americans were the greatest victims of the violence and that they longed for American growth and prosperity more than anyone. The crucial task of self-searching would begin that Sunday, which Johnson proclaimed a national day of prayer. He urged his audience to attend church and turn their desires from suppression and revenge to "order and reconciliation among men."

Driving this national period of discussion and reflection, Johnson announced, would be a new National Advisory Commission on Civil Disorders chaired by Governor Otto Kerner of Illinois. Its task, notwithstanding the core insights of which the president was so sure, would be to "investigate the origins of the recent disorder in our cities" and recommend ways to prevent or manage future outbreaks. Seven months later, the commission and its considerable staff produced a paperback best seller that warned, in its most redeployed line, found on the very first of the report's

12. President Lyndon Johnson hoped his new commission would move a broad swath of Americans, like those planted before their television sets late on July 27, 1967, to reenergize a flagging commitment to the nation's cities. (LBJ Library)

six hundred pages, that "our nation is moving toward two societies, one black, one white—separate and unequal."[2]

The assuredness—and subsequent popularity—of that conclusion, however, obscures the tortured route that brought the commission to it. After collecting almost four thousand pages of testimony from over 130 witnesses in closed hearings, talking in secret to dozens more, conducting field trips to eight cities and more detailed surveys of twenty-three, compiling even more detailed "riot profiles" of nine of those cities, speaking with over two hundred consultants and contractors and advisers, conducting two major surveys of white and black social attitudes, aggregating and analyzing these varied data, writing multiple drafts of multiple sections of a final report, discussing the data, reviewing the preliminary drafts, formulating recommendations, and wrangling over each step of that process—in fact, *because* of all that—the commission almost did not reach a consensus, almost failed in its basic task to produce a set of actionable conclusions and recommendations.

In that near ruin, however, we can glimpse the very logic of the investigative commission as an administrative *thing*, as an institutional structure that shapes the experiences and thinking of the political actors involved in it. Central to that logic is the tension between a commission's goals and its necessary method: the achievement of consensus would be worthless without the possibility of real disagreement. The commission itself needed at least some patina of ideological diversity, of course, and had to be convened outside the established structures of the federal bureaucracy. And its investigation had to reach out to a wide cast of characters, had to be open to a wide range of knowledge if it were to be taken seriously. An investigative commission, in its very form and the logic of its approach, brought its members face-to-face with the messiness of local knowledge.

That encounter would test the commission's resiliency, would push its generally moderate members to the frontier of their thinking and experience. If they could succeed in crafting a consensual vision out of this mass of data and knowledge and experience, they would be modeling unity for a nation whose temperature was rising. They might demonstrate in microcosm that the proper way to resolve the urban crisis was not through the muzzle of a gun but through reasoned negotiation among diverse interests. If the nation, in Johnson's eyes, had begun to lose its way, an investigative commission might model a path back to the Great Society. Before it was a best-selling report summed up in an often-redeployed catchphrase, the Kerner Commission was a performance.

The potential for such a performance would go unfulfilled, however, if the president were not careful in how he chose the commission's members. The casting call would have to balance the need for variety with the need for consensus. He would have to choose carefully. Before he took to the airwaves late that night in July 1967, Lyndon Johnson and his aides had spent much of the afternoon on the telephone.

Governor Kerner was in a meeting on a boat anchored in the Mississippi River when he received word that the president wanted to speak with him. First elected by a wide margin (and in the process swinging the state for Kennedy) in 1960, Kerner enjoyed a reputation as an active liberal Democrat more in the mode of the New Frontier and Great Society than of his ally, Chicago mayor Richard Daley, or his father-in-law, the legendary Anton Cermak. There were no lines of communication connecting the boat to land, so a state trooper ferried the governor back to shore, where he phoned the White House from the police station in a small riverside town. President Johnson requested he chair the new commission, and Kerner accepted on the spot.[3]

Mayor John Lindsay of New York City, though a Republican, was just as activist an executive as Kerner, and only slightly more dashing. President Johnson reached him later that afternoon at Gracie Mansion, where it was almost suppertime, and asked if he would serve as the commission's vice chairman. "Mr. President," Lindsay replied, "the country is in trouble, and when you call for help you are entitled to receive it."[4]

Johnson and his aides continued dialing, and the commission's roster filled out. In addition to the two executives—a Democratic governor and a Republican mayor—Johnson asked four federal legislators to join the commission: two senators and two representatives, two of whom were Democrats (Representative James Corman of California and Senator Fred Harris of Oklahoma) and two of whom were Republicans (Representative William McCulloch of Ohio and Senator Edward Brooke of Massachusetts). Other choices represented key citizen constituencies and stakeholders. Charles "Tex" Thornton, the chairman and director of Litton Industries, came highly recommended by his old friend Robert McNamara and represented American business interests, while I. W. Abel, president of the United Steelworkers, stood in for labor. Roy Wilkins of the NAACP, who with Senator Brooke constituted the commission's two black members, represented the civil rights establishment, while Atlanta police chief Herbert Jenkins would speak for his brothers in blue. With the bulk of the commission in place, the president tried for several hours to locate his choice for the last spot:

Katherine Graham Peden, the state commerce commissioner in Kentucky and the commission's only woman. Johnson finally found her forty minutes before his television address and didn't even tell her the names of the other commissioners. She learned them, like so many other Americans, by watching television later that night.[5]

Summoned to the White House the following day, the appointees received their charge over lunch with the president. The commission was given the task of studying the riots, Johnson explained, because the matter was too grave, too central to the security of the nation, to subject it to the whims of petty partisan politics. He promised they would not be expected to slavishly bless the administration's efforts. Rather, he expected their investigation would be guided not by conventional wisdom or the tensions and "extreme opinions" infecting the nation—which he explicitly told them to eschew—but by the evidence. He provided them a staff but made it clear that only they, the commissioners, could provide the answers. "Only if you come to the meetings of this Commission regularly, and put your shoulders to the wheel," he told them, "can America have the kind of report it needs and will take to its heart."[6]

Though the president offered up the composition of the commission as "proof against any narrowness or partisanship," his casting process soon faced some questioning. At a press conference that afternoon, a reporter told Kerner that critics had already noted the absence of black militants who, presumably, would have insider knowledge on the violence. Kerner replied that the commission hoped to have militants on its staff, "so that all voices will be heard."[7] Though the commission in fact contained no militants of any stripe, even within its narrow representative swath there existed potential for meaningful disagreement. Before the commission came together for the first time that Saturday, for example, Mayor Lindsay had said that rioting is "rooted in the problems of the poor and in urban decay," while Katherine Peden had asserted that the federal government "should carry a big stick and get tough with rioters and looters."[8] In bringing these figures together, Johnson sought to highlight such differences, while insisting that only the facts on the ground would hold sway, that Lindsay and Peden and the rest of the commissioners would have to put aside their predispositions and approach the evidence with new eyes. Only then, Johnson said that first day, could they provide a model to "guide the country through a thicket of tension, conflicting evidence, and extreme opinions."[9]

Nonetheless, the president wanted someone to keep an eye on things, so he also called David Ginsburg. A pillar of Washington's liberal community, Ginsburg was a lawyer who had helped found Americans for Democratic Action in 1947 after serving in various New Deal administrative agencies and in the war. He was in Vancouver, on vacation, when the president reached him to ask if he would serve as the executive director of his new commission. Ginsburg took a night to think about it, then drove his family down the coast to Portland, where they heard gunfire from what the commission would later label a "serious disorder" that had begun the previous day. Shocked that racial violence had reached the Great Northwest, Ginsburg flew to Washington that night.[10]

Ginsburg (who, according to an assistant, knew "batpoop" about rioting) turned to a handful of urban-policy luminaries to help him devise a work plan for the commission.[11] Among those gathered at Ginsburg's house the following weekend were Adam Yarmolinsky, James Q. Wilson, Warren Christopher, and Mitchell Sviridoff. But it was Paul Ylvisaker who seemed to have the most profound affect on the approach adopted by the commission. Ylvisaker had left a position at the Ford Foundation only five months before to become the inaugural head of New Jersey's Department of Community Affairs. As such, he had gone to Newark in the middle of its crisis to assess the situation. He organized food delivery into the riot area, where so many stores had been looted and closed, and imported from New York's Vera Institute of Justice an efficient system of establishing bail for arrestees, great numbers of whom clogged local jails and courtrooms. When violence broke out in nearby Plainfield and the police and National Guard began a door-to-door search for weapons, Ylvisaker personally made a plea that they leave the armored personnel carriers behind.[12] At Ginsburg's house that weekend, Ylvisaker spoke at length about these experiences, and Ginsburg learned many new things, especially about the role police-community relations had played in the lead-up to the riots. The discrepancy between what Ylvisaker was telling him and what he had read in the papers was remarkable, and he became convinced that the commission would have to look beyond existing accounts of the violence and conduct its own close study of each city.[13]

Next, Ginsburg arranged to begin formal hearings as soon as possible. In those early weeks, he and the commissioners made several crucial decisions about the shape they would take. It was a sensitive matter. If the commission expected honest testimony, it had to both protect the witnesses and prevent them from using the hearings as a platform for promoting their own interests. It had to gather a diversity of viewpoints and avoid the appearance of favoring any one. And cutting through all this was the need to be transparent to the American public without pandering to it or allowing witnesses to do so. Ginsburg initially proposed open hearings, since the Warren Commission, which had investigated President Kennedy's assassination, had been roundly criticized for its opaqueness. But potential witnesses balked at the prospect of testifying publicly on such an incendiary topic. So the commission decided to hold closed hearings, followed by a limited number of press conferences when necessary. In addition, select portions of testimony would be released to a hungry press, but only after transcripts were cleared by witnesses. This would ensure some transparency, provide witnesses some control over the uses of their testimony, and, the commissioners hoped, prevent them from going to the press themselves.[14]

In the first two days of hearings, the commission quickly turned its attention away from the talk of conspiracy then making the rounds in Congress and among prominent public figures and toward "the conditions that breed despair and breed violence," as the president had put it. On August 1, FBI director J. Edgar Hoover assured the commission that, though his agency would continue to investigate such charges, it had yet "received no evidence . . . to substantiate the allegations that these disturbances are part of an over-all conspiracy."[15] In the day and a half after Hoover's appearance, several administration officials—including the secretaries of Labor and Health, Education, and Welfare; Robert Weaver from Housing and Urban Development; and Sargent Shriver—testified about what they deemed the underlying causes of rioting (poverty, unemployment, decrepit housing, etc.) and the administration's efforts to remedy those ills.[16] The press was briefed on the hearings and given some key excerpts from Hoover's testimony, news of which overshadowed that of the other officials in the next day's newspapers.[17]

Having debunked the conspiracy theories and collected predictable testimony from administration officials, the commission abandoned the view from Washington and waded into the swamps of local knowledge, where the picture was murkier and more hotly contested. First up was a delegation of state officials and local activists from New Jersey, organized by Paul Ylvisaker with the understanding, as he told the commission, that its testimony would be off the record. Kerner confirmed this, and Ylvisaker introduced the delegation and explained that its members did not constitute a cohesive group. They were, rather, a set of "varied individuals, representing different points of view" who had "come from different places, and by different methods of conveyance." The only thing that bound them was "a brief telephone call and an act of faith that this was a proceeding that would not embarrass them, whatever they might say." Ylvisaker emphasized that the riots had been "seen in a thousand different ways by a thousand different people" and that, therefore, each witness could speak to only a thin slice of the action. He himself, as he sat down with his secretary only days after his stirring visits to the Newark and Plainfield riot zones, had been unable to put events in order, to construct a narrative that would capture all he had seen and done. Nothing he said, therefore, should be taken as "Gospel truth." The delegates themselves, Ylvisaker reported, had stayed up late the night before, toiling in their offices and hotel rooms to put together a "rough chronology . . . as dry and direct as it possibly can be," of events in the state. Nonetheless, he predicted before turning the microphone over to the first of them, their testimony would likely be adversarial.[18]

As president of the United Community Corporation and a longtime resident of the Central Ward and the Hayes Homes, Tim Still brought a fine-grained perspective on what had transpired in Newark. His own view was "that what started the riot was the policeman beating the cab driver at the 4th Precinct." No conspiratorial band of militants was necessary. The feeling among many black Newarkers, he explained, was that the police had free rein in dealing with their community: they could beat people, and charges of police brutality disappeared into the administrative labyrinth of city hall. But beating a man outside the precinct across from the projects, while dozens—maybe hundreds—of people looked on? That had been too much.[19]

Oliver Lofton, director of the Newark Legal Services Project, a UCC delegate agency, then explained how complaints against the police were swallowed up in the black hole of an interdepartmental investigative office in city hall. But Lofton didn't get far before he was interrupted, not for the last time.[20] Ylvisaker tried to manage the tension between the commission's need to find consensual answers and the inevitable messiness of its practice by bringing the discussion back to what he deemed basic principles. Enamored of social-scientific explanations for disorder that reduced local circumstances to national tectonic movements, he deployed analogies from the natural world to explicate social phenomena. Local details were contestable and unreliable. His narrative, by contrast, would be built on the unassailable facts of observable social dynamics, which had produced mass violence as surely as subterranean pressures produced volcanic eruptions. Ylvisaker told the commission that others would no doubt contest Lofton's view of Newark's complaint procedures, but that the important point was a broader one: tensions in Newark had been rising for years. "It is like," he began, searching for the right metaphor, "it is a glacial movement through time—the concentration of the population and the lowering of relative standards, the rising of this feeling. One could say inevitably it was going to pop somewhere."[21]

Quasi-scientific assertions were an essential element of Ylvisaker's discourse. But when confronted with local conditions and perspectives—when a devotion to community action ran him up against them—he also sounded an unmistakable note of shaken confidence. He had walked the streets of Newark and Plainfield *and* the halls of the Executive Office Building in Washington. It was a nerve-racking position to be in, shuttling between the two worlds, certain that broad national action must be taken and terrified that the lack of a unified will would undermine the effort. His confidence at one point fell apart, and he spoke briefly of "the probability that men who have used every ounce of intelligence and reason and force and money available, still may become bodies on the barbed wire next time."[22]

The irony was that it had been Ylvisaker's detailed stories of Newark, related at that initial meeting at David Ginsburg's house, that had convinced the commission's executive director to direct a large chunk of the commission's resources toward amassing detailed data on specific cities. The essential logic of the commission form of investigation demanded such a decentering of knowledge gathering, an investigative appreciation of multiple viewpoints, even if in the end the purpose was to manage everything into one consensual report. Not every commission—not every riot commission, for that matter—had acted according to that logic, but members of this one often expressed a desire to distinguish themselves from the work of their predecessors, especially those whose work had been deemed shallow or distant.[23] So despite Ylvisaker's anxious attempts to reconcile the confusing and contradictory mass of local testimony with his impulse to national action, the commission and its staff began visiting riot cities.

Over the next several months, staffers fanned out and compiled profiles of 26 riot cities, culled from the more than 160 the commission identified. Teams of six investigators, with a "large component of negroes," as Ginsburg put it (perhaps in his mind fulfilling the pledge Kerner had made during his first press conference), spent an average of five days in each, interviewing local officials, residents of the riot areas, and representatives from business and civic organizations. Their process was informal: they were passed from person to person and agency to agency, moving through the cities according to referrals rather than an established agenda.[24]

The commission, however, regarded much of this initial material as worthless, not because it didn't complicate the picture, but because it didn't do so enough. Governor Kerner's special assistant repeatedly expressed his worries about the field staff's work. He found the interview data useful, at least for establishing local "attitudes and hostilities," but the harder data often came from suspect and self-interested sources. Local chambers of commerce provided employment data, for example, and mayors and police chiefs were the main source for the reports on law enforcement. If examined too closely, he wrote in mid-October, the city data would yield "many unsubstantiated conclusions . . . and the report could be discredited, and the commissioners would suffer along with the hopes of the public."[25] In the end, the field trips threatened rather than bolstered the commission's attempts to perform a thorough and disinterested investigation. The commission's openness to the complications of local data could prove corrupting if it failed to go beyond local power structures.

As commission officials scrambled to deal with the inadequacies of the staff reports, the commissioners themselves began their own carefully orchestrated site visits. For several commissioners, these trips brought them to parts of America they'd never seen before and to people they would never have met otherwise. After the commission's investigation was complete, some of them wrote of the profound impact these experiences—so new and, very often, awkward—had on them. Senator Harris, who described himself as a white populist from a mostly white state, found himself hanging out in a black barbershop in Milwaukee and, later, talking with jobless black men on the streets of Cleveland, who told him, he remembered, "What we need is jobs, baby. Jobs. Get us a job, baby." When Harris and Lindsay visited Cincinnati, three advance men spent days setting up a secret, closed-door meeting with a group of local black radicals, who told them that recent events constituted a rebellion. The commissioners went in alone, and guards—locals, not commission staffers—were placed at the doors. "I could not imagine feeling much different," Harris wrote soon after, "had the meeting taken place in the hills of Bolivia and we had been spirited there to meet with guerillas." Afterward, out on the street, a group of crapshooters asked them if they were FBI agents. This was "a long way from Walters, Oklahoma," Harris wrote, referring to his hometown, "where no Negroes were allowed to live."[26]

Newark was one of the first cities to be visited. On August 15, John Lindsay telephoned Mayor Addonizio to politely inform him of his plans: he was coming to Newark in the morning. He hadn't phoned earlier, he explained, because he was hoping to avoid too much publicity, and he asked the mayor for a meeting late in the afternoon, when the denizens of the city hall press room would be less likely to sniff them out. The following day, he hopped a New York City police department helicopter, darted over the Hudson and Passaic Rivers, and touched down in Newark without fanfare. Several city representatives, including the city planner and two police department officials, greeted him at the heliport, but Lindsay's tour guide that day was an official from the state Department of Community Affairs.[27] Mayor Addonizio reportedly sat in his office fuming at the prospect of being upstaged in his own city by the handsome young mayor from across the rivers.[28]

The helicopter lifted off again for a short aerial tour of the riot area before Lindsay headed for the Central Ward in a fire-engine-red convertible. ("Not much of an aid to anonymity," one local reporter cracked.) His first two stops were the Newark Legal Services Project and Area Board 2 headquarters above a riot-torn drapery store on Springfield Avenue. As a carpenter noisily hammered a piece of plywood over the shattered front windows of the store, Tim Still outlined the UCC's programs for Lindsay, offered an assessment of the recent violence, and told him of Newark's enduring tensions.[29]

From there, Lindsay—jacketless, tie loosened, sleeves rolled up over his well-tanned arms—strolled up Springfield Avenue. Residents, especially young children, caught sight of his familiar face and called out for attention. A reporter for the *Newark Evening News* who caught up with the crowd wrote that Lindsay's walking tour took on "an almost festive air, much like that of a political campaign." The New York mayor shook hands with local shopkeepers and residents, while other Newarkers shouted their greetings or, if close enough, grabbed at his arm. At Sidney's Deli, a nine-year-old asked him who he was and, reassured, told the mayor he recognized him from television. Lindsay bought him a soda pop. When he asked a maintenance man at the Scudder Homes housing project what he thought the commission ought to do for the city, the custodian laughed and told him, "I'd rather not say it in public." At the Hayes Homes, he was greeted by a group of children attending a summer recreation program and joined another group of youngsters on the blacktop to shoot some hoops. Back on the street, one local hugged him and declared, "I'm going to ask my mayor why he doesn't come up here."[30]

After visiting another UCC neighborhood branch office and touring North Fourteenth Street, where he enjoyed a limeade from some kids' roadside stand while an assistant fished out a quarter for him, Lindsay headed to city hall to meet with Mayor Addonizio. What one newspaper called "a crowd of jostling cameramen and squealing secretaries" greeted him.[31] After their closed-door meeting, the mayors emerged for a joint press conference. Though they cut diametrically opposite figures, the stately Lindsay towering over the squat and rotund Addonizio, their accounts of the discussion were well coordinated. Most of it, they reported, centered on the issue of federal aid to cities and its proper delivery, and they agreed that federal money should be funneled through city hall rather than independent community action agencies. The only sign of tension came when Lindsay was asked why Addonizio hadn't been invited on the tour, and Lindsay suggested that they would not have been able to move about as freely and talk to so many people with Addonizio in tow.[32]

That slight breach of decorum had carried over from their closed-door meeting. In what David Ginsburg, who also attended, later described as a "rather guarded exchange," Addonizio had pressed Lindsay for details of his tour. Ginsburg believed Addonizio, who did not strike him as a mayor who was "right there in the middle of the people, and worried about them," was "probably offended by the kinds of stories that were carried back regarding the reaction of the people to Mayor Lindsay." It needled him to learn that Lindsay's visit was so festive, that he had been greeted warmly on his stroll along ransacked Springfield Avenue, and that he had played basketball among the high-rise towers of the Hayes Homes with youngsters who, one month before, might have been among those who stoned police officers at the Fourth Precinct. During their meeting, undoubtedly with as much tact as he could muster, Lindsay asked Addonizio whether he had ever considered establishing a review board to oversee complaints of police brutality. Addonizio grew "immediately defensive," and Lindsay took this as a sign that his Newark counterpart had neither done, nor intended to do, anything about it.[33]

Roy Wilkins was scheduled to make the next field trip to Newark. He asked Lindsay and Ginsburg if there was anything they had missed that he should be sure to see. "The best thing to do," Lindsay responded, "is put yourself in the hands of somebody who is not part of the inside structure." But, Wilkins worriedly told him, Addonizio's office had already asked him what sort of escort they could provide. Lindsay recommended plainclothes or black policemen, because an escort of uniformed white officers would suggest a relationship with city hall that the commission vehemently sought to avoid. In any case, Lindsay advised, ask the escort to wait outside while talking to the locals.[34]

Over the next few months, Mayor Addonizio emerged in the commission's deliberations as a prime symbol of the sort of unthinking, self-interestedness that it worked to undermine. His apparent distance from the black community—from the grassroots work of the antipoverty and black power movements—contrasted with the encounters the commission form of investigation had generated for its members. And despite putting on a good face for his appearance with Lindsay, Addonizio threatened to stir up controversy by scheduling a press conference to be held right after his upcoming appearance before the commission. The commissioners considered demanding that he call it off but were forced to admit that any effort to suppress him would look even worse.[35] In the end, though, Addonizio canceled the press conference and instead released his prepared statement, perhaps sensing the futility of going toe to toe with a presidential commission in the public sphere. Though that may have constituted a retreat of sorts for the mayor, his statement was not without its barbs.[36]

Addonizio opened by insisting that his administration had done everything in its power to address the ills plaguing Newark. The problem lay not in his efforts but in a wider societal disdain for cities. Cities could not save themselves, and Americans were not committed to saving them. He believed "that they would vote the cities out of existence if they could." The appropriation then before Congress for a Model Cities Program provided the faintest glimmer of hope, not only in the funds it would provide, but also in the recognition, embedded in the legislation, that local governments should control the money. "It is a far cry from the Office of Economic Opportunity which has regularly by-passed the city governments, and dealt directly with neighborhood groups," Addonizio concluded. "The cities were flat on their backs, and the OEO came along, and instead of helping us . . . it decided we were a bunch of bullies, and it gave a club to the so-called powerless to help beat us as we lay on the ground."[37]

The commissioners were largely unmoved. During a lunchtime recess, David Ginsburg noted that they were likely to hear the same message from other mayors, many of whom were offended by the Community Action Program's end run around city hall. He predicted that all of them would avoid talking about "their own problems, which are subject to their control" and urged the commission not to be taken in by their grumbling.[38] And when, after lunch, Addonizio continued his assault on the UCC ("a haven for political rejects") and the level of federal funding for, among other things, police-community relations programs, Senator Harris finally lashed out: "We have heard criticism of the county, criticism of the State, criticism of the community action programs, criticism of the Federal Government. Frankly, I'm a little stuffed with criticism."[39]

Ginsburg was right: Addonizio was far from the only mayor blaming the federal government for not adequately supporting the cities.[40] But as the commissioners gathered in December to begin considering conclusions and recommendations, they were frequently drawn back to their time with him. Roy Wilkins worried at one meeting that any criticisms the commission might level at federal spending cuts would smack of Addonizio's plea for more money. Senator Harris insisted the commission carefully focus its criticisms; otherwise it would risk looking like the mayor who had lashed out at anything and anyone. For several commissioners, Addonizio's Newark was the nightmare city, the archetype of urban crisis. When one of I. W. Abel's assistants suggested that the reports coming out of Newark were too kind, Wilkins and Herbert Jenkins agreed, citing rampant infighting within and among city agencies and between city and state governments. And when Wilkins worried that the research staff's material on Detroit lacked the drama of the reports from Newark, Senator Harris put it down to a crucial distinction between the two. Detroit was still economically healthy, he said, but Newark was "beyond salvation and hope."[41]

While the commissioners and staff continued their field trips—two more delegations visited Newark, one escorted by city officials, the other by a UCC representative—Kerner announced that the hearings would tack back toward "the broader substantive concerns" underlying violence and away from the mountain of details and disagreements threatening to overwhelm the investigators' efforts to corral it.[42] Over the next several weeks, he said, the commission would hear testimony from "experts in the field of social psychology, education, employment, job training, police-community relations, and riot control techniques." But on the first day of its new approach, the commissioners devoted their session to, as Kerner put it, "a general history of the Negro in the United States."[43]

The commission welcomed two prominent black historians: Lerone Bennett of *Ebony* magazine and Benjamin Quarles of Morgan State College. Their long-range perspective on recent events would become the vantage point from which the commission would weave out of the hundreds of individual riots one broad national narrative. Together, Quarles and Bennett established a compelling narrative structure for the violence. After them, other expert witnesses just filled in the details.

Bennett took the commissioners on a whirlwind tour of American history, a story driven by the conflict between professed national ideals and their repeated betrayal. He began in the 1660s, with the establishment of the African slave trade, passed through the racial promises and duplicities of the American Revolution, the victories of the Reconstruction years and the defeats of 1877, the courageous mass migration of black southerners to northern cities and the violence and discrimination that awaited them, the power of the *Brown* decision and its unfulfilled challenge to segregation. It was a story rife with frustrated possibility. "The result of all this, of course," Bennett concluded, "is the activity we see today in the cities of our country." The riots were "a bitter harvest of the history we have made."[44]

After Quarles offered a statement on what he deemed a broad-based desire for racial consensus, the questioning began.[45] When Senator Harris asked what they believed the basis for racial discrimination to be, Bennett said it was a hard question to answer. "Libraries are just crammed with books and studies of Negro communities, studies of the South Side of Chicago, over and over again," he said, "when in fact, I would suggest that the problem is in the North Side of Chicago." He suggested that what they really needed was "a great deal of study about what is wrong with white people."[46] When Peden asked whether blacks and whites needed to get to know each other better, Quarles pointed out that blacks already knew whites very well, and Bennett suggested that only a "problem of will" prevented Americans from enjoying "life in a multi-ethnic society."[47] And when Representative McCulloch, perhaps growing exasperated with the depth of the problems suggested by the historians, asked whether they could ever really be solved, Bennett again suggested that the nation didn't lack the resources to do so, but only the will.[48]

Shortly before the two historians' appearance, the commission had hired Robert Shellow, a little-known expert on police-community relations who had served on the staff of the National Institute of Mental Health and as a consultant to the Office of Law Enforcement Assistance, to coordinate its massive and unwieldy research program, to wade through its material, and to construct out of it some summative statement about the roots of civil disorder. As the deadline for an interim report fast approached—Shellow understood that it was to be a broad statement, without much social-scientific documentation—he shifted his team's attention from the estimated fifteen thousand pages of raw data to the writing of a broad narrative analysis.[49]

The resulting interim report, which Shellow later said "was long on attempts to cast the events of the year into a meaningful theoretical framework, but necessarily short on documentation," caused a major stir within commission ranks when it circulated late in November. Its interpretations, if made public, would no doubt whip up a storm of controversy.[50] The report's title, "The Harvest of American Racism: The Political Meaning of Violence in the Summer of 1967," pointed toward its most challenging conclusion: that the rioting had political content, that it was more than a criminal matter to be settled with police action and the proper meting out of punishment. "At one level the riots reflect simply a demand for recognition," the report claimed, while "at another the violence takes the form of political confrontation, a sort of pressure group politics in which the pressure is Negro violence; at the highest level they have a tendency to become out and out political rebellion—efforts to abrogate, though not to overthrow, the power of the state." One "way to save America," it suggested, would be to transfer control of existing antipoverty programs to local militant organizations, to imbue "young militants" with decision-making powers, and to deny local officials any veto of their programs. If the position of black youths in American society did not change, then "increasing civil disorder can be viewed as the natural state of American society in the future."[51]

Though Shellow believed the researchers could document all their conclusions if given enough time, the most common response to the report was that it had made authoritative claims based on limited and selective evidence. What the commission demanded was incontrovertible conclusions, and to release "Harvest," in one staffer's estimation, would have endangered the entire effort.[52] Another, tasked with giving his assessment to David Ginsburg, presented five general criticisms (unsubstantiated conclusions topped the list) and ten pages of specific criticisms, often expressed in outraged marginalia, most variations of "More facts" and "Facts! Facts!"[53] Ultimately, "Harvest" was rejected by the staff directors, and seems never to have been presented to the full commission. Without it, they decided to forgo an interim report altogether and to release a final report in March, months sooner than the president had requested.[54]

Complicating the situation was a funding crisis. President Johnson had been unwilling, faced with the rising costs of the war in Vietnam, to seek from Congress any supplemental funds for executive agencies. The commission's budget had been cobbled together from Johnson's emergency fund and contributions from several cabinet departments, but almost all that money had been used. Even if the commission wanted to keep its team of researchers, the money wasn't there, and they were let go.[55]

The first batch of pink slips went out on December 12, and at about 7:30 that evening, the *Washington Star* and the *Washington Daily News* received anonymous messages from a man claiming to have knowledge of the commission's inner workings. He told the papers that the White House had cut off funding and that, as a result, 120 staffers had been fired. He speculated that the White House had done this after receiving copies of "The Harvest of American Racism."[56] The *Star* ran a story the next day citing "several staff members, all of whom declined to be quoted by name," who claimed that the draft report they had helped prepare was too critical of the federal government for the president's taste. The next day, it reported that the commission's young researchers believed they had been hamstrung by an unwritten rule that forbade them from recommending any new programs or any massive new outlays of federal money. More pragmatic staffers, the paper reported, criticized the youthful radicals for thinking "they're being paid with government funds and working in a government office building in order to plan a revolution against that government."[57] The story quickly spread to other newspapers and magazines. A New York congressman repeated it on the floor of the House.[58] Kerner and Lindsay, as the commission's public faces, spent the next month denying that any staff had been fired because of pressure from the White House or any displeasure with their draft interim report.[59] The controversy inevitably died down, but the commission's carefully tended distance from political controversy had been abridged, whether by the ad hoc nature of its administrative (and therefore funding) structure, or by the way that structure had opened the commission to voices and perspectives that were deemed too incendiary to be officially reported.

In order to keep to the new timetable, the commission's writers picked up their pace. Much depended on their ability to corral the mass of data into a readable narrative. Many of them had been working on it for months, but the commission also enlisted outside help. Sometime that fall, it hired California-based journalist Robert Conot to give the city profiles a novelistic feel, a nuanced portrait of what American mass violence looked like in its recent manifestations. Conot's massive profile of the 1965 riot in Watts, *Rivers of Blood, Years of Darkness*, had been released that August, and its detailed attention to the experiences of everyday people, its colorful and engaging style, and its lambasting of the McCone Commission report's prose, which it said "had all the sparkle of a corporation report," had attracted David Ginsburg's attention.[60] Other sections also took shape. The deep historical view provided by Lerone Bennett and Benjamin Quarles was reshaped by the University of Chicago's John Hope Franklin into a draft section titled "The Roots of Racism and Alienation."[61] The list of recommendations was rewritten at least twice, once because staff higher-ups deemed it too sophomoric and again when the commissioners deemed the revision too cold and technocratic.[62]

Given the commission's urgency, the number of hands involved in writing drafts, and the flurry of revisions being made, some of the commissioners worried that the final report would be a chaotic muddle of ideas, statistics, and graphs, unreadable and assured a rightful place in the trash bin of history. Early drafts were not promising. Governor Kerner's assistant warned him that the report was growing so long that it would "scare away the very people in our Nation who must read it."[63] Representative Corman expressed the same worry, writing to Ginsburg to convince him of the need for a report that could be read in a single day, with more photos and fewer statistics and, possibly, a human-interest "Day in the Life" feature that would capture life in a riot city.[64] Mayor Lindsay was so worried no one would read the report that he suggested the commission produce a one-hour documentary film based on it.[65]

Early in the new year, after receiving several months' worth of the commissioners' suggestions, from the metaphysical to the mundane, the writers delivered a complete draft—three volumes, comprising twenty-five tabbed sections—for a final round of comments. The commissioners and their staffs labored at it for much of the next two months, and their worries and debates reached a crescendo as the March release date drew near.[66] Corman found the draft repetitious and verbose and suggested they hire one more writer to smooth it out. Agreeing, Wilkins said that every thousand words cut would improve it.[67] Commissioners debated the negative income tax, the role of white racism in the rioting, and the extent to which they should comment on national institutions.[68] Several worried that some sections might prove inflammatory and would overshadow the rest of the report. Others worried that people would read only those sections that excited them or confirmed what they already believed.[69] They debated whether they should include a price tag for the report's impressive list of recommendations. Though Lindsay advocated being forthright with the costs, most wanted to avoid what one staffer termed a "Christmas tree appearance."[70] Ginsburg continued to receive suggestions for revision late into February, and he urged Governor Kerner to accept them all or risk prolonging the debates and delaying the report.[71]

In all these discussions, the commission's legitimacy as a model for how Americans might respond to the rioting hung in the balance. It had to demonstrate that unity could be forged out of thousands of pages of testimony, dozens of city profiles, reams of research data, and the particular political persuasions of each member. Many times it seemed as though a minority report was inevitable. Chief Jenkins later admitted he had feared it all along, and Robert Conot later revealed that he had been summoned to a meeting in January 1968 at which four of the commissioners—Corman, McCulloch, Thornton, and Peden—said they were unable to support the draft recommendations and were prepared to issue a minority report.[72] Later news stories claimed that Thornton and Lindsay had regularly clashed and that Senator Harris frequently worked to ease the tension and keep them talking.[73] Through it all, David Ginsburg tried to hold the commission together, believing that anything less than a unanimous report would be disastrous.[74]

Given all the tensions inherent in the report—between the complexity of actual events and the multitude of viewpoints that passed through the commission's investigation (including those of its own members), on the one hand, and the desire to wrangle it all into a cohesive and coherent portrait of civil disorder on the other—it's no wonder that, as staff members came before the full commission in the final weeks of its deliberation to read aloud the sections they had written, Mayor Lindsay began to worry that the report lacked focus, was too conservative, and, upon release, would quickly be forgotten. He sent a memo to his colleagues in which he declared that the "major failing of the report is the lack of a sense of urgency" in such urgent times. The report—which he reportedly called "wishy-washy"—hardly seemed relevant. It was distant and academic. It did not speak to real urban lives. "This can't be just another Presidential Commission with another report," he wrote. "This is the most serious domestic crisis we have faced in the past century. It threatens the peace, stability, and growth of our society. There can be no delay. We need action."[75] In a meeting two days later, Lindsay implored his colleagues to approach the urban crisis with even more urgency than they would the war in Vietnam, since only the first posed an existential threat to the nation. They had only five more years, he told them, to save the country from possible extinction.[76]

Where Lindsay found the report too sober, Corman found it not sober enough. After reading the full draft and, apparently, Lindsay's memo, Corman wrote to Kerner to express his deep discomfort. He felt the commission's potential to make a lasting contribution to national life had dwindled. "Meeting our responsibility does not lie in an indiscriminate and unstudied attack on every problem of American society," he wrote, "but rather in a careful weighing of evidence from the disorders, a development of understanding for the frustrations and limitations of human beings in these conflicts, and a judicious setting of program priorities that respond directly to the immediate causes of riots." He charged the commission with working backward: they had uncritically accepted the staff's self-styled revolutionary recommendations and then constructed a problem to fit them. But he rejected the notion that "war-time conditions" prevailed in cities. "I emphasize that a unanimous report, without minority reports or supplemental views, is highly desirable," Corman concluded. "But, if the present course is continued, I would prefer the first option to the second."[77]

Lindsay decided to counter the minority-report threat with his own ultimatum.[78] In an all-night session before the commission's last scheduled meeting, two of Lindsay's aides drafted a summary of the report, pulling out of its deep swamp of details and recommendations and stories the points their boss deemed most urgent. The next morning, Lindsay told his fellow commissioners that he felt they had lost focus and suggested that a brief, hard-hitting summary might be just the thing they needed. He told them he had taken a shot at it and spent the next twenty minutes reading the document aloud, before asserting that it was an encapsulation of all they had been thinking. If anyone disagreed, he reportedly said, they would be the cause of discord, not him. In the end, the commission voted unanimously to accept it, with only minor revisions, as the report's opening section.[79]

As staff finalized the report for its scheduled release on the first Saturday in March, David Ginsburg prepared its path into the world. Because the Government Printing Office would not be able to produce its run in time, he arranged to have two thousand photo-offsets made for distribution to the press and Congress. The media would receive its copies on Thursday in order to give them time to prepare thoughtful stories on the report, and Congress would receive its copies on Friday. Ginsburg timed it so that Americans would open their Sunday papers to extensive coverage of the commission's wide-ranging and careful report, its bevy of conclusions, and its critical recommendations, before heading to a local bookshop or newsstand to buy the forthcoming Bantam paperback and study it for themselves.[80]

Except the plan did not work. When Ginsburg sent the *Washington Post* its copy, the paper returned it. When asked why, someone at the paper told him that a confidential source had already leaked a copy of Lindsay's summary, which the *Post* planned to print on Friday, rather than wait for the full report. Ginsburg was furious, but he was also stuck. So he immediately released the summary to all his press contacts, who scrambled to put together stories for the next day's papers.[81]

The *Washington Post*'s front-page story was headlined "Racism, Poverty Blamed for Riots: Huge Effort Is Urged by LBJ Panel," while the *New York Times* reported, "Panel on Civil Disorders Calls for Drastic Action to Avoid 2-Society Nation: Whites Criticized."[82] Both papers printed Lindsay's summary in its entirety (though without any sign that the writers knew of its origins), and both emphasized its most urgent passages. They led with paraphrases of its most provocative line, the one that claimed the "nation is moving toward two societies, one black, one white—separate and unequal," and rounded out their nut graphs with two key conclusions. First, white racism, not any radical band of conspirators, was ultimately to blame for creating ghetto conditions and, therefore, the riots. And second, only a massive, and no doubt costly, effort to redress those conditions would lead the nation away from a racially polarized future.

At the commission's inaugural event, President Johnson had said that the ultimate solution to the crisis lay in a renewed national will. We *could* solve the crisis, of course. We just had to *want* to. The commission provided a model of such desire and of the hard work it would take to fulfill it, but it had no power to compel that model's broader adoption. If Lindsay's aim in submitting the summary had been to increase the chances that the commission's work would matter to Americans, its early release proved a vital helpmate.[83] It took the most energetic part of the text and threw it out into the world, without the burden of the other six hundred pages. The summary and the blaring headlines achieved an urgency that was largely absent from the main body of the report, an urgency that, in the absence of any other mechanism, might produce a widely shared desire for the fulfillment of the commission's model.

The summary's text leads the reader in this direction. If history brought the nation to its current crisis, there had to be a clean break with the past, a fresh start. So the summary begins, as origin tales often do, with chaos. It says that the president had appointed the commission in response to the "shock, fear and bewilderment" caused by the "racial disorders." It takes readers from this initial "shock, fear and bewilderment" to the sense that they have a choice, that they are the masters of the nation's fate: they could continue down the road toward two separate and unequal societies, or they could pursue an alternative that would require "a commitment to national action—compassionate, massive, and sustained" and "from every American . . . new attitudes, new understanding, and above all, new will." In the quest for answers and the willingness to learn, the summary concludes, the commissioners "have provided an honest beginning." Now the matter lay before the rest of the nation.[84]

Americans might start by continuing through the next six hundred pages. They might demonstrate their hunger for answers by being good readers of an exhausting text, the perceived deficiencies and tedium of which had moved Lindsay to ratchet up the rhetoric. Enough copies were soon available to create out of this community of readers the ideal, more willful nation President Johnson had called for. Bantam fired up the presses for round-the-clock printing. Cases and cases of paperbacks were shipped to the coasts from the publisher's warehouse in Des Plaines, Illinois.[85] By the end of the month, there were nearly a million copies in print and sales were "still skyrocketing" with no signs of slowing, as Bantam's president wrote to Governor Kerner. "The man on the street all over the country is buying the book."[86] Bantam offered a thousand copies to each commissioner. Roy Wilkins sent them out to NAACP chapters across the country, and Chief Jenkins issued a copy to each member of the Atlanta police department.[87] Kerner, for one, received hundreds of requests for copies, to which he responded with a form letter telling people they could order a copy from the Government Printing Office ($2.00) or find it at their local newsstand or bookshop in convenient paperback form ($1.25).[88] By the beginning of the 1969–1970 school year, over twenty thousand copies had been sold to college departments for course adoption.[89] What readers would do with it remained to be seen.

For its part, the White House greeted the release with a deafening silence. Convinced of its political and financial impracticality, and stung by the implication, explained in a memo from Joseph Califano, that the administration had made little progress on civil rights, the president for the most part publicly ignored it.[90] He held no official ceremony to accept the report and called no press conferences. He never met with the commission as a whole. The most the press could pick up, it seemed, were a few off-the-cuff remarks, including ones he made to a group of black publishers. He told them that the report was the most important one of his presidency but its writers were less practical than he was. After all, he said, one might want steak three nights a week but might have money for only two.[91]

By the end of March, Mayor Lindsay had begun pointing out that money for a third steak night was going instead to feed the war machine in Southeast Asia. While campaigning for a reconvening of the commission to focus on the implementation of its recommendations, he told an enthusiastic audience of Columbia Law School students that the nation couldn't ease tensions in its cities while engaging in an "insane military escalation in Vietnam." He called on the president to end his silence on the report.[92] Lindsay kicked up such a storm that David Ginsburg, likely at the behest of the White House, asked Kerner to cool the situation.[93] Shortly thereafter, Kerner wrote to Joseph Califano assuring him that no further meetings of the commission were planned.[94] None ever occurred.

Whatever the commissioners did or said at this point, though, mattered little. The report was out in the world. People across the country, in different ways, *were* taking it seriously. For some, it inspired scornful attacks on the commission. Kerner alone received hundreds of derisive letters.[95] When the president nominated him for the federal bench just weeks after the report's release, Kerner came face to face with Senator Strom Thurmond during his confirmation hearings. Thurmond told Kerner that he did "not understand the attitude of some people today in trying to blame the white race" rather than "the individuals who took part" in the rioting.[96] Vice President Humphrey, in a speech before a convention of B'nai B'rith Women, argued that "condemning whole societies—white or black or German or Arab or Chinese—comes dangerously close to a doctrine of group guilt."[97] One Louisiana congressman deemed the report "propaganda ad nauseam," while his Senate counterpart claimed it advocated "a turn-the-other-cheek to lawlessness," as if white America had been slapped once by the riots and again by the charge of racism.[98] Syndicated columnist William F. Buckley was no less scornful. "The Kerner Report on the riots last summer," he wrote, "is likely to engage the attention of a generation of politicians and moralists as the central document of the period, accounting for our revolutionary summers and laying the blame for them squarely on the culprit—our old friend, honkey."[99]

Though public moments of dissent garnered much press attention, expressions of support flew in from many directions for several years. The Xerox Corporation, citing the commission's report, announced an intensification of its efforts to recruit and train black Americans, while Dow Chemical Corporation initiated an employee education program, using reprints of the commission's historical sketch (the one drafted by John Hope Franklin) to build awareness of the needs of "minority people."[100] The Anti-Defamation League of B'nai B'rith, apparently unmoved by Humphrey's speech to its women's auxiliary, distributed copies of the report, created curricular materials based on it, and produced a thirty-minute educational film, all in order to establish a climate suitable for the implementation of its recommendations. The Roman Catholic bishops adopted a two-thousand-word statement endorsing the report and calling on Catholics to "declare war" on racism. The radio division of the Mennonite Board of Missions and Charities made plans to excerpt the report in the July issue of its *Alive* magazine.[101] Vermont's governor proclaimed May his state's

"Response Month" and called upon all residents "to familiarize themselves with the Kerner-Lindsay Report and to look into their hearts and minds in an effort to determine what each of us can do to promote the goals of brotherhood and true equality." The Tucson Commission on Human Rights issued a pamphlet titled *The Tucson Response to the Kerner Report* detailing its plans to improve police-community relations and employment programs.[102] The board of directors at the Girl Scouts of the USA urged its local councils to study the report and "to implement in every way possible . . . the creation of a true union, a single society and a single American identity."[103] The director of the Swimming Hall of Fame in Fort Lauderdale telegrammed Kerner to tell him it had launched a summer swimming program to channel the energies of local urban youth.[104] The Urban League's Whitney Young proposed a "white people's march on Washington" at the end of April to demand congressional action on the nation's racial and urban crisis, declaring it was "up to white people to pick up the burden of leadership in making white society a decent one."[105] And when the National Association of Social Workers met in Washington just days after Young announced his proposal, members passed a resolution excoriating the association's lack of leadership in implementing the commission's recommendations, "especially those dealing with white racism as it applies to our own professional association."[106]

In January 1969, when *Social Education*, the house journal of the National Council for the Social Studies, asked the former commissioners about the steps taken to implement their recommendations over the past year, Otto Kerner cited the outpouring of support he had seen in the hundreds of letters from and many meetings with people across the country. A sufficient number of Americans, it seemed, had adopted the commission's model, and the governor was heartened. "There is great movement at all local levels that indicates that people are beginning to understand," he wrote. "It is obvious that in many areas new attitudes have developed and with it a new will."[107]

Six days after the report's release, Martin Luther King Jr. sent telegrams to commission members praising the "wisdom" of their report. "The commission's findings that America is a racist society and that white racism is the root cause of today's urban disorders is an important confession of a harsh truth," King wrote. By ignoring it, he said, "we will sink inevitably into a nightmarish racial doomsday."[108] Several weeks later, speaking at the National Cathedral in Washington about his plans for the upcoming Poor

People's Campaign, King said that one of the only things that would prevent its launch would be the full implementation of the recommendations
of the 1967 White House Conference on Civil Rights and of the Kerner Report.[109] Four days later, he was assassinated, and the question of the commission's understanding of mass racial violence was forcefully renewed.

Nearly nine months after President Johnson phoned him and one
month after the commission's report detailed for the nation how it might
prevent further urban unrest, a shaken Mayor Lindsay retreated to Gracie
Mansion. Hours earlier, upon reports of King's assassination, the mayor
had joined other New Yorkers in taking to the streets. In Harlem, he had
visited a command post from which city police tried to contain an outbreak of violence. Windows had been smashed, stores looted, buildings
burned. A four-alarmer drew the fire department to the corner of 125th
and Lenox, where firefighters were met with a barrage of rocks and bottles. Through the storm, they spied young boys sprinting down the street,
their arms wrapped around televisions and radios. Out on the sidewalks,
Lindsay waded into a surging crowd of black constituents and told them
he was sorry and sad, but violence was an unacceptable response to violence. When a scuffle broke out, his security detail shuffled him into his
limousine. Emerging a little later, the mayor encountered a smaller crowd
of Harlemites (one newspaper called them "an unruly group of youths,"
another just "several Negroes") that rained down insults and, according to
some reports, objects—sometimes "missiles," sometimes more specifically
"bricks"—on their mayor. He was hustled into the limousine again and
taken back to Gracie Mansion.[110]

In Otto Kerner's native Chicago, violence broke out on the city's west
side before spreading, on the second night, to the south. Flames engulfed
entire neighborhoods. Newspapers breathlessly reported "heavy sniper
fire" at Sixty-Fifth and Ingleside and tracked "bands of Negro youths"
roaming Sixty-Third Street. Windows were smashed, displays looted. The
perpetrators "disappeared into side streets," evading the police who had
been ordered to shoot them.[111] Buildings were set ablaze. National Guardsmen rested their bodies and repaired their equipment in the Hyde Park Armory, and a group of young Chicago activists met on the Midway in hopes
of devising a plan to stop the violence.[112]

The White House, from which nine months earlier President Johnson
had spoken to millions of American television viewers, calling for an investigation into the causes and solutions of the urban crisis, stood out against
a backdrop of black smoke. From it, whole swaths of the city were invisible.

A week later, four hundred white men, women, and children staged a

Good Friday march through the Chicago suburbs, where two years earlier King had led civil rights demonstrators through a hail of rocks and bottles. Though the gathering was interdenominational and had been organized by a Lutheran clergyman, the march took on a decidedly Catholic tone in its public displays of guilt and self-castigation. "We are simply confessing our white racism," the organizer, Rev. George Hrbek, told a reporter. "We believe the Kerner Commission is correct in stating that racism in white communities is the cause of racial crisis and we hope to dramatize this by our march and stimulate constructive action." The marchers stopped to sing eight times that day and, unlike King's marches two years earlier, not a single heckler interrupted them.[113]

SIX

The Governor's Commission

Governor Richard J. Hughes had been talking tough for days. Ever since arriving in Newark early Friday morning, just over twenty-four hours after the violence began, his strident denunciations of the looting and alleged sniping had been quoted widely in local and national media outlets. At his first evening's press conference, he condemned the looters' "holiday atmosphere" and rejected any possibility of seeing their actions as legitimate protest, insisting instead that looting constituted "a criminal insurrection against society, hiding behind the shield of civil rights." "The line between the jungle and the law might as well be drawn here as well as any place in America," he ominously declared.[1]

Over the course of the day, the gunfire increased, and Hughes's tone grew even angrier. After a police detective and a fire captain had been shot and killed—the only white people, of twenty-six total, to be killed over the course of the riots—Hughes lashed out at the black snipers presumed responsible for their deaths. "This is a criminal insurrection by people who say they hate the white man but who really hate America," he said. "This battle is joined to the finish line, but I can say now that society is going to win and that law and order will prevail." For the black residents of Newark, it was a time for choosing: "They are either citizens of America or criminals who would shoot down a fire captain in the back and then depend on people to speak in platitudes about police brutality." When asked about such charges, their numbers climbing with each hour of violence, the governor was unsympathetic. Smiling grimly, according to one reporter, he said, "I'm not surprised. It is great fashion and almost standard operating procedure" to make such accusations.[2]

Days later, once the violence ended and he had caught some rest at his family's vacation home down the Jersey shore, the governor struck a much

13. Governor Richard J. Hughes, seen here campaigning in Newark's Central Ward in 1965, was a well-regarded racial liberal and rumored Democratic vice presidential candidate. His initially vindictive response to the black rebellion in this same area two years later took some by surprise. (Monsignor William Noé Field Archives and Special Collections Center, Seton Hall University)

different tone. Back in the state capitol, he called the press to his office to tell them of his desire to "get all the facts and let the chips fall where they may." He announced the formation of "a very blue ribbon" commission to investigate the causes and facts of the rioting. The public would be reassured, he said, by the men he was appointing to serve, who would all be very serious about getting to the bottom of the riots and repairing the social order. He promised they would give "an honest report" on the allegations against law enforcement, but he also wanted them to come up with recommendations for improving the state of police-community relations in New Jersey's cities, their antipoverty and housing programs, and their school systems and economic development plans. He insisted that we "not lose sight of the social order and its deficiencies in this age of affluence for all but a few."[3]

Over the next several days, Hughes named the commissioners who would devise a blueprint for—and provide a model of—social reconciliation. At first glance, the Governor's Commission followed the same sort of limited pluralist logic in its casting as the Kerner Commission. When asked at the press conference announcing the commission if he would name any "militants," Hughes said it was unlikely but, following the logic of the commission form of investigation, militant and "all other shades of opinion" would be heard.[4] Yet within those limitations lay signs of some calculation. In naming his two immediate gubernatorial predecessors (Alfred Driscoll and Robert Meyner), he balanced out the political parties. To those executives, he added several figures from state judiciary circles, including a former state supreme court justice (William Wachenfeld), the president of the New Jersey Bar Association (John J. Gibbons), and, as the commission's executive director, an assistant US attorney (Sanford Jaffe). To chair the commission, Hughes chose a prominent liberal from the private sector, the president of New Jersey Bell Telephone Company (Robert Lilley). Three of the ten commissioners were black: a hard-nosed defense attorney and NAACP official from Jersey City (Raymond A. Brown) would serve as vice chair; the head of the Newark Legal Services Project, who had also served as the governor's community liaison during the riots (Oliver Lofton); and the theologically liberal Methodist bishop for the New Jersey area (Reverend Prince Taylor). Another clergyman, the staunchly anticommunist auxiliary bishop of the Roman Catholic Diocese of Newark (Rev. John J. Dougherty), and a newspaperman, the editor of the *Vineland Times-Journal* (Ben Leuchter), filled out the roster.[5]

Behind the Governor's Commission lay some of the same motivations driving its federal counterpart, especially its disdain for both extremism and apathy and a desire to drive a course between them. Hughes himself laid bare the commission's motivations the day after he announced its formation, in a speech about the "crisis of the cities" at a convention of the International Longshoremen's Association in Miami Beach. (The ILA was a powerful player in New Jersey politics, especially around the state's northern port areas.) He condemned as "a vocal, militant, anti-American minority" the tiny percentage of black Newarkers who had participated in the riots—"the ambushers of firemen, the killers of children, the mass looters"—*and* the local whites who had made the situation worse, "the haters, the advocates of slaughtering innocent Negroes, the drunks bearing meat cleavers and bent on killing." The immediate task, as he frequently said, was the suppression of violence, but a lasting return to order was a longer, more complicated, and more critical task. Hughes, like Lyndon Johnson, conceived the greatest obstacle to that goal not as a lack of funding or know-how but as a dwindling national will. "The real villains in the Newarks, the Watts, the Harlems, in the overall deterioration of our communities," he told the gathered labor leaders, "are greed, indifference and, perhaps, all of us who are content in our complacency to avoid thinking about the situation until it is forcibly brought to our attention by events like those which occurred in my state last week."[6]

The two commissions shared motivations and logic: they both hoped to turn Americans away from anger and violence and to renew their will to approach urban problems in a calm, thoughtful way, and they both modeled that process. But the archive for the Governor's Commission does not allow a detailed view of how those dynamics played out in the commission itself. Composed almost exclusively of hearing transcripts and official exhibits submitted by witnesses, it lacks the detailed meeting minutes and interoffice memoranda of its federal counterpart. If the Kerner archive enables a perspective from the commission looking out at the world of Newark, the Governor's Commission's records enable the opposite view: the world of Newark looking hopefully to the commission as a potential ally in its efforts to address its urban crisis.

This may be more than an archival accident, though, for the one key difference between the two commissions was that many of the central players on the commission—the governor himself, several of the commissioners, and the executive director—had close and abiding ties to Newark. If the commissioners were, on one level, representative of broad political constituencies, on another level they were very interested and involved actors in recent events, rather than remote observers descending on Newark to draw up a report. As Jaffe later put it, this "was not a commission that was operating in the abstract."[7] Unlike President Johnson's commissioners, many were natives or residents of Newark, worked there, and had witnessed the violence firsthand.[8] Though there is no reason to doubt the honesty of their investigation, few of them could be said to be disinterested. They knew Newark, many of them knew each other, and many of them knew the Newarkers who would testify before them. This familiarity bred a certain hopefulness among those witnesses who were given time to present their cases to a commission staffed with acquaintances and, sometimes, friends, and who must have thought they had a better chance of bending that commission to their perspective.

The commission's hearings, then, were a sort of narrative civil war—a riot of storytelling—in which the level of detail far surpassed that which interested the Kerner Commission. They became a site where local actors—city and police officials, black power and antipoverty activists alike—deployed the Newark riot as an immediately usable past in larger political struggles. In the greater profusion of local testimony, we see the Governor's Commission responding to the administrative logic of the commission form in a different manner than its federal equivalent. What nearly broke the Kerner Commission—the profusion of detailed data it gathered and the unavoidable interestedness of its members—gave the Governor's Commission its power. Rather than compiling a massive and perhaps unreadable report, of the kind John Lindsay felt needed rescuing from itself, the state commission produced a streamlined and hard-hitting account of the riots in which it chose sides in the most contentious struggles that had roiled Newark over the previous several years. And whereas the Kerner Commission's report had very ambiguous results—despite the multitude of local reactions, it produced little response from the White House or Congress—the Governor's Commission would move its patron to a more complicated view of his state's urban crisis and would help drive Newark and New Jersey politics (in action and reaction) in the years to come.

In his official proclamation to the commission, delivered on August 8, Governor Hughes quoted his predecessor, Woodrow Wilson, in asking the commission to speak to "the general view, the view which seems more nearly to correspond with the common interest," rather than to, in Hughes's words, "that small group of racists, white and Negro alike, who invoke violence and murder in our streets." And he asked them to pursue the "general causes underlying" disorder. But almost a third of the proclamation was addressed to a more specific theme, one that had slowly imposed itself on the governor's consciousness over the course of the riot, and that had been brewing in Newark with a renewed intensity for the past several years: "the strife," as he put it, that existed between black communities and the police. He wanted to know what part of that strife could be put down to police brutality, as so many black Newarkers had alleged, and how much was due to a general lack of respect for authority, as so many police officers alleged.[9]

It was stories of police misconduct that had moved Hughes from his tough talk to the less confident and more inquisitive stance from which he launched his riot commission. Behind the scenes, beyond the public rhetoric, Hughes was increasingly unsettled by the rising tide of accusations against those forces he had charged with keeping the "jungle" at bay. News-papers began publishing stories about such accusations on Saturday, the day after the state police and National Guard had arrived. Residents had placed dozens of calls to the Newark Human Rights Commission com-plaining of beatings, though none filed a formal complaint. A *New York Times* reporter spoke to a middle-aged black woman standing outside New-ark police headquarters, tears streaming down her cheeks, who explained that her son had been clubbed by two cops for not moving quickly enough off a street corner. She was afraid to file a formal complaint because, she ex-plained, "it would just bring more trouble down on us." A group of black men gathered nearby told the reporter about a young man who, they said, was beaten by Newark police while trying to visit his ailing mother at City Hospital. The NAACP, CORE, and the Urban League all said they had evi-dence of brutality but declined for the time being to discuss specifics, while the director of the city Human Rights Commission declared that, though their numbers might be exaggerated, he had "no doubt" that some of the charges were true.[10]

By Sunday, allegations of official retaliatory violence—beatings, mass in-discriminate shooting, destruction of property—and calls for de-escalation came to Hughes in waves. Attendees of a meeting at the Rutgers Law School pulled together by Dean Willard Heckel implored the governor to consult with people outside law enforcement circles.[11] Hughes received a telegram from the NAACP's Roy Wilkins, who wrote that the governor's support among "solid Negro citizens" was being "eroded rapidly by the shooting up of Negro business places, allegedly by the police and/or National Guards-men." Wilkins protested the "indiscriminate spraying of apartments with bullets" and warned Hughes that his public statements on the rioting had been inflammatory.[12] Wilkins wasn't the only national civil rights figure who had some words for Hughes that day. At a meeting with several com-munity leaders (including Tim Still and George Richardson) at Oliver Lof-ton's apartment, Martin Luther King called to check on Lofton and his fam-ily. When King heard that Hughes was nearby, he asked to speak to him. He told Lofton that he wanted to "give him some religion."[13]

In a press conference late Sunday afternoon, Hughes said that he found reports that his forces had vandalized black-owned businesses disturbing but as of yet only "hearsay." If anyone could provide "facts, figures, time and place," he promised to investigate.[14] Soon after, a group of forty peo-ple converged on the Roseville Armory, where the governor had set up his command post, with photos of black businesses they claimed had been shot and smashed up by state law enforcement. They carried with them slugs from .38-caliber bullets that they had found inside the stores and a telegram they had sent to the president citing the "wanton destruction of property" and "actual murders" committed by New Jersey guardsmen and police officers. But they ultimately blamed Hughes's "inflammatory statements" for fueling the violence and demanded that the federal government step in to remedy a situation threatening to spin out of control.[15]

By late Sunday night, Hughes was nearly convinced but asked his aides to track down two other community activists. Around eleven o'clock, they reached Bob Curvin and Tom Hayden by phone. Armed state troopers picked them up and drove them downtown to the Federal Building, maneuvering around the outskirts of the city to avoid the riot area. As they made their way into the building, troopers scanned the rooftops with their gun sites. Hughes listened as Curvin and Hayden detailed eyewitness testimony they had gathered of police and guard brutality. Their shared conclusion was that the continuing violence was the result of the occupation of Newark by state forces and that the community had been so brutalized that they had little to lose in fighting back. Rather than suppressing the violence, law enforcement had escalated it. Hughes seemed to listen intently, but it was not immediately clear whether he had received the message.[16]

The next day, the city made a decided turn toward normalcy. At midday, despite some sporadic reports of sniper activity, Hughes declared the riot over and ordered the withdrawal of state forces. In a notable but limited about-face, he announced that the National Guard and state police were investigating allegations of misconduct. And though the rioting had certainly been criminal, "we are not unmindful of the pressing need to turn our attention now to the serious social problems in Newark that antedate the present disturbances and that remain to be solved after them," he said. Then Hughes slipped away to his home down the Jersey shore, where, presumably, he made plans to appoint an investigative commission.[17]

The question of brutality and other forms of misconduct by law enforcement had become unavoidable, mostly because those closest to the violence—those without the luxury to view it from the safety of a police escort, let alone from a National Guard armory—were determined not to let their potential allies in state government ignore it. They had shaken Governor Hughes's assumptions about the antiriot forces he commanded and pushed him toward a deeper, more complicated approach to the violence. And when his commission opened its first day of hearings, it adopted Hughes's new, two-pronged emphasis on the underlying social causes of rioting and the urgent allegations of official violence. The commission's hearings opened on Wednesday, August 16, in the board of directors' room in the Bell Telephone building on Broad Street in Newark, and the first two witnesses were Paul Ylvisaker of the state Department of Community Affairs (DCA) and Colonel David Kelly of the New Jersey State Police, the poverty warrior and the keeper of law and order.

Ylvisaker provided a précis of the DCA, which had been established the year before in anticipation of President Johnson's Model Cities Program. Its philosophical roots lay in Governor Hughes's vision of a vigorous state government, one which would promote progress and growth, not through stifling regulation, but through close ties between Trenton and local communities. Hughes called this "Northern Democratic liberalism."[18] Its main charge, which staff handled delicately because of the fear of encroaching on other's jurisdictional territory, Ylvisaker explained, was to coordinate the approximately 440 federal grant programs available to states and to make sure New Jersey municipalities were prepared to take advantage of them. Its aim was to mediate, in other words, between Washington and cities like Newark, to shuttle between the two, as Ylvisaker himself often did.[19]

But the department also had a loose charge to keep an eye on local race relations throughout the state. That was why, Ylvisaker thought, DCA forces had been called up to Newark when the rioting broke out. "We were a convenient light brigade for the Governor," he told the commission, and they arrived "about the second day, I should think, it was about Saturday, sometime on Saturday." When one commissioner informed him of the exact time of their arrival (6:00 Saturday morning), Ylvisaker admitted that his memory of the riot was poor: "I literally can't recall the chronology of what happened from moment to moment. I have impressions, but I don't have facts." Since then, he'd appeared before the Kerner Commission and not yet resolved the tension between the uncertainties and instabilities of a microscopic view of things and the clearer picture obtained from a telescopic view, as he had put it. If he had been tasked to keep an eye on race relations in Newark, his eyes seemed to go unfocused the closer he got to the situation on the ground. Such close examination required "an entirely different kind of skill," he said. "We are going to have to go outside just about any of our experience to deal with what we have seen now in New Jersey this summer." He recommended spending a lot of time walking and talking with local residents, because they had a lot to say and because, he said, "I don't know of a single guy in this business who really knows the answers right now." The administrators and commissioners tasked with understanding and remedying the state's urban crisis, in other words, would have to push their thinking out past its current frontier, and the way to do that was to listen to local stories.[20]

Colonel Kelly had a clearer sense of his department's actions in Newark, even if he was unwilling to describe them in much detail. Kelly would appear before the commission five times, and his first day's testimony focused mostly on the preparedness of the state police (relative to the Newark Police Department especially) and on establishing a basic time line for their deployment to Newark. But over the course of Kelly's many appearances, the commissioners' questioning—typically led by Jaffe—took an increasingly critical tone. It began with one day's skeptical queries about the state police riot-training regimen and its efforts to recruit black officers and proceeded to a line of questioning that revealed that the state police had never successfully established an effective communication network with the local police department.[21] Kelly's fourth day of testimony (and the last day he was questioned about Newark, before moving on to his experiences in two other New Jersey cities) quickly turned to the question of violence, the alleged presence of black snipers, and how his forces had responded to them. Kelly had already testified that they had been ordered to fire only if fired upon, but now the commission wanted to know what *type* of fire had been returned.[22]

Much hinged on these questions. If snipers existed and had fired on law enforcement, then it was within their orders to fire back. But Kelly, under repeated questioning, seemed reluctant to provide much detail about the extent and deadliness of that retaliatory fire. He explained that the basic tactic was for police riflemen to fire into the high-rise buildings and for officers with shotguns to sweep the buildings, looking for the snipers. And when Jaffe asked whether the return fire was mass or individual, Kelly responded with a detailed description of the building searches instead, admitting that they had yielded shell casings, but no snipers. When Jaffe asked again what the riflemen down on the street were doing, Kelly said that, after the "excitement" of the first day, his forces gained confidence, felt they could better handle such confrontations, and brought their firing under control. "There was not this type of mass retaliatory fire," he claimed. "It may have been one or two conditions but I doubt very much that this even happened. It was controlled, supervised, and directed." And when asked for his assessment of the relative danger of directing ground fire up at Newark's high-rise apartment buildings, Kelly suggested the commissioners think about what might have happened if they had not returned fire, if the snipers had been free to wreak their deadly havoc. "This was the mission: to stop the fire," Kelly said. "How do you stop the fire? By returning the fire. Of course, it is entirely possible that innocent people may have gotten hurt. It is entirely possible." Later, arguing that this strategy had been effective in suppressing the snipers, he concluded that "terror should be met with sufficient force to deter the terror, and this may be the horrible true facts of life."[23]

When it came to allegations that law enforcement had shot at and otherwise vandalized black-owned businesses, Colonel Kelly was no more forthcoming with details, though he told the commission that no evidence of misconduct had yet turned up.[24] But witnesses and complainants were not so reticent, especially as the commission reached out directly to them. For one thing, Jaffe, the commission's executive director, hired four investigators to explore allegations of misconduct. Drawing on his experience as a prosecutor and on Raymond Brown's extensive network of relations in northern New Jersey's black communities, Jaffe found people who could easily move through Newark, get people talking, identify potential witnesses, and encourage them to appear before the commission.[25] For another, the commission took advantage of the fact that one of its members, Oliver Lofton, was also the executive director of the Newark Legal Services Project, a delegate agency of the UCC. During the riots, the NLSP emerged as a clearinghouse for a variety of complaints against law enforcement, other repositories—the city Human Rights Commission, county prosecutor, or the police department itself, for example—having been abandoned out of some combination of frustration and fear. In the commission's investigators and the NLSP, the community found alternative outlets for their complaints, and several community members followed them back to the commission to testify.

On two separate days, the commission heard from twelve individual business owners whose complaints were part of the growing collection of evidence gathered by the NLSP. Some of these individuals, such as Bertha Dixon, who owned a small restaurant on South Orange Avenue that was shot up several times, had been referred to the NLSP by community workers (in Dixon's case, from the Urban League). Others, such as Bow Woo Wong, whose laundry had been shot up as he watched television in the back room, had been visited by legal services staffers unbidden but not unwelcome.[26] In one case, investigators had spied a piece of plywood covering a smashed window at a dry-cleaning shop on Avon Avenue. Someone had scrawled the numbers of three police patrol cars on it, with a message that these units had shot through their front windows. When they inquired inside, they learned that Enez King's husband had written "soul" on their window, to mark their business as minority owned. (King, like

14. Earl Harris, a UCC trustee from the South Ward who was active on Area Board 3 and ran for city council in both 1966 and 1970, submitted a photo of his restaurant, which advertised its barbecue with "soul sauce." Harris claimed state and Newark police had shot up his windows. (New Jersey State Archives)

Wong, was not black, but an Apache who had moved to Newark from up-state New York when a thruway cut through her reservation). The Kings lived in an apartment above their shop, and when they heard shots early Sunday morning, they crawled to the back bedroom, where their two-year-old daughter slept. When they made it up to the third-floor rental unit, tenants watching through the windows told the couple they had seen state troopers doing it. When Enez looked out the window herself, she saw them firing into her business and into Mr. Wonderful's Lounge across the street. Around the corner, on the side of their building, she saw three police cars and took note of their numbers (530, 535, and 491). The "soul" scrawled on their window might have saved their business from the first wave of ri-oters, but not the second.[27] Almost all the witnesses testifying to vandalism by the state police and guardsmen noted that their businesses had some sort of "soul" message displayed on them. None of them doubted who was responsible.

The hundreds of pages of testimony pertaining to physical injury and loss of life at the hands of law enforcement was even more harrowing. It ranged from Jennie Carter's account of Newark police officers beating by-standers (not looters) at the corner of Springfield Avenue and Tenth Street on Thursday afternoon, to William Fields's account of seeing his cousin struck down by a hail of bullets coming down Beacon Street from Spring-field Avenue as they worked on his car. Fields said he saw the police of-ficers who fired the shots and knew they were state troopers because of the stripes on their pants.[28] Ruby Evans testified that, after she and her son were harassed and beaten by police officers (local police, not state troop-ers), she went "right on down" to the Newark Legal Services Project.[29]

By Sunday, the fifth day of violence, more and more people were doing the same. Dickinson Debevoise, Newark Legal Services founder and board president, described the scene at their offices as "chaos." They were packed with people telling stories. "Everything was just pouring into this spot," Debevoise said. As people came in, NLSP staff wrote down their stories, typed them up, checked them with the complainant, edited if necessary, arranged for them to be sworn before an attorney or notary public, then collected release signatures. When Debevoise appeared before the com-mission in early October, he brought copies of the 274 affidavits they had collected to date. He broke them down into four broad categories. There were 29 complaints involving personal indignities (14 against the Newark police, 9 against state police, 4 against the National Guard, and 2 against both state agencies), ranging from insults to death threats; 57 complaints of physical violence (37 against the Newark Police Department, 4 against state police, 1 against the Guard, 11 against some combination of agencies, and 4 unspecified), including stompings, beatings, and intentional shootings; 104 complaints of indiscriminate shooting (25 against the NPD, 35 against state troopers, 11 against the Guard, 19 against some combination, and 14 unspecified), some of which described the same incidents, including the spraying of apartment buildings, firing down streets, and shooting at or around people; and 94 allegations of the deliberate destruction of property (4 against the NPD, 41 against the state police, 8 against the Guard, 13 against some combination, and 28 unspecified).[30]

Debevoise made it clear that he recognized the political explosiveness of the complaints, but he was determined to assemble the data and make it available, while other authorities and institutions stalled. Compared to the speed and efficiency with which law enforcement moved against "the people in the ghetto," he said, they were "moving at a snail's pace, if at all," with regard to the allegations of misconduct. To Debevoise, this was "just as much a violation of the law as burning and looting and the other forms of disorder which took place." He hoped that, armed with the evidence the NLSP had provided, the commission, "which [did] not have the compelling political problems that people in day to day political life have," might break through that existing inertial politics. "And really," he concluded, "this group is one of our main hopes because if this group cannot tackle this problem and the President's Commission cannot tackle it, I really don't know who can."[31]

For all his difficulties and tense encounters with the Kerner Commission, Mayor Addonizio had not given up on the commission form altogether. When he testified before the Governor's Commission, a month after he appeared before its federal counterpart, he opened with a statement containing much the same material he had used in the wake of John Lindsay's tense visit to Newark. He again decried the lack of interest in urban issues that he believed plagued American society and argued that, though none was likely forthcoming, a massive "Marshall Plan for the cities" was the only hope they had. Donald Malafronte, the mayor's chief aid, spoke about various federally funded programs—urban renewal, manpower training, a maternity and infant health care project, and tuberculosis and venereal disease programs, for example—that had been helpful. Even some UCC programs, he said, had proved valuable. But Addonizio insisted they had obviously failed to reach a core group of the city's disadvantaged. If they had succeeded, there would not have been a riot.[32]

But failed service programs didn't tell the whole story, in city officials' minds. Of greater significance in the lead-up to the riot, in their estimation, was an apparent conspiracy among their various political opponents in the city, enabled in part by the new flows of federal money through the Community Action Program, a story Addonizio had told briefly to the Kerner Commission but upon which he and his staff now greatly expanded. He picked up the theme when asked about preriot planning. He admitted that he might have been "a little bit overconfident" about Newark's prospects for peace. "But I think that we can certainly establish the fact that there were many outside influences and individuals within our community ten weeks prior to the riot. They made appearances at various public meetings and expressed themselves rather vehemently and certainly we feel that these people contributed to the overall situation."[33]

At times, the connections between these agitators and the riots were nebulous. The head of the city's Human Rights Commission spoke about "the angry feelings permeating the community this year," as evidenced by the medical school hearings and the picketing of the Clinton Hill Meat Market in April, for example, incidents that, taken collectively, made the rally at the Fourth Precinct on Thursday night "ill-advised." At other times, city officials drew more direct connections, as when Mayor Addonizio said that he believed the medical school hearings had been "used by certain political dissidents and others from the outside to try to create the climate for a riot." They seemed to revel in naming names, as when Malafronte readily identified several antipoverty workers in CBS News film footage of the Thursday-night rally at the Fourth Precinct. (Lofton, however, corrected him on one count: an individual Malafronte identified as a UCC worker was actually a member of the city's Human Rights Commission.) Addonizio explained that he had supported the creation of the UCC and had tried repeatedly to engage it for the good of the city. But now, he said, the policy seemed to be to hire people opposed to his administration. And his administration, "having fostered this thing initially, certainly with good will and good intentions, now finds itself in a position where people are being paid through federal funds to fight" it.[34]

Keeping an eye on these local agents of dissent was Newark's Police Intelligence Unit, which had for years been investigating threats to the city's peace and order. Police Director Dominick Spina explained to the commission that the unit consisted of seven men, some who worked undercover and others who worked with community informers. They were nonpartisan: they watched organizations regardless of what place on the political spectrum they occupied, from the Ku Klux Klan on the right to the local

SDS project on the left.[35] But Spina harbored a special resentment toward the latter group, which, he claimed, had led the first-ever protest at a Newark precinct house in the summer of 1964. Though they did not subscribe to any rigid ideology, Spina explained, the Newark Community Union Project often borrowed Marxist tactics such as the doctrine (presented, he claimed, in *Das Kapital*) "that in order for the working people to take over . . . they first must subvert the police officers, they must create an aura of hostility between the police and the public, to the degree that the police can no longer function properly, and when that happens they take over."[36]

NCUP, though, had saved some of its most dastardly tactics for its planned takeover of the UCC. According to Spina, Tom Hayden and crew had quickly recognized the potential power of the local antipoverty agency. They attended trustees meetings and caused such commotion and dragged the meetings so far into the early-morning hours that regular working people would get disgusted and leave. In their absence, NCUP militants would pass whatever motions they desired. "Incidentally," Spina added, "this is a typical Communist tactic that is applied. And mind you, I'm not saying they're Communists. They're not." But, according to Spina, the tactic had given them control of Area Board 3 in Clinton Hill and Area Board 2 in the Central Ward as well as "immense influence" in Area Boards 5 and 7 and on the UCC board of trustees itself.[37] Ever since, "the UCC has had an extremely violent and disruptive kind of history here in the city." Local militants had used the antipoverty program to gain power, to raise funds, and to turn its equipment—like public address systems and mimeograph machines—to their own purposes. The most damning evidence of this was a leaflet, created and distributed by antipoverty workers from Area Board 2, that called people back to the Fourth Precinct for a protest against police brutality on the night of July 13, the night after residents had seen police officers drag a man into the precinct.[38]

The NCUP-infiltrated UCC was perhaps the most powerful and dangerous organization in Newark, according to Spina, but it was hardly the only one tracked by his intelligence officers. They also followed Robert Curvin and CORE, which had led protests at the Barringer High School construction site, had picketed White Castle restaurants up and down the East Coast for not hiring enough black workers, and had been a leading force behind the antibrutality demonstrations in the summer of 1965. He explained that Curvin had been at the Fourth Precinct the night of July 12 and was given a police bullhorn with which he was supposed to disperse the crowd. Spina claimed he didn't even try, and, what's more, he said, "we never got the bullhorn back."[39] Intelligence officers had tracked the movements of

Phil Hutchings, who had brought the Student Nonviolent Coordinating Committee to Newark, and they attended a meeting at the Black Liberation Center on South Orange Avenue four months before the riot, a meeting at which all these dissident forces had come together to organize against the relocation of the state medical school to Newark. When Raymond Brown asked him what contribution all these people had made to the violence in July, Spina answered succinctly: "They set the climate."[40]

In Spina's mind, then, the Newark Police Department, faced with such an array of dissent—irresponsible at best, incendiary at worst—deserved more credit than it had received for its efforts to head off mass violence. Dissidents had agitated enough of the community to produce a riot, but the department had also made substantial efforts to build relationships with that community. Its efforts had not been limited to surveillance and crime prevention. Under his leadership, Spina explained, the department had made unprecedented strides in connecting with black Newark. For one thing, they had come a long way in integrating the force. For another, they had established a Police Community Relations Bureau consisting of one lieutenant in each precinct whose sole duty was to act as a liaison to the community. They had reached out to neighborhood kids via summer recreation programs run by the Police Athletic League, a Junior Crimefighters club in which children met with officers to discuss character building, and a Boy Scout Explorer program. They had launched a citizen-observer project in which civil rights leaders inspected precinct houses with complete freedom and rode in patrol cars. Each precinct captain met once a month with the local Precinct Council, made up of area residents, civic leaders, and businesspeople. And, finally, Spina himself had established regular Wednesday-evening open-door office hours. They began at 7:30, and he stayed as late as necessary to hear any suggestions and complaints from the citizens he served.[41]

When Jaffe asked Spina what he might have done differently if given the chance, the police director responded that he would have done everything in his power to prevent Area Board 2 from printing the leaflets calling for a rally at the Fourth Precinct on Thursday night. "I fully believe if those damned circulars had not been distributed that the riot would not have happened that day," he said. "It might have happened some other day, but it would not have happened this day."[42]

The commission held hearings through December, and though there was one session each in January and February, the writing of the final report began before that. Most of it was done by Sanford Jaffe and his deputy director, Robert Goldmann, who came to the commission for a few months after working in New Haven with the Ford Foundation's Gray Areas program. Once they had a complete draft, the commission paid an obituary writer from the *New York Times* a couple of thousand dollars to edit the whole thing and check all the footnotes (of which there are about 850). They hired a freelance photographer and pulled some images from news archives, hoping to illustrate the report with a clear picture of what the ghetto community looked like for readers who didn't already know. The commissioners themselves received drafts and offered suggestions for revision. In the end, after discussion of some of the findings and recommendations, they unanimously accepted the document, which was titled *Report for Action*.[43]

The governor's office, unsure of some of the recommendations, was itself reluctant to print the report, so Robert Lilley arranged to have New Jersey Bell's mimeograph machines work overtime to churn out two hundred copies at minimal cost. State troopers transported several to the mayors of each riot city, as well as the state legislators representing them. On Saturday, February 10, workers at New Jersey Bell in downtown Newark loaded copies onto trucks, which were then driven around the corner to the Robert Treat Hotel, where Jaffe and Lilley had organized a press conference late enough that the story would miss the evening newspaper editions but early enough to make the popular Sunday morning papers. Readers could spend their day considering the news and what they might do about it.[44]

Reporters came from all over the world to cover the release. Lilley told them that the commission could not claim to have produced definitive answers to all the cities' problems. It couldn't even claim it knew what all the problems were. But he insisted that they had used their time concentrating on the issues that seemed to be of most immediate concern in the communities they studied. *Report for Action* prioritized those that needed immediate attention. The basic thrust of their recommendations, Lilley said, was that "the authorities must lean over backwards to involve the community in what they do." He declined to predict, when asked, whether more violence was inevitable in Newark, but he was willing to say that racial tensions remained strained and that "little has been done by the Newark administration to remove the cause of tension." Despite its sharp findings and recommendations, he did not think the report was "vindictive." Nonetheless, he concluded, "I expect there'll be some resistance. I don't expect a sweetness-and-light reception."[45]

Indeed, the report's assessment of the Addonizio administration was unsparing. After three sentences describing the interracial electoral coalition that had put the mayor in office, it notes that widespread disillusionment quickly set in among black Newarkers, even when Addonizio appointed more of them to city positions than any previous mayor. While the integration of city hall was important to many black Newarkers, the report explained, of far greater significance was how it responded to their needs. On that issue, the administration came up seriously short. Over the next several years, the report continued, the drive for black civil rights came to Newark in the form of CORE and NCUP, which led demonstrations against police brutality, employment discrimination, and decrepit housing. Then came the rising opposition to the medical school relocation, and by the time the summer of 1967 arrived, "Newark's mood was ugly." But "in spite of all the build-up and tension," it continued, "there is no evidence that the Administration made any preparations for a riot."[46] The commission ultimately found that city hall had not fully realized the bitterness growing in the black community and that that reflected "a serious lack of communication between established authority" and the community, a lack that was "one of the prime ills of Newark."[47]

The United Community Corporation, by contrast, "enjoys the support of a substantial segment of the Negro community," the commission found. Though the antipoverty program had generated controversy and tension and was far from a model of administrative efficiency, that only meant it needed strengthening, not dismantling. And the city administration's unresponsiveness or ineptitude in responding to important issues made calls for its increased involvement in the antipoverty program intolerable. The commission recommended against it. That would shake the community's confidence in the UCC, and that would mean that "the poor will be left without an institution that now is available to them and that many of them consider their own. It would also leave them with no effective link to the democratic process."[48]

Problems of the community's relationship to local municipal institutions were most evident, the commission decided, in the area of law enforcement. "Relations between the police and the nonwhite community may well be the single most decisive factor for peace or strife in our cities," it concluded. The report noted the police department's various efforts to improve that relationship but said that the programs "appear to suffer from the low priority they have in the department's activities" and thus seemed to be "token gestures rather than meaningful attempts to improve the relationships between the police and the people they serve." Whatever the sincerity of such efforts, they were far outweighed by the shortcomings they were purportedly created to address. The department's severe image problem hampered its recruitment efforts in the black community, Director Spina made too many assignment decisions based on politics rather than merit, and the few black officers on the force often faced discriminatory assignments. And each of these problems, completing the vicious circle, damaged the image of the department in the black community. The result "was virtually a complete breakdown in the relations between the police and the Negro community prior to the disorders." As a result, charges of police brutality lacked an effective avenue of communication, let alone redress. They festered, then exploded.[49]

Of the commission's thirteen official findings from its investigation of Newark, ten pertained to law enforcement. (Two others found that city government had been ill prepared and slow in its response to the violence, and another found that those who passed out leaflets calling people back to the Fourth Precinct on Thursday "showed poor judgment.") In addition to its community relations problems and its inadequate training, planning, and methods for dealing with riots, the commission faulted police for the "heavy return fire" they deployed, which, they said, made it impossible to determine the extent of sniper activity. It cited evidence of "prejudice against Negroes" among police and the National Guard, which "resulted in the use of excessive and unjustified force and other abuses against Negro citizens," including the destruction of black-owned businesses. And it found, finally, that the evidence presented did "not support the thesis of a conspiracy or plan to initiate" the riot.[50]

The commission split its recommendations for law enforcement into two categories: personnel policies and community relations. The first pertained mostly to recruitment practices and the second to opening the police department's work to the community. This included the increased use of foot patrols, mandatory nametags for officers, and improved community relations training. But most potentially volatile was the commission's intervention in the recurring debate over a civilian oversight board. It recommended that the mayor name a "five-man Board of Police Commissioners, made up of outstanding citizens representing the total Newark community . . . to receive and review all citizen complaints of police misconduct."[51]

Like its federal counterpart, the Governor's Commission addressed the bulk of its report to white America, whose willingness to address the stubborn ills that plagued society, for all its wealth and know-how, seemed to have flagged. No one, the commission scolded, could plead ignorance of the inequalities that fueled urban rioting. There was no need to quibble: these problems had been exhaustively detailed. "The shelves of government offices and academic institutions are filled with studies that shed light on them and offer avenues for solutions," the introduction reads. "The question is whether we have the will to act." The city needed "fewer promises and more action" from political leaders, police officials, employers and union heads, teachers and social workers. But, the report continued, such change was "possible only when the people in our more fortunate communities understand that what is required of them is not an act of generosity toward the people in the ghettos, but a decision of direct and deep self-interest." In the commission's moral economy, an investment in the problems of the city would generate a social profit for the suburbs. It was time for those suburbs—those spreading settlements that were so central to notions of "urban crisis"—to make a commitment to the inner cities they strangled. It was a direct appeal to white citizens, and it asked little of black Newarkers. In fact, the central issue of black equality, the introduction said, might have landed on their doorsteps sooner "had not the Negro been patient and forbearing." The choice, therefore, belonged to white New Jersey, not black Newark.[52]

Like the Kerner Commission, too, the Governor's Commission faced the difficulty of corralling the mass of evidence it had compiled into one comprehensible report. But whereas the presidential commission had relied mainly on a massive social-science research effort—in which staff compiled detailed city profiles and consulted with hundreds of expert advisors—the state commission made much more use of the personal testimony it had gathered. Its problems in compiling findings and recommendations were not rooted, therefore, in the quantity of data before it, but in that testimony's chief quality: its conflicted nature and its indifference to absolute truth. Rather than cover up such problems—say, in an urgent and confident summary section—the commission made them a central element of its report and findings. In the end, given its reliance on personal testimony, the commission conveyed a keen appreciation of how stories— not despite, but *because of* their conflicts—moved history.

Personal testimony was quoted profusely throughout *Report for Action*. The commission had spent extravagant amounts of time hearing testimony about the exact order of events during the riot, but its members were not always able to corral it all into a coherent narrative. Rather than distilling one essential truth out of it, the commission sometimes printed conflicting versions side by side. This, remarkably, was the case with what was regarded as the "trigger incident": the arrest and beating of black cabdriver John Smith and his arrival at the Fourth Precinct. When, on separate days, Smith and the arresting officers appeared before the commission, the members decided not to ask them any questions but to let each make an uninterrupted statement. The conflicts in the resulting testimony, the report stated, were "glaring and they were not resolved by the Commission." Instead, it provided summaries of the officers' testimony followed by a summary of Smith's version of events. And those versions were relayed as products of those individuals—"according to Smith," "Patrolman Pontrelli testified," "according to the Police Department arrest sheet," for example—not as a final version of events provided by the commission. The inadequacy of absolute truth to account for what happened next was demonstrated by the power of a rumor that Smith had been beaten to death, a story that circulated quickly and drew more and more people to the precinct.[53]

Similarly, on several other key issues the commission made it clear that it was acting—and that its readers should act—on information that represented not uncontested truth, but the distillation of an unruly body of evidence, including beliefs so widely shared that they had become social forces. When it came to the question of whether or not a conspiracy existed to set Newark aflame, the commission once again presented excerpts of witnesses' often contradictory testimony (in the case of Police Director Spina, he seemed to contradict himself) before concluding that it simply had received no clear evidence that such a conspiracy existed, though "other authorities, armed with stronger powers . . . may have more to say on the subject."[54] The commission refused to rule out the existence of snipers, though it noted that the extensive shooting by law enforcement made it difficult to determine the extent of their activity. And in a section that would have serious repercussions in the years that followed, the commission concluded, based on the testimony it received, the interviews it conducted, and the news articles it surveyed, not that city government (including the police department) was rife with corruption, but rather that "the belief that Newark is a corrupt city is pervasive." And that belief, true or not—and it really didn't matter for the commission's purposes, though it soon would to a grand jury—had helped strain relations between municipal institutions and the black community and bring the city to its five days of tragic violence.[55]

Initially, Mayor Addonizio appeared to be an embodiment of the commission's ideal reader: a white New Jerseyan willing to reconsider his thinking and to welcome scrutiny of his actions. At first glance, he explained in a statement, the report seemed "to represent a lot of honest, hard work, with some of it off the mark but most of it reasonable and accurate, considering the confusion and complexity of the issues." He warned its readers not to make Newark a scapegoat for issues that were national in scope and required a deep commitment from a broad swath of Americans. But he also wanted them to know that, if they felt that a dank fog of corruption engulfed his city, his administration would welcome a grand jury investigation to clear the air.[56] A couple of days later, aides reported that Addonizio supported several of the commission's most dramatic proposals, including the consolidation of police administration at the county level and a state takeover of the public schools and municipal courts. He was also reportedly reconsidering his rejection of a civilian review board and his plan to dissolve the United Community Corporation, which the commission had recommended remain independent.[57]

But three days after the report's release, Addonizio made it clear that there were limits to how far he might revise his thinking. As always, he was caught between constituencies, waffling between, on the one hand, a moderate support for civil rights, social service, and the communities that demanded them, and, on the other, the growing movement of police and their community supporters. While he still believed the commission's report to be "heart-felt and honest," he also thought that its authors had "misplaced some of their common sense" by condemning the forces of law and order while failing to censure the rioters themselves. He wished that the commission "would have taken a very strong stand against racism, black as well as white, and that it would have said again and again that riots cannot be permitted in American life." The danger was that in targeting everyone but the rioters—the city administration, local and state law enforcement, larger political, economic, and social structures—the report could be "interpreted as a mandate to riot by those impatient with democracy and our political process." Rioting could not be permitted, he repeated, but instead of emphasizing that, the commission gave police "a going-over," when, Addonizio said, "I am sure, each and every man on the force would have preferred to be safe at home rather than on the streets of Newark exchanging gunfire with rioters."[58]

Governor Hughes proved a better embodiment of that ideal reader. He received his copy of *Report for Action* the day before its public release and, though he hadn't had time to study it thoroughly, called a press conference. He declared it "a historic document" and "a moral imperative for" New Jersey.[59] Four days after the release, he convened a special meeting of his cabinet to solicit ideas on how to implement its recommendations. He wrote thank you notes to the commissioners praising the "high quality" of their work and later had them to dinner at the governor's mansion in Princeton.[60]

Less than two months later, Martin Luther King was assassinated, and Governor Hughes issued a statement mourning his death. With King's murder, he said, "the United States has lost one of its finest citizens—a man of God, a peacemaker." But he was determined that King's death would not be in vain. He urged all New Jerseyans to rid their state and nation of racism and make them places of true freedom and equality. "Let us put away the guns and violence and come together to develop and carry out a program that will make New Jersey the state it must become, and America the 'one nation, under God, indivisible, with liberty and justice for all' that it has always intended to be." As cities across America exploded with renewed violence in the wake of the assassination, Hughes announced that he would soon deliver a special message on the cities to the state legislature.[61]

King's funeral was scheduled for Tuesday, April 9, in Atlanta. Hughes decided to stay close to home and asked the UCC's Timothy Still to attend the ceremony as his official representative.[62] He wrote all Sunday night, until four o'clock Monday morning, composing his message to the legislature. When he delivered it later that day in Trenton, he denounced King's assassin ("a deranged mind") but suggested that, while this Easter week was one of death, it might also be one of resurrection. King's death might ignite a mass change of heart in America. "I think this must be the true answer," he declared, "that our real problem is indifference, a human wish not to be involved, a turning away from these problems as though they are not 'our business.'" Each person had to make it his business, had to root from his heart the indifference that had hardened it, because "the moral crisis facing us . . . certainly cannot be solved by violence or extremism."[63]

The next day, as King was laid to rest, bells rang out from Trenton's churches and synagogues marking a period of mourning. Hughes called for a moment of silence that afternoon. Many schools canceled classes.[64] For several months, violent confrontations between black and white students at Trenton Central High School had sporadically spilled out into the city. In the days immediately following King's assassination, a few scuffles broke out in the hallways, and the students who streamed into the downtown area afterward engaged in some window smashing and looting.[65] But as night fell on the day of the funeral, black youths took to city streets in greater numbers, breaking windows, looting some stores and setting others on fire. Some scrapped with local police officers, who chased small gangs of them up and down city blocks, sometimes running in circles. One group managed to invade the central police station on Chancery Street before being warned that they would be removed by any means necessary. Over one hundred people were jailed. One local newspaperman reported that crowds shouted, "Black Power!" and "Whitey, Get Out!" and "Dr. King is dead and so is nonviolence!" Streets in and out of the downtown riot area were sealed off, and the bridges across the Delaware River were patrolled by police from Morrisville, Pennsylvania, one of whom explained, "We don't want Trenton over here." The mayor set a curfew and ordered all bars and liquor stores to close and all gas stations to put gas only in cars, not in hand-held containers. From his office window in Trenton city hall, he watched the looting on State Street. Down the road, the state house's golden dome was engulfed in a heavy white smoke. Order was restored only when about 80 shotgun-wielding state troopers joined the 273-member Trenton Police Department.[66]

On Thursday, Governor Hughes visited Mrs. Mary Killingsworth in the living room of her semidetached home on Carroll Street. Her son, Harlan Joseph, had been killed on Tuesday night. A Trenton policeman, in trying to disperse a band of looters just across State Street from city hall, had fired one warning shot in the air, or maybe two, as one newspaper story reported. He claimed that as he attempted a second (or third) shot, aimed at a fleeing looter's legs, the crowd jostled his arm, and he saw a young man drop. Early reports of the shooting said that the bullet had struck the looter in the back of the head, others said in the small of his back, and the official police report said in the upper back, near his left shoulder blade, puncturing his aorta. The report also stated that various pieces of clothing from a nearby haberdashery—a gold-colored sports coat, a shirt, and a pair of trousers—had been found scattered around the looter's body. The establishment in question, the Charm-Aronson clothing and jewelry store, had indeed been looted. But friends and witnesses claimed that Harlan, rather than participating in the looting, was there trying to stop it. He was a sophomore religion major at Lincoln University. He worked at the Mercer Street Friends Center, a local social-service organization. The mayor called him "a fine young guy" and said that Joseph had been a member of his youth council. A coworker said that Joseph had planned on attending a meeting of the council that very evening to discuss ways to end the violence.[67]

Hughes asked Mrs. Killingsworth if there was anything he could do for her, and she answered that she just wanted her son's name cleared before she buried him. She told the governor that she did not believe Harlan had been involved in any looting and that several of his friends who were with him that night had assured her that he had not been. She pulled out a news clipping from the *Trenton Evening Times* about her son, in which he was quoted as saying that the Trenton Youth Council "established a means of communication which is so hard to establish in the streets of Trenton." Hughes seemed dumbfounded: "I don't know what to say, Mrs. Killingsworth. This is a tragedy. Violence is a tragedy. Innocent people get killed."[68]

Later that afternoon, the governor visited the Five Points neighborhood, where much of the violence had occurred. Unlike his patrols through Newark the previous summer, he went on foot. But not everyone was impressed. Hughes stopped at Dinky's Shoe Shine Shoppe on Warren Street, where someone yelled in at him through the doorway: "You'll have to do better than get your shoes shined down here." He walked down the street to the Famous Steak House and bought a chocolate ice cream cone.[69]

Trenton's curfew remained in place for at least another week, but the violence never again reached the level it had the night Harlan Joseph was killed. The guardsmen on alert at a nearby suburban base were gradually released from duty. At a meeting with New Jersey mayors a week after the violence in Trenton, Hughes was asked whether he favored a hard or soft line on rioting. He said that he rejected Chicago mayor Richard Daley's tactic of ordering police to shoot to cripple looters and to kill arsonists. He pointed out that a nine-year-old kid with a box of crackers could be a looter. In "the fever of a riot," he warned, "a lot of innocent people can get killed, including police." He favored, instead, an "intelligent, restrained response of arrest and detention" in order to preserve "the sanctity of life."[70]

Hughes soon delivered another special message to the Republican-controlled state legislature detailing his plan of attack on the problems of New Jersey's cities. He asked for $126 million and proposed new tax increases to pay for his proposals, many of which hewed closely to the recommendations of his riot commission. He called it "a program not for the suppression of riots but for the elimination of their cause—not a plan for disaster but a blueprint for progress." The details were impressive and broadly targeted. They included state funding for the recruitment of police cadets from ghetto areas, a network of county-level bureaus to handle complaints against local police departments, an "Affirmative Action Unit" in the state Civil Rights Division that would proactively root out discrimination rather than wait for complaints to come in, a five-year state takeover of the Newark public schools, and new state funding for housing programs, manpower training, early childhood education, school lunches, college scholarships, welfare-to-work programs, and day care. "We have reached the day of reckoning," Hughes told the legislators. "I tell you very seriously and respectfully that we must act in the two months before us or this state over the next six years will sink into stagnation and despair that will take a quarter century to overcome."[71]

A year later, with only six months left in office, Hughes returned to state assembly chambers to rebuke the legislature. Since he had delivered his "Moral Recommitment message," as he called it, back in April 1968, the legislature had responded with inaction. He accused its members of weighing his recommendations against their partisan political interests rather than the dire and obvious needs of New Jersey's urban crisis.[72] His conversion from a tough-talking commander of antiriot forces was complete, but the state government he tried to move in a more proactive direction had turned its back.

SEVEN

The PBA Commission

In September 1967, New Jersey's law enforcement community traveled to Atlantic City for the seventy-first annual convention of the state Patrolmen's Benevolent Association (PBA). The preceding summer had been a difficult one. Law enforcement personnel throughout the state had been on high alert for several months. The violence had not stopped at Newark's borders but spread tentacle-like, riding waves of rumor and hyperbole, to surrounding communities. Though specifics varied, an essential image burned itself into many officers' heads: black insurrectionists were targeting the police.

Though PBA conventions typically mixed business with equal parts sun and beach, a somber and angry tone pervaded the affair that year. Two days after Newark exploded, violence erupted twenty miles south in Plainfield, where, on Saturday evening, July 15, Officer John Gleason was run down and beaten to death by a group of black residents after he shot and critically wounded a man near a public housing project. Some said the man had confronted Gleason with a hammer. Others said he carried nothing. A couple of days later, the mayor of Elizabeth was accused of cowardice when he allowed black community leaders, rather than his own police force, to disperse crowds of looters. Later that week, when police tried to clear the streets in Englewood, a small community above the palisades lining the Hudson River, they were hit with a shower of missiles. The officer in charge at the scene suffered a severe gash when a bottle smashed the windshield of a nearby car.[1]

Just as Newark was cooling off, the violence reached Jersey City. Bands of bottle-throwing and store-looting black youths moved through downtown. Someone fired on a police cruiser and lobbed a firebomb in its direction. Mayor Thomas Whelan issued the rioters a stern warning: they were taking their lives into their own hands. As his shotgun-wielding police force scrambled to quell the small outbreaks of violence, Whelan made it clear which side was determined to prevail, regardless of the price: "Our police form our first line of defense against criminal rebellion and that line will stand firm with all the manpower and weaponry necessary to protect our people and their property. . . . Anyone who attacks a Jersey City policeman or fireman will come off second-best."[2]

The line Whelan drew had been hardening throughout the 1960s, especially in the wake of Barry Goldwater's 1964 bid for the presidency, during which he often hit at the Democratic Party's apparent unwillingness to enforce the law and maintain social order. And it would soon be reinforced by Richard Nixon, as he turned his eye toward the White House.[3] On one side of that line, in a popular version of it, police officers strictly upheld the law, while on the other, an unholy alliance of forces repeatedly challenged it. Civil rights activists, no matter how worthy their cause, had made civil disobedience their common practice, and they had been rewarded with legislative victories and vocal support from prominent liberal politicians and intellectuals. Police departments existed to uphold the law, the law established order, and you could not ignore the law without driving the nation toward anarchy. Within those departments, assaults on officers emerged as the clearest sign that America was firmly on that road.

Whelan's tough talk—especially in the midst of the apparently weak-kneed response of his counterpart in Elizabeth—earned him an invitation to keynote that year's PBA convention. By the time of the closing banquet, during the convention's business session, delegates had already unanimously adopted resolutions demanding public support of the policeman in his "cause for upholding law and order" and harsher sentencing for those who assaulted police officers.[4] Whelan used those ideas to great effect in his speech, cementing a key plank in the emerging platform of law-and-order politics. In the worst of that summer's violence, he reminded delegates, two local police officers, two of their own, had lost their lives. Detective Fred Toto had been killed on the third night of the Newark riots, shot under the heart by an alleged sniper near the Scudder Homes housing project the day before Officer Gleason was stomped to death in Plainfield. These were "human sacrifices," Whelan said, "offered up on the altar of a philosophy that says: don't get anybody mad, don't hurt anyone's feelings, and, for heaven's sake, don't expect anybody to obey the law. They were sacrificed by the philosophy that says every day is open season, not only on policemen, but on all of organized society." The great sophists of that philosophy were those who bestowed on riot cities lavish attention and rewards, like the antipoverty money that "finds its way into the pockets of those crippled and diseased hate mongers who would destroy the society from whose trough they feed."[5]

By the time Whelan delivered his keynote, charges against the state's law enforcement agencies were in wide circulation. Tom Hayden's report on what he called "the occupation of Newark" had appeared in the *New York Review of Books* in late August, the Governor's Commission was pushing the superintendent of the state police on the massive retaliatory fire employed by law enforcement during the Newark riots, and the Newark Legal Services Project had already collected, and would soon submit to the commission, hundreds of affidavits documenting police misconduct.[6] Suddenly, the defenders of social order were being pressured to answer for their alleged complicity in the recent rioting, even though, Whelan insisted, they had been its victims—or sacrificial lambs.

The PBA decided to push back. At the convention's final session, Detective William McCarthy from Jersey City introduced an emergency resolution to create a PBA "Riot Investigation Committee," a seven-member body tasked with investigating "riots, insurrections, and civil disturbances." McCarthy explained that they would take testimony from all concerned parties, in the interest of letting "the public know the truth." And the most immediate truth he wanted the public to know was that, as he claimed, all forty-five allegations of police brutality in New Jersey investigated by the FBI in the past year had been unfounded. They were, he said, "simply used to harass police officers."[7]

Over the next eight months, the Riot Investigation Committee collected testimony from hearings in several cities and gradually morphed into the "Riot Study Commission," the name that appeared on its final report in May 1968 (though in the report's text it is often called, simply, "the Committee"). Along the way, it passed through a combination of those names—"Riot Study and Investigation Commission"—and would be called, among other things, the "PBA riot hearings panel."[8] The eventual choice of "commission" suggests a dawning awareness of that form's social legitimacy as the official arbiter of the urban crisis, a legitimacy forged in their ceremonial launches, the press coverage of their proceedings, and the expectation with which many Americans awaited their findings. The PBA responded by adopting the outward form and, eventually, the name of a commission.

The PBA Commission's aims, however, were very different from those of its more liberal counterparts. Rather than destabilizing existing power relations, the PBA engaged in an effort to maintain the one institution that had been largely impervious to the encroachments of community action, the series of police-community relations programs notwithstanding. And where its counterparts' reports emerged from their close consideration of a broad range of voices and perspectives, the PBA investigation—or, as the language settled into less interested and police-like choices, the PBA "study"—took the commission form without taking to heart its political or intellectual implications, the epistemological challenges posed by the decentered ethic of community action. In a sly echo of the Kerner Commission's most famous line, which emerged out of Mayor Lindsay's confrontation with the "wishy-washy" product of that ethic, the PBA Commission would confidently conclude that, indeed, "our nation is moving toward two societies." But in this version, one of those societies was "bound by the rule of law and the other exempt from the law."[9]

It is difficult to track the progress of the PBA Commission's investigation. Its final report says that "full-scale hearings" were held in Newark, Plainfield, Englewood, and Jersey City, and that recorded testimony from sixty-five people, resulting in over two thousand pages of printed transcript, was collected. Commission members toured several cities, conducted "numerous private interviews," and gathered photographs, statistics, handbills, and other documents. Though the report says these records "will be made available to interested parties," the PBA today is not so forthcoming. And though it also says vaguely that its witnesses represented "the entire strata of involved personnel," a tally of identifiable witnesses cited in it reveals that the majority were police officers, while most others were people—like Mayors George Hetfield of Plainfield and Whelan of Jersey City—whose views were already known to be compatible with those of law enforcement, or whose views proved so in the hearings.[10]

By building its report on such a comparatively stable, uniform foundation, the PBA departed from the logic of its government counterparts, but it did so even more in its choice of personnel: each commission member was a working police officer and PBA member. Both its chair and its chief investigator were Newark officers. Several staff members, including the former Jersey City magistrate who served as chief counsel to the commission, appear to have been civilians.[11]

Like its government counterparts, however, the PBA Commission did much of its work in closed-door hearings. They began in Plainfield that November, at the city's police headquarters and then at its city hall.[12] On the first night, Plainfield police testified that they had been blocked from entering the riot area by a gang of black youth, some with criminal records, organized by Paul Ylvisaker of the state Department of Community Affairs. (Though both Ylvisaker and Governor Hughes were reportedly invited to testify, neither did.) On the second night, Mayor Hetfield testified that the violence was "planned guerilla warfare that had nothing to do with civil rights," and a local tavern owner alleged that a militant black youth group had led a boycott against his establishment until he paid them off.[13]

The final report provides no schedule of the hearings, and newspaper coverage was spotty. But it appears that after four hearings in Plainfield, the commission moved on to Newark in January 1968, where it scheduled five more. Of the few newspaper stories available, one says that witnesses would include Mayor Addonizio and residents of the Central Ward, but the only Newark civilians cited by the final report were the city's fire director, at least one other firefighter, and someone referred to simply as a "resident." On the police side, at least seven members of the Newark police department, including Director Spina, the report's most cited source, appeared at the hearings. On the first day, Inspector Melchior, who seems to be the report's second-most-cited source, told the commission that, though he had no knowledge of "planned starting dates" for the riots, he was impressed by the rioters' organization. "Young teenagers," he said, "would approach the fourth precinct in almost military formations, launch their missiles, and then withdraw."[14] Several days later, after hearing Captain Charles Kinney argue that the almost "military precision" of the rioting indicated it was definitely *not* spontaneous but the product of conspirators from within and without Newark, the commission publicly demanded the impaneling of both county and federal grand juries to hear evidence on what its chief investigator called an "interstate conspiracy."[15]

PBA officials in Newark and statewide trumpeted and praised this early finding, especially since it challenged so directly the Governor's Commission's refusal to affirm such charges.[16] When that commission's report was released several weeks before, the state's law enforcement community had greeted it with widespread derision. Before even getting their hands on a copy, the presidents of several police unions issued statements condemning the report. The head of the PBA's Newark local, Anthony Giuliano, said its eighteen hundred members were "appalled and shocked" by the "whitewashed and one-sided" report, whose allegations were "without any proof, unsubstantiated, and un-American." Members of the commission, he said, would have to explain themselves to Detective Toto's widow. The local and state PBAs, as well as their rival organization, the Fraternal Order of Police (FOP), vowed to file suit against any renewed attempt to establish a civilian review board in Newark.[17] A hastily called joint meeting of the PBA and FOP locals in Newark turned into impromptu picketing of city hall, after it was reported that Mayor Addonizio had vowed to implement the recommendations of the commission. A review board, of course, would be unacceptable, and the appointment of a black captain to head the Fourth Precinct, as the Governor's Commission had recommended, would be reverse discrimination, they argued.[18]

What the Governor's Commission report pointed to, in their minds, was the dire need for another investigation, one that would take more seriously the law enforcement perspective, one like that being conducted by the PBA Commission. While some questioned the legitimacy of that body—the Newark Committee of Concern, a coalition of civic leaders formed after the riots and led by a former United Community Corporation vice president, issued a statement arguing that "the role the PBA is undertaking is the responsibility of other agencies of government and the usurpation of these prerogatives cannot be permitted"—others became even more convinced of its indispensability.[19] Too much evidence had been disregarded, they argued, and too much trust invested in those whose agitation had led to the riots. "Why were statements of malcontents treated as gospel truth without even so much as an investigation?" Giuliano asked in a press release. "Why is the governor accepting this report as a historical document, when only seven months earlier he labeled it a criminal insurrection and declared that the line between lawlessness and law and order would be drawn here as well as any other place?" Such imponderables, he said, had led many citizens to eagerly anticipate the forthcoming PBA report.[20] Others questioned why Governor Hughes's role in leading the suppression effort hadn't been given more scrutiny, why the Newark Police Department's community relations efforts hadn't been given more recognition, why the commission hadn't called the city's antipoverty program to account for its role in the violence, and why, of course, more blame had been assigned to the police than the rioters themselves.[21] State PBA president John Heffernan assailed the Governor's Commission, which, he said, "threw a pair of loaded dice at Newark police by accepting as gospel every aspersion against police and ignoring completely evidence supporting the police." It had ignored over one thousand assaults on police officers between 1960 and 1967, he claimed, while accusing them of extreme misconduct. But "it was not the Newark police who rioted," he said. "It was not the Newark police who looted. It was not the Newark police who sniped from the rooftops and hurled bottles and rocks and Molotov cocktails."[22] The commission's conclusions were "appalling." But one thing was certain, Heffernan said: the PBA investigation would "come up with different findings."[23]

When the PBA released its report, *The Road to Anarchy*, in May 1968—the same day, as it turned out, that John Smith was sentenced to two years for his alleged assault on one of his arresting officers—the report was widely understood to be, as one reporter put it, "the policemen's answer to the reports of commissions appointed by Gov. Richard J. Hughes and President Johnson."[24] When John Heffernan called a press conference at the Robert Treat Hotel in Newark, the place where Robert Lilley had released the Governor's Commission report, the state PBA head struck a defiant pose on behalf of its sixteen thousand members. Anticipating further interference in police work from superior officers and government officials, he reminded those in attendance that each of the PBA's members had taken an oath to uphold the law and "non-enforcement" directives did not supersede that vow. When met with force, Heffernan said, PBA members would respond with superior force, regardless of such directives. In the choice between order and anarchy, the police of New Jersey had and would continue to come down on the side of order. And now, Heffernan said, the PBA was asking "all Americans, of whatever race, color, or creed, to make the same choice. In no other way can we recapture the American dream."[25]

The choice would be made easier by considering the report's two central findings, both directly contradicting the conclusions of the government commissions. The riots, the PBA said, were the product of a criminal conspiracy, and, given that, the forceful response of law enforcement was eminently appropriate. The conspiracy was made up of a range of organizations and actors, perhaps working in concert or perhaps not. The report never definitively decides. Sometimes the conspiracy sounds tight—"a conspiracy exists of radical elements, dedicated to the overthrow of our society"—and sometimes it sounds like a looser collective—"a number of organizations have played pivotal parts in the organizing and carrying out of riots."[26]

Whatever its cohesiveness, the conspiracy had left ample signs of its existence. The commission had collected fliers containing instructions for the proper assembly and use of a Molotov cocktail and others that instructed people to flood the streets by knocking the heads off fire hydrants.[27] In the months leading up to the outbreak of violence, numerous community members—at public hearings on the medical school and on the creation of a civilian review board, for example—had warned of impending violence, in words that the commission interpreted as promises rather than predictions. And when those words proved prescient, prior planning was evident in the alleged stockpiles of rocks and bottles found on the roofs of public housing projects and the bands of youth who attacked in "military formation."[28]

Some of the blame could be placed on outside agitators. The commission reported that twenty nonresidents had been arrested during the violence in Newark, "a sufficient number for mischief and disorder, particularly if they happened to be skilled and experienced leaders."[29] And they might have been, since, as many of those who met with the commission testified, Communists had been involved. This was evidenced by the "inflammatory literature purportedly printed in China" that was found in the riot area (the July issue of Robert F. Williams's *Crusader*, in which he gives his address as Peking); by the connections they had uncovered between individuals in Newark and the Revolutionary Action Movement in Philadelphia, a group said to have received large sums of money from Communist China; and by the presence of a local chapter of the Progressive Labor Party, "a splinter of the Communist party that believes in 'mass action and killing.'"[30]

But the most prominent among these allegedly Communist-inspired outside agitators was Tom Hayden. As one unidentified witness explained to the committee, Hayden "founded the Newark Community Union Project, an organization that has exploited and tried to do everything possible to cause strife in our City." The charge would have made sense to anyone on the Newark police force. Even if they hadn't been at the Clinton Hill Meat Market when picketing NCUP members refused to move away from the front door, even if they hadn't attended Hayden's trial for allegedly beating a local landlady, and even if they hadn't stopped NCUP members from blocking an intersection to demand a stoplight or arrested members for leafleting at a local high school or kept a close eye on the staff members' residence across from the Fifth Precinct building, they no doubt had at least *heard* about the agitation NCUP was stirring in the South Ward. But in case readers failed to recognize the ultimate danger posed by "the New Left movement" in Newark, the PBA Commission quoted J. Edgar Hoover's claim that its "chief passion is to destroy our government, our democratic values, our American way of life."[31]

As if that weren't enough, the Communists and Tom Hayden were joined by a host of homegrown agitators. "Anti-white black extremists and militants—Black Nationalists, Black Power advocates, Black Muslims, Orthodox Muslims, members of the United Afro-American Association, anti-white playwright LeRoi Jones—were gathering and fomenting" in the months leading up to the violence, the commission reported.[32] Yet even with such an extensive list of troublemakers, no single organization or individual deserved more blame, according to the PBA investigation, than the local antipoverty agency. UCC leaders, after all, had failed to disperse the crowd at the Fourth Precinct building on Wednesday night, when the violence began. And it was in UCC offices, on a UCC mimeograph machine, that the flier calling the community back to the precinct the following night had been printed. Its complicity in the violence, the PBA Commission charged, included meetings of the criminal conspirators hosted at its headquarters. There they had allegedly discussed the abandonment of a nonviolent philosophy, arranged to have guns smuggled into the city, and organized a cadre of lawyers from the ACLU to represent them should their plot be successfully hatched and any of the conspirators apprehended. The community action agency had been taken over by extremists and racists, and the PBA Commission found "no reason to disagree with those public officials who feel that federal anti-poverty funds are being used to finance insurrection."[33]

Little wonder, the PBA thought, that both the Kerner and Governor's Commissions had avoided any mention of government involvement or complicity in the disorders, had identified police-community relations as a primary cause of urban disorder, and dismissed out of hand the idea that a conspiracy existed. Their confident focus on police misconduct and underlying social causes had failed to shine a light on the shadowy conspiracy behind the violence, let alone to expose the shortcomings of their own liberal philosophy (don't get anyone mad, hurt their feelings, or expect them to obey the law, as Mayor Whelan had put it) or practice (the funding of local extremists). By heaping scorn on police practices, they had successfully diverted blame from themselves and threw it on the shoulders of law enforcement.

The most telling and dangerous product of this toxic stew of foreign radicalism, domestic extremism, and a shortsighted liberalism was the black sniper, and the black sniper emerged as a narrative linchpin in the PBA Commission's recounting of events in Newark. In this, the commission followed on the extensive news coverage of the riots, the vast majority of it based on police sources. Reports of snipers had filled the air. The first use of the word seems to have come from a *Newark Evening News* reporter who told of bullets whizzing by his ears as he rode with two city policemen near the corner of Springfield Avenue and Howard Street.[34] That was the only mention of snipers in the local press until Detective Toto's death. The next morning, the *Star-Ledger's* front-page headline screamed, "Police Battle Snipers," and the ensuing story reported that "the sound of gunfire was almost constant once darkness had fallen." The violence, it reported, had grown "uglier and deadlier" once the rioters had armed themselves and taken up posts atop public housing projects.[35] The *Evening News* counted

15. Police claimed that black snipers had taken aim at them, including drivers of Newark Police Department vans like this one. It had likely been used to transport arrestees to the federal post office building, where US Marshals watched over several dozen prisoners during the riots. © Media General Communications Holdings, LLC. (Newark Public Library / *Newark Evening News*)

approximately one hundred victims of gunshot wounds Friday night—including a twelve-year-old boy reportedly hit by a sniper while riding in the family car—as compared to only twenty-five the night before.[36] The *New York Times* headline read "Sniper Slays Policeman," and the lead paragraph grimly described the scene: "Gunfire crackled through the streets of this riot-torn city in renewed fury last night, bringing the toll of dead to 11, including a policeman shot by a sniper while chasing looters." Two other officers, the paper reported, had also been shot Friday night.[37]

On Saturday, city police reported that snipers had targeted City Hospital, where bullets ricocheted off an emergency room wall. Soon, the lights were dimmed, shades drawn, and nurses began toting flashlights on their rounds. One remarked: "Sometimes you'd think you're in Vietnam."[38] Snipers were reported on the upper floors of the William B. Hayes housing project, from which they laid siege to the Engine 6 firehouse at Springfield and Hunterdon, pinning firefighters inside while other companies handled their calls.[39] A few blocks to the southeast, their colleagues in Engine 12 took cover against reported sniper fire from the direction of the Prince Hall Temple.[40] On nearby Prince Street, gunfire from the rooftops of the Scudder Homes hampered firemen's efforts to battle a blaze.[41] Innumerable reports of police shoot-outs with snipers filled local and national media coverage, and news outlets printed photos of law enforcement officers as they took cover behind their vehicles, looking to the top of the photo's frame, nervously aiming their weapons at a suspected sniper's perch.[42] The *Newark Evening News* reported snipers firing on the Fourth Precinct building where the uprising began, on a police helicopter sent to the Hayes Homes to flush out the sniper, and on National Guardsmen protecting looted stores along Springfield Avenue.[43] The final tally, Police Director Dominick Spina had told the Governor's Commission, was seventy-nine separate incidents of sniper fire.[44]

Snipers themselves, however, proved slippery subjects. A state police antisniper taskforce swept rooftops and public housing projects and posted officers with "sniperscopes" at City Hospital; the National Guard toured the Prince Hall Temple looking for its rooftop gunman; rewards were posted for information leading to the apprehension of Toto's killer; *Life* magazine ran a story (which it later admitted it had fabricated) about a sniper band hiding out in a rundown tenement building; and Governor Hughes offered executive clemency to anyone accused of nonviolent plundering or looting in return for information leading to the arrest and conviction of a sniper—and yet scant evidence of their existence surfaced.[45] The case was built on some shell casings found in a housing project stairwell and the arrest of several people for possession of a dangerous weapon. In only one of those arrests was it clear that the suspect had actually fired a shot. Whether he was a sniper or not was impossible to determine.[46]

But the virtually complete invisibility of the black sniper did not stem the tide of speculation about his true identity and purpose. Rather, it became a central feature of that speculation, for weren't snipers, after all, known by their impressive stealth? Wasn't their hallmark a suddenly fallen comrade, his death sometimes accompanied by a sharp crack somewhere off in the distance? Wasn't there something familiar about that gunfire? Vietcong snipers terrorized American troops in Southeast Asia at the same time their domestic counterparts sent New Jersey's law enforcement officers scrambling for cover on the streets of Newark. The City Hospital nurse was not the only one to make sense of the gunfire by alluding to Vietnam, whose rebel Communists provided precooked referents. At times, the connections were drawn imprecisely, as when a New Jersey Department of Defense Operational Report spoke of "guerilla sniper tactics" and the sniper's ability to "[slip] away in the dark or [lose] himself in the populace to employ his tactic at another opportune time and place," or when the Newark Police Department also referred to sniper "guerilla tactics" in its official chronology of the violence.[47] Likewise, commenting on the intensity of the violence in Newark and Detroit in the *George Washington Law Review*, J. Edgar Hoover had written that snipers had played "a primary role" in the "virtual guerilla warfare" that erupted in those cities.[48] And Governor Hughes, perhaps unwittingly, had evoked the terrain upon which American soldiers fought abroad when he declared that "the line between the jungle and the law might as well be drawn here" as anywhere.[49]

At other times, as with the nurse, the connections were direct and explicit. One of her colleagues compared the emergency room to a military field hospital in Vietnam, while a National Guardsman posted outside said the situation in Newark resembled "two countries fighting."[50] Upon returning from a round trip between police headquarters and the antiriot command center at the Roseville Armory, Mayor Addonizio gave reporters his assessment of the situation: "Every time you think things are under control, sniping breaks out. It's like fighting in Vietnam."[51]

This is what gave charges that Detective Toto had been killed by a black sniper significance well beyond an officer being killed in the routine line of duty. His death at the hands of an unseen sniper meant that he—and all law enforcement troops stationed in Newark—had faced down not only the everyday criminals, the so many looters and vandals of the riots but, more perilously, an organized band of guerilla fighters intent not only on the physical destruction of the city but on the upending of the social order. The black sniper, in the eyes of so many government officials and police officers, including those who made up the PBA Commission, constituted prima facie evidence of a larger conspiracy behind the violence. His ability to jump from place to place undetected and efficiently drench Newark in terror was taken as a sign of prior planning and coordination.[52] "They were trained in cross-fire and hit-and-run techniques," Governor Hughes claimed the day the troops left Newark. "Detective Fred Toto was cut down in such a planned tactic."[53] The head of the state police also reported cross-fire and drew the same conclusion. Snipers, he later testified, were "people dedicated to a purpose . . . people assigned a mission . . . people who have made up their minds that they are going to shoot someone."[54] Police Director Spina expanded the snipers' sphere of influence by claiming that they communicated via citizen band radio with other rioters: snipers opened fire in one part of the city to attract the attention of law enforcement units so that their comrades could ransack the recently vacated area.[55] They were a small group, unburdened by heavy weaponry and quick on their feet. They were, like their counterparts in Vietnam, a well-trained, highly organized, and deadly serious revolutionary force.

Any suggestion that law enforcement officers had reacted too forcefully, then, was bound to bewilder and infuriate members of that community and their supporters. Though specialized antiguerilla tactics—countersniper teams, especially—were in short supply, ammunition was not, and police and National Guardsmen responded by joining together in massive retaliatory fire. They squatted together behind cars and mailboxes, trees and telephone poles, waiting for the next sniper shot, fearing they might be his next victim. When it rang out, they responded with hails of gunfire. A state Department of Defense official estimated that his troops had expended more than ten thousand rounds of ammunition in Newark and Plainfield, and the state police admitted firing almost three thousand rounds in Newark alone.[56] And though no local official could provide an estimate of the number of shots fired by Newark police officers, the department did have to borrow twenty cases of rifle cartridges from nearby Union City after expending much of its own.[57] To add to the confusion, officers who felt outgunned often retrieved ammunition and personal firearms (especially shotguns, of which the department owned very few) from home.[58]

Whatever the exact numbers, the result was deadly. During the siege of Engine 6, "at least 200" shots were fired up at the Hayes Homes housing project, according to the *Star-Ledger*, and the attack continued the next day.[59] When forty-one-year-old widow Eloise Spellman heard gunshots early Saturday evening, she went to her window, screamed, and fell to the floor, hit in the neck by a shotgun blast. In her Bergen Street apartment, Rebecca Brown's body was cut open by bullets as she tried to pull one of her children to safety. Down the street at the Scudder Homes project, in a separate incident, seventy-three-year-old Isaac Harrison, in town visiting family, was hit by shotgun blasts in his chest and abdomen when police opened fire on a crowd gathered on the corner. And twelve-year-old Eddie Moss was shot by National Guardsmen manning a checkpoint near his home. He was the boy originally reported to have been killed by a sniper while riding in the family car.[60]

In the end, twenty-three of the twenty-six riot deaths were caused by gunfire and eight of those by indiscriminate police fire.[61] Though it is likely that law enforcement officers faced potentially deadly gunfire, it is less likely that the source was snipers. Though it is not hard to imagine that some residents of the riot area would grab a gun and fire upon the police and National Guard—even Tom Hayden reported a man trying to shoot a police officer—Newark police director Dominick Spina, while not doubting the existence of *some* snipers, concluded that much of the gunfire charged to them most likely came from other police officers and guardsmen. That was also the conclusion reached by a team at the Stanford Research Institute hired by the Kerner Commission to study the matter. Reports of snipers in Newark, the team concluded, were "substantially exaggerated," and that exaggeration was explained by "confusion, inexperience, multiple reporting, and excessive firing by law officials."[62]

Nonetheless, the black sniper, as the leading edge of a larger conspiracy, helped provide the ground on which police could claim aggrieved status. The PBA Commission ultimately found that, in fact, "brutality did exist, but it ran *from* the community *to* the police officer." In accounts of John Smith's arrest, the incident that triggered the violence, as in the shooting death of Lester Long two summers before, was a black suspect assaulting white cops. The spark had not been provided by police, in this reading of events, but by an act of brutality *against* them.[63] And the black sniper carried that pattern through the next four days.

The PBA not only flatly rejected the government commissions' suggestion that law enforcement had overreacted and used excessive force, but countered that, actually, *not enough* force had been used. Its report chastised city officials and police leadership for not acting decisively enough outside the Fourth Precinct on Wednesday night. Their appeasement of the rapidly escalating agitation only encouraged a disregard for the law and generated a larger barrage of missiles. "This failure," the report concluded, echoing Mayor Whelan's convention keynote, "resulted in part from a previously-existing trend which counseled coddling and laissez faire attitudes by officialdom."[64] And once the agitation had exploded into full-blown rioting, someone should have made it clear that patrolmen were free to fire their revolvers if the situation warranted such response. Instead, they were confused and reluctant to use their firearms, and criminals that could have been apprehended had gotten away.[65]

Luckily, officers had gathered themselves and taken positions from which they could return fire. The government commissions had cast doubt on those tactics, suggesting the firing had been indiscriminate, unnecessary, and, at times, murderous. In return, the PBA report accused the Governor's Commission, in particular, of "emotionalizing" the issue by detailing the particularly gory shooting death of one suspected looter, in the hope that, through all the blood, readers would not be able to discern the commission's utter lack of evidence and expertise. "It is submitted," the PBA Commission offered, "that the [Governor's] Commission is in no way qualified to pass judgment on the appropriateness of law enforcement policies."[66]

In its final analysis, the PBA substituted for the Kerner Commission's grim racial prophecy the specter of a lawman's apocalypse: a nation split between those bound by the law and those exempt from it. Violence might flair between these two societies. But the real conflict pitted those who bound themselves to the law against those who willingly offered exemptions to lawbreakers—between, in other words, the police and liberal government. "The lawlessness on our nation's streets feeds on and is nurtured by the weakness of official response," they found. "As the excuses and apologies for lawlessness grow, so does the lawlessness. We charge that a conspiracy exists of radical elements, dedicated to the overthrow of our society—*and that this conspiracy is aided, perhaps unwittingly, by people at the highest levels of government and society.*"[67] While government officials had coddled rioters, negotiated with them, and legitimized their actions by calling it a protest or a rational response to oppression, PBA members held the line separating civilization from the jungle in the way that made the most sense to them. Now that they had made their case, it remained to be seen whether government officials and everyday citizens would stand with them on that line or would continue down the road to anarchy.

Left to pick up the pieces after the National Guard and state police returned to their barracks, Newark police faced a crisis of identity. They were now widely blamed for igniting and then escalating the violence. They had faced the looters, the arsonists, and most treacherously the snipers, yet somehow they had come out the criminals. The consequences were felt personally and professionally. Following the riots, the Newark Police Department suffered what Director Spina called a "mass exodus of police officers." He reported to the Governor's Commission that thirty-four officers—including a sergeant and a lieutenant—had handed in letters of resignation or taken leaves of absence that he expected would soon turn into outright resignations. Required exit interviews revealed that many had joined the Newark Fire Department, where, according to Spina, "it is nice and soft and you don't get pushed around." Morale was at an all-time low. The resigning lieutenant, who had served more than twenty years, visited Spina with tears in his eyes and a wife at home who feared for his life. Spina left no doubt what had produced such breakdowns: "This riot and the continual protests since the riot have done great harm to the morale of the police in our city."[68]

The entire profession, it seemed, had come under siege. Police tempers across the country were still boiling over the Supreme Court's *Miranda* ruling the year before. Many believed the courts had come down on the wrong side of the law, that they were now more interested in safeguarding the rights of criminals than the rights of victims and the sacred duty of the law enforcement officer. Spina, for one, ranked such court decisions as the second-most common reason officers provided for quitting the force. The top reason given was the lack of a professional pay level, especially given the current complexities of the job.[69] The state attorney general believed that the public now asked a policeman "to be a social worker, a lawyer, a member of the clergy, as well as to do his ordinary police functions . . . to know how to deal with minority elements when we have people in our society with college degrees who don't know how to deal with minority elements."[70] What's more, those same minority elements with whom officers had been asked to build a relationship had seemingly grown more hostile and threatening. Spina reported in October 1967 that the number of officers assaulted had reached an all-time high of 187 the previous year.[71]

The attempted remaking of police work—a process that was as much cultural reimagining as real and potential bureaucratic restructuring (community relations programs, civilian review boards, minority recruitment, and racial integration of the force)—had seemingly been for naught. There had still been a riot. Never embraced enthusiastically by many Newark officers or their departmental and union leadership, such efforts had been pushed on them by community activists, certain other municipal institutions like the Newark Human Rights Commission, and now, liberal investigative commissions. Despite what seemed to many officers intense efforts to improve community relations, many observers now deemed their poor relationship with black Newarkers to have been the spark that ignited the explosive mixture of poverty and racism in the ghetto.

A key goal for PBA and other police leaders, then, was to reorient police work back to crime fighting, the central element, in their minds, of law enforcement. In pursuing that goal, testifying before government commissions getting them nowhere, they made appeals directly to their remaining centers of support: Newark's white community and the municipal government. Just weeks after the state commission issued its report, the Essex County sheriff published a statement in Newark's *Italian Tribune* detailing the results of his own personal analysis of the Newark scene. For years, he wrote, he had watched Dominick Spina build Newark's police-community relations program into "one of the finest in the land." He cited the precinct councils, the open-door office hours, and the police observer program, among other measures. The sheriff had been shocked, then, "that practically nothing at all was said during the entire [Governor's Commission] report concerning the agitation by racists and subversives in the form of leaflets, speeches, demonstrations, etc., which helped set the climate for the disorder that occurred. The allegations implied are that police officers caused the disorder and compelled it by undue or excessive use of force." He himself had been a witness to the violence and had not once observed any of the police misconduct reported by the commission. And he failed to see the connection between charges of police corruption and the "insurrection," charges which, he concluded, were "totally un-American and a sad reflection on those who signed the report." In thinking this way, he was not alone, for "in all conversations I have had with thousands of people that I have come in contact with since the report was issued, there is almost a total condemnation of its findings."[72]

The sheriff had a point. Perhaps he had not spoken to literally thousands of people in the short time since the Governor's Commission had issued its report, but he no doubt had a keen sense of the political winds in Newark. In recent years, one of the stiffest had blown thousands of white citizens—most of whom a few years later would become known as urban white ethnics—out of their sizable but ever-shrinking enclaves in the North, East, and West Wards and into the streets. And they came out less because they felt directly threatened by the mounting unrest in their city than because that unrest now threatened *their* police department. So when the police once again came under fire during and after the riots of 1967, a supportive constituency of police officers and citizens already existed, even if it had lain largely dormant for two years.

So the PBA Commission took solace in political developments at the grassroots, where "a feeling of outrage among the citizenry" that the criminals had not been brought to justice, and the attendant desire to pin the blame on someone, had formed, its report said, the impetus for their investigation into the disorders' conspiratorial aspects.[73] That citizenry, however, might be taking things a little far. In a development that state PBA president John Heffernan said "greatly alarmed" him, an increasingly fearful, but defiant, citizenry—in apparent solidarity with law enforcement agencies—took to providing its own security.[74] Both Mayor Addonizio and Police Director Spina received reports from intelligence officers that Newark's white neighborhoods were becoming armed camps.[75] In an uncanny echo of the work of Black Panther chapters across the country, the Young Americans for Freedom chapter at the local Rutgers campus distributed fliers listing state gun license requirements and statutes on self-defense, along with escape routes out of the city.[76] And though the state police, who processed all applications for gun purchases in New Jersey, refused to give credit to post-riot fears, they noted an upsurge in gun applications state-wide and a slight increase in Newark following the violence.[77]

The PBA Commission also found comfort in a growing support for its perspective among more formal political institutions and actors. Its report approvingly quoted Richard Nixon, who had declared his bid for the presidency at the beginning of February. Campaigning in New Hampshire just before the primary, Nixon had attacked the government commissions for blaming "everyone for the riots except the perpetrators of the riots" and had pledged "to make it very clear to potential rioters that, in the event something starts next summer . . . the law will move in with adequate force to put down rioting and looting." (Governor Hughes responded the next day: "Platitudes aren't going to solve our problems, and Nixon is just full of platitudes.")[78] And when Nixon's campaign made a brief swing through Newark on the day after the PBA report's release, he drew the loudest applause from a crowd of two thousand at Newark's Symphony Hall when he blamed the Supreme Court for "weakening the peace forces in the country."[79]

More immediately, though, and months before presidential campaigning took off, the Newark city council had provided one clear sign that it sided with its police department on the issue of riot response. In August 1967, before considering the costs of the violence for City Hospital, the fire department, the municipal courts, or the public works department, the council approved the police department's purchase of $310,000 worth of antiriot equipment and a bond issue to pay for it. The items to be purchased included a bus for transporting prisoners, 8 public address systems, 8 videotape recorders, a bulletproof illumination truck, high-powered searchlights, 2 heavy-duty vans, 3 jeeps, 5 patrol wagons, 2 armored vehicles, 290 bulletproof vests, 7 armored suits, 50 rolls of barbed wire, tear gas grenades, gas masks, riot shields, riot sticks, and 40 AR-15 rifles.[80] "The City Council practically gave us a blank check to get any equipment that we need to put down the insurrection," Police Director Spina later said. Prior to that, the police department owned no modern helmets and only twenty-five shotguns. "So many hundreds of things we could have used and didn't have" during the recent violence, Spina lamented.[81] So pitiable was the department's collection of weaponry that many officers had dashed home during the riots to grab personal firearms. But now the city council would provide all they could ever need. By November, the department owned five hundred shotguns.[82]

PART THREE

New Directions for Community Action

EIGHT

Law and Order

On a small, crowded lawn outside city hall, a muscular German shepherd sank his teeth into the protective cover shielding a man's arm. A crowd estimated to be four hundred strong looked on admiringly. The dog's handler explained through a portable microphone that Duke packed six hundred pounds per square inch of jaw pressure and invited people to pet him. Impressed by the dog's power and trusting in his discipline, dozens did. Among them were Councilmen Frank Addonizio and Lee Bernstein, staunch advocates of establishing a canine unit within the Newark Police Department. A few minutes earlier, they had insisted that the city council break from its regular proceedings for the demonstration. When the council reconvened in chambers, its members approved a six-month trial for the dogs. The only members to vote against the trial run were the city's two black councilmen.[1]

When, in August 1967, the month before this demonstration, the city council had approved the purchase of new antiriot gear and weaponry, it had delayed action on the police department's request that the order include a canine unit. For some Newarkers, the idea stirred up ghosts of Birmingham: images of German shepherds straining at their leashes, jaws set to close on the closest civil rights protester. Newark was on edge as it was. The dogs, and the racial baggage they brought with them, might push it over. Handbills voicing opposition, at least one of which contained an image from Birmingham, circulated in the city's black neighborhoods.[2] Members of the United Community Corporation approved a resolution criticizing the council's approval of the dogs, president Tim Still explaining that "at this time, when the country faces a tense racial confrontation in many of its cities . . . the use of dogs will only add to the depressing and misguided attempts to bring about peace and order in our community."[3]

For others, those who believed Newark had yet to climb out of the lawless pit into which it had fallen, the dogs seemed a helping hand up. Chief among those supporters were, of course, members of the police department itself, as well as their allies on the city council. As crime and civil disorder emerged as social issues over the course of the decade, police departments and unions increasingly mobilized to demand greater public investment in their profession. They wanted higher salaries, better training, and, of course, better gear. Along with the tear gas and barbed wire and shotguns, a canine unit was a necessary piece of equipment in these dangerous times. But police also promoted the idea that their own civil rights—the right to do their jobs without outside interference or threat to their safety, especially— were being eroded. So the dogs also spoke to their vocational dedication to maintain order in the way they, not civil rights activists, deemed best.[4]

As such issues increased the distance between the police and "the community," as produced by community action, a relatively new force in the city mobilized in support of the last municipal institution to which it could lay clear claim. A mass citizens' movement arose in the city's remaining majority-white neighborhoods, in support of law and order broadly and their local police department specifically. These alliances called to mind the fight against a civilian review board from the summer of 1965. But in post-riot Newark, the sense of crisis for police and their supporters deepened. It drew them closer together. And in a twist on police-community relations, the lines between police officer and civilian began to blur: white activists in Newark took on the role of law enforcer, and law enforcement officers pushed the politics of rights and grievance that had begun to take hold in white communities. Traditional police-community relations work, born out of the tensions between an increasingly black population and the steadfastly majority-white police department, would soon yield to an even greater focus on crime prevention, professionalization, and police rights, as well as a strengthened solidarity with the white community from which so many Newark policeman came. Though this mixture of police professionalization and grievance, and of the police and its supporting communities, ultimately failed to bring a canine unit to Newark—the city council reversed itself early in October 1967—it formed a potent politics as the decade drew to a close, a politics that sparred with the established forces of community action in Newark as both turned an eye toward control of city hall.

The struggle between police and community action played out at all levels of government. A presidential investigative commission brought New-

ark voices to the attention of federal officials, and other commissions had
made the debate a statewide issue. And at every moment, members and advocates of Newark's law enforcement community used the opportunity to
attack community action, to try to convince the state to turn away from it
and toward a stronger commitment to the police. In their minds, the state
had been making the wrong choice for several years, and it had produced
only mayhem. Their efforts involved the promotion of certain riot narratives, as well as the emerging arguments about the proper scope of police
work and the rights due police officers in light of their riot experiences.
And though they failed to convince some state agents—the liberal commissions, most notably—they scored notable successes.

Congressional proponents of the emerging law-and-order politics began paying more attention to local law enforcement experience. The sense
that police departments and their officers faced growing threats to their
professional and personal well-being, threats that were both physical
(snipers, rioters, criminals) and administrative (review boards, community
relations programs, police observers), had been brewing on the ground in
Newark since at least the summer of 1965 and the shooting of Lester Long.
But now such grievances gained a wider hearing. That was a difference the
riots made. In fact, before any of the riot commissions heard a single witness, Newark police found a particularly receptive listener in Senator John
McClellan, Democrat of Arkansas. McClellan was interested not so much
in a broad inquiry into the causes and prevention of mass violence but
in whether Congress should enact legislation making it a federal crime to
cross state lines for the purposes of inciting a riot. When the Senate Judiciary Committee, on which McClellan was a senior member, began six
days of hearings on a bill early in August 1967, its twenty-person witness
list included sixteen police officers, two of whom were from Newark. And
though Detective William Millard spoke provocatively about his belief that
the UCC "could very well have contributed to the atmosphere that brought
on the riot," it was his Newark colleague, Patrolman Leonard Kowalewski,
who most fully made the case against community action.[5]

Kowalewski was the president of both the state and local Newark lodges
of the Fraternal Order of Police (FOP), the Patrolmen's Benevolent Association's main union rival. Where the Newark PBA boasted a membership
of eighteen hundred active and retired officers, the local FOP's rolls topped
out at just over two hundred.[6] This might partially account for the apparent
eagerness with which Kowalewski took the spotlight and touted his work.
He had begun advocating for police officers and calling attention to the
dangers they faced well before the black uprising, and it was with increas-

ing alarm that the month before it started, he had hand-delivered a letter to Mayor Addonizio warning that a race riot was imminent and that the city should immediately provide its officers helmets and shotguns and tear gas.[7] The mayor met with him late in June but, ever the optimist, did not heed his warnings. The mayor's closest aide later dismissively called Kowalewski a proponent of the "police militant view" and noted that he had not provided any evidence for his claims.[8]

Kowalewski might have failed to convince local officials, but in Washington he was determined to persuade senators that national action against militants and in support of law enforcement would be vital to the future of America's civil order. A congressional investigator with whom Kowalewski spoke shortly before his appearance had suggested that he testify about the United Community Corporation and the origins of the riots. Kowalewski did so, but he also drew out the antipoverty program's intersections with other organizations and figures. He opened his testimony by explaining that the trouble had really begun before the War on Poverty came to town, when CORE made its "vicious, insidious attack against the Newark police."[9] And from there, with McClellan doing most of the questioning, Kowalewski testified about the various organizations and demonstrations and public meetings that had raised the city's temperature and about how, through it all, city police officers were under an "unofficial order" not to arrest any militants who agitated for violence. Colonel Hassan had destroyed city property at one public hearing and was not arrested. LeRoi Jones, black nationalist writer and Newark native son, had told the city council that Hiroshima and Nagasaki would "look like Sunday school picnics after we get through with Newark," and the police were ordered to do nothing about it. Antipoverty workers had participated not only in the picketing and demonstrations that led to rioting but in the rioting itself, and the police could do nothing about it. "Regardless of what happens, no arrest. Don't antagonize them," Kowalewski explained.[10]

McClellan was shocked that Newark police would be so "cowed" by allegations of police brutality that they were now "afraid to do their job" and that this had effectively given immunity to those "elements that are preaching the destruction of our cities and rioting."[11] A few days before Kowalewski's appearance that August, McClellan had successfully introduced a resolution making the Permanent Subcommittee on Investigation, which he chaired, the Senate's official agent when it came to determining the causes of rioting. There, he would further pursue Kowalewski's line of reasoning. That the subcommittee's most famous inquiry to date had been its hearings on organized crime suggested to some observers that it would likely focus on law enforcement issues rather than the underlying social causes of violence. When one moderate Republican senator bid to limit the investigation to "economic and social" factors, colleagues soundly rejected his amendment, arguing that such a stance was tantamount to condoning lawlessness.[12]

McClellan opened his subcommittee's hearings in November 1967 by declaring that the investigation would start with the immediate, rather than the basic, causes of rioting, which he called "a tangible threat to the preservation of law and order and our internal security." The first witness called was an official with the community action agency in Houston, where two antipoverty workers had been indicted for the death of a policeman during a campus disturbance under a new Texas law that made those involved in instigating a riot responsible for any subsequent crimes committed in its course. On the hearings' second day, a Houston police lieutenant testified that antipoverty workers had taken to the streets to incite the riots.[13] Over the next year, the subcommittee heard from a parade of witnesses in that same vein: the role of law enforcement officers and the role of antipoverty workers, of police action and community action.

By May 1968, when a Newark contingent appeared before McClellan's subcommittee, the investigative commissions had firmly established the key narrative disputes: mass racial violence was the product of either underlying social ills or a criminal conspiracy. Months before, subcommittee investigators had been dispatched to Newark, and they came back with one simple conclusion: "Grievances of the impoverished people in Newark, whether real or imagined, were used by both white and Negro agitators to increase unrest." Chief among these agitators, not surprisingly, was the UCC, whose members had been spotted by Newark police at the Fourth Precinct the night officers had dragged John Smith out of their patrol car.[14] Though some Newark witnesses downplayed such talk—especially the director of the municipal housing agency and the superintendent of its schools, both of whom spoke of their efforts to address underlying social problems—Mayor Addonizio shared the investigators' general approach but couched it in a metaphor of his own making. Newark was like a Molotov cocktail, he explained. The bottle was composed of decades of poverty and urban decay. But, he continued, "the wick is most certainly supplied by the noisemakers, the unwise leader and the would-be leader, the racist and the demagogue, and by those few who have convinced themselves that violence and revolution are worthy social goals."[15]

As in the antiriot bill hearings the year before, one of the star witnesses was a Newark police officer. Captain Charles Kinney was then studying for a degree in political science at Rutgers on a police scholarship and had two years before completed the course on Communism offered by the US State Department's Foreign Service Institute. He knew conspiracy when he saw it. And he was convinced that "in Newark, certain individuals conspired and are conspiring to replace the leadership of the police department . . . to turn out of office the present city administration . . . [and] to replace the system of government under which we live in the United States of America, using any means to do so, including the use of force and violence." He provided a long list of the individuals involved. It included all the usual suspects (members of the UCC, NCUP, and CORE most prominently), but also extended the conspiracy to groups—like the Black Panther Party and the Revolutionary Action Movement—that had only thin connections to Newark. Though Kinney admitted that he lacked the evidence to arrest anyone, he was quite sure that should his report be presented to the county prosecutor, a grand jury would be impaneled. With their resources, no doubt, his conclusions would be verified.[16]

Of the twenty-four people Captain Kinney named, Senate investigators focused their efforts on one: James Kennedy, whom they called a "key employee" of Area Board 2, which covered the bulk of Newark's Central Ward. The day after John Smith was dragged into the Fourth Precinct, they told the subcommittee, Kennedy had appeared on television to announce a rally at the precinct to protest police brutality. He instructed an Area Board 2 clerk-typist to create handbills, and she ran fifteen hundred sheets of paper through the board's mimeograph machine. They came out reading, "Stop Police Brutality!" The rest of the story was well known: picket lines formed outside the precinct, and then the "demonstration deteriorated" to the point that "there was complete chaos, looting was rampant and the riot was on," as one investigator put it. "So, in effect," the Senate subcommittee's general counsel asked, "you have a situation where the organizer in area board No. 2, Mr. Kennedy, is using Federal funds and equipment such as paper and materials to create these placards and throw-aways, or fliers as they call them, to inflame a situation at the police station, which ultimately led to the riot. Is that right?" "That is right," the investigator replied, "almost all of it came from the Federal Government."[17]

Kennedy was the only one of the dozens of Newarkers implicated by such testimony invited to appear before the subcommittee.[18] The weight of that testimony fell on him heavily. For once, an antipoverty worker, rather than a police officer or city official as in other inquiries, especially those of the government riot commissions, was put on the defensive. At the time of his appearance, Kennedy was on leave from the UCC's Area Board 2, where he worked as a community researcher. Like Tim Still and Esta Williams, he lived in the Hayes Homes complex across the street from the Fourth Precinct, so he had seen what happened there. He testified that he had indeed instructed another Area Board 2 worker to print up the fliers, and he admitted that he had also probably helped distribute placards for picketers to carry. But when one committee member asked Kennedy if he thought it was an appropriate use of area board money to promote a rally that ultimately led to riots, Kennedy replied that the purpose of the rally, in fact, had been to ensure there would not be another disturbance like the one Wednesday night when the cabdriver was brought in. "I do think it is part of my job," Kennedy finished, "to try and keep the community in harmony."[19]

In the McClellan hearings, then, we can discern the terms in which many members and advocates of the law enforcement community processed Newark's disorders. Though the subcommittee did not produce a final report, its inquiry into the relationship between War on Poverty programs and violence continued until the end of the year—giving particular attention to an OEO-funded program to keep the peace among rival youth gangs in Chicago—before it turned to campus unrest and black power organizations.[20] Its attacks certainly merged with the longer-standing political dissatisfactions with community action, like those of the city councilmen and Mayor Addonizio, dissatisfactions based more in a struggle over federal funds and job-making opportunities. But for the police, the issue was more about community action's purported involvement in promoting violence and the way its broader ethic of community access to and participation in police work had threatened, in their minds, officers' safety, their professional identity, and their ability to do their jobs.

To Newark police observers, Kennedy's methods, like those of the various forces of community action in general, had proved more destructive than harmonious. Power, then, had to devolve back to the established institutions of social order, the police department especially. Ironically, departmental leadership had initially welcomed the antipoverty program to Newark and had used it to help promote their ideal relationship with black Newarkers. The Police Athletic League had cosponsored a summer youth recreation program with the UCC, for example. But a month after the riots, citing incompetence, an attempt to usurp the league's functions, and the use of an allegedly Communist-affiliated campground, Anthony Giuliano, head of both the league and the local PBA, announced that he had cut ties with the antipoverty program and called for a federal investigation into its workings.[21] And officers had, albeit with some grumbling, opened themselves to federally funded attempts to improve their relationship with the black community. Now, it seemed, that community and its civil rights and antipoverty leaders had turned against them in the most vicious of ways. While they accused police of brutality—picketing their precincts, marching through the streets demanding the department expose itself to oversight by civilians—these agitators were, according to these narratives, gathering the kindling for the city's greatest racial conflagration and, with claims of police brutality, supplying the spark. And even though law enforcement had restored order to the city, they were still at it.

Back in Newark, the record was mixed on promoting this version of events and leveraging it to reinforce the police department's institutional autonomy. The city council did not give the police department a canine unit, for example, but it did provide the funds for a mountain of new equipment. And when the Governor's Commission, to take another example, recommended both that the city finally establish a civilian review board ("a Board of Police Commissioners") and that it give black police captains command of some precincts, police prevailed against one but not the other. Several local civil rights groups—including the NAACP, CORE, and the United Afro-American Association, which was founded by UCC vice president Willie Wright—had already proposed that Captain Edward Williams, who had been promoted and put in charge of the department's Community Relations Bureau soon after the riots, be given command of a precinct. The NAACP specifically suggested the Fourth Precinct.[22] And though Mayor Addonizio initially refused their request, he changed his mind after the Governor's Commission released its report. Two days later, in a meeting with the PBA's Anthony Giuliano, the mayor said he was determined to implement the commission's recommendations. The day after that, several hundred patrolmen gathered at the Hotel Douglas to protest the move. Transferring the current Fourth Precinct commander, Captain Charles Zizza, would be discrimination in reverse, Giuliano said. About one hundred officers picketed city hall, their signs reading "Keep Zizza at 4th" and "Mayor Cops Out."[23] Though Addonizio, for the third time, rejected a review board—this time suggesting an "ombudsman" instead—Captain Williams took over the Fourth Precinct in March without incident.[24]

In their efforts to turn state institutions (including the police department itself) away from the desires of community action and toward an emerging politics of law and order, local police were given tools by an unlikely benefactor. Presidential candidates Nixon and Wallace (and to some degree Humphrey) gave them a rhetorical boost from the campaign trail, but the Johnson administration offered the material resources out of which such a turn would be implemented locally. Those resources came from a new program updating the Office of Law Enforcement Assistance (OLEA), which back in 1966 had provided Newark the grant money to launch the Newark Police-Community Relations Training Program.

The update was generated by a combination of rising crime rates, the emergence of crime and civil disorder as national issues, and calls by law enforcement for greater federal aid to combat those trends.[25] Two weeks after the rioting ended in Newark, Police Director Spina wrote to the OLEA's associate director, hoping to adequately convey "the great sense of urgency that exists" in Newark for increased police training, better equipment, and an "aggressive" community relations program.[26] In April 1968, Councilmen Addonizio and Bernstein sent a telegram to President Johnson requesting a meeting to discuss the city's finances and its police department. The force was short 255 men, they wrote, and the council couldn't afford to pay higher salaries to spur recruitment. Without federal aid, they concluded, "the months ahead look dim in the city of Newark." When the telegram was bounced to the OLEA, its acting director responded by explaining that the Safe Streets Act then under consideration would greatly expand federal aid to law enforcement.[27]

The Omnibus Crime Control and Safe Streets Act of 1968, signed into law that June, established the federal government's first major block grant program to state and local governments.[28] In New Jersey—home to Newark, which, according to the FBI, had the highest crime rate in the nation among cities larger than 250,000 people—Governor Hughes was among the first to create an administrative unit, the State Law Enforcement Planning Agency (SLEPA), to receive the grants, set statewide priorities, review proposals from local police departments, and disburse the funds.[29] For Hughes, the program offered not only a helping hand to law enforcement, which, he said in a November 1968 speech in Newark, "may perhaps have fallen behind the accelerating rate of urbanization and the complexity of modern life." It also promised "the beginning of a new and wonderful revolution in the process of government."[30] From one angle, the legislation appears an early experiment in the devolution of federal responsibilities to the states, a trend that would quicken under President Nixon. Observers often noted block grants' roots in a desire to weaken federal control.[31] Indeed, the legislation was the product of Republican insistence that categorical grants to localities, which the Johnson administration had proposed and which were well liked by Democrats, be replaced by block grants to state planning agencies, which Republicans liked better, since, at that point, they controlled a majority of state houses.[32] Looked at from another angle, though, it is hard not to see it also as "devolution" upward, from some community participation to a new state-level agency removed from local concerns. That is what the new block grants must have looked like to those in Newark—the city Human Rights Commission, for example—who had used the earlier categorical grants to run the most ambitious police-community relations programs in the city.

That may have been what law enforcement agencies liked so much about the new program. Not only did it offer new funds, but it did so in a way that was removed from potential community interference. In New Jersey, they would only have to deal with their state agency, which was staffed and advised mostly by members of the police and justice systems (though Paul Ylvisaker served on SLEPA's advisory council).[33] Though SLEPA, after an intensive statewide planning process, offered "improvement of community relations" as one of the state's official areas of emphasis, no such program was proposed in Newark.[34] The city received funding for five projects in the first round of action grants. The Human Rights Commission received money to educate Newark students about the criminal justice system, the city Department of Health and Welfare to run a drug-prevention program for high schoolers, and the Newark Police Department to fund its Youth Aid Bureau (an antidelinquency agency) and to purchase walkie-talkies and "miniature teleprinters" that would be installed in patrol cars "to send printed information back to headquarters in a shorter time than a patrolman could write it out."[35] The following year, community relations no longer appeared as a stand-alone goal in SLEPA's guide for grant applications but was subsumed under "increase the efficiency and effectiveness of the criminal justice system in crime control." And even there, it was limited to the "establishment and training of community relations units in local police departments."[36]

New federal investment via block grants was one of two revolutions in late-1960s law enforcement, as defined by early experts in the burgeoning field of police studies. Those grants included many of the specific concerns expressed by Newark police officials, including the need for better equipment, salaries, and training. The second revolution, as one scholar wrote, was "a kind of decentralized self-help campaign" consisting of police banding together in fraternal organizations, social clubs, and unions.[37] Referred to by several different names—police militancy, blue power, the police rebellion—this movement drove the emergence of a minority consciousness among officers, which often took the form of demands for police rights, often set against rights claimed by civil rights communities, like Captain Zizza's right not to be transferred to make room for Newark's first black precinct commander.[38] The movement was driven nationally by a confluence of discontent rooted in several different sources: Supreme Court decisions, violent black rebellion, soaring crime rates, student un-

16. In the late 1960s, Newark police frequently mobilized to defend their professional interests. In November 1968, many participated in a sick-out strike to protest salaries they deemed unsatisfactory. © Media General Communications Holdings, LLC. (Newark Public Library / *Newark Evening News*)

rest, the expanding scope of police work, and the lousy pay they received for it (which, according to one widely cited source, was 33 percent less than what would moderately sustain a family of four in a large city).[39] In Newark, this was exacerbated by the sense that the black community, through the War on Poverty especially, was being given resources to foment rebellion, that the police department had reached out to them in unprecedented community relations efforts, that the riot was the ultimate community refusal of those efforts, and that officers had come under fire not only from rioters but from the liberal investigative commissions. New police mobilizations, the emergence of the police unions as strident mouthpieces for the rank and file, and the discourse of police self-defense, broadly conceived, were the result.

Though it was often said that such professionalization and political organizing pulled the police even further away from the communities they served, this does not quite capture the whole of what happened in Newark. While the distance between police and "the community" (as rendered by community action) continued to widen, the police and an increasingly agitated and mobilized segment of the city's shrinking white population grew closer together. This was a sort of distorted mirror image of how police-community relations was most often conceived. The phenomenon might have begun in the anti–review board fight during the summer of 1965, but it was renewed during the riots and, with even greater force, after the release of the commission reports in the spring of 1968. As in the summer of 1965, its most conspicuous form was the rise of citizens groups that blurred the lines between civilians and law enforcement.

Perhaps the best-known of these law-and-order community groups was one founded in the midst of the disorders, when a barrel-chested former marine, a black belt in karate and lifelong resident of the North Ward named Anthony Imperiale, organized his friends and neighbors into citizen patrols along the line separating their neighborhood from the Central Ward. When the riots broke out, the identification between the police department and certain segments of the city, especially the still largely white North Ward and the Vailsburg section at the western tip of the city, grew stronger and more intimate. With all patrolmen called to twelve-hour duty—mostly touring the immediate riot area or guarding its periphery—large swaths of the city were left without police protection. By far, the greatest concentrations of damage were located in the predominantly black Central and South Wards, but there had been scattered incidents of vandalism and looting in the North and West Wards, too.[40] These relatively untouched sections of the city suffered a palpable fear of black incursion nonetheless, and some residents took to their own defense. And though the immediate danger passed relatively quickly, the broader threat to the social order it portended helped maintain the patrols well into the next decade.

The patrols took earlier visions of police-community relations to their logical end. If the anti–review board forces during the summer of 1965 insisted that the NPD was *"our* police department" and the federally funded Community Relations Training Program promoted role-playing as a means to closer police-community ties, these North Ward patrollers now seemed to be saying "we *are* law enforcement." They were not temporarily playing the role or simply claiming solidarity with those who did professionally but adopting it as a stable component of their social identity in Newark. The line between members and advocates of the law enforcement community was breaking down.

Though Imperiale ran a patio-construction company and a dojo out of a storefront on North Seventh Street, he had once wanted to be a policeman. The only thing preventing it, he claimed, was the quarter inch he needed to meet the height requirement. When the riots came to Newark, however, and with much of the regular police force occupied in other neighborhoods, Imperiale took the opportunity to play the part anyway, flavoring it with his military and martial-arts experience. He called Governor Hughes a "chicken" for not sending in troops sooner and took matters into his own burly hands.[41] In defense of neighborhood, home, and family—but also in defense of a community's identity with a broader politics of law and order and the agents thereof—Imperiale organized dozens of men into small patrol units that roamed the North Ward on the lookout for troublemakers. They called themselves the North Ward Citizens Committee (NWCC).

A typical patrol started in the early evening and ended around midnight, when some of the men went home and others returned to the dojo to debrief. Patrolmen used whatever vehicles they owned (Imperiale drove an eight-year-old black Cadillac, for example) and equipped them with two-way radios so they could maintain contact with the volunteers who staffed the telephone back at headquarters, often members of the NWCC Women's Auxiliary. Though Imperiale had at first boasted of owning a helicopter and an armored car and insisted patrolmen wear military fatigues, he quickly backtracked. Individual members undoubtedly owned guns and Imperiale himself fondly exhibited his personal collection to those who asked, but the patrols were officially unarmed. And though there was some sense of militaristic uniformity in their makeshift headgear—blackened construction helmets on which they wrote "NWCC" in white letters—most

17. Anthony Imperiale became a media celebrity after Newark's riots. With the dread of black insurrection reaching feverish heights across the country, Imperiale's apparent fearlessness made him a hero to many white Americans. © Media General Communications Holdings, LLC. (Newark Public Library / *Newark Evening News*)

observers described them as simple vigilantes. They were not above street fighting or roughing up people they deemed threats, but, in the last instance, stated policy was to call in the real actors and have the police haul the suspects away for official processing.

The patrols and the crime-fighting incidents they entailed constituted only the most publicized aspect of the NWCC's activities. Imperiale's power base was built largely on services he provided to the community even before the riots broke out and that the NWCC continued afterward. Members provided escort services for elderly residents who needed help getting to the store or a doctor's appointment. They ran a first aid squad, complete with its own ambulance, for residents of the North Ward. And they spread their ideas about community self-defense and service, setting up independent chapters in other sections of the city (the West Ward and Ironbound

Citizens' Committees) and in surrounding suburbs (the Nutley-Belleville Citizens' Committee, for example), and allying with similarly minded groups in other cities.[42]

Though the North Ward Citizens Committee grabbed widespread attention—Imperiale had been profiled by the *New York Times*, *Look*, and *True* magazines and even had a short Dutch documentary film made about him before the end of the decade—several other citizen groups contended for the local spotlight. Taking the lead on the canine corps issue, for example, was a group established by a bus driver from Vailsburg named Donald Gottwerth. Though the rioting took place about three miles from his home in the Ivy Hill Apartments on the far western outskirts of the city, it made Gottwerth sick. The bus he drove traveled up and down Springfield Avenue, and he witnessed firsthand the mobs smashing, burning, and looting his city. Like so many agitated Newarkers had done before him and would do after, he printed up a flier and distributed it to his neighbors. His goals were vague, as a police intelligence officer found out when, under an assumed name, he telephoned Gottwerth the day the National Guard left Newark. As the officer described it, "He wants to start some sort of organization to impress on the politicians of Newark, and the State of New Jersey, that the white community do[es] not like the happenings of the past few days in Newark. He also wants the politicians to stop giving concessions to the Negro." Gottwerth did, however, suggest more specifically that the city force black Newarkers to clean up the mess they had made, instead of spending taxpayer dollars to hire outside contractors to do it. He suggested, too, that Governor Hughes publish statistics regarding the number of black unemployed, the reasons for their joblessness, the number of those unable to work because they drink too much, and the number who used their welfare checks to buy huge cars that even whites could not afford. Now that the troops were leaving the city, he explained, the white community was in danger. The solution, however, was not a vigilante-type group but an organized white political pressure organization, something to let the politicians know that they should stop worrying so much about the black vote and start worrying about the white one. The intelligence officer reported that Gottwerth believed that antipoverty money had been channeled to groups directly involved in the violence and that black people were savages when in groups, and he quoted him as saying, "There is going to be a lot of trouble even after this violence quiets down because the negro is after the white man." At the time, Gottwerth was unsure what he should call his nascent organization. He suggested to the undercover police officer

214 / Chapter Eight

that it might be something like "Citizens Indignation League." He did not have much money to pour into the effort, but he would go door to door in search of people of like mind.[43]

Within two weeks, Gottwerth had found a name, convinced at least one hundred people to join him, and earned a more concerted surveillance effort. When the new group—now called Loyal Americans for Law and Order (LALO)—held its inaugural meeting at a bridal shop on South Orange Avenue in Vailsburg, a Newark police detective was in attendance. Gottwerth presided and explained to those gathered who he was and what he hoped they could do together. The detective jotted down his words. LALO's primary goal, Gottwerth explained, would be to "combine the white Americans throughout the state to meet any foolish and ridiculous demands by the Negro organizations." He stressed that the group would be independent and nonpartisan. It was also, he emphasized, not racist.[44]

With its name and general mission established, LALO just needed a cause, and the city council's waffling on the issue of a police canine unit in early September provided one. The day before the council was to consider the question, LALO held another meeting, this time in the North Ward's most cavernous meeting facility, Thomm's Continental, on the corner of Park and Mount Prospect Avenues. The police department sent three trainees to conduct surveillance, but they failed to note the number of people in attendance or their composition. Given the venue, though, the numbers must have grown, perhaps because LALO had extended its reach beyond Vailsburg and into Imperiale's neighborhood. Whatever the case, the surveillance did reveal that the featured speaker that night was Patrolman Leonard Kowalewski, fresh off his appearance before the Senate committee considering the antiriot bill. The trainees' report is sparse on detail but does list the topics Kowalewski covered. He spoke, they wrote, "about the Canine Corps, and organizations such as United Community Union [sic], and the leaders Communist affiliations. The so called Police Brutality charges, and the Police Review Boards."[45]

Over the next week, LALO members listened despondently as an overwhelmingly black crowd cheered the council's rejection of a canine unit. So they joined local PBA officials in a picket line outside city hall, with signs reading "We Want Dogs in Vailsburg," "K-9 Cuts Crime," and "Only Criminals Are Afraid of K-9." They declared that "in no way" did they accept the council's decision and promised future demonstrations.[46] Two weeks later, they organized another rally at Thomm's. Once again, the featured speaker was apparently Patrolman Kowalewski, and this time, the police observers obtained a typescript of his speech.[47]

Kowalewski opened by asking the crowd to rise for a moment of silence in honor of Detective Fred Toto. When they finished, he explained that he and Toto had been rookies together twelve years earlier. He was a partner and a friend, and his "thoughts paralleled mine," Kowalewski said. Having implied Toto's blessing for what followed, the officer explained that the deceased's favorite expression was "What's it going to be?" And now he posed the same question to them. Would it be "law and order or anarchy?" He told them that there were people in Newark "who are strides ahead in stripping you of your protection—the law." These included the Newark Community Union Project and its leader, Tom Hayden ("a bit on the 'red side'"), and the United Community Corporation (the "dissidents" who "use the mimeograph machines to produce circulars of hate, [and] federal funds for the destruction of law and order through riots and disorders"). He saw them at work outside the Fourth Precinct ("the symbol of July 4th, Memorial Day, Veteran's Day and of Democracy") the night the violence started. They led the "storming" of "this American symbol," and they had been allowed to do it because the average Newarker had sat around at home wondering when someone else would do something to stop them. But here, this night at Thomm's, something was astir, and LALO had proven that Newark police officers were not alone. "You people do my heart good," he said. "I know you're trying to stabilize this monster."[48]

LALO showed up in force at the next council meeting, where Gottwerth accused council members of "yielding to mob rule." If it continued to oppose the canine unit, he told them, "you are committing political suicide." LALO's stomping and shouting helped earn a demonstration from Duke, the muscular German shepherd. And they cheered some more when the council approved a trial run.[49]

When the council reversed itself again and rejected the dogs, the main reason was that some of Newark's Catholic clergymen had urged them to reconsider. One monsignor explained that the issue was not dogs, but the "feelings" of Newark residents, and those feelings were "unpredictable enough" to warrant the reversal. Supporters of the canine unit, many Catholic themselves, felt betrayed. Packed into council chambers, they sparred with the opposition for over five hours. Don Gottwerth told the council that any change in their position would force "civilian anticrime patrols" and warned them that LALO would "use every means to recall gutless councilmen who are laying Newark open to racial lawlessness and economic chaos." Anthony Imperiale urged them to "back up the men in blue" if they wanted law and order in the city. When the priests voiced their opposition, members of the crowd called them "Father Groppi," after the leader of open-housing marches in Milwaukee. And when the monsignor asserted that they had the support of the archbishop himself, a Newark patrolman who had recently been named chairman of the PBA's own investigative commission turned to him furiously and shouted, "You can take this back to his Eminence, the Archbishop, that William Connelly, Catholic, wants to know where he was during the riots!"[50]

With the proposal seemingly dead as far as city lawmakers were concerned, LALO began a petition drive to have the issue put to a citywide referendum. The explanatory paragraph introducing the petition equated the police, well-behaved citizenry, and America itself by invoking its Constitution. "We the People of Newark," it read, "in order to form a more perfect Police Department, establish justice for the law abiding citizen, promote Police Independence from radical pressure groups, and secure the blessings of safety to ourselves and our children, do ordain to support OUR POLICE in all matters pertaining to their effectiveness and independence." Therefore, it continued, they submitted this petition to the city council to demand the canine corps issue be put before the people of Newark. It never happened.[51]

The racially charged episodes surrounding the proposed police canine unit were the chief rallying points for the emerging politics of white and police grievance in the months after the riots. The overarching threat of mass racial violence fed a variety of defensive postures: defense against interference in police autonomy and self-determination (if they needed dogs, they should get dogs), defense against geographic incursions (citizen policing of neighborhoods), and defense against physical threats to body, family, and home. At each moment, police and civilians were joined together in this movement. They shared membership in these new organizations, marched together on picket lines, attended meetings together, reinforced each other's work on the street, and confronted the city council together. This alliance worried Police Director Spina enough that he kept a close eye on it, but it was vital to the rank and file who participated, never more so than when they took the greatest hit to their institutional autonomy and cultural sense of themselves in the first few months of 1968. That was when the North Ward Citizens Committee and Anthony Imperiale, especially, burst forth with renewed energy and attracted attention from well beyond Newark's borders.

When the Governor's and Kerner Commissions released their reports, Imperiale offered as strident a denunciation as any police or union leader. He marched outside city hall with protestors carrying signs that read "We

Want the Truth" and "NJ Riot Report is Anti-Police." He told the *Newark Evening News* that *Report for Action* "once again had made the Police Department a whipping post" and that he believed it had swept the real cause for rioting under the rug: "If there was a complete breakdown between police and the community, it was caused by Negro and white instigators, many of them not even residing in Newark." Part of the problem, he said on a CBS radio program, was that Governor Hughes himself had changed his mind about the nature of the violence, initially dubbing it a "criminal insurrection" and then retracting that statement. As for the Kerner Commission, Imperiale said, "I don't think the investigation should have been printed, because it discredited our police department and it discredited a lot of other things."[52]

Part of Imperiale's worry was that the commissions would feed an existing attempt to bring the Newark Police Department under federal receivership. During the riots, officials from the state American Civil Liberties Union had circulated a flier encouraging residents of the riot area "to preserve physical evidence of police destruction." Before store- and homeowners replaced their broken windows, the flier urged, they should take pictures of them. They should keep any shell casings they found littering the streets and sidewalks. And if they were victims of or witnesses to police brutality, they should phone the ACLU or the Newark Legal Services Project to tell their story.[53] Some of the material collected served as the basis for a suit the NLSP, ACLU, and several other organizations brought against the city, claiming "police lawlessness," as one ACLU official put it, and aiming to put the department under federal receivership. The suit was *Kidd v. Addonizio*, Kidd being Marion Kidd, the woman who had founded the Area Board 3 Welfare Mothers Committee's consumer buying club.[54]

In April 1968, when the state chapter of the ACLU held its annual meeting at Newark's Military Park Hotel, the North Ward Citizens Committee joined the Women's Organization for the Return of Law and Decency (WORLD) on a picket line. Though founded in February 1968 by two male police officers, WORLD was "dedicated to demonstrate by any and all lawful and peaceful methods that the majority of women are firmly united by their role of motherhood to make the community a better place in which to work and live."[55] It was sometimes spoken of as the NWCC's "sister" organization and sometimes as its women's auxiliary. Whatever the exact nature of the relationship, they were united against those who threatened the one city institution still dedicated, as they saw it, to maintaining peace and order in Newark.

The trouble began when the ACLU's state education director showed up for the meeting an hour early to take care of last-minute details. NWCC and WORLD members had already gathered in front of the hotel, many wearing military fatigues and helmets, and some carrying signs reading "ACLU Are Pinks" and "Untie Policemen's Hands." As the official passed through their picket line carrying her own ACLU signs, she was shoved by a man trying to rip them from her arms. When she made her way into the hotel, she phoned Henry di Suvero, the ACLU's state director. When he arrived, she pointed out her assailant, and di Suvero asked a police sergeant at the scene to arrest the man. The sergeant reportedly responded that he had the man's name, he knew about the accusation, but he wouldn't be taking him in.

As he regrouped, di Suvero felt a slight bump, as he put it, from someone on the picket line, and a woman angrily accused him of shoving her. Then a man in a civilian dress shirt came off the line, placed di Suvero under arrest, and escorted him to a nearby patrol car with the help of another off-duty policeman. While in custody, one account of the incident says, di Suvero "was struck by the man who heads the vigilante group," undoubtedly meaning Imperiale himself. Di Suvero was charged with assaulting the woman (who, it turned out, was the sister-in-law of the arresting officer, who, it turned out, was one of WORLD's founders), resisting arrest, using loud and offensive language, threatening a police officer, and assault and battery on the arresting officer.[56]

At the end of the week, the state ACLU filed a federal lawsuit seeking to "break the nexus" between the Newark Police Department and the city's "vigilante" groups, specifically the NWCC and WORLD. At a press conference at national ACLU headquarters in New York City, di Suvero declared that "Newark is now a vigilante-controlled city." The immediate impetus for the suit had been his arrest, but the complaint alleged that during and since the city's riots, "white vigilante groups" in conjunction with the police had been violating the constitutional rights of the city's black citizens and their allies. "What we see happening in Newark," the national ACLU director explained, "is similar to what has happened in many Southern cities— the police and vigilante groups working hand in hand." The suit was based on section 1983 of the Ku Klux Klan Act of 1871, as interpreted by a 1961 Supreme Court ruling. Under that section, individuals can sue state actors for violating their civil rights.[57] The suit therefore argued that the line had blurred between the police department and these citizen groups to such an extent that the latter had effectively become state actors. But by insisting on applying the label "vigilante" to these organizations—marking them as groups acting in the interest of the prevailing order, but outside of it—the

ACLU established rhetorically what they sought judicially: a separation between the state and the neighborhood groups acting as its agents.

Governor Hughes shared the ACLU's concern. Three weeks after it filed suit, he sent a bill to the state legislature that would establish stiff penalties for anyone participating in the "paramilitary" activities of "vigilante" groups, including training in guerilla warfare and collecting or distributing weapons for that purpose. The immediate spur to Hughes's action was a meeting with Mayor Addonizio, Police Director Spina, and several other city and state officials to address rising racial tensions in Newark. LeRoi Jones joined the meeting for two hours, and Imperiale for about one. Governor Hughes had intended to focus the meeting on the current crisis, but it quickly spun out to the broader issue of citizen law enforcement. He was blunt about his proposed legislation: it was aimed primarily at Anthony Imperiale and the North Ward Citizens Committee. According to the governor, Imperiale objected to being called a vigilante and argued that his organization served many social functions, only one of which was the maintenance of law and order in Newark. "I told him," the governor later told the press, "that the brown shirts in Germany started the same way." When he implored Imperiale to dissolve the NWCC, the North Ward leader told him that was beyond his power.[58]

Soon after the meeting, Spina himself announced that his officers were now forbidden to join "extremist groups." He refused to identify any such groups by name, but reminded officers that they should show "greater restraint and caution than the average citizen." PBA president Anthony Giuliano vowed to resist the order, charging that it was a violation of officers' constitutional rights. While the PBA did not promote extremist groups, he said, "we do discourage any moves to penalize police and relegate them to second-class citizenship."[59]

The ACLU's suit, the governor's bill, and Spina's ban were crucial tests of state boundaries: would the state accept the expansion of its monopoly on legitimate force practiced by the white citizens of the North Ward and their community policing efforts? Governor Hughes understood that the legitimacy of the state as presently constituted was at stake. "Under no circumstances can our society depart from the principle that protection of the public is exclusively the province of fully authorized public officials," he said after urging the state senate to act on his bill. "No private citizen has the right to act as a vigilante and attempt, without legal authority or any obligation to the public, to exercise police powers."[60] The senate approved Hughes's bill two days later, and the assembly quickly followed. The ACLU's suit, however, dragged on for two more years before being dismissed as moot in 1970 because, by then, the police officials named were no longer in office.[61]

The suit was moot in another sense. On the same day the senate approved the antivigilante bill, June 24, 1968, Anthony Imperiale announced he would order the cessation of the NWCC's main law enforcement activity—its street patrols. He declared that the pending legislation had nothing to do with his decision, that the patrols had been successful, and that two-thirds of the city, by his own estimate, had been made safe again. Now the NWCC would shift its focus to a new project: Imperiale's candidacy for the city council in an upcoming special election. If he could not join the state as a quasi-police officer, he would do so as an elected official on a platform consisting of, in his words, "law and order and obedience to the law, the untying of policemen's hands and the removal of politics from the police department." Imperiale called this recourse to the ballot box "the American way of doing things," and contrasted his move with that of "the black radicals who advocate stomp, burn, and bang-bang."[62]

In reality, Imperiale had begun laying the groundwork for his turn to the ballot box months earlier. Since at least February 1968, the Newark Change of Government Association had been gathering signatures on a petition to set in motion the process by which the city's municipal charter could be reformed, exactly as the forerunners of community action, like Willard Heckel and Alan Lowenstein, had done in the mid-1950s. The energy behind the movement seems to have been provided primarily by the NWCC and LALO. In the middle of May, Samuel Raffaello, head of the new Change of Government Association and Imperiale's attorney and eventual campaign manager, filed a fifteen-thousand-signature petition with the city clerk. He argued that the current form of government "leads to a dictatorship" and that "the present mayor and council are ineffective, weak and vacillating."[63]

Raffaello's dubious logic aside, it is not clear what motivated the call for charter reform. Though George Richardson argued it was a "racist attempt to turn the clock back," the old form of government, under which city commissioners were all chosen at large and a mayor was chosen from among them, might have eventually worked against Imperiale in a now majority-black city.[64] But the vision might have been shorter term, Imperiale believing he could turn out more voters, regardless of larger trends in Newark's racial demographics. And in any case, the potential payoff was clear: he could become mayor, of course, but he might also have had his eyes on being the commissioner in charge of public safety and, therefore, the police department. Whatever the case—and Imperiale seems not to have publicly revealed his motivations—the petitions turned out to be so riddled with duplications, nonresidents, and unregistered voters that over six thousand names were cut by the city clerk, and the reform effort failed.[65]

In August 1968, three months before the special city council elections, Imperiale got his first taste of electoral victory. The Model Cities Program in Newark by that time had established, under intense community pressure, a new mechanism for ensuring some community participation in its workings. An elected Model Cities Neighborhood Council would share veto power over programs with the city administration. (The latter's Community Development Administration would still run all the programs, however.) The designated redevelopment area included half the Central Ward and parts of the North Ward, making Imperiale eligible, based on his residency, to run. When the votes were tallied, he had won more than any other candidate in *any* of the thirteen districts up for grabs.[66] In a bizarre editorial, the *New York Times*, while noting the election of "one white extremist leader," nonetheless called the results "one of the most encouraging developments in another bleak summer of racial tension."[67]

Within weeks of the Model Cities election, the *Times'* optimism proved premature. In the early morning hours of August 25, 1968, the brick-paved six-hundred block of North Seventh Street was rocked by bombs placed in two drain pipes and under a parked car outside Imperiale's headquarters. The explosions shattered windows and air-conditioning units up and down the street. They blew the hood off a car. No one was injured, and Imperiale himself was having a drink with a friend in a local tavern. As friends swept up the shattered remains of the dojo's front windows, Imperiale vowed to increase the patrols that he had reinstated (calling them an escort service) just days before the election. The patrols had always been the key to his celebrity, were quite possibly the reason for his resounding victory at the polling place, and once again seemed necessary for the protection of the North Ward. On weeknights, there would now be ten rather than four patrols, and on weekends fifteen or twenty rather than ten. "After this," Imperiale said, "the people are demanding they be increased."[68]

When it was bombed, Imperiale's dojo was festooned with a banner identifying it as the campaign headquarters for his pursuit of an at-large city council seat and informing passersby that the Imperiale ticket advocated "law and order for everyone." The day after, Imperiale drove down to city hall and filed a petition for the November 5 election. He had collected almost two thousand signatures, over six hundred more than needed. If he were elected, he promised, "you can be sure appeasement will not be found in my vocabulary."[69] When he returned to North Seventh Street, he talked to the press about the bombing. He said he believed black militants had done it and warned that he would not be responsible for what his neighbors might do if something like this happened again. "You know, it's ironic," he said. "They label our organization racist and vigilantes, but we've never done anything like this." But he also turned to his aides and told them, "Our job is to keep things calm."[70]

Over the next two months, Imperiale campaigned relentlessly for law and order, the "untying" of policemen's hands, and in support of George Wallace's presidential candidacy. It worked. Once again, he won more votes than any other candidate. (Taking the second of the two open at-large city council seats was Anthony Giuliano, by then the former president of Newark's PBA local.) Supporters crammed into Imperiale's headquarters for his victory rally. He ominously promised them that if Mayor Addonizio did not stand up to "the radicals," he would be in big trouble. "We're going to support the police, right or wrong."[71]

Producers at NBC television asked Imperiale to appear on their *Man in Office* news program several days after the election. He told viewers that, as councilman, he would "strive toward meeting with conservative and moderate Negroes" in Newark. He claimed that those moderate forces had fallen victim to an unfettered black radicalism that all levels of government had appeased, while simultaneously and hypocritically attacking the North Ward Citizens Committee. He vowed to go into the Central Ward and let its residents know that they must get together. When asked about the findings of the recent riot commissions, Imperiale argued that the pinning of blame on white racism revealed only that "somewhere along the line we've got a bunch of liars and a bunch of hypocrites." He had seen the arson and the looting, he reminded the interviewer, and Detective Fred Toto had been a friend.[72]

But the issues that propelled Imperiale to the city council did not go away, and in May 1969, a night of looting in the South Ward followed the shooting of a black teenager by a police officer, this time a black one. Police were accused of brutality in their response to the looting, which mostly occurred in the area around Clinton Avenue and Bergen Street. Mayor Addonizio asked the United Community Corporation to deploy peacekeepers to the area. When calm was restored and the curfew lifted, he praised the UCC for its efforts. This time, there was no gunfire, and no one was killed.[73]

Imperiale was not pleased with how things went down. He felt that Addonizio should have used more force earlier in the outbreak. He felt that, as he said, "we've been kneeling too much to the perpetrators of arson, looting, and physical assault on decent citizens. People must be made to respect the law and respect the rights of all citizens even if the Police Department must use excessive force." The mayor's latest approach to rioting and its suppression had convinced him of one thing, though: Addonizio had to go. To that end, Imperiale announced his bid for the mayoralty.[74]

NINE

Departures

In the eyes of many government and police officials, blame for the Newark riots rightly fell somewhere within an undifferentiated mass militancy and its efforts to bring the black community into the workings of city institutions. Newark was a hotbed of such experimentation, and people came to town to participate in its ferment. Among them, there are differentiations to be made—such was the nature of experimentation—even if their accusers rarely did so. Though there was a period during which a remarkably broad range of actors intent on furthering the cause of black power (an idea that itself contained multitudes) tried their hand with various forms of community action, some did so with more skepticism than others, and some did so not at all. For many proponents of community action, the riot became the lens through which they judged the relative merits of the experiment. In its wake, they had to decide whether their newly and sharply honed views would keep them in Newark or draw them elsewhere. While much of Newark's political ferment moved in one direction—toward city hall—some pointed themselves in another.

Among the most influential and well known of these sojourners were Tom Hayden, the New Left luminary who had come to Newark with a handful of Economic Research and Action Project colleagues to organize an interracial employment campaign, and Nathan Wright Jr., a middle-aged Episcopal priest and black power theorist, better known for his poetry, pacifism, and professorial demeanor than any fist raising. Though opponents often lumped them together with the larger host of riot enablers, they had come to Newark from very different places, performed very different work while there, and, when it came time to leave, traveled very different routes.[1] Though their stays in Newark were relatively brief, each affected the city's political development in small but lasting ways and, through their writings, brought it before a national audience. Their personal political movements into and out of Newark helped define the contours of Great Society liberalism, just as it began to bear its most significant fruits.

By the time he arrived in Newark in 1964, Nathan Wright Jr.'s notions of black power had already begun to coalesce. The son of a solidly middle-class couple who had met at the Tuskegee Institute, he had been raised in a strong tradition of black self-help.[2] Upon being drafted into the army in 1945, Wright declared himself a pacifist, and two years later he became the youngest member of the Congress of Racial Equality's Journey of Reconciliation.[3] In the fall of 1947, he moved east to attend the Episcopal Theological Seminary in Cambridge, Massachusetts. Within a year, he launched a local CORE affiliate, organized tests of antidiscrimination policies at local hotels and restaurants, and in the early 1950s was named CORE's New England field director.[4]

Soon after, Wright began channeling his energies more into his pastoral and academic work than direct-action campaigns. After earning his bachelor's degree from the Episcopal seminary, he was ordained a priest in December 1950 and became the rector of Saint Cyprian's Church in Roxbury. There, he immersed himself in the life of his parish. He became close with the family of a young Louis Farrakhan, met Malcolm X, and helped them recruit local teens who, he thought, would never be reached by the Christian church.[5] Yet Wright's thinking on black power was given shape more by his struggle to discern the proper role of the church in urban black neighborhoods than it was by emerging forms of radicalism. That struggle consumed him for the next twenty years and took shape across a range of writings, from his early sermons and poetry to the later books that earned him a national audience, and shifted over time from theological to sociological considerations.[6]

As the 1960s dawned in Roxbury, Wright devised a new mission for the urban church—a liturgical renewal that would stoke the divine light in each congregant—and began pushing it out into the streets.[7] At the core of his thinking lay a "theology of transfiguration," which, in a 1963 *Christianity Today* essay, he contrasted with a "theology of identification." In an identification model, he explained, "God's gracious condescension" to become human in the figure of Jesus served as the sole model for the church's urban work: the church moved into inner cities and patronized them as congregations in need of special services. But, Wright reminded readers, the incarnation was only the first part of the story and, in terms of the church's urban mission, far less important than the resurrection. The impulse should be not only to serve but to *uplift* in the distinctly Christian sense of redemption, "the ultimate uplift of all life to the plane where God would have it be."[8] What, exactly, the church was to do on the ground, in the streets of its cities, was not yet clear. Nor was Wright's theology yet explicitly tied to any notion of a specifically *black* power. But by the time he left Boston and moved to Newark in 1964—to get down "into the thick of things," as he later explained—he was on the verge of making that connection.

The Newark Episcopal diocese hired Wright to head its new Department of Urban Work. The previous December, a three-alarm fire had devastated St. Philip's Church in the Central Ward. Founded in 1847 as a predominantly black parish, it had thrived during the postwar years while the nearby congregation at Trinity Cathedral—one of the oldest in Newark and the headquarters of the Newark diocese—was depleted by white migration out of the city. The rector of St. Philip's and the local bishop spied an opportunity in the fire: why not merge the congregations? After taking communion together in October 1966, members of both congregations approved their plan. Since the black congregation outnumbered its downtown white counterpart, the diocese's central parish became majority-black overnight.[9]

Wright took the opportunity afforded by this racial shift to make concrete his new theology of black transfiguration. In a move that flirted with prevailing forms of community action, he proposed a community-organizing effort that would encompass the black communities of Newark, Jersey City, and Paterson. Rather than plug into existing organizing projects, which, in Newark at least, were predominantly neighborhood based, Wright's proposed tri-city organizing agency would work on an explicitly racial logic. The problem, as he saw it, was that the black community was not a geographical entity. Its problems could not be addressed city by city (let alone neighborhood by neighborhood) by isolated agencies but had to be confronted by a larger, unified organization. But like those other efforts, especially those connected to the War on Poverty, Wright saw the need for a larger coordinative rather than programmatic structure. He aimed to bring black people together, not to tell them what to do. In a proposal for the new organization, Wright wrote that it would provide a much-needed "power fulcrum for change" that would provide for the "self-development of the Negro people out of a total culture of poverty."[10]

When Stokely Carmichael raised the cry of black power in June 1966, and many Americans shuddered at what they perceived to be a shocking turn in the civil rights movement, Wright greeted the development with only the shock of recognition. Soon after, during a meeting in Harlem of black clergymen to discuss the growing controversy over black power, he pointed out that the fundamental idea, if not the phrase itself, was any-thing but new. After noting that the idea of power suffused black history from slave rebellions and John Brown to W. E. B. Du Bois and A. Philip Randolph, he warned against forming a hasty consensus on black power's meaning and urged that it be allowed "flexible implications, for no two individuals can perceive of, and assert, their own validity and place in pre-cisely identical ways." And if the nation could successfully develop the un-tapped human resources of its black citizens, black power would play "a restorative and conserving force in American life." He made the case that black power need not be destructive and violent but could be creative and redemptive.[11]

In relatively peaceful Newark, in the months before the summer of 1967, Wright used the recent waves of violence in other cities to articu-late his vision most fully. In *Black Power and Urban Unrest: Creative Pos-sibilities,* he sought to recast black power and emphasize its ties, as he saw them, to Christianity and deep national traditions at a time when racial violence had amplified its alarming "surface qualities" and called attention to the failings of postwar liberalism. The key historical turning point had come during World War II, Wright argued, when the racial radicalism of the interwar years yielded to racial liberalism. Since then, integration had not brought black Americans into the economic mainstream, and public and private agencies had worked more toward the amelioration of ghetto grievances than the adjustment of basic power relations. Liberal efforts—including the Great Society, in which Wright saw little more than the provi-sion of basic services to the ghetto—had produced "almost a race of beg-gars" and "a slave mentality of dependence." In this context, rioting was "an ironic sign of hope," evidence that black Americans' innate humanity had not been completely quashed. He concluded that liberalism's failings, not black power, had caused the riots. Only black power, then, and not more liberalism, would end them.[12]

By the time *Black Power and Urban Unrest* was published in early July 1967, Wright was well known within black political and theological circles. When Adam Clayton Powell Jr. formed a committee to formulate plans for the first National Conference on Black Power, he made Wright a member. And after Powell, because of mounting legal troubles, resigned his position as chair of the committee, the members voted to have Wright replace him, though only after some debate that reportedly centered on the question of whether Wright was too "bourgeois" and moderate to hold the position. For the time being, the more radical committee members told him, his connections and access to resources were needed and, in the end, he listened to and respected their perspectives.[13] Tensions continued throughout the spring, as committee members chided Wright for exercising dictatorial powers.[14] Despite the friction, the committee largely held together because at the heart of its vision was a commitment to black unity. Wright was apparently not the best practitioner of this ideal, but he was among its greatest theoreticians and publicists. In a position paper written for the committee, he declared the basic purpose of the black power conference to be "unity, not unanimity" and urged his colleagues to think of "our common mind" as having many crosscurrents, but as nonetheless "motivated and shaped by a singleness of purpose."[15]

Operational unity ultimately carried the day, and the committee finalized plans for a four-day conference beginning July 20, 1967. Because of its relative affordability and proximity to large concentrations of black Americans and because Wright could secure the use of local facilities (including the Episcopal diocese's Cathedral House) as conference headquarters, Newark was chosen as the host city.[16]

Tom Hayden grew up in at least modest comfort in tree-lined Royal Oak, Michigan, which he might have described as Camus did the setting of his novel *The Plague*: "Glamourless, soulless, the town of Oran ends by seeming restful and, after a while, you go complacently to sleep there."[17] Though politics, as he later explained, passed largely over his young head, he imbibed an inchoate sense of alienation from postwar Beat and youth cultures. It was "the boring and prearranged nature" of his suburban, middle-class existence "that caused the first tiny irritations." Since it seemed to him that "everything important had to be discussed" outside "the proper institutions," that irritability would drive him away from home and church and toward new frontiers in political and personal experience, first at his town's local youth hangouts and eventually, by a circuitous route, to the other side of the world.[18]

The most important stop on that journey was his first encounter with the Student Nonviolent Coordinating Committee. He met several members at the 1960 convention of the moderate (and covertly CIA-funded) National Student Association. "Fresh from beatings and jail . . . they quoted not Marx but the Talmud, not Mao but Camus," he remembered. They were models of commitment and action, students who acted on their own initiative and made decisions democratically and, seemingly, without fear. Looking back later, he wrote that "this was a key turning point, the moment my political identity began to take shape."[19]

That identity was also forged in relationship to the corruptions of the state. If young civil rights activists were Hayden's model of personal commitment and democratic participation, the possibilities of their politics often ran against a seemingly immovable Democratic hegemony built on a foundation of southern alliances. As a field secretary for the newly formed Students for a Democratic Society, Hayden traveled to McComb, Mississippi, in 1961. There, he was deeply affected by the young civil rights activists who met under the cover of night and draped thick blankets over their windows for safety, and he endured his first beating while curled up in a protective, nonviolent crouch. Soon after, aching and swollen, he traveled to Washington, DC, to meet with Justice Department officials. He told Assistant Attorney General Burke Marshall of the need for federal protection of civil rights workers. When Marshall responded by asking if there were any way to persuade the activists to leave those dangerous areas, Hayden "began to feel that we had been officially abandoned."[20]

Later that year, in a jail cell in Albany, Georgia, his McComb experience still raw, Hayden thought hard about his role in the southern civil rights movement. Rather than traveling around from campaign to campaign and jail to jail for SDS, an organization that was "little more than a mailing list," he decided it was time to carry SNCC's model of organizing forceful cadres of local leaders to new sections of the country.[21] At the University of Michigan, about forty student activists committed themselves to building such a movement and asked Hayden to write a draft manifesto for a new SDS. In its final form, adopted at the organization's summer gathering the next year in Port Huron, the manifesto located hope in its "regard [for] men as infinitely precious and possessed of unfulfilled capacities for reason, freedom, and love." In this, SDS self-consciously diverged from what it deemed the mid-twentieth century's proclivity to see "man" as highly manipulable and "inherently incapable of directing his own affairs."[22] Given the centrality of this proclivity, citizens' awakening to their own virtue and power would have to be fostered and organized by a new class of historical agents. It would not grow out of received ideology or, given a ruling liberal regime that fostered cold war with the Soviet Union and détente with southern segregationists, the state but would be sought in the authentically human encounters of what C. Wright Mills called "face-to-face publics." The social system these young activists sought was "a democracy of individual participation" in which each person would "share in those social decisions determining the quality and direction of his life" and in which society would "be organized to encourage independence in men and provide the media for their common participation."[23]

After his southern sojourn, with a new call to action in place and repeated national crises—the Cuban Missile Crisis, the dogs and bombs of Birmingham, the assassination of a president—demonstrating the possibility and the *need* for radical change, Hayden encouraged fellow student activists to "leave all that academic crap behind" and transplant the ERAP organizing model pioneered in Chester, Pennsylvania, to inner cities around the country.[24]

Hayden, of course, went to Newark. He arrived in the oppressive heat of July 1964, after an all-night drive, and looked around the first black ghetto he would come to know intimately. Stepping out into the street, he was struck briefly by the physical landscape—"scores of furniture stores, foul-smelling markets, and cheap record shops lined the baking streets of tar"— but more powerfully by the people he saw: "Young people holding school books in one hand and holding radios to their ears with the other crossed the street. Mothers carried large bags of groceries while trying to keep trailing children out of the traffic. A few men stood outside a bar in animated argument. A police car slowly cruised by, the officers glancing at me, the only white who was clearly not a merchant."[25] Here he and a host of others would work to build an authentic community that would confront the power structures muffling human potential. While much of the local state apparatus eyed them warily, one slim administrative arm of the federal War on Poverty reached out to them, and they tentatively grasped it in the hopes that it might serve as one medium for their "common participation."

A few short months after the publication of *Black Power and Urban Unrest* and a week before the National Conference on Black Power opened, Nathan Wright found himself where he had wanted to be when he took the job in Newark: the thick of things. The Wright family had moved into a house in bordering Orange (because of Newark taxes, he later explained), and every day Wright would drive from his nearly all-white suburban neighborhood along Springfield Avenue to the downtown offices of the Episcopal diocese. On the evening of July 13, Wright, his wife, and their teenage daughter climbed into the family car to make the trip to his office to pick up a package. They knew of the previous night's disturbance at the Fourth Precinct but realized only as they were leaving that they would pass close by. Curiosity outweighing caution, they approached the intersection of Springfield and Belmont at around 9:30. They parked the car and got out. Small crowds of thirty to fifty people, mostly men, were gathered on each of the four corners. They heard a loud thud and the sound of glass raining down on concrete, and "almost immediately there was chaos," Wright later wrote. "Men ran by with bottles of liquor in their hands and under their arms. The intersection swarmed with people suddenly out of nowhere." He sent his wife and daughter home in a cab, but stayed behind "to see at firsthand something of what I had studied and taught as the anatomy of black urban distress."[26]

Alone, Wright circled back to Springfield Avenue, followed it to the corner of Bergen Street, and came face to face with hundreds of people tensely milling about a police roadblock. A bottle shattered in the street a distance from the intersection. It was precisely 10:05, Wright remembered. One of the officers manning the roadblock pulled a rifle from his patrol car and fired aimlessly up into the surrounding buildings. Wright pulled his car to the curb, got out, stormed up to the officer, and scolded him. He told the officer that his indiscriminate shooting was not only against orders but was provoking the crowd to greater heights of anger. "Looking with pity at the policeman who, still holding his rifle, towered over me, I added in a moralistic tone of sadness, 'Shame, Shame, Shame!'" Wright had had enough. He returned to his car and drove out of Newark, the sounds of the crowds along Springfield Avenue and the wailing of sirens fading out behind him.[27]

On the evening of July 12, 1967, Tom Hayden was outside a friend's Newark law office, tossing around a football. While Hayden went long, a call came in reporting trouble in the Central Ward. The pair arrived at the Fourth Precinct just in time to see the first Molotov cocktail light up its outer wall. They watched the crowds milling about the Hayes Homes in a scene Hayden later compared to the storming of the Bastille.[28] For the next several days, he walked among crowds of rioters, asking questions and collecting testimony.

The more he moved about and the more people he talked to, the more obvious it became that the violence in Newark was of two kinds. As the state police and National Guard arrived, the riot had turned from the almost joyous attack on property perpetrated by black residents to the storm of lethal gunfire unleashed by the occupiers. As the weekend drew to a close and Governor Hughes searched for alternatives to the violence, Hayden and Bob Curvin were invited to meet with him. State troopers carrying automatic weapons picked Hayden up at the Newark Legal Services office, and as they traveled around the outskirts of the city, Hayden understood how the troopers could believe themselves to be engaged in war. "Each group of blacks turning the corner might be the enemy," he later wrote. "None could be talked to or trusted. It was an urban Vietnam."[29] As in Vietnam, the escalation would have to stop, so Hayden and Curvin emphatically urged the governor to call an immediate end to the occupation. The next morning, Hughes did.[30]

A month later, the *New York Review of Books* published Hayden's account of the riot, all supported, as it said, by newspaper and eyewitness accounts, under the title "The Occupation of Newark." It was a strongly narrative piece, rarely pausing to reflect on social conditions in the city or Hayden's writerly motivations. He divides the riot into two periods, the first couple of days, during which "people felt as though for a moment they were creating a community of their own," and, after darkness fell late Thursday and Governor Hughes declared the city in "open rebellion," the subsequent occupation and terror. The conclusion was clear: "the military, especially the Newark police," had not only triggered the riot but had brought to bear a murderous force "not in response to snipers, looting, and burning, but in retaliation against the successful uprising of Wednesday and Thursday nights." On the issue's cover, the *Review* printed a diagram of a Molotov cocktail: a glass bottle one-third full of dirt and "soap powder," two-thirds full of "gasoline (from pump)," and plugged with a rag and a clothesline fuse.[31]

Once the violence in Newark had confirmed their worst fears about black power, state and local officials hastily called for the National Conference on Black Power's cancellation.[32] Nathan Wright remained adamant that to move, let alone cancel, the conference would be "inflammatory." The riots notwithstanding, he argued, the conference still enjoyed the support of many church and business groups and, rather than fuel more violence, would actually help stem the tide. All other efforts having failed, he said, "the basic problems of the Negro community are in the hands of Negroes themselves to deal with."[33] A conference call to the other members of the planning committee confirmed Wright's inclination: they refused to bow to the power structure that, they believed, had caused the violence in the first place. Conference-goers supported their decision: not one registrant canceled in the wake of the rioting. In fact, registrations skyrocketed, surpassing 450 in the days before the conference (only 200 had been expected) and eventually exceeding 1,000.[34] On the appointed day, delegates arrived in droves. Barricades still lined certain streets, but a sign hanging in the front window of a downtown beauty school informed all passersby, "We have faith in Newark and all its people."[35]

Registration forms had invited "all segments of the black community" to attend and many did: delegates represented over 190 organizations, mostly from the United States, but several from overseas.[36] For the *Newark Evening News*, this diversity registered most clearly in the delegates' personal appearance and garb: Ron Karenga's flawlessly shaved head, other delegates' Afros, and others' more "conventional hairstyles"; sandals and high-heeled shoes; dungarees and "conventional business suits."[37] But the range of ideas attendees espoused and the organizations they represented surpassed the diversity of outward appearance. "From the 'little-old-ladies-in-tennis-shoes' of the civil rights movement—the Urban League—and its partner in conservatism, the NAACP, to the bearded militants of RAM (Revolutionary Action Movement) and the young firebrands of SNICK ('man, don't call us "Non-Violent"—call us SNICK'),'" wrote one planning committee member, "black people registered as delegates. Wearing somber Ivy-leagued sum-

18. Nathan Wright Jr. and Ron Karenga at the National Conference on Black Power, July 20, 1967. Wright strove to achieve what Karenga called "operational unity" within the movement, even though his own emerging market-based notions of empowerment positioned him near the movement's outskirts. (AP)

mer suits, flamboyant African robes, open-neck sport shirts, faded blue jeans, hippie beads and mini-skirts, black people sat together and swapped dreams."[38] Dick Gregory opened the conference on Thursday, July 20, by telling those gathered that "some colored folks gonna see some niggers and some niggers gonna see some Uncle Toms, and each one gonna find out he didn't know how beautiful the other one could be."[39]

Upon arrival, delegates paid their registration fee of twenty-five dollars (meals included) and signed up for their choice of fourteen workshops. Areas of expertise and concentration varied widely, from the potential role of black youth in bringing about black power to that of black professionals; from black power through black politics to black power through economic development; and from black power in the home to black power in the city and the world. Resolutions were to be hammered out in the workshops and then presented at a final plenary session to be accepted or rejected by the whole body of delegates.[40] Only two meetings were open to the public, but the press was briefed each day. Wright explained the reasoning behind the closed-door format in a statement released shortly before the conference opened. Black power was not about rejection of or withdrawal from American society, he wrote, but about black solidarity for the good of the entire nation. The conference, therefore, would "be an assembly of black Americans, as in an intimate family gathering, to set our own house in order and to work for the unity of Black People and the greatest good for all Americans."[41]

The promise of a constructive unity didn't escape the eye of the editorial board of the *New York Times*, which ran two glowing columns about the conference on its third and fourth days. One noted the many meanings of black power in evidence and concluded that the conference "was probably the most diverse group of Negroes ever to assemble in this country."[42] "The words 'black power' suggest chauvinism and militancy for some dark purpose," the other began. "They need not. . . . The National Conference on Black Power now meeting in Newark could do much to bring a constructive meaning to the phrase."[43]

But with barricades still up along Springfield Avenue and the graves of riot victims still fresh, some people refused to regard the closed-door meeting of black power advocates with any hope or warmth. The tensions that gripped the city closed in around the conference. A tense standoff between white policemen and a group of several dozen delegates ended only when the conference's press officer convinced the police inspector on duty to withdraw his men. At a press conference later that day, one white newspaper reporter, arriving late and finding the doors locked, climbed through a ground-floor window only to be pushed back out by conference staffers. Both near skirmishes made the front page of the *Newark Evening News*.[44] On the second day, a white Newark resident picketing the conference out of a sense of "moral obligation" was pummeled by a young conference delegate. SNCC chairman Rap Brown broke it up before the police arrived, and no arrests were made. But the story made the *New York Times*, and the *Evening News* made sure to print a picture of the victim in the hospital, a nurse dressing the gash in his head.[45]

No incident, however, received as much coverage as the violence that marred Saturday's press conference. Newspaper accounts agreed on several basic elements: a group of black men entered the first-floor room of Cathedral House and destroyed some news cameras, sending press and conference delegates alike scrambling for the nearest door or window, before Newark police showed up, only to be quickly withdrawn. Past that, the reported details may have varied, but the alarmist tone held steady. One local paper called the attackers "a dozen screaming [conference] participants," another just "angry Negro delegates." They were described as wearing any combination of helmets, dashikis, sunglasses, and machetes. The *New York Times* reported that they removed the film loads from the overturned press cameras, while the *Evening News* reported that one attacker had jumped up and down atop a camera and another smashed a lens with a chair. The *Star-Ledger* giddily labeled it "a fist-swinging, chair-throwing melee." On the last day of the conference, Charles Kenyatta, the founder of the Harlem Mau Mau, admitted to a UPI reporter that the demonstration had been his brainchild.[46]

Press alarmism only increased once reporters got hold of the conference resolutions, which were read at the final plenary session and received with expressions of support for those who had devised them but were not formally accepted by the conference as a whole.[47] One resolution in particular, frequently described as having been shouted through during the final session (it did not emerge from a workshop but was introduced from the floor), garnered the most attention. It read, "BE IT RESOLVED THAT a national dialogue be initiated on the feasibility of establishing a separate homeland in the United States for Black People."[48] Local newspapers all noted in the text of their stories that the resolution called only for discussion, but their headlines were more alarming. The *New Jersey Afro-American* ran the headline "Black Power Leaders Call for a 'Separate Nationhood,'" while the *Evening News* declared, "Separate Negro State Asked by Black Power Conference" and called the manifesto "a summary of many bitter denouncements of the white society." The *Star-Ledger* ran the not entirely false but nonetheless misleading headline "Black Power Delegates May Seek Separate State" and informed readers that "the nearly 1,000 Negro delegates wound up the conference by approving resolutions with strong anti-white, anti-Christian and anti-draft tones." The article turned the diversity of the conference's delegates on its head: this extremism was particularly alarming because a seemingly wide spectrum of black thought had agreed on it.[49]

Editorial pages quickly set upon the conference. Though the editors of the *Evening News* claimed that "the conference attempted to set Negroes against whites, to widen the gulf rather than narrow it," and their colleagues at the *New Jersey Afro-American* judged it "more like a kid's masquerade party, as people you had known all your life as Johnnie Jones or Smith corrected you with 'I am Mr. Gobbledegook of Africa,'" the *New York Times'* change of tone was the most pronounced.[50] From praise of the delegates' diversity in its earlier editorials, the *Times* moved to an excoriation of the "open black racism that dominated" the conference, claiming that the resolutions were evidence of a "radicalization of the moderates."[51] From its hopeful and longing glance to the conference as the best chance to end the violence that had just then spread from Newark to Detroit, the editors now condemned "the irresponsible Negroes who prevailed" at the conference and who had "sent forth a drumbeat of hostility around the country."[52]

Wright took these reactions in stride. The *Times'* "precipitous change in appraisal," he explained in a follow-up letter to conference participants, "reflected a prevailing white nervousness about the unique closed-door gathering of black people, coupled with several gross and unfortunate misunderstandings." In the end, he came across as unsurprised and remarkably nonplussed. The conference, after all, "fundamentally had nothing to say to white Americans. It was an introspective conference involving ongoing dialogue within the family of black Americans concerning our own needs, weaknesses, and opportunities."[53]

Among the opportunities the conference generated for Wright was a new book contract. A white editor at the New York publishing house of Holt, Rinehart and Winston had tried to crash the conference and been expelled. Though his stay was short, he saw enough to convince him that the conference chairman could write a considerably learned and influential book on the causes of and solutions to race riots.[54] In the spring of 1968, the publisher released Wright's second major statement on black power, *Ready to Riot*, but the editor's hopes for the book proved only half right: it was indeed learned, but it enjoyed little influence in an atmosphere rank with the fear of black rioting.

Where *Black Power and Urban Unrest* was calmly and clinically developed,

Ready to Riot reads more like the product of the evening Wright spent along Springfield Avenue, mixed with equal parts frustration and determination in the wake of the National Conference on Black Power. The writing is more tempestuous, and his building of an argument around the specificities of Newark lends the book an immediacy and an urgency its predecessor lacks. Nonetheless, its treasure trove of statistical and qualitative data on Newark's postwar development served to bolster the earlier book's central argument: rather than promote peaceful empowerment, postwar liberalism had unjustly suppressed black potential and unwittingly produced violence.[55]

Wright's argument had not changed much, but its packaging had. Though he began *Ready to Riot* describing the National Conference on Black Power as "a call for reasoned assessment . . . out of the immediate fury and frustration of the moment," and though he professed an ardent devotion to nonviolence even while seeking a better understanding of that fury, the book's front dust-jacket panel bears a simple close-up of a tightly clenched fist, its skin drawn tautly over angry knuckles, emerging from a sea of blackness. And though Wright maintained his insistence on black power as a creative force for national rejuvenation, the back of the book jacket features a photo of a black man standing atop a well-composed pile of trash—a flattened carton of Ajax laundry detergent, a canister of Diamond Crystal Salt—as if he had just brought the world crashing down around him with his bare hands. He is trapped in an empty lot. Tenement buildings barricade him in on three sides. The book's reader blocks his last avenue of escape. The man's fist is raised, but not in a black power salute. He shakes it menacingly at the reader, as if to say, "You are next."[56]

Less than two months after Tom Hayden's initial report from Newark ran in the *New York Review of Books*, Vintage released a slim paperback version in bright red covers and titled *Rebellion in Newark: Official Violence and Ghetto Response*. Hayden's narrative was largely unchanged—more detail was added in a few places, especially pertaining to arrest statistics and the trials that followed—but it came newly framed with a greater purpose. After walking the riot area, he decided to leverage his modest celebrity "to suggest to 'the outside world' a way of understanding the violence that took place." That understanding, the book insists, derived not from the intellectual wanderings of a white New Leftist but from the experience of his black neighbors under military occupation. Not entirely of Newark but not entirely of "the outside world" either, Hayden would help transmit that understanding of the riot to his community of readers.[57]

Hayden offered them a set of conclusions and further questions. He asked them to make their way through his book in much the same way he had made his way through Newark's riot. He appealed to their presumed desire "to understand without prejudice." They would encounter two central themes, each relating to rioting's essential nature, as he saw it. First, rioting was more than antisocial behavior. It was, rather, "a new stage in the Negro protest against racism," the "logical outgrowth" of a broader American failure to support racial equality. Second, readers needed therefore to turn their attention from the immediate and frightening black violence toward the "original and greater violence of racism." He asked them to consider whether the country, "thirty years after the New Deal and five years after the rediscovery of poverty," was capable of "dealing with the social problems being violently protested in the slums." If after the two greatest state interventions against poverty, Newark still exploded, where could one turn?[58] The riots made Hayden's experimental engagements with the American state—especially the Newark Community Union Project's work in Newark's antipoverty program and its brief foray into electoral politics via George Richardson's United Freedom Democrats—appear all for naught. These efforts had failed to relieve the repressive pressures on the ghetto, and the ghetto, in response, had exploded. It was clearer than ever to Hayden that the community would have to do the work itself, often in spite of the state. This was a conclusion that he had most clearly discerned not two years before on a trip to North Vietnam.

In November 1965, Hayden had arrived at an NCUP staff meeting with a proposal. He had recently received a call from Yale historian and Quaker pacifist Staughton Lynd. "Brother Tom," Lynd inquired, "how would you like to go to Hanoi?" North Vietnamese officials had invited Communist historian Herbert Aptheker to organize a small American delegation, Aptheker had invited Lynd, and Lynd turned to Hayden to round out the group. But Hayden worried his participation would expose NCUP to whatever red-baiting might accompany his trip. But after he and other staff organizers consulted with members, Hayden became convinced that the trip would be worth any potential backlash. He quickly raised $2,000 from wealthy NCUP supporters and applied for his first passport.[59]

Ignoring federal travel restrictions, the three departed a few days before the holiday bombing pause in North Vietnam. Their visit was billed as a fact-finding trip seeking to discern Vietnamese negotiating positions. For that, each might face a $5,000 fine, five years in prison, and the revocation of his passport, in addition to prosecution under the Logan Act (which could bring a $3,000 fine and three years in prison) for practicing citizen diplomacy. To Hayden and Lynd, the trip was worth the risk. They weren't sure what regular citizens could do to advance understanding between the two sides, but they felt compelled to try.[60] After all, as they would later write, nuclear war was predicated on "the refusal to 'recognize' regimes which the American Government does not like and ends with the stereo-typed view of an unknown 'enemy.'" In this context, "freedom of travel is essential so that Americans can discover if in reality they have, in the words of Cassius Clay, 'anything against them Vietcong.'"[61]

Their proclaimed freedom of travel produced what Hayden and Lynd, in their published account of the trip, *The Other Side*, called "an important byproduct" of their fact-finding mission. They quickly forged, with some surprise, an empathy not only with neutral, non-Communist Vietnamese but also with the "more fully 'other' members of the other side, spokesmen for the Communist world." These Americans and Communists were both varieties of revolutionary: they both cared for the poor and oppressed, and their socialism was more expressive than ideological. Their first translator in Hanoi sang for them a song he had written about the young daughter of Norman Morrison, the Quaker activist whose act of self-immolation under Robert McNamara's Pentagon window that November was well known in Vietnam. In return, Hayden and Lynd showed him and his comrades how to circle up and sing "We Shall Overcome." They later reported that they had been told hundreds of times on their travels that "there were possi-bilities of the beginnings of dialogue among people a world apart." Only on a tour of the surrounding countryside, where they detoured around a bombed-out bridge and visited the wreckage of a school, did local residents coldly turn their backs on them. That visit was cut short when an American plane was spotted nearby, and they were hurried back to Hanoi.[62]

More so than Aptheker's account of the trip, Hayden and Lynd's book lingered on the interpersonal encounters rather than the policy details that emerged from them.[63] In forging a clearer picture of the South's guerillas—who they were and why they fought—their main source was a small cadre of National Liberation Front (NLF) soldiers they interviewed over tea dur-ing an arranged meeting in a hotel lobby ringed with television cameras. Though not impressed with the sophistication of their ideas, the Ameri-cans reported that their alleged enemies nonetheless spoke with "an in-tensity which we could only compare to that of SNCC workers discussing civil rights in the United States." The soldiers spoke of how the repressive Diem regime had violently snuffed out the hopefulness that had followed the Vietnamese victory at Dien Bien Phu. A twenty-six-year-old woman, a veteran of over thirty battles, told them that people had been pressed into military service under Diem, raped and tortured, and even disemboweled. At first, she explained, the struggle against Diem took the form of political protest. But the more they protested, "the more terrorism and suppression increased." So they tentatively turned to violence, first using bamboo sticks and then eventually guns. "If you were in our position," she said, "you would have no other way than what we are doing."[64]

Upon returning stateside, Hayden gathered his thoughts. He gave speeches about the war (at least one of which was in Newark itself) and participated in teach-ins.[65] In Newark in March 1966, he wrote a widely read preface to Aptheker's account of their trip. In it, he established many of the ideas that would help him understand the Newark riots a year later. America's motives in Southeast Asia, he wrote, were "so thoroughly warped" that it was prepared to use the hydrogen bomb—a weapon of mass and indiscriminate violence—against a popular people's revolution. Only with the enemy's destruction would "the United States be ready to go ahead fully with its blueprint for a Great Society in Asia." In response, Hayden continued, the Vietnamese asked that "the citizens of all the Great Societies" see them not through the lens of national interests as defined by the state but as they saw themselves. The Great Society, in other words, could be built on the dead bodies of the Vietnamese, or it could be built on the empathic understandings of ordinary Americans willing to travel— whether by book or by plane—to the other side. "Our government will do what it will do," Hayden concluded, "but our words and deeds will show that we ourselves are not at war with Vietnam."[66]

But walking among Newark's urban rebels and sipping tea with Communist guerillas raised tough questions for thinkers rooted in the non-violent tradition. When Hayden and Lynd gathered their thoughts in *The Other Side*, which was not published until February 1967, they confronted this conundrum head-on: could they continue to profess nonviolence while supporting the resistance in Vietnam? Feeling distant from those who would glibly condemn or praise the NLF, their inclination was toward critical support, though even that prompted discomfort. What struck them, despite knowing there was no shortage of ferocity on either side of the conflict, was the Vietnamese guerillas' lack of vengeful and stereotyped hatred for Americans. They were certainly violent, but they had turned to violence "reluctantly, after other methods had failed at terrible cost to break the iron grip of repression." If "the violence of guerillas is a reaction to the violence of life under colonial domination," Hayden and Lynd wrote, "this is the same pattern, in an extreme form, that appears in our own society when . . . Negroes rebel in a place like Watts."[67]

What happened in Newark four months after *The Other Side*'s publication, then, was not entirely a surprise. In *Rebellion in Newark*, Hayden revisited the question of violence and placed it before a specific audience. In addition to his appeal to a community of readers interested in viewing the riots without prejudice, Hayden presented a methodological proposition specifically to fellow activists. As he had once asked his Newark colleagues to experiment with nonviolent antipoverty and electoral politics, he now asked whether the time had come to reconsider that approach. The rebellion, he wrote, represented "the assertion of new methods of opposing the racism that politics, nonviolence, and community organization have failed to end." They were causing "a crisis of strategy, and perhaps of conscience," among movement leaders, who would have to decide—their other experiments having failed—whether violence was a legitimate response to oppression.[68]

A pattern of official violence and violent response thus joined the streets of Newark and the jungles of Vietnam. If the American state, despite its professed intentions for peace, for racial justice, and for more justly distributed affluence, countenanced violent repression, then it was up to individuals to ignore the state, consider (or even visit) the other side, and forge transnational, interracial, and interclass communities of empathy and truth. So Hayden encouraged readers to leave their prejudices behind and follow him on a tour of Newark's riot area. And if those empathic travelers could not steer the state toward justice, the instructions for building a Molotov cocktail were ready at hand.

Wright enjoyed a modest renown in the months and years after the National Conference on Black Power. In addition to the coverage of the conference in various newspapers and magazines, an entry in the *New York Times'* Man in the News series, and several offers for consultancies and teaching positions, he increasingly attracted the attention of political insiders who shared his critique of postwar liberal interventions in black life, interventions that he believed stifled rather than fostered black empowerment. Republican Senator Charles H. Percy of Illinois, who had succeeded former New Dealer Paul Douglas in 1966, in particular took notice.[69] It may have been this entrée into high politics that turned Wright increasingly toward a vision of black power based more in the capitalist marketplace than the black community. Though a Senate freshman, Percy was already well known for an ambitious proposal to increase home ownership in the nation's "slum" areas. The bill established a foundation that would raise capital by selling government-backed debentures and then lend it to local nonprofit housing associations, which in turn would rehabilitate and sell "slum" homes. Buyers would need only a nominal down payment and enjoy low interest rates. Government had a role to play in this plan, but the funding was largely private, and the initiative was taken by local non-profits, who would provide construction-job training and ensure resident participation in the program. Despite surface similarities, the difference between this plan and the Community Action Program was that between loans and grants and between a focus on housing and a focus on community development as however the community defined it. It was the difference between seeing the community primarily as a housing market or a marketplace of ideas and desires. It offered an alternative to community action, and Republicans rallied around Percy's plan as the Johnson administration's commitment to the War on Poverty faltered.[70]

One of Percy's assistants had read *Black Power and Urban Unrest*, and when he was tasked with leading the legislative effort on the housing bill, reached out to Wright to testify on its behalf. By the assistant's account, Wright's "moving testimony on the need for black people to have the chance to own their share of America had a powerful effect on the Senators and on me."[71] In a speech before the Community Renewal Society in Chicago later that year, Senator Percy called Wright "a voice of responsible conservatism" and suggested that the radicalism of America's slum areas was really the same thing as conservatism. They were both, after all, committed to individual freedom, local initiative, and responsibility.[72]

When presidential candidate Richard Nixon began laying out his own vision of black power—which was, he said, not the "black power as some extremists would interpret it—not the power of hate and division, not the power of cynical racism, but the power the people should have over their own destinies, the power to affect their own communities, the power that comes from participation in the political and economic processes of society"—Wright took notice.[73] To the extent that Nixon emphasized a "re-alignment" of political forces rather than "the false unity of consensus," he opened the door to Wright, who, though certainly disagreeing with Nixon on issues of law and order, for example, found a kindred disdain for the Johnson administration's alleged insistence on keeping those communities in a state of dependency.[74] For Nixon, the solution lay in the heady combination of black pride, opportunity, entrepreneurship, ownership, and jobs that he called "black capitalism." In a national campaign address in April 1968, Nixon argued, as Wright would, that the goal of true black power was not separation from but membership in the American mainstream. The proper role of government, he asserted, was to help build bridges between the black community and that mainstream, especially in the form of loans and tax relief to businesses (especially black-owned businesses) that built, hired, and trained in the ghetto. "Helping provide these incentives is the proper role of government," Nixon said. "Actually doing the job is not."[75]

Wright met the president-elect in January 1969 at the Pierre Hotel in New York City, along with the Southern Christian Leadership Conference's Ralph David Abernathy, John Johnson of the Johnson Publishing Company, and several other select black public figures. Nixon promised them that his efforts to improve the social and economic conditions of black Americans would surpass those of previous presidents and hinted that he would be appointing several to high posts in his administration. Though Wright was less than impressed with Nixon's choice of Daniel Patrick Moynihan as urban affairs advisor (having a white man advise the incoming president on black affairs constituted "plantationism"), he otherwise offered Nixon much praise.[76] He later reported that Nixon had told them that "what turned [him] on about black power was its bringing of a new sense of hope, confidence, and of self-respect."[77] The president-elect was talking—was perhaps even appropriating—Wright's language.

Within months of Nixon's inauguration, Wright left Newark to become the inaugural chair of the Afro-American Studies Department at the State University of New York at Albany. There he argued for the increased empowerment of black students in university life and began writing a syndicated newspaper column entitled "Black Empowerment."

In the wake of Newark's black rebellion, Tom Hayden turned more and more of his attention to his antiwar work. In his apartment on Jelliff Avenue in Newark, a map of Vietnam hung on one wall and shelves sagged under the weight of books on the conflict. After an invitation from North Vietnamese officials, he helped organize a meeting between prominent American antiwar activists and representatives from Hanoi and the National Liberation Front in Bratislava in September 1967. (At least two local Newark organizers, in addition to Hayden, attended.)[78] There, an NLF official suggested a prisoner release, and two months later, three American POWs were released to Hayden in Cambodia. At that time, Averell Harriman was in charge of POW matters at the State Department, and he asked Hayden to Washington to thank him for his efforts. Intending to make the most of the opportunity, Hayden impressed on State Department officials the need for a renewed push for negotiations before the war escalated any further. He later recalled that the urgency of his message failed to impress them, so he "went back to Newark dejected," seeing no end of the violence in sight. "It was time," he wrote, "to think about the next step of protest."[79]

Whether that next step would involve violence was an open question for Hayden, but he was considering it after the apparent failures of the liberal strategies and alliances he had forged in Newark. As he thought back on those events and began planning for confrontation with the Democratic Party machinery in Chicago, his language often suggested he was now, like others in the New Left, more inspired by Che Guevara and Frantz Fanon than Camus.[80] In his appearance before the Governor's Commission on Civil Disorder that December, Hayden was asked whether, in the absence of any useful response to community demonstrations, social conflict was necessary. When he nodded, he was then asked whether he believed violence to be a legitimate instrument of social change. Though a very dangerous instrument, Hayden responded, it was certainly among those necessary for change.[81] That was something he learned during his travels to the other side of America's conflicts in Vietnam and Newark.

Those Great Society liberals with whom Hayden had some influence, though, seemed not to get it. Jack Newfield, an early SDS member who was friends with both Hayden and Robert Kennedy, gave Kennedy a copy of *Rebellion in Newark* and later reported that the senator, who was generally sympathetic to the book and with whom Hayden had seen eye to eye on community action, did not "care for the parts that seemed sympathetic to violence."[82]

In spring 1968, Lyndon Johnson named Averell Harriman his personal representative to new Vietnam peace talks and Sargent Shriver his new ambassador to France. Four days after the announcement, Martin Luther King was shot and killed in Memphis. Hayden raced to Washington to meet with Harriman and Shriver before they departed for the talks. He arrived as the city was burning. He impressed on Harriman the potential for a political solution and promised to press Hanoi to release more American POWs. Harriman—showing little worry or anxiety—sat before his office window, his gray hair lit by the fires burning in the capital's ghettos. Later, Hayden rode out to the suburbs with Shriver, watching those fires out the back window of the limousine.[83]

Progressive momentum, Hayden later wrote, was also at a standstill in Newark. But the pause would prove temporary, as "blacks would regroup, on their own, in the quest for political power." With the war continuing unabated in Vietnam, he saw the abandonment of the social reform programs with which he had tentatively aligned himself. The cost was too great for the country to bear, even if white Americans were so inclined. But in such situations, "good intentions tend to collapse."[84] The only solution would be black political power. That, ultimately, was what the rebellion in Newark sought, even if that admission forced Hayden to dance along a thin line separating the understanding and the condoning of violence. Looking at the Newark situation pragmatically, rather than taking a dogmatic position on the question, Hayden thought it clear that the violence had usefully shaken the power structure. But now that the dust had cleared and the bodies had been buried, the community would best be served by organizers who could channel the energy of the rebellion into "a more organized and continuous revolutionary direction." Violence might help shatter the status quo, he argued, "but only politics and organization can transform it."[85]

Hayden, however, was not the organizer to do it. He remained in Clinton Hill well into the spring of 1968 but felt increasingly that a white organizer was no longer needed or wanted in a black community. Reflecting on the period barely five years after, Hayden insisted that, as black self-determination became the center of the movement in Newark, the best proof of having created a valuable organization in the city was to phase himself out of it, to orient himself "away from having a traditional kind of power."[86] In May 1968, he announced that he had left Newark for good. "I did what I wanted to do here," he said. "I helped build an organization of self-help in the community."[87] He soon moved to Chicago, where the question of violence and social revolution remained unresolved four months later, when the police charged demonstrators gathered there for the Democratic National Convention.

Both Hayden and Wright left Newark that spring, neither seeing any hope in community action as it was then structured in Newark. Hayden, overcoming the skepticism of many a New Leftist, had experimented with it, using Clinton Hill's antipoverty area board to help organize residents around their shared desires. But as he considered the violent events of summer 1967 and as he increasingly turned his attention toward events in Southeast Asia, he saw the writing on the wall: the desire to suppress revolutionary violence would eclipse any calls for self-determination or empowerment from those communities, let alone any state programs that might begin to give it to them.

Wright, on the other hand, though welcoming black power's abundant ideological possibilities, never countenanced its alliance with the Great Society in Newark. To him, the liberal American state could only suppress, and never empower, the black community. But unlike Hayden, he never countenanced violence. So in his later years, Wright became a prominent conservative, whose promotion of a market-based conception of "empowerment" as the solution for the ongoing urban crisis was feted by Ronald Reagan and earned him a spot on the cover of the *New York Times Magazine* in 1981 alongside Thomas Sowell and other "new black conservatives."[88]

Their relatively brief and overlapping sojourns in Newark were not without their legacies, and their departures not without their ironies. For they had each, in small but notable ways, demonstrated the possibilities that lay at the intersection of community action and black power. The neighborhood project that Hayden was instrumental in launching had demonstrated that local black residents could indeed find something valuable in their participation in a federal program, even with the inevitable tensions and conflicts. And that alliance would continue to bear fruit after Hayden's departure. While he headed for Chicago and more violence, the local organizing of which he had been an important part continued.

Wright's legacy, even if ignored by much of the press, was his strident insistence and his demonstration, despite what that press would have its readers believe, that black power was a creative and peaceful rather than destructive force. Though his strategy for obtaining black power soon drew him away from Newark and toward political camps that held little sway there, those black activists who continued local organizing work continued to demonstrate that essential truth. First on display at the National Conference on Black Power, where even Rap Brown (the "violence is as American as cherry pie" Rap Brown) insisted attendees keep the peace, that insight would inform black power organizing in Newark as it turned its sights toward city hall.

Though Hayden's tentative turn toward violence and Wright's steadier turn toward conservatism were both indicative of national political trends on the left and right at the end of the 1960s, subsequent events in Newark suggested that the Great Society's brand of community action still held much currency there, especially as it was pushed beyond its participatory ethic toward a politics of control.

TEN

Control

The fundamental contours of community action's struggles for increased black participation in Newark's institutional power structures were much in evidence at the Fourth Precinct on the evening of July 12, 1967. The seemingly simple matter of the cabdriver—a scenario whose basics may have played out many times before—contained the key elements of that history: an injustice, a communal demand for redress, a recalcitrant institution, an effort to crack open that institution, the threat felt by its guardians, and their violent response. Antipoverty and civil rights leaders were called to the scene, and several of them gained admittance to the precinct. But there were also those who may have given up on the potential for such openings to yield much of value. The police response gave their assessment considerable weight. The door was ultimately barred. Burn the institution down.

Whatever the nature of the rioting that followed, whatever its proximate and ultimate causes, it provided a space in which the forces of community action demonstrated their ability to shape events on the ground in a way that stands in marked contrast to the vindictive and deadly response of state and local law enforcement. Such disorder allowed for the assertion of community action as an alternative way of governing the city and for the generation and circulation of narratives that made the case for that alternative. Over the next year, reactionary forces would seek to contain these developments, offering their own versions of what happened and what it meant. In this interpretive struggle, proponents of community action and their adversaries deployed the riots as an immediately usable past. Just as supporters of law enforcement saw cause for shoring up their defenses, the gathering forces of black power in Newark used the violence as evidence of what happened when the black community was denied access to the city's institutional structures, whether the housing authority, city hall, or

19. On Sunday, July 16, 1967, civil rights and antipoverty leaders called a press conference demanding a withdrawal of National Guard and police forces from the riot area. It was one of many attempts by resident activists to control the narrative of the violence. Seated are, left to right: Jesse Allen (UCC/Area Board 3/NCUP); James Hooper (CORE); Donald Tucker (UCC/Area Board 5); Marion Kidd (UCC/Area Board 3); and Phil Hutchings (NCUP/Area Board 3/SNCC). © Media General Communications Holdings, LLC. (Newark Public Library / *Newark Evening News*)

the police department. They would increasingly stake a peaceful future on the achievement of black *control*, rather than just participation. They set out to demonstrate this by promoting their own activities during the riot, by circulating alternative readings of the violence, and when the chance arose, by helping keep the lid on a city many thought would explode again.

In many ways, the year after the riot was community action's most successful season in Newark, when its local proponents stretched its possibilities into community peacekeeping and up to the threshold of electoral politics. On the national level, however, this was community action's mean season, when the ethic and administrative structures of participation were abandoned for fear of racial violence. Control of what was left of liberalism's investment in urban America was turned back over to its traditional keepers. As its participatory script was being rewritten in Washington, community action in Newark turned toward a politics of the ballot box.

William Wolfe, Cyril Tyson's replacement as director of the United Community Corporation, was on vacation in Wisconsin when the rioting started. But his associate director, Donald Wendell, made sure that officials at the federal Office of Economic Opportunity knew what was going on. He compiled a report detailing the actions of UCC leaders at the Fourth Precinct and sent it to the OEO's regional office, which soon sent its own memo on to Sargent Shriver in Washington.[1] Another OEO official, in town on a previously planned field visit, accompanied Wendell and Oliver Lofton to the precinct on Thursday, the second night of violence. He reported that it was ringed by police keeping "large disorderly groups" at bay and that UCC officials did "their utmost" to calm the situation.[2] Despite those efforts, the violence was reignited that night and burned through the weekend.

Through it all, UCC leaders worked to limit its extent and consequences, and OEO officials took note. After Tim Still ordered the staff to get themselves involved "in quieting down the ghetto," they established a command post at UCC headquarters on Branford Place, kept it open around the clock, organized several "community committees" to gather information in the riot area, and recruited about two hundred volunteers for peacekeeping patrols. They wore green armbands and distributed fliers urging residents to "Play It Cool!" Workers from the Legal Services Project arranged a release procedure for arrestees and took down nearly three hundred statements alleging abuse or vandalism by law enforcement. When the state Department of Community Affairs and the Red Cross arranged to have food delivered to the riot area, the area boards served as distribution points. The UCC rented station wagons and trucks to transport the food, as well as its own workers and, sometimes, the injured throughout the city. One state official telegrammed Sargent Shriver to say that "the UCC did its job and we are proud of the part played by this corporation."[3]

On Saturday, as the police and National Guard raised the death toll, two OEO officials toured the area boards and helped coordinate food distribution. Residents told them that they were well aware of the UCC's direct involvement in helping them in those dark days. "Many of these people, upon learning that I was an OEO representative," one of the officials wrote, "indicated what a comforting feeling it was to know that there was some place where they could turn in their hour of need." Soon after the violence ended, he predicted that the UCC—its executive committee, trustees, and area boards—would play a vital role in repairing the city. Without their direct participation, he concluded, "the situation within the Central Ward area and the Negro community in Newark, in general, would have been far more chaotic."[4]

When he got to City Hospital on the night of July 12, the UCC's director of community action could not find the cabdriver. When he called the Fourth Precinct to find out what had become of him—he'd actually been taken to Beth Israel in the city's South Ward instead—the dispatcher, upon learning his identity, called him "one of those agitators causing all the trouble." That dispatcher was among the first, but far from the last, to draw connections between the rioting in Newark and the local community action agency.[5] Such readings, built on years of tension between the UCC and its allies on one side and municipal and police officials on the other, and given new urgency by the riot, would soon drastically reshape community action nationwide.

The process began the day after the state police and National Guard left Newark, when Senator Winston Prouty of Vermont, at a Senate subcommittee hearing on the antipoverty program, read from a telegram that Newark police director Dominick Spina had sent to President Johnson, Sargent Shriver, Governor Hughes, and several UCC officials almost a month before. In it, Spina had protested the UCC's "fomenting and agitating against the organized and democratic government and agencies of the City of Newark" and claimed that UCC employees' jobs had been threatened if they refused to participate in "picketing and demonstrations." Such action, he concluded, would "undoubtedly lead to riots and anarchy in our city."[6] Prouty never explained how the telegram came into his possession, but its contents were soon picked up and circulated to a much larger audience by the *Washington Post*.[7] Later that day, Prouty's Republican colleague in the House, James C. Gardner, a freshman from North Carolina, told a news conference that political activities within the antipoverty program had been worrying him for some time. "I now find," he said, "that there is evidence that OEO-funded agencies, with the tacit approval of Sargent Shriver, are tied directly to the violence that has broken out in many of our cities. I am speaking specifically of the recent violence in Newark." Under questioning from reporters, he cited Spina's telegram as his evidence.[8]

Two days later, Gardner met with Frank Addonizio and Lee Bernstein at the Saint Regis Hotel in New York City, seeking material to bolster his case. The councilmen took Gardner on a tour of their city's riot area the following day, and afterward the congressman declared he had "proof positive" that the UCC's political agitation had caused the riots. He promised to present that proof to the House Education and Labor Committee, on which he served, and to draw up legislation that outlawed such activity by any federally funded antipoverty program. As Gardner headed back to

North Carolina (where, ironically, rioting had broken out in Durham the same day), Bernstein once again made the case for bringing the UCC under the control of the city administration. "This way elected officials have some control over the programs," he said. "As it's set up now, city officials don't have anything to say."[9]

When Gardner returned to Washington, he took up the issue in congressional hearings considering amendments to the Economic Opportunity Act. Newark played an outsize role in the legislative revisions that emerged. When Sargent Shriver testified that allegations of antipoverty workers fomenting violence were "simply not true," Gardner accused him of whitewashing the OEO's political activities. He had recently spent hours speaking with Mayor Addonizio, Gardner explained, and was convinced that "you people are agitating the poor sections of our cities . . . to go out and demonstrate against the authorized authority in that city, and what happens, it gets out of hand. This happened in Newark." As evidence, Gardner cited the "Stop Police Brutality" flier produced by Area Board 2 and police reports of UCC personnel at the Fourth Precinct. When Gardner declared that "there cannot be so much smoke and not be fire," Shriver told the committee members that, if they believed the OEO hadn't done everything they legally could to investigate and respond to such allegations, Congress should change the law.[10]

As the House committee considered ways to do so, three positions emerged, each embracing the general notion of a federal intervention in poverty alleviation—and so each broadly "liberal" in the modern American sense—but each advocating that a different combination of actors take up the task. Shriver defended the current setup, in which the OEO mandated the maximum feasible participation of the poor, while strongly encouraging involvement from city officials. House Republicans, meanwhile, proposed an "Opportunity Crusade," which would abolish the OEO and distribute its programs to the old-line government departments that community action had been designed to disrupt.[11] This idea threatened to split the Democrats between those who favored maintaining the antipoverty program in its current form and those, mainly southerners and urban machine–friendly northerners, who despised the disruptions community action had caused in their districts.

A third position emerged on the day Newark councilmen Addonizio and Bernstein appeared before the committee, when Representative Roman Pucinski, a close ally of Chicago mayor Richard Daley, who had from the start controlled the community action agency in his city, asked Bernstein if he would support an amendment that would render the poverty program "fundamentally controlled by the responsible elected public officials in a community." Bernstein, predictably, said yes because, as he explained, "you cannot put money and power in the hands of groups—and we are seeing it happen in Newark now—who are not directly responsible to the people."[12] Representative Edith Green of Oregon, whom the *Washington Post* had recently dubbed the "pivotal Democrat" for her independent-minded willingness to buck her party, picked up the thread and vowed she would never vote for such an expenditure of federal funds. The poverty program, she said, should be accountable to the normal democratic process of elections and political representation.[13]

During an open legislative meeting in October, Representative Green introduced an amendment that allowed local elected officials to reconsider the independence of their community action agency. They could take it over, if they wished, or leave it as was. According to a *Washington Post* reporter, the proposal "quickly heated up the atmosphere." One congressman called it "nothing but a Christmas tree for politicians." And when Chicago's Pucinski asked what made the Community Action Program "so sacrosanct that you can't trust it to public officials," a colleague responded, "Daley domination." When the amended bill reached the House floor, a Republican advocate of the Opportunity Crusade angrily labeled Green's contribution the "bossism and boll weevil" amendment. But Pucinski reminded his colleagues that, without it, other cities might suffer the fate of Newark, where "renegades took over the community action board and set the stage for mass disturbances."[14]

In December 1967, both chambers of Congress passed the bill, the House by the largest margin since the Economic Opportunity Act's initial passage in 1964. OEO officials were reportedly instructed to stridently denounce the Green Amendment as a ploy to cement the support of southern Democrats. The opportunity for mayors to take control of their local community action agencies was the price of saving the OEO from being spun off into the old-line bureaucratic agencies. OEO survived, but community action was imperiled.[15]

As Congress considered community action's fate, UCC leaders made two moves that suggested they remained strongly committed to it. First, the executive committee asked for William Wolfe's resignation. He had been suspended in May and, since replacing Cyril Tyson, had never settled comfortably into the UCC's culture. When Wolfe complied with their request, the *New York Times* reported that the operative split was "between those who wanted to emphasize the substance of the antipoverty programs—that is, job training, employment, aid for children and the elderly—and those who believed the mission of the agency to be community organization and leadership development."[16] Second, on the day Wolfe resigned and Representative Gardner visited with Councilmen Bernstein and Addonizio, the trustees voted unanimously to demand that OEO launch an investigation of the UCC in order to "clear up all doubts about activities within the antipoverty program."[17]

OEO investigators visited Newark during the second week of August. After meeting with UCC, city, and police officials, they reported that they could find "no evidence to support charges that UCC or any of its employees participated in or planned the riot." In fact, they continued, efforts by UCC leaders to maintain calm were widely acknowledged. Yet they also discovered why the agency was so susceptible to such allegations: its administrative structure was shockingly lax. Administrative innovation, in the investigators' view, did not mean the utter absence of structure, but that was exactly what Cyril Tyson's area board model had produced. Rather than providing coordination and guidance to the area boards, the UCC central office left them "to their own devices." The result was that they were "up for grabs in a number of political power struggles." In the South Ward, Councilman Bernstein controlled the board, for example, while the Newark Community Union Project had taken over in Clinton Hill and the Central Ward. Worst of all, the report continued, the new executive director, Donald Wendell, and "the ever-present chairman," Tim Still, were *proud* of this structure and didn't want to provide any more guidance to the area boards.[18]

The investigative team had a fine needle to thread. Community action had produced homegrown, innovative approaches to fighting poverty in Newark, and they had no programmatic criticisms. In fact, they strongly praised the Blazer work-training program, the Newark Pre-School Council, and the Legal Services Project. But the decentered area board structure had stretched community action to its breaking point: it made a joke of administrative efficiency (the UCC had recently lost out on $400,000 for submitting a grant late) and generated too much political strife. The team's recommendations, therefore, were not programmatic but administrative: the UCC should be abandoned and an OEO taskforce brought in to reconstitute community action in Newark under a new agency, which would more closely supervise the area boards and in which municipal government would have "an appropriate role and voice."[19]

As even the investigators admitted, however, the local political scene in Newark was too fragile for such a dramatic move. So Tim Still worked out a complicated deal that saved the UCC but changed it, much like the Green Amendment would soon do with the national Community Action Program. After closed-door meetings with high OEO officials dispatched to Newark by Shriver, Still agreed to form a special reorganization committee to devise a plan to reduce the size of the large and inefficient UCC board of trustees and to hire a new executive director and give him more power.[20] Days later, Still publicly announced the formation of the committee, whose members included both UCC stalwarts and close allies of Mayor Addonizio. Nonetheless, he and Wendell made their distaste for the OEO's proposals clear. Cutting the board of trustees and transferring more power to the executive director, Still said, "would be the worst thing we could do at this point," presumably because it would rile the area boards, whose powers would be reduced. At the reorganization committee's first meeting, Wendell recommended instead that they *further* decentralize the UCC's structure by creating a number of autonomous *neighborhood* boards.[21]

At a special membership meeting at Abyssinian Baptist that September, the trustees and about two hundred members were divided over the course they should take. Willard Heckel assailed the OEO, suggesting it might be better to shut down the UCC than "to knuckle under to ridiculous terms." Others, however, thought it better to maintain the program, even if in altered form. For his part, the UCC's treasurer, a vice president at Prudential Insurance, pointed out that OEO was right in at least one regard: the UCC, he said, had been "spectacularly inefficient." As if to prove the point, the vote scheduled to choose new trustees was postponed because of a technical error. If inefficient, the UCC remained committed to its politics: the only other action that night was the approval of a resolution criticizing the city council's recent decision to establish a police canine corps.[22]

Later that month, the OEO released nearly $2 million to the UCC, but with a reminder of the terms of their agreement, which was to be fulfilled by October 21. Over the next several weeks, the reorganization committee revamped the UCC's central administration and fiscal operations, and its personnel committee submitted the name of a potential new director to OEO for approval.[23] It could not have hurt that the candidate, L. Sylvester Odom, was at the time the chief of technical assistance for the Community Action Program at OEO. Trustees tangled over the hiring during a meeting at Our Lady of Perpetual Help two days before the deadline. In two hours of intense debate, some argued that they were surrendering to the OEO and ignoring local talent. A representative from Area Board 4 in the Dayton Street neighborhood saw no need to hire someone "who will need somebody to go with him to show him where Belmont Avenue is." In the end, though, the board hired Odom.[24] With that, the UCC had only one more obligation to fulfill, and the voting for a smaller, more efficient board of trustees was scheduled for its annual summer membership meeting.

The reorganization of community action in Washington and Newark was driven by narratives of both the uprising's deeper causes and its immediate starting point. Police Director Spina's telegram portending the cataclysm and Councilmen Addonizio and Bernstein's quick assignment of blame had helped drive developments in Congress and had led the UCC to open itself up for investigation. Those ideas about community action's responsibility for the riot, however, did not go unchallenged or unanswered. They were only one side of the interpretive civil war that accompanied and outlasted the five days of violence.

Identifying the riot's starting point is a matter of narrative, not science. There are a range of choices—when John Smith was arrested or beaten, when the crowds gathered at the precinct on July 12, when they returned the next day, when the first Molotov cocktail was thrown or window smashed, when the police stormed the crowd—among which must be the communal act of interpretation that occurred when nearby residents, stepping out into the cooler evening air after a sweltering day, saw two white police officers drag a black man into the precinct house. They did not know what led to that moment, and there were, as always, other possible, if less likely, interpretations. But the one they chose was that they had witnessed an act of, or the immediate aftermath of, police brutality. That interpretation no doubt quickly circulated among and beyond the crowd, causing it to swell. Within hours it was put into print, and the agent of that textualization was the clerk-typist at the local antipoverty area board who mimeographed the "Stop Police Brutality!" leaflets.

This area board was perfectly positioned to relay and reinforce the belief that the riot's spark was an act of police brutality. Its employees were plugged in to communal readings of the cabdriver incident, it had the equipment to quickly and cheaply churn out the leaflets, and it had the means to easily distribute them among its immediate constituents and, through some of the other area boards (Phil Hutchings and Hayden reportedly helped distribute it, using the latter's Volkswagen), an even wider audience.[25] And the fliers, by calling people together for a demonstration at the Fourth Precinct helped consolidate an interpretive, political community.

Over the next several months, a small cottage industry in mimeogra-

20. The leaflet printed by employees of Area Board 2, simply designed and easily circulated, provided residents an opportunity to come together around a shared reading of events at the Fourth Precinct. (New Jersey State Archives)

phy maintained the circulation of such riot narratives on a very local level. Mimeograph machines were standard office equipment in the 1960s. They could be had relatively cheaply and were easy to use. Those qualities made fans of many artists and activists, for whom the relatively primitive technology was an ideal way to produce alternative cultural and political forms in the age of mass media. A sign on the wall at SDS national headquarters, for example, read: "Our Founder, the Mimeograph Machine."[26] The OEO's 1965 *Community Action Workbook* listed them as an example of the "simple office equipment" that nonprofessional workers could be employed to operate.[27] They were material embodiments of community action's larger administrative structure: a vessel waiting to be filled with content.

In the middle of August 1967, amid the debates over the UCC's role in rioting, a black man left two stacks of fliers on a window ledge inside the White Castle hamburger shop at the corner of Elizabeth and Hawthorne Avenues in the South Ward. He was likely targeting the black children and teens that congregated there for a late-night snack on the one day a week that a nearby roller-skating palace reserved for black patrons. Each leaflet was marked "Black Survival" and warned of the costs, financial and existential, associated with white control of the city. The first detailed the recent decision of the "devilish beasts [who] run our lives in Newark" to purchase hundreds of thousands of dollars of new police equipment and to pay officers for the overtime they worked during the riots. The city council, in other words, was using their own tax money for equipment that would, no doubt, be turned against them and "to pay those animals to beat on our heads."[28]

The second also counseled preparedness—its header read, "Get Ready for the Devil!"—and gruesomely exhibited the strange fruits of a failure to do so. Opposite the written text was a photo of the corpse of James Rutledge, who, the flyer said, had surrendered with his hands up just before police shot him dozens of times during "the Rebellion." In the photo, his naked body lies prone on a table in a clean, institutional setting. Just below the chest, his skin is pulled back in two wrinkled folds revealing some indiscernible gore and what appears to be a plastic or metal plate, whose stark whiteness draws the eye to the gaping wound. Bullet holes riddle his upper chest and one arm.[29] The overall effect is of a brutally tortured body, ripped open and exposed. The audience for which it was intended knew how to read the photo as easily as the people outside the Hayes Homes on July 12 knew how to read what they saw. It was solid evidence that black people in Newark should prepare themselves for battle, because surrendering would get them as far as it had Rutledge.

Police Director Spina soon claimed that the UCC had provided the gruesome photo used in this flier, but that was not entirely accurate. In the Newark Legal Services Project's efforts to provide evidence of police misconduct, a young law school student named Junius Williams (who had first come to Newark as an NCUP organizer and who ran the VISTA program at the NLSP) had asked a photographer to go to the funeral home where Rutledge was laid out and take pictures of his wounds for evidentiary purposes. The photographer gave one set of prints to the NLSP, where they were placed in a safe and never moved, and kept the remaining prints and negatives himself to distribute as he saw fit. He took no payment for his services, he later explained, "because I personally believed that it was important to the black citizens of the civil disturbances which occurred in this city." But he did not say to whom he had given the photos.[30] His was a surprising use of a request from a UCC delegate agency, but not one the UCC had authorized. Sometimes community action had unpredictable outcomes.

Among those individuals combining accessible office equipment—though it is not clear if it was the UCC's—and new post-riot ideas about black survival was Willie Wright, UCC vice president, trustee, and former head of Area Board 2. Back in the summer of 1965, he had established the United Afro American Association as an outlet for ideas that were perhaps too militant for the UCC. Willard Heckel, who mentored Wright in the early days of the antipoverty program, later remembered this as a period in which Wright "ate white politicians." When Councilman Bernstein testified at the House hearings on amending the Economic Opportunity Act, he asked them to imagine "the most militant person you can think of." Wright, he said, "is worse."[31]

Soon after the riots, Wright took up the cause of black self-defense. While Anthony Imperiale patrolled the North Ward, looking to help out the local police, Wright established the Community Black Patrols to guard against them. He claimed about thirty members. They wore white shirts, black ties, and pith helmets with "CBP" stenciled on the front and "UAAA" on the side. They were unarmed, but Wright refused to rule out a potential change in that policy. Two weeks after the riots, he told an Associated Press reporter that they'd be ready "the next time the white man walks into the black community." And then he said, "This is what I am advocating around my town: get yourself a piece of gun and put it in the bottom drawer or something and have it fully loaded, and then if some joker breaks into your house like they broke in Plainfield, let him have it."[32]

The director of the OEO's northeast regional office called upon the UCC to suspend Wright, pending a hearing on the statements attributed to him. They "are so completely opposed to everything that OEO stands for," she said, "that I have also asked [the UCC] immediately to disavow any sympathy with those statements and with any other action which would precipitate new violence."[33] Though she denied it later, she told one UCC official that the likely outcome of a refusal to suspend Wright would be a cessation of federal funds. When Sargent Shriver asked for a legal opinion on the possibility of imposing a receivership on the UCC, the idea didn't get very far. But it made plain the threat presented by Wright's radicalism, to both the UCC and the OEO itself.[34]

The resulting dispute between UCC and the OEO was both jurisdictional and ideological: it was fought mainly over who had the administrative power to fire Wright, but the propriety of his speech was also contested. The UCC executive committee refused to suspend Wright for two reasons. First, he was not an employee of the UCC but a trustee duly elected by the community. Second, they did not feel they could or should "police the private views" of their thousands of constituents.[35] After the trustees meeting, board president Tim Still told a local reporter that, though he disagreed with Wright on many things, they agreed on the issue of self-defense. "I think that the philosophy in this country is that every man should be able to protect his home and his family," he said. "In my opinion the conduct of the state police here during the riots was like Nazi storm troopers."[36]

Over the next several weeks, as the dispute intensified, police found the "Black Survival" handbills at the White Castle in the South Ward and began picking up fliers produced by Wright's United Afro American Association. One advertised a meeting to protest police brutality at its headquarters just below Wright's apartment on South Sixth Street. It said that both victims and eyewitnesses would be present and that "only *black* brothers and sisters will be admitted." Two others featured a caricatured Uncle Sam, a spiky devil's tail protruding from his striped pants and nails sharpened into pointed claws. But in neither is he particularly threatening. Though in one he is associated with substandard housing and police brutality, it's clear that he is more frightened than frightening. A large black hand, with a recently broken manacle around its wrist and "black power" etched on the fleshy base of its thumb, puts the squeeze on Sam. In another, he trembles and sweats as he strains to hold a door closed against the black figure with a spiked wooden bat behind it. "The natives are getting restless," he says.[37]

The issue of Wright's suspension came to a conclusion at a UCC trustees meeting at Area Board 1 offices on Central Avenue on August 17. Wright was granted the top spot on the agenda, and he railed against the OEO, suggesting that Shriver was trying to burnish his national reputation at his expense. He also suggested that every black man "get yourself a machine-gun, cause you're gonna need it. Every black man should buy a tank and put it in his back yard." Then Wright introduced a resolution demanding amnesty for all those arrested during the riots. When Tim Still put it up for a vote, it passed, and so too, once again, did a refusal to suspend Wright.

Only one trustee registered a strong dissent. Walter Dawkins, the head of the Blazer work-training program, asked what would happen if the OEO withdrew its funds and the UCC was destroyed. Then all the Willie Wrights of the world, he said, could not "do a damn thing for them."[38]

A spokesman for Sargent Shriver, however, told the *New York Times* that the OEO director was resigned to the fact that there was nothing he could really do about Willie Wright.[39] In any case, Willie Wright was done with the OEO. "The poverty program is not meant to uplift the lives of black people and the OEO knows this," he told his fellow trustees. "Sargent Shriver can take the whole damn poverty program and shove it down the Mississippi River."[40] Most of the trustees continued to push the program toward its greatest promise, but Wright, for one, had given up on it. Over the next few months, he was investigated by both the Kerner Commission and the IRS after insinuating he had access to a hidden cache of "heavy weapons."[41] In early September, he traveled with Tom Hayden to the peace conference in Bratislava.[42] And he made the local papers shortly after Halloween when, despite widespread fears that the holiday would turn violent, Newark had remained calm. Wright praised black Newarkers for keeping the peace and demanded that, since they had shown respect for law and order, law and order now needed to show them some respect by putting a black police captain in charge of a precinct house.[43]

In February 1968, when Captain Zizza was transferred out of the Fourth Precinct to make room for Captain Williams and members of the police unions angrily picketed city hall, many feared the city was on the brink of more violence. Reports of sporadic episodes came into UCC offices, and L. Sylvester Odom, not even four months into his directorship, released a statement heading off any attempts to link the agency with the violence. He reminded people that the record was clear on such attempts: the UCC had never condoned or participated in violence.[44] In fact, the winter had been comparatively quiet for the UCC. With the immediate post-riot crises largely settled, it had managed finally to approve the first set of area board–designed and run projects, including job training programs, youth recreational centers, and consumer education courses.[45] But if anyone had any lingering doubts about the UCC's relationship to violence, the question would be settled before summer arrived.

On March 27, 1968, Martin Luther King came to Newark. The visit was ostensibly part of a buildup to the public launch of the Poor People's Campaign in late April, and though he did visit the apartments of two welfare families and stopped for a coffee break at United Community Corporation headquarters, much of King's public speaking centered on black rather than poor power. "Stand up with dignity and self-respect," he told a raucous crowd of students at South Side High School. "Too long black people have been ashamed of themselves. Now I'm black, but I'm black and beautiful." He moved into the Central Ward and knocked on Amiri Baraka's Spirit House door and encouraged him to push for a forceful political coalition between militant and traditional civil rights forces. King ended his visit at Abyssinian Baptist, where the crowd, crammed into the aisles, vestibules, and balconies, burst into cheers when he declared, "The hour has come for Newark, N.J., to have a black mayor." King's appearance at Abyssinian stretched late into the night. He left early the next morning for Atlanta, then Memphis.[46]

The night of King's assassination a week later, anxieties in Newark spiked. Sporadic looting and youth violence broke out, and Police Director Spina ordered a partial mobilization of city police. The National Guard and state police were put on alert. Mayor Addonizio summoned community leaders to city hall for a closed-door meeting that night, and they followed up the next morning at UCC headquarters on Branford Place. Sylvester Odom, the executive director of the UCC, cochaired the meeting with the mayor. Attendees ranged from the moderate to the militant, from political officeholders and city officials to community representatives. Among the former were officials from the city's Human Rights Commission and several city councilmen. Among the latter were Willie Wright and Amiri Baraka. The mayor eventually met with this ad hoc Committee on Community Tensions at UCC headquarters at least a dozen times over the next week, and his administration took no action concerning potential racial violence without consulting them. At a meeting the day after King's assassination, Addonizio told close to one hundred community representatives that his administration could do its job "only by convincing the memberships here that we'll do exactly what they want."[47]

What they wanted was the same thing he wanted: to keep the peace during the most widespread racial violence in US history, when National Guard helicopters skirted the rooftops of Pittsburgh's Hill District; guardsmen reported to Wilmington, Delaware's, armory; and most famously, entire city blocks burned within sight of the White House. Youngstown. Buffalo. Chicago. Cincinnati. Few American cities were untouched. It seemed folly to suggest the fires would not spread to Newark.

The UCC organized a special peacekeeping force of local teens, some of whom had participated in the violence the previous summer. They re-

ported to Area Board 2, the city's largest, where they slipped black armbands around their biceps, affixed colorful stickers identifying themselves
as peacekeepers to their clothing, pocketed a small stipend for food (most
of which was donated by local businesses), and grabbed stacks of flyers
printed by the UCC's information agency reading: "Dr. Martin Luther
King Jr. has lain down his life for every man. The greatest tribute that we in
Newark can pay our 'fallen warrior' is to reaffirm our belief in the goals for
all humanity, for which Dr. King labored."[48] Baraka attended the organizational meeting and told the teens that Spirit House, like UCC headquarters and the mayor's office, would be open around the clock for gatherings,
conversations, and even movies. Telling them that "we don't want any of
our kids getting their heads blown off," he urged them to avoid violence.[49]
The patrols lasted through the weekend, and the city was peaceful.

That Sunday—Palm Sunday—was the long-standing date of a community "march for understanding" first proposed two months before by
Willie Wright. It now served double duty as a memorial to the slain civil
rights leader. Approximately twenty-five thousand marchers—more than
half of whom were reportedly white nonresidents, many arriving on one
of the forty buses chartered for the occasion—formed a loop that began at
the Essex County courthouse on Market Street and wound its way past the
Fourth Precinct, the Hayes Homes, and the still-visible wounds of the riot.
Willie Wright and Mayor Addonizio walked together behind a banner that
read, "Walk for Understanding—People Care." A few steps behind them,
one white man and one black man carried a large photograph of Martin
Luther King, draped in purple. The procession was so long that those at
the front could look down Prince Street and see others still making their
way along West Kinney. A few people sang "We Shall Overcome," and others called out to bystanders, urging them to join the march. But for the
most part they proceeded in silence. Afterward, when they gathered back at
the courthouse, UCC president Tim Still told the marchers that what they
witnessed that day in the riot-torn Central Ward "cries out for partnership
of those of us who believe in the dignity of man." But his was a particular type of partnership, for he asked the white marchers to support *black*
candidates, *black* voter registration drives, and "the development of *black*
community corporations in which the *black* community can serve the economic needs of its people."[50]

The mayor and the Committee on Community Tensions met just after
the march and again the next day. They discussed plans to memorialize
King and arranged to send a delegation of Newarkers to the funeral that
Tuesday. They adopted a resolution praising the organizers of Sunday's

walk, and the mayor singled out Willie Wright for commendation. Addonizio sounded almost giddy when he declared the atmosphere in the city "better than ever. . . . People are actually smiling at each other, and there's a general feeling of brotherhood." Nevertheless, he decided not to travel to Atlanta himself, preferring to "stay close to the situation" in Newark.[51] And when Governor Hughes asked Timothy Still to be his personal representative at the funeral, Still declined when he learned the delegation would not make it back to Newark by nightfall.[52]

The first fire was reported shortly after 2:30 p.m. on April 9, while mourners were gathered at King's funeral. Acrid smoke drifted down Springfield Avenue from the corner of Bergen Street, the epicenter of the previous summer's riot. Within an hour, five hundred teen peacekeepers hit the streets in three-person patrols. At 5:30, someone ordered police to brandish their shotguns out patrol-car windows. At 5:40, someone else rescinded the order. Mayor Addonizio went to UCC headquarters to meet with Still, Wright, Baraka, and other community representatives. He agreed not to impose a curfew, and Baraka agreed to record a message, to be played over loudspeakers, urging residents to keep calm. Wright, however, stormed out of the meeting, refusing to help keep the city calm when the police, carrying shotguns, threatened to blow the city wide open. At 6:45, Police Director Spina ordered all officers to return their shotguns to their precinct houses. Officers were placed under general orders to use restraint, and a police inspector intoned over the radio, in words usually reserved for the city's black community, "Keep cool. Keep calm."[53] To the credit of the police department, there was only one confirmed shot fired during the violence after King's assassination: a warning shot fired into the air two days after the funeral.[54]

Addonizio spent all night speeding from one potential crisis to the next, doing what he could to keep a lid on the city. After the meeting with the UCC, he drove to the North Ward to visit Anthony Imperiale at his headquarters. When he noticed a gun in Imperiale's hands, he chased him inside and they bristled at each other in what one newspaper called a "near-scuffle." Back in the Central Ward, Addonizio watched a small band of youngsters smash a department-store window. He summoned a police cruiser carrying a black minister with a loudspeaker to the scene, and the children moved along. On Howard Street, he ordered a group of policemen to disperse. "There is no riot and no talk of a riot," he told them. "A show of police force only makes it worse." As he headed back to UCC headquarters, a group of about three hundred youngsters sprinted down Springfield toward downtown. About fifty broke off and climbed the stairs to the UCC offices to complain to antipoverty officials about police behavior. The rest continued down to the Four Corners, Newark's busiest intersection, where one hundred policemen were waiting for them. But no violence ensued. The officers waded into the crowd and talked with the kids, and within an hour downtown was empty again.[55]

After a short rest, Addonizio headed out for a last swing through the city at two o'clock in the morning. At the corner of Hunterdon and Clinton, a group of police officers had gathered in a tense face-off with workers from the UCC and a man who accused an officer of smashing a youngster in the mouth with his gun. The mayor ordered the alleged assailant's badge number be taken down for further investigation. Then he ordered the police to leave the area and the UCC workers to take it over. As the police withdrew, they chattered angrily over their radios about the UCC.[56]

Through the day of King's funeral and on into the next morning, a total of 195 fires were lit in Newark, at least 20 of them multiple-alarm blazes, and almost all attributed to arson. At least 150 people were left homeless. Many of them were taken to UCC headquarters, where they found food and shelter. Area Board 2 coordinated a free diaper service for the displaced. Firemen worked all night in helmets redesigned since the previous summer to better cushion the blow from rocks and bottles and bricks, and the city's fire director ordered a precautionary evacuation of the firehouse that had allegedly come under sniper fire the previous July. Both measures proved unnecessary. Rather than hostility, firemen had to contend with black youngsters rushing into homes adjoining fires to evacuate residents. Others helped carry heavy hoses to burning buildings and helped direct traffic.[57]

Newark was calmer the next day. Fifty-eight fires were reported, and sporadic looting broke out along Clinton Avenue. The UCC sent out between six hundred and eight hundred patrols that night, and the Committee on Community Tensions requested an hour to clear Clinton before the police were ordered in. About seventy-five peacekeepers, armed with nothing but bullhorns, hit the scene. The police were never sent.[58]

The following day, the city was calm.

When the *New York Times* sent a journalist to Newark to tell the story of the city's "responsible militants," Tim Still told him that the black community had kept the peace, that they—not the police, not the city administration, not the military—had decided that the situation was intolerable. And so, the former boxing champ explained, they paid black people to go out, "bust . . . some heads," and put an end to it before it really got started.[59] And when *Time* magazine wanted to understand what had happened in Newark, it too asked Still. "If any man burns those poor Negroes' homes down, I say goddamn his soul to hell," he said. The black community would take care of the arsonists themselves. "When we're through with them, we'll turn them over to the police."[60]

The spring and summer of 1968 would prove a mixed blessing for the UCC. Newark's experience after King's assassination demonstrated not only community action's commitment to communal peace, but more important, its ability to deliver it, if the police exercised restraint. Though Senator McClellan still hauled James Kennedy down to Washington a month later to grill him about his alleged role in starting the previous summer's riots, perhaps more significant to the UCC's fate than such investigations were the legislative limitations placed on community action's participatory mandate. "Feasible" would soon become less open to local interpretation. Even so, community action in Newark was not without its victories, even if limited ones.

The first of those threatening developments was the Model Cities Program, the showpiece of President Johnson's new Department of Housing and Urban Development.[61] One of the key questions surrounding the program—key for those architects on the task force that devised it, for the congressional committees considering the legislation, and for the local officials and residents who stood to benefit from it—was whether or not, or in what form, the Great Society's participatory ethic would infuse Model Cities. Among those voicing strong support for citizen participation were Walter Reuther, who served on the task force that devised Model Cities; Robert Kennedy, who served on the Senate subcommittee that considered the legislation; and Mayors Lindsay of New York and Cavanagh of Detroit, both of whom testified at those hearings. But none provided more unqualified support for participation than Sargent Shriver, who said at the hearings that, when it came to the urban crisis, he was committed to two cardinal principles: "First, the crisis of the city is the crisis of the poor. There is no extraordinary crisis on Park Avenue. Second, democracy based on full participation of the poor offers the only viable solution to that crisis."[62]

In the end, under the new legislation, each city would establish a City Demonstration Agency, which was directly responsible to city hall. Instead of mandating the maximum feasible participation of the poor in program development and execution, Model Cities required an even vaguer "meaningful citizen participation." In Newark, the Addonizio administration quickly submitted an application, and the mayor appointed his executive assistant, Donald Malafronte, to head the local Community Development

Administration. As he awaited word on the application, Addonizio appeared before the Kerner Commission and explained that Model Cities was "a far cry from the Office of Economic Opportunity." Instead of bypassing city government, it was "one of the few programs which recognizes that city governments need to be strengthened and not abused." Malafronte later called Model Cities "the antidote to the rioting and the community action."[63]

Soon after HUD named Newark one of its initial demonstration cities in November 1967, Mayor Addonizio met with HUD secretary Robert Weaver to tell him about the centerpiece of his Model Cities plan: the relocation of the state medical school to the Central Ward, where it would be the largest single project in the designated demonstration neighborhood.[64] After the contentious hearings the previous spring, the area had officially been declared a blighted urban renewal site. The city just needed approval from HUD and the federal Department of Health, Education, and Welfare (HEW) to reassign that urban renewal site from residential to public purposes. That reassignment would free up the federal grants that would pay for nearly half the campus's construction costs.

But as 1967 turned to 1968 and the city awaited the feds' decision, neighborhood opposition to the medical school plan regrouped, reorganized, and brought in reinforcements. Most importantly, the Committee against Negro and Puerto Rican Removal, the group launched by Louise Epperson, was joined by the Newark Area Planning Association (NAPA), which was organized by Junius Williams, the law school student who organized the VISTA volunteers at the Newark Legal Services Project. After studying the feasibility of the city's existing plans, NAPA and other opponents sent a telegram to Robert Weaver asking that HUD withhold all urban renewal funds from Newark because the data submitted by the city was "fraudulent": the city did *not* have enough replacement housing and the school did *not* need 150 acres.[65] This self-directed community opposition soon won an important concession. At the end of 1967, the state medical school reduced the amount of acreage it demanded and shifted the proposed renewal site toward downtown, where it would presumably displace fewer residents.[66]

The project's entanglement with Model Cities soon gave the opposition a significant boost. After a team of federal officials visited Newark early in January 1968, Governor Hughes received a letter from HEW and HUD undersecretaries laying out the conditions the state would have to meet in order to receive the necessary federal grants. They included guarantees of adequate replacement housing, of employment opportunities for local residents, and, most important, of community participation in the planning and development of the college.[67]

The next month, Hughes announced a new series of public hearings on the medical school. Through much of February 1968, a team of community negotiators, composed of representatives from NAPA and the Committee against Negro and Puerto Rican Removal, along with a few from the UCC and the Newark Legal Services Project, and backed by crowds of community participants, met with officials from state and local government, the Newark Housing Authority, and the medical school to hammer out an agreement on the process by which the school might relocate to Newark. The issue of replacement housing was central, but community negotiators also pushed for long-term solutions to urban renewal's undemocratic methods. Oliver Lofton advocated the creation of "a community based umbrella group" to help plan renewal sites, for example. And when Louis Danzig, director of the Newark Housing Authority, balked at the inevitable inefficiency of such a community-based process, Junius Williams said he'd grown tired of development driven by "some lone person sitting behind an agency desk, dealing and wheeling with the land," without anyone to check him. The time had come to change that.[68]

The negotiations ended early in March with an agreement that was remarkable not only for the concessions (in terms of site size, job training opportunities, community health care services) it contained, but also for the mechanisms of community participation it established in what had seemed, before the riot, an unstoppable urban renewal juggernaut. The agreement recognized that "the low-income and disadvantaged sectors of the community" were now "prepared to share responsibility for the future" of their own health care. The media for their participation would include a "Newark community health council," comprising nine community representatives (three each chosen by the UCC, the Model Cities Program, and the community at large), to develop comprehensive health care plans for low-income residents; a Citizens Housing Council to devise a plan to rehouse those dislocated by the school; and a "review council" to assess potential construction contracts to ensure that at least one-third of all journeymen and one-half of all apprentices building the new campus would be drawn from underrepresented racial groups.[69]

Perhaps most impressively, given city officials' determination to overturn community action, the agreement reshaped the very structure of Newark's Model Cities Program. The victory wasn't complete. Community negotiators did not come away *controlling* the program, but they gained new powers within it. The agreement established an "ad hoc committee of community representatives"—five from the UCC, five designated by the negotiating team, ten from the community at large, and five designated by city government—tasked with developing "a broad-based community group to serve as the vehicle of community participation under the Model Cities guidelines." Remarkably, the city agreed that this yet-to-be-determined body would share veto power over projects developed by the official Model Cities agency.[70] The ad hoc committee soon devised a plan for a Model Neighborhood Council, whose members would be elected from residents of voting districts in the demonstration neighborhood. The elections, held that summer, were the ones that gave Anthony Imperiale his earliest electoral victory in Newark. But the council also included several other veterans of community action, including Junius Williams (NCUP, UCC, Newark Legal Services), Louise Epperson (Committee against Negro and Puerto Rican Removal), and Zain Matos (one of the UCC's original incorporators and coordinator of its job training program).[71]

The medical school agreement was no doubt a victory for the participatory ethic of community action. This massive urban renewal project in the Central Ward would now be policed by residents and their representatives. The irony of this victory, however, was that there turned out to be so much to police. The juggernaut, in the end, wasn't so easily turned, especially since it involved not only massive amounts of public money but also the racial recalcitrance of local labor unions. Construction began with cheap modular units on a small parcel of land on the north side of Twelfth Avenue. This "temporary" campus (the units are still there today) would be used until the larger permanent campus across the street was finished. Though members of the construction review council objected, the temporary campus went up without the required minority apprentices and journeymen. Early in January 1969, members of the council demanded that federal officials study the workforce before releasing any more funds for campus construction. "We have been short-changed all the way," one member said. "Until this situation is corrected, construction, in our opinion, is proceeding illegally."[72]

Newark's implementation of the Green Amendment to the Economic Opportunity Act proved more of an impediment to community action than the Model Cities Program. In the summer of 1968, just as the area boards launched their programs and the UCC demonstrated its ability to manage community tensions, the agency took a decided turn away from the participatory heights reached in its first few years of existence.

The most immediate threat—the opportunity afforded by the Green Amendment for municipal governments to take over their local community action agencies—proved toothless in Newark and, for that matter, many other cities. When the OEO commissioned a private research firm to report on the effects of the amendment a year and a half after its passage, it found that only three of the fifty-three localities studied had created a new public agency to replace the existing private one.[73] To the head of the OEO's Community Action Program office, however, the effects were much more subtle. In his reading of the report, local officials were reluctant to take over antipoverty programs for fear of a community backlash but were biding their time until the War on Poverty came up for reauthorization, at which point they would push for greater influence.[74]

In Newark, Mayor Addonizio, who had reportedly considered closing down the UCC in the immediate aftermath of the riots, decided not to take it over. Instead, he waited to see what another key change to the Economic Opportunity Act would yield. Instead of maximum feasible participation of the poor, community action governing boards were now to be divided among the poor, city government, and business and civic groups, each getting roughly a third of the seats. When he announced that the UCC would remain independent, Addonizio noted that what had divided them in the past was not goals, but methods. With this new setup, he said, they had begun "uniting our methods as well."[75]

In June 1968, the UCC held its first elections since the OEO investigation, its own reorganization efforts, and the amendment of the Economic Opportunity Act. The board had been reduced from 114 trustees—all either representatives of area boards or elected at large—to 45 trustees broken down into three segments: 16 were representatives of the poor; 15 came from city government (including the mayor and all 9 city councilmen); and 14 represented a range of private organizations, including churches, labor unions, and business groups. Area boards were brought under stricter control. They now had to make their financial records available to the central UCC office, and their constitutions could no longer conflict with that of the UCC as a whole. But perhaps most riling was the UCC's new power to suspend any area board it found in violation of these policies. Several people at the meeting voiced strident objections to this reorganization of power but, faced with the prospect of losing funding altogether, could do little to stop it. Most disturbing was the effect it seemed to have on the membership. Timothy Still, who was reelected to another term as president, said he hoped the UCC would continue to exert influence in the community, but he lamented that, because of the new guidelines, "many people who were enthusiastic have already left." Only 190 of the 12,000 voting members had even bothered to show up for the meeting that night, and to Still the reason was clear. The new restrictions, he said, had "frozen out grassroots participation."[76]

Still died suddenly and tragically of a heart attack three weeks later. Mayor Addonizio, who called his death "a tragic loss not only to his family but in this city and to our society," declared a week of mourning and ordered all flags flown at half-staff and public buildings draped in black.[77] At the funeral, UCC director Sylvester Odom said that Still "clearly understood his own times, and set himself resolutely to the task of fashioning new responses to ever-changing conditions."[78]

The disadvantages of a short and peripatetic formal education and of life in Newark's public housing had fueled rather than stymied Still's self-starting politics of social service (after he hung up his gloves, he ran the Dukers Athletic Club, which channeled the energies of many local teens into boxing) and community organizing (he cofounded the Hayes Homes Tenants Association). As black political power grew in the Central Ward, he went to work with the local politicians—Irvine Turner and Hugh Addonizio among them—who relied on black votes for their electoral victories. And when those politicians disappointed him, Still was among those who recognized in the Community Action Program an opportunity to build an independent black political base that would leverage federal funds and connections—would in fact stretch them to their breaking point—to challenge the extant political system in Newark. We see in Still's life, then, several of the major mileposts in the history of Newark's black politics.

One might speculate what Still would have done next, in the wake of what he took to be community action's evisceration. He likely would have agreed with the city's mainstream black newspaper, which had recently editorialized on the city's shifting political winds. Newark's experience after the King assassination, the editor wrote, had led many observers "to understand that very subtly and without advertising, the power had taken a shift in Newark from the white structure to the black community."[79] And maybe Still would have looked, as many others began to do, beyond independent community organizations and toward city hall itself.

Just days after the UCC's fateful membership meeting, a three-day gathering that opened on June 21, 1968, provided the surest sign to date that the politics of community action had taken a decisive shift from participation to control. A black political convention, building off the energy and diver-

sity of the previous year's National Conference on Black Power, brought together a diverse group of activists and politicians for the explicit purpose of
nominating candidates for upcoming city council elections that November.
Phil Hutchings, whose Black Liberation Center on South Orange Avenue
had attracted the attention of police intelligence officers during the medical school fracas, gave his first public address since succeeding Rap Brown
as SNCC's national spokesman. On the convention's final day, he told the
crowd of nearly five hundred gathered at West Kinney Junior High School
that a takeover of all levels of government was necessary for black power to
be meaningful. Newark—this "urban Mississippi"—was a "key city" in that
larger process. "If we can't get black power here," he said, "we can't get it
anywhere."[80]

The immediate force that brought these streams together, however, was
comparatively new. They called themselves the United Brothers and were
an outgrowth of political discussions that took place each Sunday at Le-
Roi Jones's Spirit House cultural center in the Central Ward. Jones had returned to his native Newark in late 1965 from New York City and quickly
established Spirit House as a dynamic center of an emerging black cultural nationalism. After teaching at San Francisco State during the spring
1967 semester, Jones returned once again to Newark just in time for the
riot. In its wake, a childhood friend of Jones's—a Springfield Avenue merchant whose store had been shot up by the National Guard—mobilized
his substantial network of local contacts and recruited a number of politically minded men "whose imaginations had . . . been turned on by the fact
of Newark's black majority," as Jones later wrote. Their recruiting efforts
yielded a team of local community activists and more traditional political
leaders, several with experience in the antipoverty program. It was not a
movement built from scratch but an organizing and reorientation of existing streams, including that of community action. Among the dozen or
so men (and they were all men, as the name implied) who attended the
initial United Brothers meeting were several who had steered their political
careers through the antipoverty program (though the antipoverty program
certainly didn't exhaust their political experiences in Newark), and they
no doubt brought with them the experience gained from their multiple
battles with city hall over control of the program.[81] They included Kenneth
Gibson, a city engineer and UCC vice president, for whom the antipoverty
program was an outgrowth of his civil rights work with the Newark Coordinating Council and who ran for mayor against Addonizio in 1966; Theodore Pinckney, a director at the Neighborhood Youth Corps and member
of the UCC's Committee on Community Tensions; Donald Tucker, head of

the Ironbound area board; Earl Harris, a UCC trustee who had run against Lee Bernstein for the South Ward city council seat in 1966 and was active in Area Board 3; Harry Wheeler, a schoolteacher and onetime UCC trustee; Eulis "Honey" Ward, chairman of the Central Ward Democratic Party and UCC trustee; and Junius Williams, whose introduction to Newark politics had come by way of NCUP and its control of Area Board 3.[82]

Jones himself, by that point, appreciated both the promises and disappointments, the potential and its seemingly constant frustration, of the antipoverty program. He had been entangled in it well before returning to his hometown, and it had opened his cultural work to a wider world of Great Society politics. The Black Arts Repertory Theatre/School that he established on 130th Street in Harlem in March 1965 had survived its first few months largely on ticket sales generated by Jones's plays and a benefit jazz concert whose acts included Sun Ra, John Coltrane, and Archie Shepp. But very soon, the school hit upon a major windfall.[83] That summer, the OEO gave Harlem's community action agency, HARYOU-ACT (Cyril Tyson's former employer had since merged with Associated Community Teams in a move that granted Adam Clayton Powell Jr. more control over the poverty program in Harlem), money to run a summer program dubbed Project Uplift, and HARYOU-ACT gave a portion of it to Jones's Black Arts Theatre for a youth arts project. Some four hundred children attended classes in playwriting, poetry, music, painting, and black history. The project bought portable theater equipment, sponsored jazz concerts and performances of Jones's plays, set up street-corner poetry readings, and organized sidewalk art exhibitions. It was all a traveling show, put together and taken apart by a technical crew hired from among local residents trained in the backstage arts, moving from site to site by truck. One assessment of Project Uplift found that in no other program that summer were enrollees so enthusiastic. Jones was enraptured. He later hailed it as a recycling of the New Black Arts back into the community, where, despite its avant-garde label, the people really dug it.[84]

As in Newark's antipoverty program, however, so in Harlem's. Local actors had shaped the War on Poverty in their own image, lending it a sharper political and racial edge than even community action's staunchest proponents could tolerate. Soon after Project Uplift ended in September, the OEO cut off the flow of money into Harlem, and HARYOU-ACT, in turn, cut off the Black Arts Theatre/School. Ostensibly, the reason was that the community action agency had been neglectful, if not deceitful, in its bookkeeping. But the *New York Times* reported in September that HARYOU-ACT regularly employed black separatists, nationalists, and Muslims, a practice the agency's director readily admitted, since those people were just as much a part of Harlem as any other residents.[85]

A growing chorus of complaints about the plays being performed by the Black Arts Theatre/School and paid for with federal money intensified the scrutiny. Letters from around the country arrived at OEO headquarters in Washington complaining about the project.[86] Yet the OEO's deputy director of public affairs remarked that the agency would "rather see these kids fussing on the stage than on the streets."[87] The complaints culminated in the demand by a Bronx congressman that Shriver "state specifically" whether he had authorized or even supported the HARYOU-ACT grant given to LeRoi Jones. Federal money had gone to produce "plays that advocated Negro revolution and murder of white people and portrayed the whites as homosexuals and degenerates," the congressman proclaimed on a local television news program. "If this is the way that the taxpayer's money is going to be spent, then I'm opposed to it—violently opposed."[88]

Under increased pressure, the OEO line grew firmer. As always, the official tactic was to distance the OEO from the independent, community-based projects it funded. One press release called the plays the theater produced "crude and racist in character" and went to great lengths to point out that the theater was only one small part of a much larger antipoverty effort in Harlem.[89] When Shriver appeared before a congressional committee in March 1966, he testified that the theater "produced vile racist plays in language of the gutter unfit for the youngsters in the audience" and singled out the controversy as one of the few disappointments in the War on Poverty's short history.[90]

For Jones, the War on Poverty was a great disappointment in his still young black nationalist career. To him, it had been a fickle financier, ironically taking little interest in how its money was spent until it was channeled into something truly meaningful for the black community. He later wrote in his autobiography that the Black Arts organizers, himself included, had been "too honest and too naïve for our own good. We talked revolution because we meant it; we hooked up programs of revolutionary and progressive black art because we knew our people needed them." But it was not without some regret that he recalled their failure to "science out how these activities were to be sustained on an economic side." When the press uncritically repeated the charges of "black racism," the funding dried up, and Jones could no longer sustain what he believed to be "the most obviously successful arts and culture program any poverty program ever had." What he lacked, he later acknowledged, was the knowledge of "the art and science of politics and how to run an institution."[91]

In his autobiography, Jones constructs the year and a half between his return to Newark and the outbreak of the riots as a period of multilayered growth: he formed new personal relationships, greatly expanded his cultural output, and, most importantly, began to forge connections between that cultural work and political organizing. Inspired by the discipline of Ron Karenga's US Organization, Jones delved into local Newark politics as both an active observer and an organizer.[92] With Spirit House as home base, he built a Stirling Street block association and distributed the mimeographed *Stirling St. Newspaper*. When he discovered that many neighborhood children had trouble reading, the block association complained at the local school, brought neighbors down to board of education meetings, "and began to raise hell."[93] Jones began to untangle the complicated political power lines in the city, learned who paid homage to what political boss, attended antipoverty meetings, spoke out on the medical school controversy, and, predictably, attracted the attention of the police department.

Early Friday morning, July 14, 1967, as the rioting entered its third day, Jones and two friends—Charles McCray and Barry Wynn—were pulled over by police officers as they drove through the Central Ward in Jones's green Volkswagen van. Reports of shots fired from a similar vehicle had allegedly been reported, and when the three professed their innocence, the police turned violent. They turned up two revolvers and arrested the three on weapons charges.[94] Of the 1,967 employees of the UCC and the 3,345 full-time participants in its activities, McCray had been the only one arrested during the riots in July. He was an accountant at the UCC's central office.[95] And though the OEO demanded he be immediately suspended, UCC officials refused, noting that they were not required to do so unless McCray were convicted.[96] The day after all three were convicted in early November, McCray went to UCC headquarters and began cutting a mimeograph stencil for a flier that called Jones "a political prisoner." "Black People," it warned, "we sat back and permitted these devils to kill/murder brother Malcolm X. We *cannot allow* the extermination of another black leader!!"[97] He was suspended from the UCC that day.

In January 1968, Jones was sentenced to two and a half years, McCray and Wynn to eighteen months. The sensational aspects of the trial—just before sentencing, the judge read from Jones's poem "Black People": "All the stores will open up if you will say the magic words. The magic words are: Up against the wall mother fucker this is a stick up!"—and the press's coverage of it tended to obscure Jones's turn to the ballot box and his continued engagement with local politics in Newark. As he continued his efforts to "science out" a sustainable black politics, several of the opportuni-

ties presented to him came directly from Great Society programs, which
he, like so many others, turned to his own purposes. He served on the Title
I Advisory Committee at the Robert Treat School, whose purpose was to
help design programs under a mandate from the 1965 Elementary and Secondary Education Act, or, as he put it in testimony before the Governor's
Commission, "attacking the educational structure because . . . the change
of consciousness is the key to have black people possess the power they
need to change their lives." There was no contradiction in using federal
funds, he told the commission, "because we want that money to change the
school into an image of the black man's needs."[98] When the community
negotiations over the medical school ended in the reshaping of the local
Model Cities Program, Jones joined the committee that devised the mechanism by which community participation would be assured. (When he himself ran for a seat on the Model Neighborhood Council later that summer,
however, he was trounced, to Anthony Imperiale's great enjoyment.)[99] And
while the United Brothers crafted their own fliers to help keep Newark cool
in the aftermath of the King assassination, Jones also attended meetings of
the UCC's ad hoc Committee on Community Tensions.[100]

Still, Jones was among those who realized very soon after the riots—as
Congress considered stories of the UCC's involvement with the violence
and ways to assure greater representation of elected officials in the program—that the best way to ensure true community action was for the community to not only participate in Newark's institutional structures, but to
take them over. When asked about the War on Poverty in his appearance
before the Governor's Commission, Jones—or Amiri Baraka, as he had recently been rechristened—said he was in favor of any money coming into
the black community. But he concluded that the poverty program provided
"the illusion of progress, the illusion of self-control" because "any instance
where actual control by black people of the monies or the services" appeared imminent was "automatically thwarted." If the UCC had decided to
print fliers defending him, it should have been allowed to do so if it "were
really empowered by black people to act upon their best interests." And if
they had gone into Harlem and asked residents what they thought of his
plays, they would have learned how popular they were. Instead, "it was determined by white people that the plays that they saw were unfit for black
consumption." So now, he concluded, the basic need of the black community was not antipoverty money. It was "unity and power."[101]

The politics of community action, therefore, was generative of the black
power politics that developed in Newark over the course of the mid-1960s
and that cemented into an electoral campaign in the summer of 1968. It

wasn't the sole progenitor of that politics, for sure, but it was a crucial one. The intense post-riot struggles over the control of the antipoverty program, the dawning realization that the UCC was no longer a viable venue for political dissent, and the ever-hardening sense that "the community" and the municipal "power structure" were divided by irreconcilable interests and that the former should take over the latter, helped turn black power politics in Newark toward city hall. So when Baraka opened the June 1968 black political convention at West Kinney Junior High, he sounded the call for black unity and voter mobilization. "If we unite just this once," he told the convention, black Newarkers could control city government by the end of the decade.[102]

The convention aimed to elect black Newarkers to city office, but it also gave to the black community the power of selecting candidates for the first time. It failed to achieve the former—both Donald Tucker and Theodore Pinckney, both United Brothers, both former UCC workers, were soundly defeated that November—but the latter proved infectious, and before the convention ended, organizers were talking of another at which they would take aim at the mayoralty.[103] They soon scheduled the Newark Black and Puerto Rican Political Convention for November 1969.

In the days leading up to this second convention, over one hundred individuals and organizations signed their names to a pledge of support that was printed in the local daily newspapers. The signatories included, of course, Amiri Baraka (as LeRoi Jones) and the United Brothers, as well as several cultural-nationalist institutions connected with Baraka's circle in Newark. But, under the banner of "UNITY IN THE COMMUNITY!" a wide range of people and associations publicly supported the convention: UCC workers, CORE officials, clergymen, businessmen, established and up-and-coming politicians, local block and tenant associations, black teachers' and policemen's organizations, the Urban League, the Central Ward Democrats, the Rutgers-Newark Black Alumni Association, the Metropolitan United Methodist Ministry, and on and on.[104] On the first day of the convention, the *Evening News* described the audience as "a cross-section of the black community" (excluding the tenth it figured was Puerto Rican) and noted the presence of both ministers and youngsters in "African garb."[105] Like the National Conference on Black Power two years before, the convention gathered under one roof an ample expanse of people engaged with black political power in Newark.[106]

Instead of the three hundred attendees expected by Bob Curvin, chair of the convention's planning committee, over seven hundred people showed up to cheer repeated calls for black unity and power. Raymond Brown—

formerly of the Governor's Commission and Baraka's attorney during his riot trial—gave the keynote. "Are you going to forget your bickering and your ambitions, and realize only one black man can win next year?" Brown asked. "Get yourselves together," Ossie Davis commanded. "Stand tall, walk proud and let the man know a new black man is here. . . . Let us take the simple fact that we are black and make that cat blow his mind."[107]

On the second day, delegates began laying out a platform that embodied their hopes for a black-controlled Newark. They looked to old desires and generated new ones. After years of agitation, this was their best chance for a civilian review board, and their demand for one provided the *Evening News* its headline the next day. They urged the elimination of the police director's post and the establishment of a board of civilian police commissioners to take its place. In the wake of the medical school controversy, they called for the reorganization of the city's Central Planning Board and the inclusion of black and Puerto Rican residents on all boards that made decisions affecting the city's housing program. The creation of a Newark Capital Development Corporation to work with a minority business advisory council, support for a statewide agency running all welfare programs, citywide student councils and comprehensive youth programs—the delegates approved all of it.

On the last day of the convention, delegates took a pledge—read by Hilda Hidalgo, UCC trustee and former candidate on George Richardson's 1965 United Freedom Ticket—to support the convention's candidates. Then twenty young women, campaign hats perkily perched on their heads, tossed small bits of paper in the air as they walked to the stage carrying signs reading, "Let's Get Ourselves Together." Behind them, to what one newspaper described as a "wild ovation," Kenneth Gibson arrived. He was the city engineer and UCC vice president who had lost his bid for the mayoralty in 1966. But the memory of that defeat did not dim his mood this night as he was voted the convention's mayoral candidate. "When you elect me," he confidently told the audience, "you'll be getting an expert for the same price you've been paying to corrupt amateurs." He joined seven city council candidates—all but one of whom had experience working in the city's antipoverty program—to form what was dubbed the "Community Choice" ticket. The convention ended with the black and Puerto Rican crowd chanting together in Spanish and then Swahili: *Venceremos! Harambee!*[108]

CONCLUSION: COMMUNITY ACTION
AND THE HOLLOW PRIZE

To the extent that community action—in the War on Poverty, in the struggles to crack open the police department to citizen review, and in the shaping of riot narratives—had helped build and empower a particular definition of "community" in Newark, the election of the city's first black mayor
might seem its most significant victory. Ken Gibson rode that definition
all the way to city hall on the Community Choice ticket. As the *Newark
Evening News* pointed out the day after the victory, Gibson's triumph was
the product of a local black freedom movement that began in the early
1960s.[1] The administrative avatars of community action in Newark were
key players in that movement. They provided new resources—physical, financial, and political—for many of those involved: the Great Society liberals in Washington bent on disrupting local power structures they deemed
undemocratic and, often, racist; local liberals who looked to administra-
trative reform to accomplish the same end; an older black political class
that had made gains in the local Democratic Party in the postwar years; a
younger generation of activists who took their inspiration from more recent manifestations of the struggle; and residents who simply recognized
an opportunity to put their political desires and interests at the center of
the antipoverty program. Community action furthered key narratives of the
1967 riots that placed police violence at the center of the action, narratives
that were, in turn, subsets of the more general notion that city hall and the
(black) community were locked in a struggle for control of the city.

   Gibson's victory was celebrated because of what it meant for black
politics—he was the first black mayor of a major northeastern city—and
for its apparent defeat of a politics of corruption and white reaction. The
"pervasive feeling of corruption" cited by the Governor's Commission had
proved perceptive, and in December 1969, in the middle of his campaign,

Mayor Addonizio and fourteen others—including reputed Mafioso Tony "Boy" Boiardo and Councilmen Bernstein, Addonizio, and Turner—were indicted on charges of extortion and conspiracy.[2] The mayor passionately defended his integrity, but his life in politics had suffered a fatal wound. After fending off the challenge from Anthony Imperiale by emphasizing the North Ward leader's extremism and association with violence, a desperate Addonizio reached out to him late in the campaign. The final election was scheduled for a Tuesday in June, and the mayor's corruption trial was scheduled to start that Monday. So on Sunday, Addonizio ended a long day of campaigning at Ferrara's Hall in the North Ward, where he accepted Imperiale's endorsement. "I'll break my back and my fat belly to work for this man," Imperiale told the raucous crowd, "and you'd better do the same."[3]

The mayor's late coalition building, however, could not arrest the political momentum carrying Gibson toward victory. The sense that this was community action's major accomplishment—a political rather than economic triumph—is in keeping with many contemporary assessments. The ethic had opened political spaces in which local communities could exercise significant power over program design and development, not only in the War on Poverty, but in shaping agendas coming out of commission investigations, congressional hearings, and local community meetings and workshops. A 1970 study commissioned by the OEO captured a wider sense of the Community Action Program's efficacy. Based on interviews with hundreds of antipoverty workers in fifty cities (including Newark), its basic conclusion was that "community organization efforts by Community Action Agencies are the most productive path to bringing about institutional change." It encouraged the OEO to "to get out of the business of running and administering services" and to get about mobilizing the poor to push and prod local institutions. "Forty dollars per poor person in services," it said, "is not worth as much as forty dollars per poor person in increased demand for those services."[4] The influential economist and public policy analyst Sar Levitan wrote in 1969 that, in the end, the antipoverty program "may ultimately be evaluated more for its role in the political mobilization of disadvantaged citizens than for the number of dollars it puts into their pocketbooks."[5] Even Daniel Patrick Moynihan, who bemoaned the local conflicts engendered by the Community Action Program, conflicts that he misguidedly saw rooted in the "intellectual colonialism" of social scientists and the allegedly confused goals of community action's architects rather than local conditions in places like Newark, nonetheless deemed political conflict and "the formation of an urban Negro leadership echelon" as its most salient products.[6]

For all that, community action would soon show its limitations. For one, it was not as galvanizing a political force as it *might* have been. In a city recently awakened to a historic shift in its racial demographics from a white to a black majority, the resources and opportunities provided by community action were most forcefully seized by the top-billed players in that drama.[7] If community action's great success in Newark was its contribution to black political unity, its biggest failing may have been that it largely excluded the city's growing Puerto Rican community. But that wasn't for a lack of effort among Puerto Rican leaders and activists themselves. In early 1966, a group of over eighty residents, Spanish and non-Spanish speakers alike, came together to address the problem. They surveyed over two hundred local families and concluded that, while the United Community Corporation provided many opportunities and services for the city's poor, it lacked "specialized efforts" and failed to "recognize the underprivileged Spanish-speaking people of Newark as a distinct ethnic group with special temporary handicaps." To Spanish speakers, the UCC looked much like the federal bureaucracy that community action had been created to disrupt. "Language barriers, red-tape, uncoordinated services, and impersonality," they reported, "deter the Spanish community from participating" in its programs. They proposed, then, the creation of a Field Orientation Center for the Underprivileged Spanish (FOCUS), which would refer members of that community to newly coordinated programs aimed at their needs. They sought $285,000 from the OEO to rent office space and hire a staff of twenty-five full-time workers and thirteen part-timers.[8] But when FOCUS opened its doors on Broad Street in November 1967—after a delegation protested a delay in funding by picketing UCC headquarters—it had a budget of only $24,000 and a staff of three.[9]

Puerto Rican leaders also pushed for greater representation on the UCC board of trustees, with even less impressive results. The board reserved one seat for a representative of the Spanish-speaking community, but Hilda Hidalgo and Zain Matos, the trustee who held that seat and who was one of the original signers of the UCC's incorporation papers, worked to have that number increased to six. The East Ward city councilman urged the UCC to do it, a group of thirty community leaders issued a scathing demand, and a group of young militants called Puerto Rican Youth United picketed the 1969 membership meeting and then occupied UCC headquarters.[10] Their efforts were joined by two of the original United Brothers in a last-ditch attempt to return Newark's community action agency to the community. Yet in August 1969, the trustees rejected their proposed expansion of the board.[11] A little more than a year later, Hidalgo and a group of her Rutgers students surveyed Newark's Puerto Rican community and found that the most prominent Puerto Ricans in the city were Gibson's deputy mayor Ramon Añeses and FOCUS executive director Antonio Perez. And though of the more than half of respondents who knew FOCUS, 80 percent had a positive opinion, only 10 percent were even aware of the UCC, and 96 percent of those had no opinion of it.[12]

If Latinos have since emerged as a major political force in Newark, therefore, some of the roots of their political consciousness surely lay in the organizing that occurred not within the community action program but on its margins, demanding it live up to its promise of community action for *all* Newarkers. If many black Newarkers look to 1970 as the year they attained municipal power, the city's Latino and immigrant populations might see it as a moment of significant achievement and valuable alliances—Añeses lost the council election but joined Gibson's administration, for example—but not as the moment at which they gained full representation in city politics. The tensions that developed between the black and Latino political communities in Newark were certainly not as hostile or violent as those between the black and white communities in the 1960s. But neither were they fully resolved.[13]

Though there were, of course, white antipoverty leaders in the UCC, and there were area boards in neighborhoods with substantial white populations, the hostility to community action engineered by Councilmen Addonizio and Bernstein (with, perhaps, Mayor Addonizio at their backs) and the outright rejection of a board in Vailsburg meant that white Newarkers largely missed the opportunities, both political and financial, it provided. So when, in the 1970s, they became more and more conscious of their minority status in the city and used it as a means of community organizing—often positioning themselves between white and black America, as *ethnics*—a frequent grievance was that few antipoverty resources or services had been made available to them. "All we really want is what the blacks have been getting," one North Ward resident told the *New York Times* in 1971. "Cleaning off Columbus's statue in time for the parade isn't enough any more."[14]

In 1971, Anthony Imperiale rode such sentiments to the state house, first as an assemblyman, then a senator, first as an independent, then as a Republican. And he almost rode them to city hall when he ran against Ken Gibson in 1974 and received 44 percent of the vote.[15] But his neighborhood-organizing prowess was surpassed in the 1970s by a young North Ward Democratic Party activist named Stephen Adubato, who channeled that discontent into his own community organization. With financial support from Rutgers and the National Center for Urban Affairs, Adubato opened the North Ward Educational and Cultural Center in the summer of 1971. Since, as he said later that year, there were no Italians in the UCC or Model Cities, the center would help local Italians get into college, find jobs, and gain leverage within the local antipoverty programs.[16] (Annoyed, Imperiale pointed out that, by that time, he'd already been organizing services for the North Ward's Italians for several years.)[17] The North Ward Center has since served as a communal base for Adubato's career in local and state Democratic politics, even, ironically, as the neighborhood changed from Italian to Latino over the ensuing years.

Even had the politics of community action overcome its limitations, other developments would have kept it from mounting a serious challenge to structural poverty. By the late 1960s, the antipoverty program was being steered away from community control, and the political power it had generated over the course of the decade was achieved in a city that seemed the exemplary "hollow prize": the proposition made by political scientists in the late 1960s and early 1970s that the election of black mayors would not mean black control of cities, but rather a form of "colonial indirect rule," as the best-known of those scholars put it.[18] In a city whose finances have been so reliant on property taxes, less and less power accrued to city hall in the years of deindustrialization and depopulation. The *New York Times*, in so many stories it ran during the early days of Gibson's administration, cited a miserable triumvirate of Newark ills: it had the highest per capita crime rate in the nation and the most "slum housing" per capita, and a third of its population was on welfare. Within five years, in a *Harper's* magazine ranking of the nation's most populous cities across a range of indices, Newark—which ranked dead last in nine categories and in the bottom five in nineteen—earned the title "worst of all" American cities.[19]

Gibson did what he could. He brought some stability and renewed integrity to city hall and lobbied hard for a share of President Nixon's new federal revenue-sharing largesse. But he learned quickly what Mayor Addonizio had been complaining about all those years: the city could not survive without injections of outside aid. Less than three months after his inauguration, he discovered an impending $60 million budget deficit, and city hall sources began speculating that Newark would become the first city in American history to file for bankruptcy. Gibson made a dramatic plea to the state legislature in Trenton that December. When Governor William Cahill, a moderate Republican, signed the resulting aid package—a mix of new tax authorizations and state grants—he warned that Newark's near bankruptcy was a sign "of the storms ahead, approaching urban storms that can bring our major cities and our sovereign states to financial destruction."[20]

For those who had hoped that a black administration would be more attuned to communal desires, the disappointment came quickly. Few were as disenchanted as Amiri Baraka, who, even before the first Newark black political convention was held, had said that the best way to prevent the rise of a black neocolonial class would be "consensus" and "decentralization," the practice of determining everything "according to what blocks of people say—houses, streets—rather than in terms of some kind of abstract artery-hardened form."[21] Seeking a position from which to challenge the Gibson administration, Baraka and his nationalist allies turned to the UCC. Even in depleted form, the community action agency appeared a viable political space in which dissidents might leverage federal resources against city hall. For several years in the early 1970s, activists with the Committee for a Unified Newark (CFUN) campaigned for and won high office in the anti-poverty program, criticizing the mayor from its pulpit, designing programs to advance a nationalist agenda, and, as new UCC president and CFUN leader David Barrett said upon his election in 1970, making the UCC "truly a community organization" where people would "speak from positions of power rather than protest."[22] After one term of Gibson's mayoralty, Baraka concluded that his former political ally had become a member of "the bureaucratic EE-LIGHT" in an "unadministratable city. Unadministratable, because the system that animates it is unadministratable. The system of profit for the few and poverty for the many."[23]

But by the end of Gibson's first term, the federal Community Action Program would be reduced to a shell of its former self. The devolution of administrative power and knowledge development would never reach the lengths it had in the mid-1960s. It was the victim of two seemingly contradictory conservative critiques of modern American liberalism: that it is so liberating that it has little concern for the collective social order, or so reliant on state power that it is insufficiently committed to liberty. Over the ensuing decades, community action suffered from conservatism's search for a more properly balanced "ordered liberty."[24] On the one hand, in many critics' minds, CAP had promoted intergroup conflict rather than the common good. The conservative response was to rein it in and promote investment in the forces of law and order. On the other hand, CAP constituted a further incursion of state paternalism rather than greater freedom and opportunity for the poor. The conservative response was to turn to the capitalist market and promote private investment in the inner city, a move prefigured in Nathan Wright's vision of black power and abetted by the Democratic Party's embrace of a new suburban-centered meritocratic politics geared to the postindustrial economy.[25] The closing of liberalism's frontier, therefore, opened the door to a resurgent conservative politics promoting public security and private capitalist development.

The process of reeling in community action—of restoring order—had begun with Model Cities, which in Newark, even with the concessions won by community activists, was largely controlled by city hall, and continued apace with the 1967 amendments to the Economic Opportunity Act.[26] President Nixon, at the insistence of Daniel Patrick Moynihan, the director of his Urban Affairs Council, agreed to keep the OEO around for a while, to see if it could be reformed into what Nixon called a more effective "incubator" of innovative poverty programs, which could then be moved to existing executive departments.[27] It quickly became clear that for him and Donald Rumsfeld, his new OEO director, "innovation" was not to be generated at the neighborhood level but via state and, especially, local governments, while Rumsfeld himself retained the power to determine which programs were significantly imaginative to warrant federal funding. In this way, developments within the Nixonian OEO reflected the president's distaste for federal bureaucracy and his desire to strengthen the role of states and localities in public problem solving.[28] To call Nixon a "liberal" on domestic affairs, as seems the vogue, is fair enough if consideration is limited to spending (which he increased) and a general belief in government action (which he mostly shared).[29] But at a time when local liberals in places like Newark and national liberals like Robert F. Kennedy and Walter Reuther argued for the maintenance of community participation, Nixon, out of distaste for the federal bureaucracy *and* for community action, returned the decision-making powers to local and state bureaucracies, which to Great Society liberals were just as inefficient as—and, in fact, more corrupt and violent than—their federal counterpart. Nonetheless, Rumsfeld, who as a congressman had voted against the Economic Opportunity Act and who claimed that the OEO's office walls were covered with Che Guevara posters when he arrived, later wrote that the OEO itself was an extra layer of bureaucracy with which he was simply "uncomfortable."[30]

Soon enough, the administration dispensed with that "extra" layer. Several programs were delegated to old-line departments: the Job Corps to Labor and Head Start to Health, Education, and Welfare. What was left of the OEO itself, which was essentially the funding of local Community Action Agencies, became, with very little attention, the Community Services Administration (CSA) in 1975. The variety of programming the OEO had once supported was narrowed over the next few years, as community ac-

21. Mayor Gibson and Harry Wheeler, Newark's manpower director, reviewing funds
from federal block grants under President Nixon's Comprehensive Employment
and Training Act in 1975. Though welcome, such programs were funded at
levels insufficient to address the city's rampant unemployment and were often
beset by allegations of patronage and corruption. (Newark Public Library)

tion yielded to community services, with nutrition, senior services, youth
employment, and home weatherproofing the most prominent. In 1981,
the Economic Opportunity Act was repealed by Reagan's budget-slashing
Omnibus Budget Reconciliation Act, and the CSA became the victim of
what the *New York Times* termed "the first wholesale elimination of a major
independent agency since the end of World War II."[31] Its limited role was
limited even more as it moved into a new Office of Community Services
within the Department of Health and Human Services, where it remains to
this day.[32]

That 1981 legislation, advancing the cause of federal block grants, also
consolidated seventy-seven separate social grant programs into nine, at a
funding level that was about 25 percent less than the separate programs.[33]
(Upon learning of these cuts, one local Newarker asked, "Has the riot
started yet?")[34] These Community Services Block Grants now fund the local Community Action Agencies that have managed to survive. Whether

the Community Economic Opportunity Act, introduced in early 2014 by Representative Betty McCollum of Minnesota and combining block grants to states with a revived mandate for "maximum feasible participation," can revitalize community action remains to be seen.[35]

The effects have been felt locally in Newark. After the last-gasp efforts to sustain the UCC's community action orientation, its program was quickly reduced to service provision. Though services were of course precious in a city as poor as Newark, the funding was spare and, without community participation in the program, subject to repeated rounds of administrative misbehavior later in the 1970s.[36] Still, the UCC survives to this day, and though it doesn't play as prominent a role in Newark political life as it did in the 1960s, its ability to survive and provide services and, more recently, expand into the arena of community development, despite the financial cutbacks and past corruption in its ranks, makes it one of the longest-lasting antipoverty organizations in the city.

As funding for community action dried up or was diverted, investments in law enforcement and public security grew. Law-and-order politics yielded its greatest fruits at the national level, as an accompaniment to, or maybe the umbrella under which, the decimation of community action occurred. One sign of community action's administrative and ethical demise came two years into Gibson's mayoralty. The Law Enforcement Assistance Administration had awarded Newark a $20 million grant, under a new program to aid cities with high crime rates. The program emphasized crime fighting and promoted better communications systems, the expanded use of helicopters, and new police training techniques. In November 1972, the local grant director in Newark resigned his post, claiming that government officials had threatened to withhold funding because his approach to crime fighting—he wanted to use the money to deal with unemployment and school dropouts—didn't channel the money to police work.[37]

Despite new federal aid programs, the Newark Police Department remained embattled, and there would be fewer and fewer residents willing to come to its aid, let alone organize massive petition drives and marches. Allegations of brutality and general disregard for the well-being of black and Latino Newarkers continued apace, through the violence that accompanied the proposed construction of Kawaida Towers, a housing development designed by Amiri Baraka according to black cultural nationalist values in 1972; a police attack on residents protesting the city's pathetic garbage collection practices that same year; and a smaller but still deadly riot that broke out in September 1974, pitting Puerto Rican residents against police and city hall.[38] (This last was the final straw for Baraka, who turned against

Gibson and black cultural nationalism and toward a third-world Marxist perspective calling for greater unity between black and Puerto Rican residents.)[39] Activists have kept alive the call for a civilian review board over the ensuing decades, as various police directors and their various reforms— including a much-praised turn to the big-data techniques of CompStat, increased surveillance, and "business management strategies"—have come and gone.[40] And yet the department remained embattled in ways that no reform seemed able to remedy. For much of the past four decades, it has remained largely impervious to community action.

These developments on the side of order—the reeling in of community action, the "devolution" into block grants for states and municipalities, and the bolstering of law enforcement—have been accompanied by developments on the side of liberty, or market-based notions thereof, especially in community development. Since the 1960s—at least since the medical school controversy—development has been increasingly driven by the competitive demands of a postindustrial and globalized market economy, in which public funding has been reduced and private investment spies opportunities in seemingly decayed cities. The place-based development approach that emerges sees neighborhoods' exchange value more than their political value. In such an atmosphere, where neighborhoods' "market imperfections" are meant to be corrected, they are viewed more as financial than political resources, more as commodities than communities.[41] Subsequent city administrations have worked through this approach. It's impossible to avoid it. Developers and investors offered generous tax concessions have built new sports venues, hotels and restaurants, several major corporate headquarters, and most recently, a mixed-use development project of charter schools, affordable and market-rate housing, and retail called Teachers Village.[42] One sign of how fully this approach to development has supplanted community action is that recent bipartisan legislation expanding tax credits for job creation and incentive grants for developers was called the New Jersey Economic Opportunity Act of 2013. Governor Chris Christie signed it into law after vetoing provisions that mandated prevailing wages for construction and maintenance workers on supported projects.[43]

Such considerations might make 1960s-style community action seem like a bold but ultimately doomed experiment, one bright shining moment sandwiched between the bureaucratic onslaughts of postwar liberalism, urban renewal, and machine politics, on the one hand, and the financial onslaughts of market-based development and neoliberal politics on the other. While the contradictions of the former helped drive community action, the widespread popularity of the latter may seem to have snuffed it out. Yet, just as community action's energy was not created out of nothing, so was it not wholly destroyed by subsequent developments. We just have to look in the right places and be willing to value not only social movements' "great victories"—since, though not hollow, they are often imperfect—but also, as Manuel Castells put it, their lasting effects "in the breaches produced in the dominant logic, in the compromises reached within the institutions, in the changing cultural forms of the city, in the collective memory of the neighbourhoods, and, ultimately, in the continuing social debate about what the city should be."[44]

To see this in Newark, we might start by going back, one last time, to Tim Still. A few days before he passed away in July 1968, he had been elected vice president of a new community organization in the Central Ward.[45] He had likely been recruited to the cause by Willie Wright, who was a parishioner at Queen of Angels, a black Catholic church with a history of community activism and a corps of young white priests committed to that work.[46] Among the latter was Father Bill Linder, who shared with Still a growing dissatisfaction with the direction in which community action was heading. To him, its decentralized structure had generated too much competition and controversy to offer much help to those in need. To Still, the controversy and various reforms suffered by the UCC in the year after the riots threatened to make it a source of disillusionment rather than change.[47] The *New* Community Corporation, as it was called, would be more flexible than community action in its approach to fund-raising (it would have to be, as public funding dried up), yet maintain its participatory ethic. In its earliest days, the NCC pulled together a mixture of public and private funding—including money raised by selling symbolic five-dollar shares in the corporation to area suburbanites—to build housing in the Central Ward. Residents participated in the design of the housing project, which broke ground in 1972. They also convinced NCC officials that day care was a prime need in the neighborhood, and in 1969 the NCC established its first Babyland day care center in the basement of the Scudder Homes public housing project. The prime moving force behind the establishment of Babyland was Mary Smith, a UCC trustee who had helped organize the first three area boards back in 1965 as a member of its Community Action Task Force.[48]

Two years before, other UCC leaders had launched another community development corporation, the Tri-City Citizens' Union for Progress (an outgrowth of meetings convened by Nathan Wright to discuss his own proposed tri-city organizing agency). Designed as an alternative to the large-scale demolition offered by urban renewal, Tri-City rehabilitated existing housing near West Side Park, promoted black home ownership, and organized residents to be their own advocates. Like the NCC, they were pragmatic with their fund-raising efforts, drawing on both public and private funds, which they raised through a financing office they called Priorities Investment. Its first president was Oliver Lofton, director of the Newark Legal Services Project and soon to be one of Governor Hughes's riot commissioners. One of Tri-City's three cofounders was Rebecca Andrade, who had founded the UCC's Newark Pre-School Council and served, with the NCC's Mary Smith, on its Community Action Task Force.[49]

With black nationalist politics on the rise, white organizers left Lower Clinton Hill in the summer of 1968. They went in various directions, but several of them ended up in Newark's still largely white Ironbound neighborhood. There, they continued to work on welfare rights issues and established the Ironbound Youth Project, which included a teen community center and Independence High School, and recruited SDS members and VISTA volunteers to work in the neighborhood.[50] A more lasting impact came from the work of Derek Winans, a native Newarker whose long career of activism had taken him from the Harvard College Young Democrats, the Kennedy campaign, and the Essex County Americans for Democratic Action to the Newark Coordinating Committee, which grew out of the protests at the Barringer High School construction site in 1963, and the United Community Corporation. He worked closely with the Newark Community Union Project in Clinton Hill, where he served as chair of Area Board 3's personnel committee and was elected to the central UCC board. As community action was dismantled, he too moved his work to the Ironbound, where he focused on the needs and desires of young mothers. He and other neighborhood activists launched a preschool program in 1969, the first endeavor of the new Ironbound Community Corporation. The ICC has since combined social services, community organizing, the trilingual skills of its staff, and a pioneering attention to urban environmental justice into powerful neighborhood mobilizations in a predominantly immigrant community.[51]

A thread of community action has run through Newark city hall, too. Ken Gibson kept a lock on office until 1986, when South Ward councilman Sharpe James, who began his political career as chairman of the UCC's Area Board 9, unseated his former antipoverty and Community Choice ticket colleague with a campaign that emphasized the lack of development outside downtown, in the neighborhoods.[52] More recently, Mayor Ras Baraka, son of Amiri, has revived some of Newark's community action ethic and at least one of its central proposals. In April 2015—over half a century after the campaign for civilian oversight of police work began at a meeting in St. James AME Church, and despite protests from local police unions— Mayor Baraka signed an executive order establishing a Civilian Complaint Review Board, which will investigate complaints against the police department and make recommendations to the police director. Its membership is to be shared between city officials and representatives of five community organizations, including the Ironbound Community Corporation and the ACLU. This action grew out of decades of agitation by the ACLU, the local People's Organization for Progress (which proudly declares itself an outgrowth of "the struggles of the African-American community during the late sixties and seventies for justice"), and others, which, in turn, culminated in a Department of Justice investigation of the police department and a landmark consent decree.[53]

Community action, therefore, has had an institutional presence in Newark since the 1960s, sometimes in city hall, but more steadily outside it. The UCC and FOCUS, New Community, Tri-City, the Ironbound Community Corporation, Steve Adubato's North Ward Education and Cultural Center all still exist today. And they have been joined by other groups that share a general orientation to neighborhood-based organizing and development, even if their ties to the community action struggles of the 1960s are not so direct, including the Unified Vailsburg Services Organization in the West Ward and La Casa de Don Pedro in the Lower Broadway area of the North Ward, both founded in 1972. Any accounting of their accomplishments in Newark would have to include the housing saved and the housing built; the Superfund and brownfield sites cleaned up or remediated; the day care centers, schools, and after-school programs that have educated thousands of Newark children; the work training offered and the businesses established; the health care services provided; and the rich cultural life that has been maintained and celebrated. And it must include the ways in which this work continues to value the lives, desires, and knowledge of community residents at least as much as it values the land they live on.

Though this story of community action began with a president, it ends in Newark's neighborhoods among various community groups and workers, because that is where we will find most clearly the participatory ethic and structures that, however briefly, remade local politics under the Great Society. It is there, even amid pragmatic accommodations to prevailing modes of development and notions of economic opportunity, that we find organizations carrying on the work of building self-sufficiency and self-determination, critiquing the methods and goals of urban public policy, and providing a broad array of services to those who stayed in or continued to come to Newark. And it is there that we will find the main source of whatever equity and capital remains in Newark's neighborhoods as they continue through their urban crises.

ACKNOWLEDGMENTS

I'll start with the dedicatees: three people I lost recently who shaped me as an individual and a historian, who modeled so convincingly how to be in the world, imparted a love of storytelling, and forever wore smiles. Amid all the relief of finishing this book, there's a sharp pain in knowing they won't read it.

My grandparents Fran and Lou Krasovic, both orphans, found each other as teenagers at a grange-hall dance in 1935 and spent the next seventy-five years together. They were both inveterate tellers of tales, some taller than others, all enchanting. Hanging out on their back porch, listening to them talk of coal towns, the Home for the Friendless, farm life, moving to New Jersey, cross-country travels, assorted family hijinks—this was what got me hooked on stories. Their love of reading (him: history and adventure; her: romance) made it all right for me to be a bookworm. The grace and humor with which they lived tough lives have left me no excuses. I try to live up to their example every day.

The first time I presented a piece of my research in Newark, I looked up from (very anxiously) reading my paper and saw Clement Price smiling. And he never stopped making me feel welcome in the profession, in Newark, at Rutgers. When he passed away in 2014, some people described him as a "cheerleader" for Newark, but I wasn't so sure. He *was* a careful student of the city, a critical scholar and public intellectual, a model citizen. "Cheerleader" suggests more the offer of undeserved, but nonetheless energetic and sincere, support. Clem was, then, my cheerleader, and I try to deserve it every day.

Among the many things I owe to Clem Price is my presence at Rutgers University–Newark, where I've had the amazing good luck to land among extraordinary colleagues at an exciting time for the university. My first stop was the Institute on Ethnicity, Culture, and the Modern Experience (now the Price Institute). Since then, I've happily worked side by side with Marisa "Farasha" Pierson and Laura Troiano, the two most skillful guides through the tangles of university bureaucracy, thoughtful program developers, and supportive colleagues I could hope for. What's more, they're creative, funny, brilliant friends. Alison Kolodny and Aftan Baldwin helped me with innumerable tasks and helped make 49 Bleeker so much more a home than a workplace. I was fortunate enough to overlap with Amy Bach for a couple years and several beers and to follow an amazing, humbling group of Dodge Fellows, an extended Price Institute family. Thanks to Charles Russell for helping me get here and for always being there when I have a question or need advice. And to the sagacious Sherri-Ann Butterfield, my guardian angel: thanks for always answering my calls and texts.

After being reared in graduate school on horrifying tales of life in academic departments, I'm still pinching myself for having joined the Federated Department of History at Rutgers and the New Jersey Institute of Technology and the Program in American Studies. I could not imagine more wonderful colleagues, and I thank every last one. I owe a special debt to Robert Snyder, whose faith and feedback pushed this book forward at key moments. For reading, providing writing models, and general advising, thanks also to Beryl Satter, Whit Strub, Tim Stewart-Winter, Mary Rizzo, Jim Goodman, Ruth Feldstein, and Tim Raphael. Karen Caplan looked out for me at a real low point—major thanks. The incomparable Christina Strasburger, Rabeya Rahman, and Georgia Mellos look out for all of us.

The interests that eventually coalesced into this book first took shape at Michigan State, where David Bailey, Dean Rehberger, Richard Thomas, Peter Levine, and Mark Kornbluh led me up a steep learning curve. One of them must have called ahead to New Haven and explained how much patience having me as a student required, because I encountered inexhaustible wells there. Matthew Frye Jacobson's intellectual flexibility and commitment remain inspirations. Trying to keep up with Jean-Christophe Agnew in conversation and on the basketball court was equal parts exhilarating and exhausting. Glenda Gilmore's interest in this project extended well beyond the time I was technically her student, even to a recent lunch when she pulled out a red pen and started reading some of my writing (provoking involuntary nervous twitching on my part). Other faculty members who helped with this project, sometimes unwittingly, with words of encouragement and critique that still bounce around my brain, include Robert Johnston, Jonathan Holloway, Nancy Cott, John Demos, and David Brion Davis.

My time in graduate school was incredibly rich in friendship, making those years so fulfilling and enjoyable in ways that went well beyond the academic and that have continued even as the geographical whims of the job market have had their way with us. I have to thank especially Lucia Trimbur, Brian Herrera, Sandy Zipp, Aaron Sachs, Kip Kosek, Roxanne Willis, Dan Gilbert, Lara Cohen, Amanda Ciafone, Amy Reading, Jay Farmer, Josh Guild, Brenda Carter, Rebecca Davis, Christine Evans, Beth Linker, Nick Parrillo, Geoff Pynn, Adam Solomon, and, of course, Vicki Shepard.

A handful of others read the manuscript, in whole or in part, and gave me vital feedback. Howard Gillette's multiple careful readings whipped it into much tighter shape. He was an ideal reader: knowledgeable and generous. Alison Isenberg's encouraging response meant the world to me. Julian Zelizer made a suggestion for revision late in the game that was spot on, even if I tried to resist it for a while. One coffee with Paige McGinley changed the way I thought about investigative commissions. Series editors Becky Nicolaides and Jim Grossman gave me invaluable encouragement and ideas. And to the one reader who remains anonymous, many thanks for your incredible wealth of knowledge and eye for detail.

At the University of Chicago Press, Tim Mennel let me write what I wanted to write, valued it, judiciously assessed it, and nudged it forward with great kindness and skill. Thanks also to Nora Devlin, Jenni Fry, and Ashley Pierce for all their production and marketing skills. Eagle-eyed George Roupe saved me from numerous errors of fact and style.

For financial assistance with research and publication, thanks to Rutgers University–Newark; Yale University; the Beinecke Rare Books and Manuscripts Library at Yale; the estate of Robert M. Leylan; the Lyndon Baines Johnson Foundation; and the New Jersey Historical Commission.

Libraries and archives were homes away from home, sometimes for weeks at a time. Being there, amid the boxes and folders and papers, was my favorite part of the process. It's hard to beat the Newark Public Library for its holdings, sense of history, and public commitment. Thanks to the late, great Charles Cummings, who, on my very first visit, made a point of coming out and greeting me personally with a warmth I'll never forget. Those who have ably carried on his work and helped me immensely include George Hawley, Dale Colston, Brad Small, and James Osbourne. And special thanks to Tom Ankner, whom I must have driven crazy, though you would never know it for his good-natured calm. At the New Jersey State Archives, thanks especially to Donald Cornelius for answering thousands of annoying little questions about why I couldn't look at all the records, and to Joanne Nestor. Thanks to Allen Fisher at the LBJ Library for guiding me through the collections and, again, answering thousands of little questions; and also to Lauren Gerson, Sarah Haldeman, Barbara Constable, and the rest of the staff members in the reading room. Many thanks to Jose DaSilva and Joyce Lanier at the Newark City Archives; Brianna LoSardo and Alan Delozier at the Archives and Special Collections Center at Seton Hall University; Stephen Plotkin at the John F. Kennedy Library; Cheryl Schnirring at the Abraham Lincoln Presidential Library; Lois Densky-Wolff at what was then the University of Medicine and Dentistry of New Jersey archives; and Jennifer McGillan and Linda Forgash at the Jewish Historical Society of New Jersey. Thanks to Harry Miller at the Wisconsin Historical Society; Linnea Anderson at the University of Minnesota's Social Welfare History Archives; Erin Sloan at the Carl Albert Congressional Research and Studies Center at the University of Oklahoma; the Center for American History at the University of Texas; and Mary Beth Brown at the Western Historical Manuscript Collection at the University of Missouri for sending me materials. And, finally, thanks to the staffs at the National Archives in College Park; Yale's Beinecke and Sterling Libraries, especially the microtexts room; the Dana, Alexander, and Kilmer Libraries at Rutgers University, especially Alexander's special collections and microfilm rooms; the New Jersey State Library; the New Jersey Historical Society archives; the Schomburg Center for Research in Black Culture; NYU's Tamiment Library; the Walter P. Reuther Library at Wayne State; Lafayette College's Special Collections and College Archives; Rider University's Moore Library; and the library at the College of New Jersey. Brian Hohmann's last-minute research help was deeply appreciated.

For additional help with photos, thanks to Vinessa Erminio, Amanda Glickman, Matthew Lutts, and Joe McCary. For the wonderful maps, thanks to Mike Siegel at the Rutgers Cartography Lab.

Though they don't always show up in the text or notes, many former and current Newarkers (whether by residence or employment) consented to interviews, responded to random e-mails looking for clarifications and confirmations, "let me" corner them at public events, joined me for coffee or meals, and generally just wowed me with their generosity, even when (*especially* when) they disagreed with an interpretation or point of fact. Chief among these has been Robert Curvin, whose mixture of encouragement and criticism keeps me on my toes. Many, many thanks also to Walter Afflitto, Lawrence Bilder, Brendan Byrne, Richard Cammarieri, Bob Cartwright, Walter Chambers, Samuel Convissor, Theodore Dachowski, Dickinson Debevoise, Victor De Luca, Rebecca Doggett, Louise Epperson, Corinna Fales, Ronald Gasparinetti, John J. Gibbons, Carol Glassman,

Gustav Heningburg, Harold Hodes, Phil Hutchings, Sanford Jaffe, Ledlie Laughlin, Monsignor William Linder, Roger Lowenstein, Robert Machover, Donald Malafronte, Eric Mann, Tyler McClain, Betty Moss, Jonathan Prinz, George Richardson, Vincent Testa, Cyril Tyson, Madge Wilson, Chi Wright, and Nancy Zak.

Others arranged for me to present my work and read, commented on, and questioned it. A special thanks to Warren Grover, Tim Crist, Linda Epps, and everyone else at the Newark History Society. And I owe a special debt to Tom McCabe, Newark expat and soccer (history) god, who read a lot of this with a discerning eye and was always game to explore a new corner of the city, especially if it contained a bar. Elizabeth Aaron paid me the kindest compliment after reading a chapter. Thanks also to Damon Rich, Linda Morgan, Zemin Zhang, Sally Yerkovich, Niquole Primiani, Sara Cureton, Linda Nettleton, and Ted Lind.

Many, many thanks to all those who made the actual writing possible: to several coffee shops from Newtown to Newark; to Trudy Hale and the many birds of Norwood; especially to Collette Gosselin, who provided living and writing space when contractors kicked us out of our house and police kicked me out of empty classrooms. And to Helen Silsburn, for always being right there, anytime I need her.

Several wonderful friends provided child care at our most desperate moments. So thanks to the following families: the Steele-Hollars, Steinbergs, Carneys, Cubanos, and Paces. And, again, Collette Gosselin.

One of the great things about studying Newark and coming back to New Jersey has been the proximity to family and old friends. Thanks especially to Rich Labot, Peter Hamilton, and Marc Pereira (who early on taught me where to find the best Portuguese food in the city). It's been a joy learning how much Bill and Kathy Dowling appreciate history and the arts.

My family always comes through with love, reassurance, vacations, and lots of much-needed laughter. Few things give me greater pleasure than knowing how happy my parents are at this point in their lives. Stan, Veronica, and Erica are the greatest blessings. The affection I have for them as an adult must be directly proportional to the terror we caused each other as children. Great blessings, too, are the people they've brought into my life: Grainne, Jim, Terry, Sean, Ciara, Auggie, and Bea. And thanks to the Meixner/Conger clan: Ed, Marge, Julie, Chris, Hailey, and Hannah. Your generosity with the checkbook and a scrub brush, your uniquely midwestern charms, and your general wackiness are all deeply appreciated.

And finally, Emily and Efram. Somehow, Efram always finds the exact balance between sadness and joy at the work that went into this book, letting me know he wished I didn't have to spend so much time on it and, despite that, expressing a deep curiosity about the process of writing and the end product. He enriches every moment of my life with his creativity, introspection, and general goofiness. He's exactly what I want him to be: a better person than me. And that's largely because of Emily, who makes everything possible. I could not have finished this without her. Her stability steadies me, and her love of and dedication to her work inspire me. She trusted me completely and never once asked why I was taking another walk or watching another TV show instead of writing. All the time, she remained a remarkable teacher, a productive scholar, and a best friend. I'm not about to run off to find a book this time. Instead, I happily proclaim: you guys are the loves of my life.

ABBREVIATIONS USED IN NOTES

ALPL: Abraham Lincoln Presidential Library, Springfield, IL
CAP: Community Action Program
GPO: Government Printing Office
GSCCD: Governor's Select Commission on Civil Disorders Records (NJSA)
JFKL: John F. Kennedy Library, Boston, MA
JHSNJ: Jewish Historical Society of New Jersey, Whippany, NJ
JWJC: James Weldon Johnson Collection, Beinecke Library, Yale University
LBJL: Lyndon B. Johnson Library, Austin, TX
LEAA: Law Enforcement Assistance Administration Records (NARA)
LOP: Michael Lipsky and David J. Olson Papers (WHS)
NACCD: National Advisory Commission on Civil Disorders Records (LBJL)
NARA: National Archives and Records Administration, College Park, MD
NEN: Newark Evening News
NJAA: New Jersey Afro-American
NJHS: New Jersey Historical Society, Newark, NJ
NJSA: New Jersey State Archives, Trenton, NJ
NJSL: New Jersey State Library, Trenton, NJ
NJSPBA: New Jersey State Patrolmen's Benevolent Association
NPL: Newark Public Library
NWP: Nathan Wright Jr. Papers (SCNYPL)
NYT: New York Times
OEOR: Office of Economic Opportunity Records (NARA)
OLEA: Office of Law Enforcement Assistance Records (NARA)
RUA: Rutgers University Archives
RUL: Rutgers University Libraries
SCNYPL: Schomburg Center, New York Public Library

SL: *Star-Ledger* (Newark)
TET: *Trenton Evening Times*
TLNYU: Tamiment Library, New York University
WHS: Wisconsin Historical Society, Madison, WI
WP: *Washington Post*

NOTES

INTRODUCTION

1. Richard N. Goodwin, *Remembering America: A Voice from the Sixties* (Boston: Little, Brown, 1988), 272; Tom Wicker, "Johnson Pledges 'Great Society,'" *NYT*, April 24, 1964, 14; "Excerpts from Johnson's Address to Georgians," *NYT*, May 9, 1964, 12; "President Urges a 'Great Society,'" *NYT*, May 10, 1964, 73.

2. Goodwin, *Remembering America*, 267–71; Robert M. Warner, *The Anatomy of a Speech: Lyndon Johnson's Great Society Address* (Ann Arbor: Michigan Historical Collections, 1978), 1; Wicker, "President Urges New Federalism," *NYT*, May 23, 1964, 1.

3. Lyndon Johnson, "Remarks at the University of Michigan," May 22, 1964, *Public Papers of the Presidents: Lyndon Baines Johnson, 1963–1964* (Washington, DC: 1964), 704–707.

4. Hallmarks of this era's literature on metropolitan expansion include Christopher Tunnard and Henry Hope Reed, *American Skyline: The Growth and Form of Our Cities and Towns* (1955; reprint, New York: New American Library, 1956); Tunnard, "America's Super-Cities," *Harper's* 217 (August 1958): 62–64; Jean Gottmann, "Megalopolis; or The Urbanization of the Northeastern Seaboard," *Economic Geography* 33, no. 3 (July 1957): 189–200; Walter H. Whyte, ed., *The Exploding Metropolis* (Garden City, NY: Doubleday, 1958); Edward Higbee, *The Squeeze: Cities without Space* (New York: William Morrow, 1960); Gottmann, *Megalopolis: The Urbanized Northeastern Seaboard of the United States* (Cambridge, MA: MIT Press, 1961); Luther Halsey Gulick, *The Metropolitan Problem and American Ideas* (New York: Knopf, 1962); Scott Greer, *The Emerging City: Myth and Reality* (1962; reprint, New Brunswick, NJ: Transaction, 1999); Mitchell Gordon, *Sick Cities: Psychology and Pathology of American Urban Life* (New York: Macmillan, 1963); C. E. Elias et al., *Metropolis: Values in Conflict* (Belmont, CA: Wadsworth, 1964); Victor Gruen, *The Heart of Our Cities; The Urban Crisis: Diagnosis and Cure* (New York: Simon and Schuster, 1964).

5. Johnson, "Remarks at the University of Michigan," 705; US Senate, Committee on Government Operations, Subcommittee on Intergovernmental Relations, *Impact of Federal Urban Development Programs on Local Government Organization and Planning* (Washington, DC: GPO, 1964), iii. For the expansion of the federal role in urban development, see Bernard J. Frieden and Marshall Kaplan, *The Politics of Neglect: Urban Aid from Model Cities to Revenue Sharing* (Cambridge, MA: MIT Press, 1975), 15–18.

6. Johnson, "Remarks at the University of Michigan," 706.
7. Roger Lowenstein, phone interview by author, May 14, 2013; Robert M. Warner, *The Anatomy of a Speech: Lyndon Johnson's Great Society Address* (Ann Arbor: Bentley Historical Library, 1978), 3.
8. "Yale Study Maps a 34,000,000 'City,'" *NYT*, March 27, 1955, 49.
9. For broad overviews of these developments in Newark, see Harold Kaplan, *Urban Renewal Politics: Slum Clearance in Newark* (New York: Columbia University Press, 1963); John T. Cunningham, *Newark* (Newark: New Jersey Historical Society, 1988), 307–312; Brad R. Tuttle, *How Newark Became Newark: The Rise, Fall, and Rebirth of an American City* (New Brunswick, NJ: Rutgers University Press, 2009), 119–154.
10. "New Reform Bills Signed by Driscoll," *NYT*, June 9, 1950, 4.
11. City of Newark, Mayor's Commission on Group Relations, *Newark: A City in Transition*, vol. 1 (Newark, 1959), 1–3.
12. "Northern City Looks at Its Race Problem," *U.S. News & World Report* 46 (April 20, 1959): 64–66.
13. Milton Honig, "Discrimination Protests Rising in Newark," *NYT*, June 16, 1963, 59.
14. Junius Williams, *Unfinished Agenda: Urban Politics in the Era of Black Power* (Berkeley, CA: North Atlantic Books, 2014), 97.
15. Wendell E. Pritchett, "Which Urban Crisis? Regionalism, Race, and Urban Policy, 1960–1974," *Journal of Urban History* 34, no. 2 (January 2008): 266–286; Robert A. Beauregard, *Voices of Decline: The Postwar Fate of U.S. Cities* (New York: Routledge, 2003), especially 150–178. The key literature on postwar liberalism's contradictions, as they played out in cities, includes Arnold Hirsch, *Making the Second Ghetto: Race and Housing in Chicago, 1940–1960* (New York: Cambridge University Press, 1983); Kenneth T. Jackson, *Crabgrass Frontier: The Suburbanization of the United States* (New York: Oxford University Press, 1985); Thomas Sugrue, *The Origins of the Urban Crisis: Race and Inequality in Postwar Detroit* (Princeton, NJ: Princeton University Press, 1996); Lizabeth Cohen, *A Consumer's Republic: The Politics of Mass Consumption in Postwar America* (New York: Knopf, 2003); Robert O. Self, *American Babylon: Race and the Struggle for Postwar Oakland* (Princeton, NJ: Princeton University Press, 2005); Matthew J. Countryman, *Up South: Civil Rights and Black Power in Philadelphia* (Philadelphia: University of Pennsylvania Press, 2006).
16. More and more writing has been tracking this local community-federal government dynamic, especially in histories of the War on Poverty. See, for example: Nancy Naples, *Grassroots Warriors: Activist Mothering, Community Work, and the War on Poverty* (New York: Routledge, 1998); Rhonda Y. Williams, *The Politics of Public Housing: Black Women's Struggles against Urban Inequality* (New York: Oxford University Press, 2005); Annelise Orleck, *Storming Caesar's Palace: How Black Mothers Fought Their Own War on Poverty* (Boston: Beacon, 2006); Noel Cazenave, *Impossible Democracy: The Unlikely Success of the War on Poverty Community Action Program* (Albany: State University of New York Press, 2007); Kent B. Germany, *New Orleans after the Promises: Poverty, Citizenship, and the Search for the Great Society* (Athens: University of Georgia Press, 2007); Thomas Kiffmeyer, *Reformers to Radicals: The Appalachian Volunteers and the War on Poverty* (Lexington: University Press of Kentucky, 2008); Susan Youngblood Ashmore, *Carry It On: The War on Poverty and the Civil Rights Movement in Alabama, 1964–1972* (Athens: University of Georgia Press, 2008); Robert Bauman, *Race and the War on Poverty: From Watts to East L.A.* (Norman: University of Oklahoma Press, 2008); William S. Clayson, *Freedom Is Not Enough: The War on Poverty and the Civil Rights Movement in Texas* (Austin: University of Texas Press,

2010); Orleck and Lisa Gayle Hazirjian, eds., *The War on Poverty: A New Grassroots History* (Athens: University of Georgia Press, 2011); Wesley G. Phelps, *A People's War on Poverty: Urban Politics and Grassroots Activists in Houston* (Athens: University of Georgia Press, 2014).

17. On the centrality of legibility for state functioning, see James C. Scott, *Seeing Like a State: How Certain Schemes to Improve the Human Condition Have Failed* (New Haven, CT: Yale University Press, 1998).

18. Frederick Mosher, "The Changing Responsibilities and Tactics of the Federal Government," *Public Administration Review* 40, no. 6 (November–December 1980): 541–548; James Fesler, "Public Administration and the Social Sciences, 1946 to 1960," in *American Public Administration: Past, Present, and Future*, ed. Frederick Mosher (University: University of Alabama Press, 1974), 97–141; Lester Salamon, "Rethinking Public Management: Third-Party Government and the Changing Forms of Government Action," *Public Policy* 29, no. 3 (1981): 255–275; Brian R. Fry, *Mastering Public Administration: From Max Weber to Dwight Waldo* (Chatham, NJ: Chatham House, 1989). Precursors to community action in the 1960s include the decentralized planning ideas and projects of the Tennessee Valley Authority and the Bureau of Agricultural Economics during the New Deal and various overseas development projects established by the United States during the Cold War. Both are covered in Daniel Immerwahr, *Thinking Small: The United States and the Lure of Community Development* (Cambridge, MA: Harvard University Press, 2015).

19. On pragmatism, experimentation, and irony as postwar liberalism's "social style," see Michael Trask, *Camp Sites: Sex, Politics, and Academic Style in Postwar America* (Stanford, CA: Stanford University Press, 2013).

20. On task forces, see Nancy Kegan Smith, "Presidential Task Force Operation during the Johnson Administration," *Presidential Studies Quarterly* 15, no. 2 (Spring 1985): 320–329; Lyndon B. Johnson, *The Vantage Point: Perspectives of the Presidency, 1963–1969* (New York: Holt, Rinehart, Winston, 1971), 326–327. Philip S. Hughes of Johnson's Bureau of the Budget said, "Johnson's use of the task forces was a major innovation whose significance has been missed. The task force was the basic tool which made much of the success of the Eighty-ninth Congress." Quoted in William E. Leuchtenberg, "The Genesis of the Great Society," *Reporter* 34, no. 8 (April 21, 1966): 38. Measurements of grant activity, which was haphazard and uncoordinated, vary in their details, but the boom of the mid-1960s is clear across studies. George E. Hale and Marian Lief Palley, *The Politics of Federal Grants* (Washington, DC: Congressional Quarterly Press, 1981), 12–13; Lawrence D. Brown et al., *The Changing Politics of Federal Grants* (Washington DC: Brookings Institution, 1984), 6–20; Donald F. Kettl, *Government by Proxy: (Mis)Managing Federal Programs* (Washington, DC: Congressional Quarterly Press, 1988), 53; J. Richard Aronson and John L. Hilley, *Financing State and Local Governments*, 4th ed. (Washington, DC: Brookings Institution, 1986), 49–50; Bernard J. Frieden and Marshall Kaplan, *The Politics of Neglect*, 15; Edward Berkowitz, "Losing Ground? The Great Society in Historical Perspective," in *The Columbia Guide to America in the 1960s*, ed. David Farber and Beth Bailey (New York: Columbia University Press, 2001), 105; Mosher, "The Changing Responsibilities and Tactics of the Federal Government," 542. On the increase in the proportion of congressional sessions given to public hearings in the 1960s, see Christopher J. Deering and Steven S. Smith, *Committees in Congress*, 3rd ed. (Washington, DC: Congressional Quarterly Press, 1997), 158–159. On the growth in numbers of advisory and investigative commissions, see Michael Lipsky

and David J. Olson, *Commission Politics: The Processing of Racial Crisis in America* (New Brunswick, NJ: Transaction, 1977), 91.

21. Other studies that find a relationship between liberalism and black power that was more than antagonistic include Devin Fergus, *Liberalism, Black Power, and the Making of American Politics, 1965–1980* (Athens: University of Georgia Press, 2009); Karen Ferguson, *Top Down: The Ford Foundation, Black Power, and the Reinvention of Racial Liberalism* (Philadelphia: University of Pennsylvania Press, 2013).

22. Daniel Patrick Moynihan, *Maximum Feasible Misunderstanding: Community Action in the War on Poverty* (New York: Free Press, 1969). There is evidence of many more dissenters in the chapters ahead. Perhaps the earliest study of the Community Action Program, funded by a 1967 grant from the Office of Economic Opportunity, found among community action agency (CAA) board members widespread acceptance of protest as a legitimate CAA activity and use of federal funds. See Florence Heller Graduate School for Advanced Studies in Social Welfare, *Community Representation in Community Action Programs*, Report no. 2 (August 1968), 19–20.

23. See, for example, Eric Hobsbawm, "The City Mob," in *Primitive Rebels: Studies in Archaic Forms of Social Movement in the 19th and 20th Centuries* (New York: Norton, 1965), 108–125; E. P. Thompson, "The Moral Economy of the English Crowd in the Eighteenth Century," *Past and Present* 50 (February 1971): 76–136; Natalie Zemon Davis, "The Rites of Violence," in *Society and Culture in Early Modern France* (Stanford, CA: Stanford University Press, 1975), 152–188.

CHAPTER ONE

1. John Kenneth Galbraith, *The Affluent Society* (Boston: Houghton Mifflin, 1958); Michael Harrington, "Our Fifty Million Poor: Forgotten Men of the Affluent Society," *Commentary* 28 (July 1959): 19–27; Harrington, *The Other America: Poverty in the United States* (New York: Macmillan, 1962); Leon Keyserling, "Two-Fifths of a Nation," *Progressive* 26 (June 1962): 11–14; Harry M. Caudill, *Night Comes to the Cumberlands: A Biography of a Depressed Area* (Boston: Little, Brown, 1962); Homer Bigart, "Kentucky Miners: A Grim Winter," *NYT*, October 20, 1963. For the influence on Kennedy, see Michael L. Gillette, *Launching the War on Poverty: An Oral History* (New York: Twayne, 1996), 1–11, 33; Barbara Newell, notes to interview with Robert Lampman, June 16, 1965, WHS; James L. Sundquist, "Origins of the War on Poverty," in *On Fighting Poverty: Perspectives from Experience*, ed. Sundquist (New York: Basic Books, 1969), 20; Arthur Schlesinger Jr., *A Thousand Days: John F. Kennedy in the White House* (Boston: Houghton Mifflin, 1965), 1009; Sar A. Levitan, *The Great Society's Poor Law: A New Approach to Poverty* (Baltimore: Johns Hopkins University Press, 1969), 12–13.

2. Carl M. Brauer, "Kennedy, Johnson, and the War on Poverty," *Journal of American History* 69, no. 1 (June 1982): 98–119. For even more evidence of Kennedy's reading habits, see 103n12. In addition to the works cited, my account of the formation of the Community Action Program is particularly indebted to Levitan, *The Great Society's Poor Law*; Sundquist, *On Fighting Poverty*; Peter Marris and Martin Rein, *Dilemmas of Social Reform: Poverty and Community Action in the United States* (New York: Atherton, 1967).

3. John F. Kennedy, "Remarks in Heber Springs, Arkansas," October 3, 1963, *Public Papers of the Presidents: John F. Kennedy, 1963* (Washington, DC: GPO, 1964), 762.

4. On emphasizing the institutional over the presidential in political history, see Julian Zelizer, "Beyond the Presidential Synthesis: Reordering Political Time," in *A Com-*

panion to Post-1945 America, ed. Jean-Christophe Agnew and Roy Rosenzweig (Malden, MA: Blackwell, 2002), 345–370. On the Great Society writ large, see Zelizer, *The Fierce Urgency of Now: Lyndon Johnson, Congress, and the Battle for the Great Society* (New York: Penguin, 2015).

5. William M. Capron in Poverty and Urban Policy Conference transcript, Brandeis University, June 16–17, 1973, 141–142, JFKL. See also Robert Lampman in Gillette, *Launching the War on Poverty*, 6–8; Brauer, "Kennedy, Johnson, and the War on Poverty," 109.

6. Capron in Poverty and Urban Police Conference transcript, 142–143, 169–170; Heller in Gillette, *Launching the War on Poverty*, 12.

7. Stephen K. Bailey, "Managing the Federal Government," in *Agenda for the Nation*, ed. Kermit Gordon (Washington, DC: Brookings Institution, 1968), 304–309; Rowland Egger, "The Period of Crisis: 1933–1945," in *American Public Administration: Past, Present, Future*, ed. Frederick Mosher (University: University of Alabama Press, 1974), 73–78; Brack Brown and Richard J. Stillman III, *A Search for Public Administration: The Ideas and Career of Dwight Waldo* (College Station: Texas A&M University Press, 1986), 45. Two key players in the formation of the Community Action Program later identified the Bureau of the Budget as the program's strongest supporter within the executive branch. Richard Boone, "Reflections on Citizen Participation and the Economic Opportunity Act," undated [1975], n. 6, "CCC, Boone, Cit. Particip. Paper 1975" folder, box 20, Center for Community Change Collection, Walter Reuther Library, Wayne State University; David Hackett oral history transcript, October 21, 1970, 90–92, JFKL.

8. David Bell oral history transcript, July 11, 1964, 4–9, JFKL.

9. William Cannon in Poverty and Urban Policy Conference transcript, 172–178.

10. John Knowles, *A Separate Peace* (New York: Bantam, 1959), 11.

11. David Hackett oral history transcript, July 22, 1970, 2–7, 10, 14–17, JFKL; Evan Thomas, *Robert Kennedy: His Life* (New York: Simon and Schuster, 2000), 38–39.

12. Laurence Leamer, *The Kennedy Women: The Saga of an American Family* (New York: Villard Books, 1994), 393, 415–416, 575; Hackett oral history transcript, October 21, 1970, 66–67.

13. Hackett oral history transcript, October 21, 1970, 72–74, 94–95, JFKL; Edward Schmitt, *President of the Other America: Robert Kennedy and the Politics of Poverty* (Amherst: University of Massachusetts Press, 2010), 69–71.

14. "Robert Kennedy Meets Gang Members Here," *NYT*, March 9, 1961, 6; John P. McKenzie, "Shirt-Sleeved Bob Kennedy Goes Slumming," *WP*, March 9, 1961, A1.

15. Hackett oral history transcript, October 21, 1970, 67–70.

16. Notes from interview with Richard Boone, January 30, 1969, 1, Notes folder, box 1, Richardson White Papers, JFKL; Hackett to Robert Kennedy, January 8, 1962, "Key Documents 1961–1965" folder, box 4, Daniel Knapp Papers, JFKL.

17. Boone interview notes, January 30, 1969, 1–2, Notes folder, box 1; Boone, statement before NACCD, October 6, 1967, 1, "Pres. Advisory Comm. on Civil Disorder" folder, box 26, Center for Community Change Collection, Reuther Library.

18. Richard A. Cloward and Lloyd E. Ohlin, *Delinquency and Opportunity: A Theory of Delinquent Gangs* (Glencoe, IL: Free Press, 1960); Alice O'Connor, *Poverty Knowledge: Social Science, Social Policy, and the Poor in Twentieth-Century U.S. History* (Princeton, NJ: Princeton University Press, 2002), chapter 4; James Gilbert, *A Cycle of Outrage: America's Reaction to the Juvenile Delinquent in the 1950s* (New York: Oxford University Press, 1988), 127–42.

19. Noel A. Cazenave, *Impossible Democracy: The Unlikely Success of the War on Poverty Community Action Programs* (Albany: State University of New York Press, 2007), 20–21; Daniel Knapp, notes from interview with Ohlin, December 11, 1967, 2–3, box 51, Knapp Papers, JFKL.
20. Notes from interview with Ohlin and Leonard Cottrell, February 21, 1969, 3–5, Notes Misc. folder, box 7, Richardson White Papers, JFKL.
21. Emma Harrison, "U.S. to Aid Plan for Youths Here," *NYT*, December 16, 1959, 46.
22. "East Side Groups Weigh Slum Role," *NYT*, April 3, 1960, 127.
23. Hackett oral history transcript, October 21, 1970, 73, JFKL.
24. PCJD Memo on Grant to New York City and Mobilization for Youth, Inc., May 31, 1962, "Hackett: Memorandum and Notes (1)" folder, box 7, Richardson White Papers, JFKL.
25. "Remarks by Eunice Kennedy Shriver: Commencement, Santa Clara University," June 2, 1962, accessed March 31, 2012, http://www.jfklibrary.org/Asset-Viewer/Archives/JFKPOF-032-016.aspx; "Home-Front Peace Corps Is Proposed," *WP*, June 3, 1962, A12; Eunice Kennedy Shriver oral history transcript, May 7, 1968, 21–22, JFKL.
26. Boone interview notes, January 30, 1969, 2, Notes folder, box 1, Richardson White Papers, JFKL.
27. Hedrick Smith, "President Spurs Home Peace Corps," *NYT*, November 18, 1962, 1; Eve Edstrom, "Domestic Aid Corps Considered," *WP*, November 17, 1962, A1.
28. Boone interview notes, January 30, 1969, 3, Notes folder, box 1, Richardson White Papers, JFKL.
29. Boone and Milton Ogle, "A Volunteer Component for the Eastern Kentucky Program" (1963) quoted in Thomas Kiffmeyer, *Reformers to Radicals: The Appalachian Volunteers and the War on Poverty* (Lexington: University Press of Kentucky, 2008), 39, 35–36. See also Boone interview notes, January 20, 1969, 3–4, Notes folder, box 1; Mark Furstenberg interview notes, January 22, 1969, 2–3, Notes Misc. folder, box 7; both Richardson White Papers, JFKL.
30. Boone in Poverty and Urban Policy Conference transcript, 245.
31. Ibid., 245–246; Boone interview notes, January 30, 1969, 3, Notes folder, box 1, Richardson White Papers, JFKL; Boone, "Reflections on Citizen Participation and the Economic Opportunity Act," n.d. [1975], 7–8n5, "CCC, Boone, Cit. Particip. 1975" folder, box 20, Center for Community Change Collection, Reuther Library. Boone noted in this essay that, when the Office of Economic Opportunity was established, it very deliberately established direct ties with local tribal councils rather than working through the Bureau of Indian Affairs. On Robert Kennedy's trips through poor areas, see Schmitt, *President of the Other America*, 82–86.
32. Boone, statement before NACCD, October 6, 1967, 8, "Pres. Advisory Comm. on Civil Disorder" folder, box 26, Center for Community Change Collection, Reuther Library.
33. Hackett oral history transcript, October 21, 1970, 83–84, JFKL; notes from Virginia Burns interview, November 28, 1967, 1–4; notes from Sanford Kravitz interview, December 11, 1967, 6; both box 51, Knapp Papers, JFKL; notes from Hackett interview, January 27, 1969, 5, Notes folder, box 1, Richardson White Papers, JFKL.
34. Notes from Kravitz interview, December 11, 1967, 2–5; Burns interview notes, November 28, 1967, 2; both box 51, Daniel Knapp Papers, JFKL.
35. Kravitz in Poverty and Urban Policy Conference transcript, 33–34.

36. Notes from Mark Furstenberg interview, January 22, 1969, 3, Notes Misc. folder, box 7, Richardson White Papers, JFKL.

37. Brauer, "Kennedy, Johnson, and the War on Poverty," 109–112; Jack Anderson and Les Whitten, "Jonah and the Federal Whale," WP, September 11, 1976, D7.

38. William M. Capron in Poverty and Urban Policy Conference transcript, 40–41, 144–145, 154.

39. For more on the role of social science, see O'Connor, Poverty Knowledge, 124–136. A growing literature has established connections between the construction of community action and international development projects. See Alyosha Goldstein, Poverty in Common: The Politics of Community Action during the American Century (Durham, NC: Duke University Press, 2012); Sheyda Jahanbani, "One Global War on Poverty: The Johnson Administration Fights Poverty at Home and Abroad, 1964–1968," in Beyond the Cold War: Lyndon Johnson and the New Global Challenges of the 1960s, ed. Francis J. Gavin and Mark Atwood Lawrence (New York: Oxford University Press, 2014), 97–117; Immerwahr, Thinking Small.

40. Barbara Newell, notes from Robert Lampman interview, June 16, 1965, WHS.

41. Quoted in Brauer, "Kennedy, Johnson, and the War on Poverty," 113–114; Lyndon B. Johnson, The Vantage Point: Perspectives of the Presidency (New York: Holt, Rinehart, Winston, 1971), 69–71.

42. Boone interview notes, January 30, 1969, Notes folder, box 1, Richardson White Papers, JFKL.

43. Hackett to Heller, December 1, 1963, Legislative Background: Economic Opportunity Act of 1964, box 1, White House Central Files, LBJL.

44. Adam Yarmolinsky oral history transcript, July 13, 1970, 1–10, and October 21, 1980, 3–5, LBJL. Yarmolinsky knew Shriver from Kennedy's 1960 campaign, and he had become a special assistant to Secretary of Defense Robert McNamara in the new administration before moving to the antipoverty task force.

45. William Cannon (Budget Bureau) and Richard Boone in Poverty and Urban Policy Conference transcript, 234, 238–239.

46. Boone and Adam Yarmolinsky in Poverty and Urban Policy Conference transcript, 255; Yarmolinsky oral history transcript, July 13, 1970, 11, LBJL. In 1966, Yarmolinsky wrote to the task force member who had drafted the legislation to confirm his memory of the origins of the phrase. He was right. Yarmolinsky to Norbert A. Schlei, April 8, 1966; Schlei to Yarmolinsky, April 13, 1966; both "OEO Yarmolinsky" folder, box 87, Yarmolinsky Papers, JFKL.

47. William Capron and Adam Yarmolinsky in Poverty and Urban Policy Conference transcript, 43, 241–242.

48. Boone, "Reflections on Citizen Participation and the Economic Opportunity Act," undated [1975], 4, "CCC, Boone, Cit. Particip. Paper 1975" folder, box 20, Center for Community Change Collection, Reuther Library.

49. Notes from David Grossman and Fred Hayes interview, February 6, 1969, 2; notes from Furstenberg interview, January 22, 1969, 2; both Notes Misc. folder, box 7, Richardson White Papers, JFKL. See also Hackett oral history transcript, October 21, 1970, 100, 105, JFKL.

50. See Kiffmeyer, Reformers to Radicals.

51. Hackett oral history transcript, October 21, 1970, 97–99, JFKL.

52. Jack Conway oral history transcript, April 10, 1972, 14–15, 54, 71–80, 90, JFKL; Nelson Lichtenstein, Walter Reuther: The Most Dangerous Man in Detroit (Urbana: University of Illinois Press, 1995), 212–213, 368–369, 384–389.

53. Jack Raymond, "President to Ask a Billion in Aid for Appalachia," *NYT*, April 26, 1964, 1.

54. Lichtenstein, *Walter Reuther*, 389–390.

55. Conway, statement before the House Committee on Education and Labor, April 28, 1964, 1, 4, OEO Poverty Legislation folder, box 87, Yarmolinsky Papers, JFKL. Sanford Kravitz recalled Conway's use of the three-legged-stool image with the mayors. Minutes, American Academy of Arts and Sciences Seminar on Poverty, March 3, 1967, 10, Seminar on Poverty 1966–67 folder, box 88, Yarmolinsky Papers, JFKL.

56. Cloward quoted in Cazenave, *Impossible Democracy*, 75, 119.

57. Bigart, "Report Due Today on Youth Agency," *NYT*, August 21, 1964, 56.

58. PCJD press release, February 4, 1963, Newsletters and Progress Reports folder, box 1, Eleanor Charwat Papers, JFKL; MFY Field Visit Report, April 4, 1963, Field Visits folder, box 6, Richardson White Papers, JFKL; Gertrude Goldberg, "Summary of Report on Visiting Homemakers: Emphasizing the Use of Indigenous Persons in a Social Work Program," July 1963, Mobilization for Youth folder, box 7, Richardson White Papers, JFKL.

59. Cazenave, *Impossible Democracy*, 119–120.

60. "Lower East Side Plans Rent Rally," *NYT*, January 12, 1964, 80.

61. Harold H. Weissman, "Education Innovation: The Case of an External Innovating Organization," in *Employment and Educational Services in the Mobilization for Youth Experience*, ed. Harold H. Weissman (New York: Associated Press, 1969), 216–218; notes from George Brager interview, December 4, 1967, 3, box 51, Daniel Knapp Papers, JFKL.

62. Gene Currivan, "Principals Assail Juvenile Agency," *NYT*, January 31, 1964, 29. Bernard Russell, one of Hackett's guerillas, later recalled that MOM protested the "Dick and Jane" textbooks the schools used; notes from interview with Russell, November 29, 1967, box 51, Knapp Papers, JFKL.

63. Currivan, "Principals Assail Juvenile Agency," 29.

64. "Hearing Is Planned on Youth Program," *NYT*, February 3, 1964, 17.

65. Leonard Buder, "Boycott Cripples City Schools," *NYT*, February 4, 1964, 1. For context on the boycott, see Clarence Taylor, "Conservative and Liberal Opposition to the New York City School-Integration Campaign," in *Civil Rights in New York City: From World War II to the Giuliani Era*, ed. Taylor (New York: Fordham University Press, 2010), 95–117.

66. For an accessible account of this rioting, see Janet L. Abu-Lughod, *Race, Space, and Riots in Chicago, New York, and Los Angeles* (New York: Oxford University Press, 2007), 171–178, which, in turn, is largely (though not exclusively) based on Fred C. Shapiro and James W. Sullivan, *Race Riots: New York, 1964* (New York: Crowell, 1969).

67. "Mobs Fight Police Again in Brooklyn and Harlem Area," *NYT*, July 22, 1964, 1.

68. "City Investigating Agency for Youth on the East Side," *NYT*, August 16, 1964; William Federici, Edward O'Neill, and Henry Lee, "Anti-JD Agency Probed for Red Ties," *Daily News*, August 16, 1964, 2; Bigart, "City Hunts Reds in Youth Project on the East Side," *NYT*, August 17, 1964, 1.

69. Bigart, "City Hunts Reds"; and Bigart, "Youth Project Chief Is Called to Capital," *NYT*, August 18, 1964, 1.

70. Bigart, "FBI Rechecking Youth Workers," *NYT*, August 20, 1964, 46; Bigart, "9 in Youth Project Linked to Leftists," *NYT*, August 19, 1964, 1.

71. Bigart, "Youth Project Chief Is Called to Capital," 1, 15.

72. Shriver, letter to the editor, *NYT*, August 21, 1964, 28.

73. Adam Yarmolinsky in Poverty and Urban Policy Conference transcript, 249–250.

74. Brager and Leonard Cottrell quoted in Martin Tolchin, "Youth-Agency Aim Stirring Debate," *NYT*, August 22, 1964, 22. Cottrell later said that this belief came from a faith in the competence of local residents, that they knew how to articulate their own needs and desires. But he also recognized that, to some extent, these local groups had run away with the staff of MFY. He used MOM as his example. See notes from interview with Lloyd Ohlin and Leonard Cottrell, February 21, 1969, Notes Misc. folder, box 7, Richardson White Papers, JFKL. Richard Cloward, who with Ohlin had devised the original opportunity thesis and who was MFY's research director, later said that whatever worthwhile change had occurred on the Lower East Side had been generated by conflict, not cooperation. Notes from interview with Cloward, December 5, 1967, box 51, Daniel Knapp Papers, JFKL. For his part, David Hackett came to believe that no one "outside of the small group that we worked with really understood what we were up to, and we suffered two or three years later because of this misinterpretation." Hackett oral history transcript, October 21, 1970, 76, JFKL.

CHAPTER TWO

1. Minutes of the Newark antipoverty meeting, July 29, 1964, folder 20, box 2, Cyril Tyson Papers, SCNYPL; "City Preparing Drive on Poverty," *SL*, July 30, 1964, 8; "Newark Seeking Its Share of Anti-Poverty Program," *NEN*, July 30, 1964, 22; Addonizio, GSCCD hearing transcript, September 29, 1967, 97–98. Larry Houston identified as a "guerilla" in Daniel Knapp, notes from interview with Virginia Burns, November 28, 1967, 4, box 51, Knapp Papers, JFKL.

2. Heckel statement, May 15, 1964, folder 4, box 59, Mason Gross Papers, RUA; Julia Rabig, "The Laboratory of Democracy': Construction Industry Racism in Newark and the Limits of Liberalism," in *Black Power at Work: Community Control, Affirmative Action, and the Construction Industry*, ed. David Goldberg and Trevor Griffey (Ithaca, NY: Cornell University Press, 2010), 60–62.

3. Rutgers Urban Studies Center, Application to the Ford Foundation for the Operation of the Urban Studies Center, 52, box 48, folder 2, Richard Schlatter Papers, RUA; Samuel Convissor, interview by author, May 23, 2012.

4. Rutgers Urban Studies Center, Supplement to Report for Period Ending June 30, 1962, 5, folder 1, box 48; 1962–1963 Annual Report, 27, 47–50, folder 3, box 48, Schlatter Papers, RUA. Also Bob Shabazian, "South Side Area Is Chosen for Social Conditions Study," *NEN*, September 9, 1962, 1; "New Unit Meets on Urban Renewal," *NEN*, November 3, 1962, 2; Donald Malafronte, "Newark Maps Field Test on Delinquency Problem," *SL*, April 7, 1963, 4. For further evidence of a strong participatory ethic, see Convissor testimony, Senate Subcommittee on the National Service Corps, *National Service Corps* (Washington, D.C.: GPO, 1963), 161–163; Minutes of Meeting of the Committee on Human Aspects of Urban Renewal, May 28, 1962, 2–3, box 48, folder 1, Schlatter Papers, RUA.

5. Rutgers Urban Studies Center, Application to the Ford Foundation, 50; "New Unit Meets on Urban Renewal," *NEN*, November 3, 1962, 2; "Group Seen Aiding City," *NEN*, February 15, 1963, 31.

6. Dorothy Tabourne, "Projects Proposed to Aid Youngsters," *NEN*, April 26, 1964, 40; Convissor interview, May 23, 2012.

7. Heckel resume, folder 14, box 2, Eldridge Papers, NPL; Heckel, "The Bill of Rights," in *Monographs*, Governor's Committee on Preparatory Research (Trenton: State of New Jersey, 1947), 1–2, 42.

8. Lowenstein, *Alan V. Lowenstein: New Jersey Lawyer & Community Leader* (Piscataway, NJ: Rutgers University Press; New Brunswick, NJ: New Jersey Institute for Continuing Legal Education, 2001), 199–203; Charter Commission of the City of Newark, *Final Report* (Newark, 1953), 9–10; "Plan Drive for Charter," *NEN*, February 14, 1953, 5; William May, "Citizens' Cold, Hard Work Won the Fight for Newark," *NEN*, January 17, 1955, 4.

9. On honesty and efficiency, see "Ellenstein in Board Race," *NEN*, February 15, 1953, 2; "Views Told on Charter," *NEN*, June 10, 1953, 24; Angelo Baglivo, "New City Rule Is Showing Good Results," *NEN*, January 17, 1955, 4.

10. Helen B. Pendleton, "Cotton Pickers in Northern Cities," *Survey* 37, no. 20 (February 17, 1917): 569–571; Clement A. Price, "The Afro-American Community of Newark, 1917–1947: A Social History" (PhD diss., Rutgers University, 1975); Price, "The Struggle to Desegregate Newark: Black Middle Class Militancy in New Jersey, 1932–1947," *New Jersey History* 99, no. 1–2 (February 1981): 215–228; William M. Ashby, *Tales without Hate*, 2nd ed. (Metuchen, NJ: Upland, 1996); Kenneth T. Jackson and Barbara B. Jackson, "The Black Experience in Newark: The Growth of the Ghetto, 1870–1970," in *New Jersey since 1860: New Findings and Interpretations*, ed. William C. Wright (Trenton: New Jersey Historical Commission, 1972), 36–59; Robert Curvin, "The Persistent Minority: The Black Political Experience in Newark" (PhD diss., Princeton University, 1975); Curvin, "Black Ghetto Politics in Newark after World War II," in *Cities of the Garden State: Essays in the Urban and Suburban History of New Jersey*, ed. Joel Schwartz and Daniel Prosser (Dubuque, IA: Kendall/ Hunt, 1977); Kevin Mumford, "Double V in New Jersey: African-American Civic Culture and Rising Consciousness against Jim Crow, 1938–1966," *New Jersey History* 119, no. 3–4 (Fall–Winter 2001): 22–56; Marion L. Courtney, "Civil Rights at the Grassroots," *American Unity* 12, no. 5 (May–June 1954): 10–13. For one direct protest, led by black clergymen, against the commission form, see Price, "The Afro-American Community of Newark," 30, 159, 163–164.

11. Stanley B. Winters, "Charter Change and Civic Reform in Newark, 1953–1954," *New Jersey History* 118, no. 1–2 (Spring–Summer 2000), 42–47; Lowenstein, *Alan V. Lowenstein*, 208; "Mayor, Council Plan Endorsed by CIO Unit," *NEN*, June 26, 1953, 7.

12. Charter Commission, *Final Report*, 4, 56.

13. Curvin, "Persistent Minority," 30–31; Winters, "Charter Change and Civic Reform," 55–56; Curvin, "Black Ghetto Politics in Newark," 153–155, 159n35.

14. Curvin, "Persistent Minority," 30–37; Curvin, "Black Ghetto Politics in Newark," 155–156.

15. Curvin, "Persistent Minority," 41–42; Winters, "Charter Change and Civic Reform," 61; Shabazian, "Carlin Puts Record on Line," *NEN*, May 7, 1962, 12; Douglas Eldridge, "Addonizio Says Victory Will Be His Tomorrow," *NEN*, May 7, 1962, 13; Baglivo, "Addonizio by 24,183," *NEN*, May 9, 1962, 1; Gerald Pomper, "Ethnic Group Voting in Nonpartisan Municipal Elections," *Public Opinion Quarterly* 30, no. 1 (spring 1966): 85–90.

16. Curvin, "Persistent Minority," 42–50; Milton Honig, "Discrimination Protests Rising in Newark," *NYT*, June 16, 1963, 59; "Camden St. School Split Sessions Hit," *NEN*, July 29, 1964, 8.

17. "Voter Rally in Newark," *NEN*, July 30, 1964, 1, 3; Donald Warshaw, "Negroes Hold Quiet Vote Rally in Newark," *SL*, July 30, 1964, 1, 7.

18. Cyril D. Tyson, *2 Years before the Riot: Newark, New Jersey and the United Community Corporation, Inc., 1964–1966; The Full, Real Story of the Anti-poverty Program* (New York: Jay Street, 2000), 18–22.

19. Certificate of Incorporation of United Community Corporation, August 10, 1964, folder 10, box 1, Eldridge Papers, NPL.

20. GSCCD hearing transcript, December 8, 1967, 57; Curvin, "Persistent Minority," 44n2; "City Girds for Hot Election Tuesday," *NJAA*, October 30, 1965, 1.

21. Richardson affidavit, May 28, 1968, US Senate, Permanent Subcommittee on Investigations, *Riots, Civil and Criminal Disorders* (Washington, DC: GPO, 1968–1969), 1777; GSCCD hearing transcript, December 8, 1967, 57–59.

22. Honig, "Newark Rejects Inquiry on Police," *NYT*, April 7, 1963, 66; Richardson, GSCCD hearing transcript, December 8, 1967, 59–61; Curvin, "Persistent Minority," 44n2. See chapter 4 for more on this episode.

23. Newark Exhibits Q and S, box 3, series 33, NACCD; Harry Burke, "Clash Brings Request to Halt Barringer Job," *NEN*, July 3, 1963, 1. Also, Rabig, "The Laboratory of Democracy," 48–59.

24. "Truce Is Reached on Barringer Job," *NEN*, August 14, 1963, 1; Eldridge, "Barringer Dispute Up to Negotiators," *NEN*, August 15, 1963, 1; Curvin, *Inside Newark: Decline, Rebellion, and the Search for Transformation* (New Brunswick, NJ: Rutgers University Press, 2014), 74–78.

25. Richardson in *Troublemakers*, VHS, directed by Robert Machover and Norm Fruchter (1966). In 1963, in his first foray into insurgent politicking, Richardson had led the New Frontier Democrats in a challenge to the Essex County machine and lost badly, garnering only 10,000 votes in a county whose black population numbered about 300,000. *Advance*, October 2, 1965, 10, JWJC; Curvin, *Inside Newark*, 85–86.

26. The others were Peter Schuyler and John Collier. See Curvin, *Inside Newark*, 76–77, 81.

27. Eldridge, "Advisory Panel of 53 Named in City's Anti-Poverty War," *NEN*, September 15, 1964, 14; Tyson, *2 Years before the Riot*, 27; Gibson remarks at Newark History Society panel discussion, May 5, 2014; Prinz, interview by author, April 11, 2006.

28. Tyson, *2 Years before the Riot*, 20.

29. Tyson, interview by author, April 27, 2006; Tyson resume, folder 14, box 2, Eldridge Papers, NPL.

30. Tyson, *Power and Politics in Central Harlem, 1962–1964: The Harlem Youth Opportunities Unlimited Experience* (New York: Jay Street, 2005), 93–94, 239–243; Tyson, *2 Years before the Riot*, 20–21, 52; Sydney H. Schanberg, "HARYOU Will Get U.S. and City Fund," *NYT*, August 26, 1964, 1; "Acting Director of HARYOU Quits," *NYT*, November 13, 1964, 18.

31. HARYOU, Inc., *Youth in the Ghetto: A Study of the Consequences of Powerlessness and a Blueprint for Change* (New York, 1964), 388, 391; Tyson, interview by author, April 27, 2006; UCC board of trustees minutes, November 18, 1964, folder 20, box 2, Tyson Papers, SCNYPL; Tyson, *2 Years before the Riot*, 7, 24, 30; Eldridge, "Beats Gun in Poverty War," *NEN*, November 19, 1964, 23.

32. "First Antipoverty Board Set Up in Central Ward," *NEN*, February 25, 1965, 11; "Antipoverty Unit Formed," *NEN*, February 26, 1965, 13; "Clinton Hill Forms Antipoverty Board," *NEN*, February 27, 1965, 14. Membership statistics from Tyson, *2 Years before the Riots*, 77–79.

33. Bruce Stave, *The New Deal and the Last Hurrah: Pittsburgh's Machine Politics* (Pittsburgh: University of Pittsburgh Press, 1970); Lyle W. Dorsett, *Franklin D. Roosevelt and the City Bosses* (Port Washington, NY: Kennikat, 1977); Roger Biles, *Big City Boss in Depression and War: Mayor Edward J. Kelly of Chicago* (DeKalb: Northern Illinois University Press, 1984); Steven P. Erie, *Rainbow's End: Irish-Americans and the Dilem-*

mas of Urban Machine Politics, 1840–1985 (Berkeley: University of California Press, 1988), 223–235; "RFC Aid Asked to Cities by Mayors," *NYT*, February 18, 1933, 2; John J. Gunther, *Federal-City Relations in the United States: The Role of the Mayors in Federal Aid to Cities* (Newark, DE: Associated University Presses, 1990), 23–30; Sidney Fine, *Frank Murphy: The Detroit Years* (Ann Arbor: University of Michigan Press, 1975), 363–365.

34. Discussion between Moynihan and Sanford Kravitz in Minutes, American Academy of Arts and Sciences Seminar on Poverty, March 3, 1967, 9–10, "Seminar on Poverty 1966–67" folder, box 88, Adam Yarmolinsky Papers, JFKL; Yarmolinsky and William Cannon in "Poverty and Urban Policy" transcript, 244–254, JFKL.

35. "Council Votes Poverty Funds but 'Strings' Draw Attacks," *NEN*, November 5, 1964, 19.

36. "Will Lift Conditions on Poverty Fund," *NEN*, November 18, 1964, 57; UCC board of trustees minutes, November 18, 1964, folder 20, box 2, Tyson Papers, SCNYPL; Eldridge, "Beats Gun in Poverty War," *NEN*, November 19, 1964, 23.

37. Tyson, *2 Years before the Riot*, 52–7.

38. Shabazian, "2 Newark Councilmen Rap Salaries in Poverty Budget," *NEN*, February 2, 1965, 1, 12; "Political Influence Charged in Anti-Poverty Aid Cutback," *NEN*, February 2, 1965, 12; UCC membership meeting minutes, February 1, 1965, box 2, folder 16, Eldridge Papers, NPL.

39. Tyson, *2 Years before the Riot*, 108–109; UCC executive committee meeting minutes, May 10, 1965, box 2, folder 16, Eldridge Papers, NPL.

40. Eldridge, "Anti-Poverty Unit Advised: Avoid Politics, Publicity," *NEN*, May 28, 1965, 5.

41. Mayor's Remarks Made before UCC, May 27, 1965, box 1, folder 9, Eldridge Papers, NPL.

42. "City Poverty Agency Elects 21 Trustees," *NEN*, May 28, 1965, 5; Carol Glassman oral history transcript, May 28, 1965, 14–18, TLNYU.

43. Shabazian, "Larger Voice to City, Poor," *NEN*, August 3, 1965, 1.

44. "To Ask Study Unit for Poverty Drive," *NEN*, August 4, 1965, 21; "Antipoverty Study Is Set," *NEN*, August 5, 1965, 12.

45. Eldridge, "Denies Program Needs City Funds," *NEN*, August 22, 1965, C5; Tyson, *2 Years before the Riot*, 167–170.

46. "Mayor, Defending UCC, Upholds Probe by Council," *NEN*, August 27, 1965, 29.

47. "Anti-Poverty Probers to Visit Newark," *SL*, September 1, 1965, 14.

48. "Anti-Poverty Units," *NEN*, August 29, 1965, C5; Allan Spetter, "Newark Poverty Agency Creates 6th Local Board," *SL*, September 1, 1965, 14.

49. Walter Waggoner, "Newark Antipoverty Program to Be Investigated," *NYT*, September 4, 1965, 22.

50. "Prepared Statement of Dean C. Willard Heckel," September 9, 1965; transcript, meeting of Municipal Council Committee to Study the Anti-Poverty Program, 6, 15, 36; both box 1, folder 1, Eldridge Papers, NPL; Eldridge, "Argue Poverty Jobs," *NEN*, September 10, 1965, 1; Spetter, "Rutgers Dean First Witness in Poverty Hearings," *SL*, September 10, 1965, 6.

51. Eldridge, "City Bars Funds," *NEN*, October 7, 1965, 1. See also Fred Powledge, "Newark Aides Seek Antipoverty Role," *NYT*, November 1, 1965, 1.

52. Eldridge, "Antipoverty Snag Cited," *NEN*, November 2, 1965, 1. Both the city's corporation counsel and a state antipoverty official declared the committee's constitutional argument without legal merit.

53. Ben A. Franklin, "Mayors Challenge Antipoverty Plan," *NYT*, June 1, 1965, 30; Franklin, "Mayors Shelve Dispute on Poor," *NYT*, June 2, 1965, 20; Joseph A. Loftus, "Mayors Assured of Poverty Role," *NYT*, June 8, 1965, 49; OEO, *Workbook: Community Action Program* (March 1965), section III.A, 5–6.

54. Powledge, "Newark Aides Seek Antipoverty Role," *NYT*, November 1, 1965, 1.

55. Loftus, "Wide Policy Role for Poor Opposed by Budget Bureau," *NYT*, November 6, 1965, 1; Powledge, "Alarm Is Voiced Here," *NYT*, November 6, 1965, 1; Prinz, letter to editor, *NYT*, November 14, 1965, E11.

56. William C. Selover, "The View from Capitol Hill: Harassment and Survival," in *On Fighting Poverty: Perspectives from Experience*, ed. James L. Sundquist (New York: Basic Books, 1969), 181; Eldridge, "Poor Seen Holding Antipoverty Reins," *NEN*, November 8, 1965, 3.

57. Eldridge, "Jersey's Poverty Programs Praised by Federal Officials," *NEN*, November 9, 1965, 24.

58. Humphrey to Heckel, November 27, 1965, quoted in Tyson, *2 Years before the Riot*, 304.

59. "Report of the Council Committee to Study the Anti-Poverty Program for the City of Newark," December 1965, preface, 2–5, 9, box 1, folder 1, Eldridge Papers, NPL.

60. "Report of the Council Committee," preface, 11; Baglivo, "Wants UCC Replaced," *NEN*, December 7, 1965, 1; Charles Sullivan, "Council Probe Raps Newark Poverty Arm," *SL*, December 8, 1965, 12.

61. John Farmer, "City Antipoverty Blasted by Powell," *NEN*, December 9, 1965, 17.

62. "All Local Poverty Boards in Works," *SL*, December 8, 1965, 12.

63. "Report of the Council Committee," 11.

64. "Newark's Poverty Dispute," *SL*, December 10, 1965, 1.

65. Mayor's Commission on Group Relations, *City in Transition*, 3:39–42; Nathan Wright Jr., *Ready to Riot* (New York: Holt, Rinehart, Winston, 1968), 17–18, 25–30.

66. "Newark's Poverty Dispute," *SL*, December 10, 1965, 1; "Few Attend in Roseville," *NEN*, December 10, 1965, 16; minutes, UCC trustees meeting, December 16, 1965, 2, folder 22, box 2, Tyson Papers, SCNYPL.

67. Mayor's Commission on Group Relations, *City in Transition*, 3:43; Wright, *Ready to Riot*, 21, 35–38.

68. UCC executive committee meeting minutes, December 15, 1965, 3, folder 16, box 2, Eldridge Papers, NPL; Eldridge, "Antipoverty Board Approved in Weequahic by Split Vote," *NEN*, December 16, 1965, 18.

69. Mayor's Commission on Group Relations, *City in Transition*, 3:11, 43; Wright, *Ready to Riot*, 23, 30–32; Bruce Bailey, "Spina Probes Klan Recruiting," *SL*, January 7, 1966, 1.

70. UCC executive committee meeting minutes, December 15, 1965, 3, folder 16, box 2, Eldridge Papers, NPL; "Poverty Dissent," *NEN*, December 17, 1965, 20; "Vailsburg Opposes Poverty Aid," *SL*, December 12, 1965, 21.

71. Spetter, "Poverty Truce Stands Despite New Criticism," *SL*, December 24, 1965, 1; Eldridge, "UCC Reply to Critique," *NEN*, December 23, 1965, 1; Eldridge, "New Blasts Shake Antipoverty Truce," *NEN*, December 24, 1965, 9. Still also helped Councilman Turner write a dissenting minority report. "Minority Report of Councilman Irvine I. Turner," December 1965, 4, folder 1, box 1, Eldridge Papers, NPL; Eldridge, "Turner Backs Poverty Unit against Council Attacks," *NEN*, December 12, 1965, C6.

72. Statement of the UCC, December 23, 1965, 32, 77, Newark Non-Governmental Documents file, NPL.

73. Tyson, *2 Years before the Riot*, 492–493; Eldridge, "UCC Adopts Budget Cut to $1.5 Million," *NEN*, December 3, 1965, 16; "Poverty Dissent," *NEN*, December 17, 1965, 20.
74. Spetter, "Newark Poverty Agency Rejects City Block Plan," *SL*, January 28, 1966, 11.
75. Spetter, "Poverty Board Meeting 2-Hour Shouting Match," *SL*, January 18, 1966, 4.
76. Eldridge, "Clark Says Project Can't Please All," *NEN*, January 12, 1966, 36.
77. "Pre-School Council Seeks Staff for $2 Million Program," *NEN*, July 28, 1965, 17; Tyson, *2 Years before the Riot*, 121–124.
78. Minutes, board of trustees, February 17, 1966, 3, folder 24, box 2; report from community action director to executive committee, March 17, 1966, folder 13, box 3; "Analysis of Programs Approved in Newark, 1965" folder 25, box 3; "Facts about UCC," folder 14, box 3; all Tyson Papers, SCNYPL.
79. Heckel speech, attached to Newark Police Department Administrative Submission, Charles Kinney to Robert Donnelly, November 29, 1967, folder 1, box 59, Mason Gross Papers, RUA; Eldridge, "Anti-Poverty Unit Advised," *NEN*, May 28, 1965, 5; telegram, August 1, 1967, "Civil Rights—Riots 1967 Folder 2 of 2," box 37, Subject Files, Records of the Director, CAP Office, OEOR; "Alumni—Minority Student Groups Meeting summary," May 28, 1968, folder 4, box 78, Mason Gross Papers, RUA.
80. Minutes, UCC board of trustees, 4, December 16, 1965, folder 22, box 2, Tyson Papers, SCNYPL.
81. Eldridge, "Slap at City Hall," *NEN*, February 18, 1966, 1; Waggoner, "Newark Revives Antipoverty Rift," *NYT*, February 19, 1966, 56; Glassman, "A Night of the People," *New Left Notes* 1, no. 7 (March 4, 1966): 1.
82. Shabazian, "Addonizio on Top, Carlin in Runoff," *NEN*, May 11, 1966, 1; Curvin, *Inside Newark*, 86–87, 129–130.
83. Office of Economic Opportunity, *The Quiet Revolution*, n.d. [spring 1966], 11, exhibit 9, series 2, NACCD.
84. US House of Representatives, *1966 Amendments to the Economic Opportunity Act of 1964*, part I (Washington, DC: GPO, 1966), 145–147, 151–152.
85. US Senate, *Amendments to the Economic Opportunity Act of 1964 (Washington, DC: GPO, 1966)*, 505–506; Loftus, "Shriver Losing 6 Key Poverty Aides," *NYT*, August 21, 1965, 19.
86. Nan Robertson, "Shriver Defends Program to the Poor," *NYT*, April 15, 1966, 1; Eugene Carson Blake, press statement, April 14, 1966; "What Happened at the Convention," undated typescript; both "CCAP Training—General Background, 1965–1966 #1" folder, box 3; and Boone, summary of remarks, 3, "CCAP Training—General Background, 1967" folder, box 3; all Citizens' Campaign Against Poverty Collection, Reuther Library.
87. Minutes, UCC executive committee, July 28, 1966, folder 1, box 3, Tyson Papers, SCNYPL. On the final decision to go to Washington, see Saul Schwarz to Abe Sudran, August 23, 1966, folder 6, box 804, United Jewish Federation of Metrowest Papers, JHSNJ.
88. Operation Concern newsletters, September 1966, folder 6, box 1, Eldridge Papers, NPL; Spetter, "A Jersey March in DC," *SL*, September 27, 1966, 1.
89. Powell quoted in Meyer Fine to Abe L. Sudran, September 27, 1966, folder 6, box 804, United Jewish Federation of Metrowest Papers, JHSNJ.
90. Michael Mosettig, "Bringing Some 'Concern' to Officialdom," *SL*, September 27, 1966, 7; United Community Corporation, *UCC Program Report, 1966–67*, 5–6, box 12, GSCCD.

91. Loftus, "Senate-House Conferees Allocate $1.75-Billion Antipoverty Authorization," *NYT*, October 12, 1966, 30; John Kifner, "U.S. Aid for Poor in City May Drop," *NYT*, October 22, 1966, 16; Lillian Rubin, "Maximum Feasible Participation: The Origins, Implications, and Present Status," *Annals of the American Academy of Political and Social Science* 385 (September 1969): 25–26.

92. A version of these OEO guidelines became law later that year. It mandated a *minimum* of one-third be representatives of the poor, a *maximum* of one-third be public officials, and the rest be made up of representatives from the private sector. "Community Action Memo No. 81," February 15, 1968, reprinted in OEO, *Organizing Communities for Action under the 1967 Amendments to the Economic Opportunity Act* (Washington, DC: GPO, February 1968); Rubin, "Maximum Feasible Participation," 25–26.

93. Tyson to Prinz, July 18, 1966, folder 14, box 2, Eldridge Papers, NPL.

94. UCC release and statement, July 28, 1966, folder 14, box 2, Eldridge Papers, NPL; UCC program listing, "Civil Rights—Newark—UCC 1967" folder, box 37, Subject Files 1965–1969, Records of the Director, CAP Office, OEOR.

95. Eldridge, "UCC Head Knows Poor's Needs," *NEN*, November 13, 1966, 33; *UCC Program Report, 1966–67*, 3, box 12, GSCCD.

96. Eldridge, "Poverty Agency Suspends Top 3," *NEN*, May 26, 1967, 1; Committee to Save Your Jobs, "William K. Wolfe: Newark's Quisling," folder 14, box 2, Eldridge Papers, NPL. See also Malafronte, GSCCD hearing transcript, October 23, 1967, 97; October 27, 1967, 51–2, GSCCD.

CHAPTER THREE

1. GSCCD hearing transcript, November 6, 1967, 70–73.

2. Hayden, *Reunion: A Memoir* (New York: Random House, 1988), 106; "President's Report," *SDS Bulletin*, March–April 1963, SDS Papers, reel 35, folder 4a, 19; Wittman and Hayden, "An Interracial Movement of the Poor?," in *The New Student Left: An Anthology*, ed. Mitchell Cohen and Dennis Hale (Boston: Beacon, 1966), 216–217. On development of ERAP: James Miller, *Democracy Is in the Streets: From Port Huron to the Siege of Chicago* (Cambridge: Harvard University Press, 1994), 144, 187–196; Kirkpatrick Sale, *SDS* (New York: Random House, 1973), 95–115; Jennifer Frost, *"An Interracial Movement of the Poor": Community Organizing and the New Left in the 1960s* (New York: NYU Press, 2001), 7–25.

3. "Prospectus for a Newark Organizing-Research Project," 3, series 2B, reel 10, folder 2; Newark Committee on Full Employment, "Draft Statement of Purpose," May 6, 1964, series 2B, reel 14, folder 81; both SDS Papers.

4. Mayor's Commission on Group Relations, *Newark: A City in Transition*, 3:10–14; Wright, *Ready to Riot*, 47–51; *We Got to Live Here*, VHS, directed by Robert Machover and Norm Fruchter (1965).

5. Hayden, "Organizing the Poor," letter to Ken Bacon, undated, series 2B, reel 10, folder 9, SDS Papers.

6. Frost, *"An Interracial Movement of the Poor,"* 69, 95–103.

7. "Report: Newark Project," June 30, 1964, 1, series 2B, reel 10, folder 2, SDS Papers. On the JOIN versus GROIN debates, see Miller, *Democracy Is in the Streets*, 202; Richard Rothstein, "A Short History of ERAP," March 1966, 2, series 2B, reel 11, folder 21, SDS Papers. Later, Rothstein wrote that by the end of 1964, the GROIN approach had been adopted by all ERAP projects. Rothstein, "Evolution of the ERAP Organizers," in *The New Left: A Collection of Essays*, ed. Priscilla Long (Boston: Porter Sargent, 1969), 278–279.

8. NCUP newsletter, n.d. [April or May 1965], Newark Exhibit DD, box 3, series 33, NACCD; *Advance*, September 25, 1965, 1, JWJC.
9. Glassman oral history transcript, May 14, 1965, 6–8; Jill Hamberg oral history transcript, February 18, 1965, 23–6, and March 11, 1965, 16–17; both TLNYU.
10. NCUP newsletter, n.d. [April or May 1965], Newark Exhibit DD, box 3, series 33, NACCD. Because of the publicity Wells's case attracted, she was offered several new places to live and several jobs. She soon moved into a bigger apartment with better facilities. *Advance*, October 9, 1965, 2, JWJC.
11. NCUP newsletter, no. 11, n.d. [January 1965]; NCUP press release, n.d. [January or February 1965], Newark Exhibit DD, box 3, series 33, NACCD; Hamberg oral history transcript, February 11, 1965, 10–12, TLNYU.
12. NCUP press release, n.d. [late January 1965], Newark Exhibit DD, box 3, series 33, NACCD; exhibit C39, box 13, GSCCD; Hamberg oral history transcripts, February 11, 1965, 5–6, 15, 25–26; February 18, 1965, 1, 6; March 4, 1965, 4–5; March 18, 1965, 2; April 1, 1965, 4–6; April 29, 1965, 5, TLNYU; SDS work list mailing, January 23, 1965, file 82, reel 14, series 2B, SDS Papers.
13. "Report: Newark Project," June 30, 1964, 1, file 2, reel 10, series 2B, SDS Papers; NCUP flier, n.d. [June 1964], exhibit C28, box 13, GSCCD; Hayden in GSCCD hearing transcript, December 8, 1967, 26–27.
14. Spina, GSCCD hearing transcript, October 30, 1967, 136–137.
15. *ERAP Newsletter: Newark Report*, August 2, 1964, file 2, reel 10, series 2B, SDS Papers; Hamberg oral history transcript, April 29, 1965, 1, TLNYU; "Probe of Rights Unit Asked," *NEN*, July 23, 1965.
16. Glassman oral history transcript, May 14, 1965, 19–24, TLNYU.
17. *Summer Report: Newark Community Union*, n.d. [Summer 1964], 4–5, file 82, reel 14, series 2B, SDS Papers.
18. Hayden, *The Port Huron Statement: The Visionary Call of the 1960s Revolution* (New York: Thunder's Mouth, 2005), 53.
19. Rennie Davis, "The War on Poverty: Notes on Insurgent Response," in Cohen and Hale, *The New Student Left*, 168–169.
20. Eric Mann, interview by author, March 7, 2006; Glassman oral history transcript, July 2, 1965, 15–17, TLNYU; Hamberg oral history transcript, March 4, 1965, 18, TLNYU; Hayden, *Reunion*, 138–141.
21. "Clinton Hill Forms Antipoverty Board," *NEN*, February 27, 1965, 14.
22. Hamberg oral history transcript, February 11, 1965, 1–4, TLNYU; NCUP newsletter, no. 15, folder 13, box 23, SDS Papers, WHS.
23. Glassman oral history transcripts, May 28, 1965, 8–9, 14–22, and June 11, 1965, 4, 13–14; Hamberg oral history transcripts, February 11, 1965, 16–17; March 4, 1965, 2–3, 6–15, 19–22; March 18, 1965, 4–5, 15–24; April 8, 1965, 15; April 22, 1965, 15–19; April 29, 1965, 1–3; all TLNYU; NCUP newsletter, undated [March 1965], Newark Exhibit DD, box 3, series 33, NACCD; "Clinton Hill Forms Area Board," *NEN*, February 27, 1965, 14; "City Antipoverty Agency Elects 21 Trustees," *NEN*, May 28, 1965, 5.
24. This account draws heavily on *Troublemakers*, VHS, directed by Robert Machover and Norman Fruchter (1966); *Advance*, October 2, 1965, 4, JWJC.
25. "Picket Landlord," *NEN*, December 12, 1965, 44; *Troublemakers*, VHS.
26. Robert Machover, interview by author, December 8, 2005.
27. Richard Rothstein, in an essay that traces the multiple disappointments suffered by ERAP, identifies their effect on the Community Action Program as the one exception

in an otherwise general failure to effect change in liberal-labor institutions. Rothstein, "Evolution of the ERAP Organizers," 278n2.

28. *With No One to Help Us*, directed by Eugene and Carol Marner (1967), http://archive.org/details/WithNoOneToH (accessed June 22, 2012); *Advance*, October 2, 1965, 6, JWJC.

29. "Pickets at Grocery Arrested," *SL*, April 2, 1967, 5; "19 Pickets Seized," *NEN*, April 2, 1967, 1.

30. NCUP's organizing around welfare issues seems to have begun in the summer of 1965. Glassman oral history transcript, May 14, 1965, 17–18, TLNYU.

31. I draw much of the following account of the welfare mothers' committee from *With No One to Help Us*. Also Tyler McClain (Wyla's son), interview by author, October 20, 2005.

32. Area Board 3 Welfare Committee Flier, n.d., Newark Exhibit DD, box 3, series 33, NACCD; Tyson, *2 Years before the Riot*, 624.

33. *With No One to Help Us*; Tyson, *2 Years before the Riot*, 724.

34. *With No One to Help Us*.

35. Ibid.

36. GSCCD hearing transcript, December 8, 1967, 78–79; Hayden, *Reunion*, 139–141.

37. *Troublemakers*, VHS. There's some irony here that NCUP staffers organized people to support a decision that had already been made; Mann interview, March 7, 2006.

38. Minutes, UCC board of trustees, August 19, 1965, 4–7, folder 22, box 2, Tyson Papers, SCNYPL; Tyson, *2 Years before the Riot*, 166–171.

39. Tyson, position paper, July 8, 1965, reprinted in Tyson, *2 Years before the Riot*, 147–148.

40. *Troublemakers*, VHS; photo spread, *NJAA*, October 9, 1965, 20. All four of the Freedom Singers also either were members of or worked for the consumer buying club of Area Board 3's Welfare Mothers Committee.

41. GSCCD hearing transcript, December 8, 1967, 61–2.

42. "CORE Backs Freedom Unit," *NEN*, October 13, 1965, 38; *Advance*, October 16, 1965, 2, JWJC; Eldridge, "CORE Leaders Chart Plans," *NEN*, January 24, 1965, 27.

43. UCC notice of annual meeting, folder 14, box 2, Eldridge Papers, NPL; Tyson, *2 Years before the Riot*, 157, 164.

44. Curvin, interview by author, January 31, 2006; "City Poverty Agency Elects 21 Trustees," *NEN*, May 28, 1965, 5; GSCCD hearing transcript, October 17, 1967, 4–5; Tyson, *2 Years before the Riot*, 132; August Meier and Elliott M. Rudwick, *CORE: A Study in the Civil Rights Movement, 1942–1968* (New York: Oxford University Press, 1973), 363; Hamberg oral history transcript, February 18, 1965, 6, TLNYU; Hayden, *Reunion*, 157–159.

45. GSCCD hearing transcript, November 6, 1967, 54–59, 72–73.

46. Curvin interview, January 31, 2006; Meier and Rudwick, *CORE*, 236, 239–240; "Hoffmann-LaRoche, CORE Set Truce," *NEN*, November 19, 1964, 33; "CORE, Drug Firm Reach Agreement," *NJAA*, December 5, 1964, 20.

47. Meier and Rudwick, *CORE*, 330; Inge Powell Bell, *CORE and the Strategy of Nonviolence* (New York: Random House, 1968), 178–181.

48. Eldridge, "CORE Leaders Chart Plans," *NEN*, January 24, 1965, 27.

49. Meier and Rudwick, *CORE*, 154; GSCCD hearing transcript, October 17, 1967, 3–4; "New Faces on Board of Newark-Essex CORE," *NJAA*, May 29, 1965, 7.

50. "CORE Unit Backs UCC," *NEN*, December 14, 1965, 38. Similarly, at the CORE Northeast Regional Conference held in Philadelphia in April 1966, delegates passed

a resolution demanding that the OEO interpret "maximum feasible participation" to mean that three-fifths of every local community action board be composed of poor persons; that the OEO refuse funding to any agency not meeting that requirement; that it simplify forms so that nonprofessional people could apply for antipoverty money; and that it provide 100 percent of the funds required by any program administered by the poor. See "Minutes, Regional Conference—Philadelphia," May 3, 1966, 12, Curvin Papers, WHS.

51. "Driver Killed by Cop as He Tries to Flee," *SL*, June 13, 1965, 21; "Probe in Killing by Policeman Set by Byrne," *SL*, June 15, 1965, 8.

52. Curvin interview, January 31, 2006; quotation from CORE's transcript in Ron Porambo, *No Cause for Indictment: An Autopsy of Newark* (New York: Holt, Rinehart, and Winston, 1971), 42–44; Ernest Johnston, "CORE Planning Rent Strike with Demonstration," *SL*, June 25, 1965, 8.

53. "CORE Demands Probe of Slaying," *SL*, June 15, 1965, 8; Harris MacBeth, "CORE Threatens Shooting Protest," *SL*, June 17, 1965, 9.

54. "Mayor Suspends Cop in Traffic Slaying," *SL*, June 18, 1965, 1; Tex Novellino and Bruce Bailey, "Cops, Mayor Still at Odds," *SL*, June 22, 1965, 1.

55. "Martinez Is Reinstated on Finding of No Bias," *NEN*, June 22, 1965, 1.

56. Johnston, "Review Board or We Protest, CORE Says," *SL*, June 23, 1965, 1.

57. Johnston, "Brutality a 'Fact,' CORE Tells Rally," *SL*, June 24, 1965, 4; "CORE Planning Rent Strike," *SL*, June 25, 1965, 8; "CORE Tours Newark Urging March Support," *SL*, June 30, 1965, 1.

58. Novellino and Don Warshaw, "Grand Jury Hears 10 More in Shooting," *SL*, June 25, 1965, 1.

59. Glassman oral history transcript, July 2, 1965, 8–15, TLNYU; Novellino, "Rights Marchers Demand Ouster," *SL*, June 27, 1965, 4; Ward Ulrich, "Picket Two Hours for Review Board," *SL*, June 28, 1965, 4; Ishmael Reed, "The Raunchy Crusade . . . Kicked About and Strapped," *Advance*, September 25, 1965, 3, JWJC.

60. Audrey Fecht, "Grand Jurors Clear Martinez in Shooting," *NEN*, June 30, 1965, 1; Newark Police Department, *Rules and Regulations, 1966*, 38, section 9:6, NPL.

61. Walter Sopronik, "Demand Made at Park Rally," *NEN*, July 1, 1965, 1; Johnston and MacBeth, "CORE Stages a Protest for Police Review Board," *SL*, July 1, 1965, 1; memo, Newark Police Department patrol division, deputy chief of police to commanding officers, June 30, 1965, "Policies—1965" folder, box 2, Newark Police Department Collection, NPL.

62. "Other Groups Join in CORE March," *SL*, July 20, 1965, 9; "Where Do We Go from Here?" *NJAA*, July 17, 1965, 1, 16; "Jobs Panel Asks Police Agreement," *NEN*, August 1, 1965, C6.

63. Johnston and Sullivan, "CORE Rally Attracts 750," *SL*, July 22, 1965, 1.

64. Johnston and Novellino, "10 Arrested at City Hall Sit-In," *SL*, July 30, 1965, 1; Baglivo, "Stage Sit-In at City Hall," *NEN*, July 30, 1965, 1.

65. Eldridge, "Police Review Board Talk Generates Heat, Little Light," *NEN*, July 14, 1965, 21; Johnston, "Review Board Hearings Begin," *SL*, July 14, 1965, 13; Eldridge, "Police Review Board Forum to Need Two More Hearings," *NEN*, July 21, 1965, 18; Johnston, "Third Hearing on Review Board," *SL*, July 28, 1965, 17; Eldridge, "Police Review Board Hearings End Quietly," *NEN*, August 4, 1965, 20; Johnston, "Newark Holds Last Meeting on Review Board," *SL*, August 4, 1965, 8.

66. "Mayor's Decision," *NEN*, September 8, 1965, 1; Spetter, "Rights Unit Readies Cop

Board Data," *SL*, September 8, 1965, 8; Spetter, "Mayor Pledges Decision Soon on Police Board," *SL*, September 9, 1965, 6.

67. Addonizio, "Statement on a Police Review Board for Newark," September 15, 1965, exhibit C34, box 13, GSCCD. See chapter 4 for more details.

68. "Leaders Seek Alternatives to Newark Plan," *NJAA*, October 9, 1965, 1; Eldridge, "Police Favor System; Rights Leaders Split," *NEN*, September 16, 1965, 13; *Advance*, October 9, 1965, 2, JWJC.

69. Minutes, UCC board of trustees, September 16, 1965, 3, folder 22, box 2, Tyson Papers, SCNYPL.

70. Eldridge, "Police Favor System," *NEN*, September 16, 1965, 13; "CORE Raps Mayor's Plan," *NJAA*, September 25, 1965, 1. Opponents had a point. An agent from the Newark FBI office explained that the bureau's jurisdiction only extended to cases of civil rights violations and would be unlikely to include a police officer's use of force. "City to Send FBI 'Brutality' Cases," *NEN*, September 16, 1965, 1.

71. Cicetti, "CORE Panel Hits Addonizio on Review Board Decision," *NEN*, October 12, 1965, 16.

72. Lois Densky-Wolff, *The First Quarter Century: UMDNJ, 1970–1995*, University of Medicine and Dentistry of New Jersey Archives, George F. Smith Library of the Health Sciences, Rutgers Biomedical and Health Sciences, Newark; William Madden, "Medical School Faces Eviction," *SL*, December 10, 1965, 12; Bailey, "State Med School to End Jersey City Ties Jan. 1," *SL*, December 24, 1965, 5; Thompson, "Med School Leaving," *NEN*, December 24, 1965, 1.

73. Newark Central Planning Board, *Master Plan 1964: City of Newark, N.J.* (Newark, 1964), 94–95.

74. Robert Kalter, "Newark Needs Land Fast," *SL*, November 15, 1966, 1; Shabazian, "Land Available," *NEN*, November 25, 1966, 1.

75. Shabazian, "City Pledges Land Med School Asked," *NEN*, December 23, 1966, 1.

76. Kaplan, *Urban Renewal Politics*, 26, 29, 36.

77. Louise Epperson, interview by author, July 7, 2001. The first mention of the land deal in the *Newark Evening News* came on December 23, 1966, a Friday. If Epperson did first learn about this from a Sunday paper, it might have been the January 1, 1967, edition, which contained a story about five hundred letters the city sent to site residents informing them of an impending appraisal of their homes.

78. William Doolittle, "Med School Site Eyed by Board," *NEN*, January 11, 1967, 30.

79. Rudy Johnson, "Central Ward Stirs," *NEN*, January 15, 1967, C12.

80. "Residents Hit Med Site Plan," *NEN*, January 19, 1967, 16; "Central Ward Protest Removal Plan," *NJAA*, January 28, 1967, 1; "Medical Site Survey Made," *NEN*, January 18, 1967, 20; Shabazian, "City Eyes Land for College," *NEN*, January 1, 1967, 1; Novellino, "Med College Bills Ready for State," *SL*, January 22, 1967, 1.

81. Eulis "Honey" Ward, chair of the Central Ward Democratic organization, was a co-chair of the Committee against Negro and Puerto Rican Removal and a founding trustee of the UCC. Harry Wheeler, a local schoolteacher, served on several UCC committees and headed the UCC's Summer Block Recreation Program in 1966. See Tyson, *2 Years before the Riot*, 39, 66, 650. Alvin Oliver, the UCC's community action director at the time, was also listed as a committee member; see Johnson, "Central Ward Stirs," *NEN*, January 15, 1967, C12.

82. Eldridge, "Reaction Favorable to Medical School," *NEN*, April 21, 1967, 33; Malafronte, GSCCD hearing transcript, October 23, 1967, 46–50.

83. Kaplan, *Urban Renewal Politics*, 34.
84. See A Veteran of Newark's Blight Wars, "Fighting the 'Blight,' or Urban Resistance to Authoritarian Social Change," unpublished essay, NPL.
85. Thompson, "Protests Disrupt Newark Hearing," *NEN*, May 23, 1967, 8; Peter Farrell, "Eggs and Shouts Wreck Hearing," *SL*, May 23, 1967, 1; NACCD hearing transcript, August 22, 1967, 753–757; GSCCD hearing transcript, October 23, 1967, 69–70.
86. GSCCD hearing transcript, November 6, 1967, 75–80; "Teacher Put under Probe," *NEN*, May 19, 1967, 1. For Hassan's post-Newark career, which included various federal grants in other cities, see Arnold Forster and Benjamin R. Epstein, *The New Anti-Semitism* (New York: McGraw-Hill, 1974), 49–58; "Hassan Jeru-Ahmed and the Black Man's Army of Liberation" file, Richard H. Ichord Papers, Western Historical Manuscript Collection, University of Missouri–Columbia.
87. Thompson, "Protests Disrupt Newark Hearing."
88. Ibid.
89. Farrell, "Eggs and Shouts Wreck Hearing"; Spina deposition, January 2, 1968, 43–52, "Depositions Newark" folder, box 4, series 32, NACCD; Thompson, "Protests Disrupt Newark Hearing."
90. Farrell, "A New Hearing on Med School," *SL*, May 25, 1967, 13; Johnson, "Hearing on Med School Site Rescheduled," *NEN*, May 25, 1967, 14.
91. Shabazian, "City Council Votes Contract for Medical College Land," *NEN*, May 26, 1967, 7.
92. "Jack and Jills Donate $1,307 to Essex SNCC," *NJAA*, February 11, 1967, 1; Eldridge, "ACLU Leader Appointed to Newark Antipoverty Job," *NEN*, January 19, 1967, 11; Eldridge, "Silently, Militant SNCC Has Started Newark Drive," *NEN*, April 2, 1967, 31; Phil Hutchings, interview by author, April 12, 2006.
93. Bob Queen, "Most Devastated Eastern City," *NJAA*, July 15, 1967, 1.

CHAPTER FOUR
1. "Radio Address by Director Michael P. Duffy," January 16, 1936, Newark Police vertical file, NPL.
2. Bureau of Municipal Research, *Police Problems in Newark: Report of a Survey Conducted at the Request of Honorable John B. Keenan, Directory of Public Safety, Newark, N.J.* (Newark: Bureau of Municipal Research, 1943), i, 42.
3. Robert M. Fogelson, *Big-City Police* (Cambridge, MA: Harvard University Press, 1977), 13–39; Michael K. Sparrow et al., *Beyond 911: A New Era for Policing* (New York: Basic Books, 1990), 34–37; William J. Bopp, *"O. W.": O. W. Wilson and the Search for a Police Profession* (Port Washington, NY: Kennikat, 1977).
4. Sparrow, *Beyond 911*, 37–40, 50–51.
5. A. F. Brandstatter and Louis Radelet, *Police and Community Relations: A Sourcebook* (Beverly Hills, CA: Glencoe, 1968), introduction (unpaginated).
6. Samuel Walker, "The Origins of the Police-Community Relations Movement: The 1940s," *Criminal Justice History* 1 (1980): 225–246; David Patrick Geary, *Community Relations and the Administration of Justice* (New York: John Wiley and Sons, 1975), 373–374; Myra A. Blakeslee, "New Jersey Workshops in Human Relations," *American Unity* 10, no. 1 (September–October 1951): 10–12.
7. Edward J. Mowery, "Police Morale Collapses," *SL*, January 19, 1958, 1.
8. Mowery, "Newark Lives in Fear," *SL*, January 20, 1958, 1; "No Incentive for Newark Cops to Do a Good Job," *SL*, January 21, 1958, 1; "60 Pct. of Newark Called Crime

Jungle during Night Hours," *SL*, January 22, 1958, 1; "Police Radio Cars Often Late on Calls," *SL*, January 23, 1958, 1.

9. Dorothy Guyot, *Coping with Crime in Newark*, rev. ed. (Evanston, IL: Northwestern University Center for Urban Studies, 1983), 82–84, 90; Sullivan, "NY Cop Nominated," *SL*, October 12, 1958; Baglivo, "Carlin Picks Police Head," *NEN*, October 12, 1958, 1.

10. "Police Department Morale Is Better," *SL*, October 12, 1958, 1.

11. Ned Schnurman, "Tools Available but Rarely Used," *NEN*, October 20, 1958, 1. The other entries in the series were "News to Analyze Department's Role," *NEN*, October 12, 1958; "Lesson Possible from Cincinnati," *NEN*, October 13, 1958; "Trying to Set House in Order," *NEN*, October 14, 1958; "Discipline Found a Major Problem," *NEN*, October 15, 1958; "Secondary Jobs Breed Difficulty," *NEN*, October 16, 1958; "7-Week Course Given Rookies," *NEN*, October 17, 1958; "Emergency Calls Face Roadblocks," *NEN*, October 18, 1958; and "Traffic Setup Loosely Drawn," *NEN*, October 19, 1958.

12. "Open-Minded on Weldon," *NEN*, October 12, 1958, 14; Guyot, *Coping with Crime in Newark*, 90–91; Baglivo, "Weldon Confirmed by Council," *NEN*, November 6, 1958, 1.

13. On reform efforts prior to Weldon's tenure, see Alfred G. Aronowitz, "Police Dept. Reorganized," *NEN*, July 1, 1956; Joseph B. Sugrue, "Police Reorganization in the City of Newark," *New Jersey Municipalities*, May 1957, 5–9, in Newark Police vertical file, NPL; Schnurman, "Trying to Set House in Order," *NEN*, October 14, 1958.

14. Andrew Briod, "Weldon Man of Wide Experience," *NEN*, October 12, 1958, 14; David McAndrew, "Reorganizes Police Force," *NEN*, May 24, 1959.

15. Guyot, *Coping with Crime in Newark*, 97–98.

16. Mayor's Commission on Group Relations, *First Annual Report, 1954*, folder 10, box 3, Daniel S. Anthony Papers, NPL; Blakeslee, "New Jersey Workshops in Human Relations," 10.

17. Mayor's Commission on Group Relations, *Annual Report, 1956*, 5–6, Newark Documents Collection, NPL; Schnurman, "7-Week Course Given Rookies," *NEN*, October 17, 1958, 1. It's not clear when these classes ceased, but the commission's annual reports from 1962 and 1963 (the next reports I was able to locate) make no mention of *any* police-community relations training programs.

18. "Newark Police Institute on Community Relations," brochure, "Police Institute Programs" folder, box 11, National Conference of Christians and Jews Collection, Social Welfare Archive, University of Minnesota.

19. Devaney, "Prejudice, Discrimination and Delinquency," Devaney folder, box 9, National Conference of Christians and Jews Collection, Social Welfare Archive, University of Minnesota.

20. Baglivo, "Spina Favors Canceling NCCJ Courses," *NEN*, September 14, 1962, 1; "Cops to Get New School," *NEN*, September 17, 1962, 4; "Civil Rights Unit to Gather Facts," *NEN*, September 9, 1962, 16.

21. US Commission on Civil Rights, *Hearings before the United States Commission on Civil Rights: Newark, New Jersey*, September 12, 1962, 468–471.

22. Tom Barrett, "Political Musical Chairs: Newark Police Head Left Standing," *New York Herald Tribune*, May 13, 1962, Newark Police vertical file, NPL; Guyot, notes from interview with Donald Malafronte, undated, 2, "Guyot Interviews" folder, box 1, Newark Police Department Collection, NPL.

23. Spina, GSCCD hearing transcript, October 30, 1967, 4–5; Guyot, *Coping with Crime in Newark*, 106.

24. Baglivo, "Spina Favors Canceling NCCJ Courses."

25. "Cops to Get New School," *NEN*, September 17, 1962, 4; "Newark Cancels Course to 'Humanize' Patrolmen," *NYT*, September 18, 1962, 29. Devaney continued his efforts at the state and regional levels. See, for example, Report of Proceedings, Northeast Institute on Police and Community Relations, "Police-Community Relations 6 of 6" folder, box 69, General Correspondence, 1965–1968, OLEA.

26. National Commission on Law Observance and Enforcement, *Report on Lawlessness in Law Enforcement* (Washington, DC: GPO, 1931), 112; Price, "The Afro-American Community of Newark," 150–151; Bureau of Municipal Research, *Police Problems in Newark*, 51.

27. Mayor's Commission on Group Relations, *First Annual Report, 1953*, 14, folder 10, box 3, Anthony Papers, NPL.

28. Chester Rapkin and Eunice and George Grier, *Group Relations in Newark, 1957: Problems, Prospects, and a Program for Research* (New York: Urban Research, 1957), 67.

29. Mayor's Commission on Group Relations, *Newark: A City in Transition*, vol. 2 (March 1959), 97.

30. US Commission on Civil Rights, *Justice* (Washington, DC: GPO, 1961), 1, 105, 112–113.

31. Anthony Lewis, "New Curbs Sought on Police Cruelty," *NYT*, March 21, 1962, 27.

32. Quoted in *Hearings before the United States Commission on Civil Rights*, 460.

33. "CORE Leaders Call for Store Boycott," *NEN*, September 9, 1962, 16; "Police Brutality and Bias Charged at Newark Rally," *NYT*, September 9, 1962, 73.

34. Jack Trugman, in *Hearings before the United States Commission on Civil Rights*, 445–459.

35. Eldridge, "Panel on Police," *NEN*, February 23, 1963, 1; "Need for Advisory Board Aired by Newarkers," *NJAA*, March 2, 1963, 1. On the history of Philadelphia's board, see: Bruria Tal, *Civilian Oversight of Police in Philadelphia: The First Fifty Years* (2003), 8, http://www.phila.gov/pac/PDF/HistoryofOversight.pdf; James R. Hudson, "Police Review Boards and Police Accountability," *Law and Contemporary Problems* 36, no. 4 (Autumn 1971): 525–527.

36. "Phila Advisory Bd. Head to Speak Here on Friday," *NJAA*, February 23, 1963, 1; Eldridge, "Panel on Police"; "Need for Advisory Board Aired by Newarkers"; "Seek Board to Eye Police," *SL*, February 23, 1963, 3.

37. Malafronte and Robert Cole, "Newark Police Brutality: Is It Fact of Fiction?," *SL*, February 24, 1963, 5.

38. "PBA Head Raps Plans for Police Review Board," *SL*, February 26, 1963, 7.

39. "Mayor Weighs Plan on Police Board," *NEN*, March 1, 1963, 33; "Newark PBA Urges Ouster of Board Chief," *SL*, March 2, 1963, 3; "Rights Leader Won't Resign to Satisfy Cops," *SL*, March 3, 1963, 7; "Police Board Fight Joined," *NEN*, March 3, 1963, 17.

40. "Disputes Need for Police Board," *SL*, March 6, 1963, 6; "PBA Leader: Review Board Hampers Law," *SL*, April 1, 1963, 3.

41. "RFK Cites Rise in Cop Cases," *NJAA*, March 9, 1963, 1; "Demand Ouster of Rights Leader," *SL*, March 8, 1963, 9; "Civil Liberties Wants Police Review Board," *SL*, March 8, 1963, 9; Lee Johnson, "The Police, the Public, the PAB, and the Pressure," *NJAA*, March 30, 1963, 20; Alexander Mark, press release, March 3, 1963; meeting minutes, Newark Human Rights Commission, March 19, 1963; Mark, statement on police advisory board, March 19, 1963; all folder 10, box 3, Anthony Papers, NPL.

42. Eldridge, "Review Board Out," *NEN*, April 7, 1963, 1; Milton Honig, "Newark Rejects Inquiry on Police," *NYT*, April 7, 1963, 66.

43. "Newark Police Head Asks Single Station," *NYT*, January 5, 1964, 82; Guyot, "Discussion of Changes which have taken place over the years," typed notes, 1979, loose document, box 1, Newark Police Department Collection, NPL; City of Newark, *Capital Program, 1966–1971*, 55, box 9, GSCCD.

44. Guyot, Malafronte interview notes, undated, 5, "Guyot Interviews" folder, box 1, Newark Police Department Collection, NPL.

45. "Mayor and Advisory Bd.," *NJAA*, April 13, 1963, 1.

46. Novellino, "Addonizio Rejects Review Board," *SL*, April 7, 1963, 1; "Richardson to Keep His Job, Says Addonizio," *NJAA*, April 20, 1963, 1; "Newark NAACP Split," *NYT*, June 21, 1963, 14; Richardson, GSCCD hearing transcript, December 8, 1967, 59–61; Curvin, "The Persistent Minority," 44n2.

47. US Commission on Civil Rights, *Hearings: Newark, New Jersey*, September 12, 1962, 470.

48. Baglivo, "Spina Favors Canceling NCCJ Courses for Police," *NEN*, September 14, 1962, 1; "Newark at Top of Crime List," *SL*, March 12, 1963, 5.

49. Eldridge, "Review Board Out," *NEN*, April 7, 1963, 1; minutes, Newark Human Rights Commission, June 18, 1963, 3–4, folder 10, box 3, Anthony Papers, NPL.

50. For an overviews of these efforts, see *Advance*, October 9, 1965, 9, in which the author gives much credit to Spina, even if they yielded, in his mind, unimpressive results; and Guyot, *Coping with Crime in Newark*, 122–124.

51. Guyot, *Coping with Crime in Newark*, 115–116.

52. GSCCD hearing transcript, October 30, 1967, 38–39.

53. "Spina Planning to Arm Cabbies," *SL*, March 14, 1963, 7; Guyot, *Coping with Crime*, 116.

54. "New Voices to Fight Crime," *SL*, May 23, 1967, 9.

55. "Newark Cops Must Brush Up on Civil Rights," *SL*, February 24, 1963, 6; "Lecture Series to Aid Cops in Fighting Own Bias," *SL*, March 25, 1963, 8; "Community Relations Training Given 800 Policemen," *NJAA*, April 2, 1963, 3.

56. Spina deposition, January 2, 1968, 19, "Newark Deposition" folder, box 4, series 32, NACCD.

57. Ibid., 13–16.

58. Ralph Matthews, "How the Police Observer Got Her 1st Taste of Death," *NJAA*, June 19, 1965, 1.

59. Johnston and Novellino, "Judge Refuses to Reinstate Cop," *SL*, June 19, 1965, 1; "A Time for Sanity," *NJAA*, June 26, 1965, 1.

60. "Pickets Step Up Protest," *NEN*, June 21, 1965, 1.

61. Theodore Dachowski, interview by author, April 13, 2006.

62. United Citizens of Newark against a Civilian Review Board, press release, July 1, 1965, photocopy in possession of author, courtesy of Theodore Dachowski; "New Group Would Bar Police Review," *NEN*, July 2, 1965, 7.

63. United Citizens of Newark against a Civilian Review Board, press release, July 1, 1965, photocopy in possession of author, courtesy of Theodore Dachowski.

64. Harris MacBeth and Bruce Bailey, "Group Marches against Review Board," *SL*, July 30, 1965, 1; Baglivo, "Paraders Hit Review Board," *NEN*, July 30, 1965, 1; Dachowski interview, April 13, 2006.

65. *NJAA*, July 3, 1965, 1.

66. "Raps CORE in Suspension of Policeman," *SL*, June 18, 1965, 8.

67. Robert Thompson, "Flees Cops, Shot Dead," *NEN*, September 15, 1965, 1.

68. Addonizio, "Statement on a Police Review Board for Newark," September 15, 1965, exhibit C34, box 13, GSCCD.

69. Ibid. Addonizio specifically said he'd seek funds from the antipoverty program, but Newark actually ended up applying through a different Great Society initiative.

70. Lyndon Johnson, "Special Message to the Congress on Crime and Law Enforcement," March 8, 1965, *Public Papers of the Presidents: Lyndon Baines Johnson, 1965* (Washington, DC: GPO, 1966), 263–271.

71. Naomi Murakawa, *The First Civil Right: How Liberals Built Prison America* (New York: Oxford University Press, 2014), 79–80, 87.

72. "Opinion at Home and Abroad," *NYT*, October 31, 1965, E13.

73. Maurice Carroll, "FBI Computers Rush Crime Data to Police," *NYT*, January 28, 1967, 9.

74. "9 City Policemen to Enroll in Course in Puerto Rico," *NYT*, February 19, 1967, 56.

75. "Unfilled Human Rights Post Stirs Up Council Squabble," *NJAA*, December 21, 1963; Eldridge, "City Finds It Printed Zinn's Parting Blast," *NEN*, July 15, 1965, 17; Ralph Zinn, *Human Relations Profile: Newark, 1965* (Newark, 1965).

76. Newark Human Rights Commission, *Newark Police-Community Relations Program* (Newark, 1967), 3.

77. Application for Police-Community Relations Training Program, 1–3, exhibit C35, box 13, GSCCD.

78. Newark Human Rights Commission, *Newark Police-Community Relations Program*, 7–8, 75.

79. Robert F. Allen et al., "Conflict Resolution—Team Building for Police and Ghetto Residents," *Journal of Criminal Law, Criminology, and Police Science* 60, no. 2 (1969): 251.

80. Newark Human Rights Commission, *Newark Police-Community Relations Program*, 61.

81. Ibid., 61–63.

82. Ibid., 22–23, 27–28; Threatt in GSCCD hearing transcript, November 6, 1967, 20–23, 163–164.

83. Newark Human Rights Commission, *Newark Police-Community Relations Program*, 31–33. The report noted that, despite his experience with Rustin that day, this officer was a constructive participant.

84. Ibid., 44.

85. Ibid., 46–51, 135–137; "6 Policemen on a Mission of Goodwill," *SL*, April 5, 1967, 17.

CHAPTER FIVE

1. "Transcript of Johnson's TV Address on the Riots," *NYT*, July 28, 1967, 11. Television schedule: *NYT*, July 27, 1967, 71; *WP*, July 27, 1967, D17.

2. NACCD, *Report of the National Advisory Commission on Civil Disorders* (New York: Bantam Books, 1968), 1.

3. Kerner oral history transcript, June 12, 1969, 10–12, LBJL; Bill Barnhart and Gene Schlickman, *Kerner: The Conflict of Intangible Rights* (Urbana: University of Illinois Press, 1999), 1–4; Robert P. Howard, *Mostly Good and Competent Men: Illinois Governors, 1818–1988*, 2nd ed. (Springfield, IL: Institute for Public Affairs, 1999), 279–285.

4. Max Frankel, "President Forms Panel to Assess Causes of Riots," *NYT*, July 28, 1967, 11.

5. Beirne Lay, *Someone Has to Make It Happen: The Inside Story of Tex Thornton, the Man*

Who Built Litton Industries (Englewood Cliffs, NJ: Prentice-Hall, 1969), 175–176; Wilkins oral history transcript, April 1, 1969, 8–9, LBJL; Herbert T. Jenkins, *Presidents, Politics, and Policing: Oral History Interviews on Law Enforcement and a Career in Public Life Spanning Fifty Years* (Atlanta: Center for Research in Social Change, Emory University, 1980), 17–18; Katherine Graham Peden oral history transcript, November 13, 1970, 13–16, LBJL.

6.   White House press release, July 29, 1967, Malvina Stephenson Collection, box 3, folder 5, Congressional Archives, Carl Albert Center, Norman, Oklahoma; "LBJ: 'Civil Peace Has Been Shattered,'" *WP*, July 30, 1967, A8.

7.   Frank C. Porter, "Both Short-Term and Future Goals Given Riots Panel," *WP*, July 30, 1967, A1.

8.   Both quoted in William Chapman, "Johnson Meets Probe Panel," *WP*, July 29, 1967, A8.

9.   White House press release, July 29, 1967.

10. Michael Lipsky, Ginsburg interview notes, April 23, 1968, 1–2, folder 2, box 4, LOP; NACCD, *Report*, 113, 158n2.

11. Lipsky, David Chambers interview notes, April 24, 1968, 3, folder 2, box 4, LOP.

12. NACCD hearing transcript, August 9, 1967, 316–317, 360–364; GSCCD hearing transcript, August 16, 1967, 8–15.

13. Lipsky, Chambers interview notes, April 24, 1968, 1; Lipsky, Ginsburg interview notes, April 23, 1968, 5.

14. Lipsky, Steven Kurzman interview notes, March 20, 1968, 1–2, folder 2, box 4, LOP; Lipsky, Ginsburg interview notes, April 26, 1968, 3–4; Peden oral history transcript, November 13, 1970, 23, LBJL; Robert Conot, "When Domestic Disorders Blazed across the Major Cities of America," *Los Angeles Times*, February 28, 1988.

15. NACCD hearing transcript, August 1, 1967, 4, 84. On the commission's continuing investigation of the conspiracy question, see exhibit 3, series 2, box 1, NACCD; Kerner to Hoover, February 22, 1968; Hoover to Kerner, February 27, 1968, "NACCD 2/28/69–3/13/68" folder, box 387, LBJ Papers, LBJL. Johnson may have twisted Hoover's arm on this testimony—one of Johnson's assistants recommended that he get the conspiracy question out of the way quickly so that they could keep "the heat on Congress not to run away from your programs." Douglass Cater to Johnson, July 28, 1967, "NACCD 11/23/63–9/30/67" folder, box 386, LBJ Papers, LBJL. For examples of the conspiracy charge, John Herbers, "Congress Chiefs Ask Riot Inquiry," *NYT*, July 26, 1967, 1; "Antiriot Bill Gets a Push in the Senate," *NYT*, July 27, 1967, 1; "Bill to Curb Riots Approved by House Committee," *NYT*, July 12, 1967, 23; Paul Hoffman, "Moynihan Blames Low Status, Not Race, for Riots," *NYT*, July 25, 1967, 22.

16. Lipsky, Ginsburg interview notes, April 23, 1968, 4–5, folder 2, box 4, LOP; James Corman, "The Riot Commission's Report," *Arizona Law Review* 9, no. 3 (Spring 1968): 348; Jenkins, *Presidents, Politics, and Policing*, 51.

17. See William Chapman, "Hoover Suspects Outsiders," *WP*, August 3, 1967; Roy Reed, "Riot 'Agitators' Cited by Hoover," *NYT*, August 3, 1967.

18. NACCD hearing transcript, August 9, 1967, 223–227.

19. Ibid., 230–241.

20. Ibid., 242–246.

21. Ibid., 246–247; also 257–259.

22. Ibid., 366.

23. Lipsky, Ginsburg interview notes, April 23, 1968, 13–14, folder 2, box 4, LOP;

Peden oral history transcript, November 13, 1970, 17, LBJL; William Chapman, "FBI Chief Reports No Riot Plot," *WP*, August 2, 1967, A1; NACCD, *Report*, 483.

24. Ginsburg to McGeorge Bundy, October 29, 1967, "Otto Kerner: Official Correspondence" folder 2, box 1392, Kerner Papers, ALPL; Lipsky, Kurzman interview notes, March 21, 1968, 3, folder 2, box 4, LOP; NACCD press release, October 1, 1967, "Alvin Spivak: Press Releases" folder 1, box 1393, Kerner Papers, ALPL. One staffer later wrote that the number of black people on these city teams was rather low: about ten. See Charles H. King, *Fire in My Bones* (Grand Rapids, MI: Eerdmans, 1983), 132–133.

25. Kyran McGrath to Kerner, October 13, 1967, "Otto Kerner: Official Correspondence" folder 3, box 1392, Kerner Papers, ALPL. His worries soon spread to the commissioners themselves. See McGrath to Kerner, October 30, 1967, "Otto Kerner: Official Correspondence" folder 2, box 1392, Kerner Papers, ALPL. See also McGrath to Kerner, October 20, 1967, "Otto Kerner: Official Correspondence" folder 3, box 1392, Kerner Papers, ALPL.

26. *Bill Moyers Journal*, PBS, March 28, 2008, transcript, accessed October 27, 2011, http://www.pbs.org/moyers/journal/03282008/transcript1.html; Fred R. Harris, *Alarms and Hopes: A Personal Journey, A Personal View* (New York: Harper and Row, 1968), 6–16; Lipsky, Jay Kriegel interview notes, June 20, 1968, 3–4, folder 2, box 4, LOP. See also Kerner in *Issues and Answers*, ABC, March 3, 1968, transcript, "Paper: Kerner: 'ABC—Issues & Answers'" folder, box 1397, Kerner Papers, ALPL; Corman, "The Riot Commission's Report," 352.

27. Ginsburg, NACCD hearing transcript, August 22, 1967, 655–656; Eldridge, "Lindsay Tours Newark," *NEN*, August 16, 1967, 1.

28. Eldridge, "Newark Takes to Lindsay," *NEN*, August 17, 1967, 4; "City Hall Still Hot from Lindsay Cold Shoulder," *NEN*, August 19, 1967, 5.

29. Joseph Carragher, "Newark Needs Money, Addonizio Tells Lindsay," *SL*, August 17, 1967, 1; NACCD hearing transcript, August 22, 1967, 656–657; Eldridge, "Lindsay Tours Newark."

30. Eldridge, "Lindsay Tours Newark." A Lindsay aide admitted to one incident of hostility: a group of young black men heckled Lindsay from a street corner. Eldridge, "Newark Takes to Lindsay."

31. Eldridge, "Newark Takes to Lindsay."

32. Ibid., 1, 4; Carragher, "Newark Needs Money, Addonizio Tells Lindsay," *SL*, August 17, 1967, 1.

33. NACCD hearing transcript, August 22, 1967, 658–664.

34. Ibid., 668–669.

35. See NACCD hearing transcript, August 22, 1967, 604–605.

36. "Addonizio: Suburbs Don't Care," *SL*, August 23, 1967, 1.

37. NACCD hearing transcript, August 22, 1967, 612–617.

38. Ibid., 666–667.

39. Ibid., 690–691, 695, 699–700, 740–741, 751–752.

40. Patrick Healy, "The Alternatives to America's Urban Crisis," *Nation's Cities* 6, no. 5 (May 1968): 9.

41. NACCD meeting minutes, December 7, 1967, 8–9, 11, 14; December 8, 1967, 2; "Kyran McGrath: Minutes of Meetings of ACCD Staff" folder, box 1392, Kerner Papers, ALPL.

42. Novellino, "Newark Toured by 5 LBJ Panelists," *SL*, August 24, 1967, 1; Shabazian, "Riots Panel Pays Visit to Newark," *NEN*, August 23, 1967, 1; Shabazian, "Gov.

Kerner Says Insurance Key to Riot Area Business," *NEN*, September 29, 1967, 29; "LBJ Riot Panel Chief Finds Central Ward Still Hurting," *SL*, September 29, 1967, 4. On his trip to Newark, Kerner also met with local "radicals" hostile to city hall, including Willie Wright and Charles McCray, two UCC officials who would become very controversial figures in the aftermath of the riot (see chapter 10). Barnhart and Schlickman, *Kerner*, 210–211; Isaac Hunt to staff, October 17, 1967, Official Correspondence folder, box 1392, Kerner Papers, ALPL.

43. NACCD hearing transcript, September 12, 1967, 999.

44. Ibid., 1002–1003, 1015.

45. According to August Meier and Elliott Rudwick, this optimistic, moral reading of American history was a hallmark of Quarles's approach and of a post–World War II intellectual milieu shaped by Gunnar Myrdal's "emphasis on the unifying consensus in American values." By contrast, Bennett's work was a product of a later generation inspired by the drama of 1960s protest. Meier and Rudwick, *Black History and the Historical Profession, 1915–1980* (Urbana: University of Illinois Press, 1986), 116, 122, 176.

46. NACCD hearing transcript, September 12, 1967, 1031–1032.

47. Ibid, 1043–1049.

48. Ibid, 1057–1058, 1061.

49. Shellow, "Social Scientists and Social Action from within the Establishment," *Journal of Social Issues* 26, no. 1 (Winter 1970): 208–211; Lipsky, Shellow interview notes, March 20, 1968, 2–5, 8–10, folder 2, box 4, LOP. For more on Shellow, see Ellen Herman, *The Romance of American Psychology: Political Culture in the Age of Experts* (Berkeley: University of California Press, 1995), 216–217; Shellow, "Essentials to Police Prevention of Civil Disturbances," April 3, 1966, "Police-Community Relations" folder, box 69, General Correspondence, 1965–1968, OLEA; "Reinforcing Police Neutrality in Civil Rights Confrontations," *Journal of Applied Behavioral Science* 1, no. 3 (1965): 243–254.

50. Shellow, "Social Scientists and Social Action from within the Establishment," 211.

51. Shellow et al., "The Harvest of American Racism: The Political Meaning of Violence in the Summer of 1967," 153–156, 166–171, box 1, series 7, Commission Research Studies, NACCD.

52. Lipsky, John Koskinen interview notes, April 25, 1968, 10–11, folder 2, box 4, LOP. See also Lipsky, Anthony Downs interview notes, April 24, 1969, 3–4, folder 2, box 4; Lipsky, Ginsburg interview notes, April 26, 1968, 3, folder 2, box 4; David J. Olson, Hans Mattick interview notes, November 28, 1969, 1, folder 3, box 4; all LOP.

53. Kyran McGrath to Ginsburg, Shellow, et al., December 1, 1967, "Memo: Dec 1, 1967" folder, box 1394, Kerner Papers, ALPL.

54. Press release, December 10, 1967, "Alvin Spivak: Press Releases" folder 1, box 1393; and meeting minutes, December 9, 1967, "Kyran McGrath: Minutes of Meetings of ACCD Staff" folder, box 1392; both Kerner Papers, ALPL. Other commissioners subsequently confirmed this explanation. See Edward W. Brooke, "Social Education Asks," *Social Education* 33, no. 1 (January 1969): 24; Peden oral history transcript, November 13, 1970, 23, LBJL.

55. Lipsky, Ginsburg interview notes, April 23, 1968, 3; Lipsky, Kurzman interview notes, March 21, 1968, 11–12; both folder 2, box 4, LOP. Shellow said soon after that the firings were due to budget concerns combined with the speedup. See Lipsky, Shellow interview notes, March 20, 1968, 11, folder 2, box 4, LOP; Shellow, "Social Scientists and Social Action from within the Establishment," 212. Kerner, however,

denied that the speedup was due to funding concerns, though this might have been an effort to avoid antagonizing the White House. See press briefing, January 10, 1968, 18, "Alvin Spivak: Press Releases" folder 2, box 1393, Kerner Papers, ALPL.

56. Al Spivak to Ginsburg, undated, "ACCD (Thank You) 1968" folder, box 1408, Kerner Papers, ALPL.

57. Newspaper clippings, *Washington Star*, December 13, 1967, December 14, 1967, "Otto Kerner: Official Correspondence" folder 1, box 1392, Kerner Papers, ALPL.

58. Morton Mintz, "Riot Probe Firings Stir Exchanges," *WP*, December 14, 1967, A1; Ethel Payne, "Riot Commission Disbanding," *Chicago Defender*, December 18, 1967, 19; "Riot Panel: High Aims, Low Budget," *Newsweek*, December 25, 1967, 9.

59. Spivak to Kerner et al., January 9, 1968, "Memo: Jan 9, 1968" folder, box 1394, Kerner Papers, ALPL.

60. Robert E. Conot, *Rivers of Blood, Years of Darkness* (New York: Bantam Books, 1967), 416; Lipsky, Ginsburg interview notes, April 23, 1968, 10–11, folder 2, box 4, LOP.

61. NACCD meeting minutes, December 9, 1967, 1–5, "Kyran McGrath: Minutes of Meetings of ACCD Staff" folder, box 1392, Kerner Papers, ALPL.

62. Lipsky, Victor Palmieri interview notes, March 22, 1968, 1–3, folder 2, box 4, LOP.

63. McGrath to Kerner, September 29, 1967 [*sic*], "Otto Kerner: Official Correspondence" folder 4, box 1392, Kerner Papers, ALPL. (This letter must be misdated; it refers to a December draft of the report.) See also Brooke in NACCD meeting minutes, December 7, 1967, 8, "Kyran McGrath: Minutes of Meetings of ACCD Staff" folder, box 1392, Kerner Papers, ALPL.

64. Corman to Ginsburg, October 17, 1967, "Otto Kerner: Official Correspondence" folder 2, box 1392, Kerner Papers, ALPL.

65. Lindsay to Kerner, December 26, 1967, "Otto Kerner: Official Correspondence" folder 3, box 1392, Kerner Papers, ALPL.

66. Ginsburg to commissioners, January 1, 1968, "Memo: Jan 1, 1968" folder, box 1394, Kerner Papers, ALPL. On the commissioners' reading process: Fred Harris, first rough draft, "The Kerner Commission Report One Year Later," n.d. [1969], folder 10, box 281, Fred Harris Collection, Congressional Archives Collection, Carl Albert Center, University of Oklahoma; Herbert T. Jenkins, "A Commission Member Speaks," *Police Chief* 35, no. 5 (May 1968): 36; Jenkins, *Presidents, Politics, and Policing*, 20; Peden, oral history transcript, November 13, 1970, 23–24, LBJL.

67. NACCD meeting minutes, January 11, 1968, 10, "Kyran McGrath: Minutes of Meetings of ACCD Staff" folder, box 1392, Kerner Papers, ALPL.

68. Lipsky, Koskinen interview notes, April 25, 1968, 7–8, folder 2, box 4, LOP; Jenkins, *Presidents, Politics, and Policing*, 22; Lipsky, Chambers interview notes, April 24, 1968, 5, folder 2, box 4, LOP.

69. See, for example, NACCD meeting minutes, January 30, 1968, 2, "Kyran McGrath: Minutes of Meetings of ACCD Staff" folder, box 1392, Kerner Papers, ALPL.

70. McGrath to Kerner, February 2, 1968, "Otto Kerner: Official Correspondence" folder 1, box 1392, Kerner Papers, ALPL; NACCD meeting minutes, December 9, 1967, 8; January 9, 1968, 4; January 30, 1968, 5; all "Kyran McGrath: Minutes of Meetings of ACCD Staff" folder, box 1392, Kerner Papers, ALPL; McGrath to Kerner, February 1, 1968, "Otto Kerner: Official Correspondence" folder 2, box 1392, Kerner Papers, ALPL.

71. Multiple telegrams, Ginsburg to Kerner, February 20, 1968, "Otto Kerner: Official Correspondence" folder 2, box 1392, Kerner Papers, ALPL.

72. Jenkins, *Presidents, Politics, and Policing,* 22; Conot, "When Domestic Disorders Blazed across the Major Cities," *Los Angeles Times,* February 28, 1988.
73. David Wise, "On Humphrey's Team, Harris-in-a-Hurry," *NYT Magazine,* August 18, 1968; Charles Mangel, "The Remarkable Mr. Harris," *Look* 33, no. 6 (March 18, 1969), 75.
74. Lipsky, Ginsburg interview notes, April 23, 1968, 11–12, folder 2, box 4, LOP.
75. Lindsay to commission members, January 9, 1968, "Memo: Jan 9, 1968" folder, box 1394, Kerner Papers, ALPL; Andrew Kopkind, "White on Black," in *The Politics of Riot Commissions, 1917–1970,* ed. Anthony Platt (New York: Macmillan, 1971), 389.
76. NACCD meeting minutes, January 11, 1968, 12, "Kyran McGrath: Minutes of Meetings of ACCD Staff" folder, box 1392, Kerner Papers, ALPL.
77. Corman to Kerner, January 13, 1968, "Otto Kerner: Official Correspondence" folder 1, box 1392, Kerner Papers, ALPL.
78. Paul Ylvisaker claimed this was his idea. Olson, Ylvisaker interview notes, June 17, 1968, 6, folder 6, box 4, LOP.
79. Lipsky, Kriegel interview notes, June 20, 1968, 1–2, folder 2, box 4, LOP; Vincent Cannato, *The Ungovernable City: John Lindsay and His Struggle to Save New York* (New York: Basic Books, 2002), 206.
80. Kerner to Albert Watson, March 11, 1968, "Memo: March 11, 1968" folder, box 1394, Kerner Papers, ALPL; Lipsky, Ginsburg interview notes, April 26, 1968, 5–6, folder 2, box 5, LOP.
81. Lipsky, Ginsburg interview notes, April 26, 1968, 5–6, folder 2, box 5, LOP; Fred Harris, first rough draft, "The Kerner Commission Report One Year Later," n.d., 2–3, Fred Harris Collection, Congressional Archives Collection, Carl Albert Center, University of Oklahoma. The White House was likely the source for the leak. The day before the *Post* informed Ginsburg of its scoop, Joseph Califano, the president's top domestic aide, suggested to Johnson that he authorize a leak in an attempt to diminish the report's overall impact. See Califano to Lyndon Johnson, February 28, 1968, "NACCD 2/28/68—3/13/68" folder, box 387, LBJ Papers, LBJL. Victor Palmieri, the commission's deputy director, later claimed that Ginsburg, who was frequently defending himself against charges that he was a White House stooge, had leaked the summary. Palmieri oral history transcript, October 26, 2004, 22–23, Newsome Oral History Collection, National Bankruptcy Archives, University of Pennsylvania.
82. William Chapman, *WP,* March 1, 1968; John Herbers, *NYT,* March 1, 1968.
83. Roy Wilkins later wrote, "I can still see John Lindsay, mayor of New York, yellow legal pad in hand, going over them [the words of the summary] with us. Without him, the commission would have been seriously reduced in its bite and effectiveness. The bad news had to be delivered. You had to be honest." Wilkins, *Standing Fast: The Autobiography of Roy Wilkins* (New York: Viking, 1982), 329.
84. NACCD, *Report,* 1–2, 29.
85. Bantam press release, March 4, 1968, "ACCD 1968" folder, box 1408, Kerner Papers, ALPL; "Riot Report to Go on Sale Next Week," *WP,* March 2, 1968, A6.
86. Oscar Dystel to Kerner, March 28, 1968, "ACCD (Thank You) 1968" folder, box 1408, Kerner Papers, ALPL.
87. Esther Margolis to Chris Vlahaplous, April 30, 1968, "ACCD (Book) 1968" folder, box 1408; Herbert T. Jenkins to Oscar Dystel, May 9, 1968, "ACCD 1968" folder, box 1408; Roy Wilkins to Dystel, May 22, 1968, "ACCD (Thank You) 1968" folder, box 1408; all Kerner Papers, ALPL.

330 / Notes to Pages 148–50

88. There are hundreds of such letters in "ACCD (Book) 1968" folder, box 1408, Kerner Papers, ALPL. The price of the GPO edition was printed in the introductory pages of the Bantam version.

89. Letter and attached sales report, Marc Jaffe to Ginsburg, August 20, 1969, "National Advisory Commission on Civil Disorders" folder, box 9, Kerner Family Papers, ALPL. Ginsburg, in response to the sales report, soon wrote to Kerner to say that "we seem to be doing considerably better in academia than we are on the Hill." Ginsburg to Kerner, September 2, 1969, "National Advisory Commission on Civil Disorders" folder, box 9, Kerner Family Papers, ALPL.

90. Califano to Johnson, February 28, 1968, "NACCD 2/28/68–3/13/68" folder, box 387, LBJ Papers, LBJL.

91. Johnson to Califano, February 26, 1968, "NACCD 1/26/68–2/27/68" folder; "Notes on Meeting with Negro Editors and Publishers," March 15, 1968, "NACCD 3/14/68–6/15/68" folder; both box 387, LBJ Papers, LBJL. Also, Max Frankel, "President Calls Report on Riots Worthy of Study," NYT, March 7, 1968, 1, 34.

92. Richard Reeves, "Lindsay Renews Criticism of War," NYT, March 26, 1968, 20; Reeves, "Mayor, in Denver, Warns of Rioting," NYT, March 31, 1968, 44. Other commissioners were also disappointed, if a bit less strident. See, for example, Wilkins oral history interview transcript, April 1, 1969, 11–13, LBJL; John Henry Cutler, Ed Brooke: Biography of a Senator (Indianapolis: Bobbs-Merrill, 1972), 292; Edward W. Brooke, Bridging the Divide: My Life (New Brunswick, NJ: Rutgers University Press, 2007), 173.

93. Califano to Johnson, April 10, 1968, "NACCD 3/14/68–6/15/68" folder, box 387, LBJ Papers, LBJL.

94. Kerner to Califano, April 25, 1968; bound transcript of interview with Kerner, undated (May 1968), 16–17; both "ACCD (Thank You) 1968" folder, box 1408, Kerner Papers, ALPL.

95. "Kerner Commission: Dissent" folder, box 7, Kerner Family Papers, ALPL.

96. "Kerner Defends Riot Report," WP, March 29, 1968, A6; "Kerner Confirmed," WP, April 12, 1968, A18.

97. "Humphrey Says Riot Panel Errs," NYT, March 25, 1968, 44.

98. "Kerner Panel Report Stirs Shockwaves," WP, March 2, 1968, A1; "Riot Panel Plan Scored," NEN, March 2, 1968, 1.

99. Buckley, "Why All Blame on Honkey?," Los Angeles Times, March 18, 1968, A5.

100. Xerox Corporation, memo, May 2, 1968; Larry Nye (Dow Chemical) to Kerner, February 12, 1970; both "Kerner Commission Business Firms & Labor Groups" folder, box 7, Kerner Family Papers, ALPL. What follows is just a sampling of the immense amount of material expressing support for the implementation of the commission's report found in the Kerner Family Papers, ALPL, especially boxes 7, 8, 9.

101. Memo, Sam Elfert to Anti-Defamation League (ADL) regional offices, April 11, 1968, "Kerner Commission: Commission Correspondence" folder, box 7, Kerner Family Papers, ALPL; ADL, "Minutes of New York Area Program Community Meeting," April 11, 1968, "Memo: May 11, 1968" folder, box 1394, Kerner Papers, ALPL; Edward Fiske, "U.S. Catholic Bishops Endorse Riot Report," NYT, April 24, 1968, 1; Eugene K. Souder to Kerner, May 24, 1968, "ACCD (Thank You) 1968" folder, box 1408, Kerner Papers, ALPL.

102. Governor Philip H. Hoff, proclamation, April 15, 1968; Tucson Commission on Human Rights, "The Tucson Response to the Kerner Report," September 9, 1968;

both "Kerner Commission: Governmental Bodies" folder, box 7, Kerner Family Papers, ALPL.

103. Holton R. Price to Kerner, telegram, May 26, 1968, "Kerner Commission: Social Work Organizations" folder, box 8, Kerner Family Papers, ALPL.

104. Buck Dawson to Kerner, March 4, 1968, "ACCD 1968" folder, box 1408, Kerner Papers, ALPL.

105. Peter Kihss, "A March on Capital by Whites Proposed," *NYT*, April 24, 1968, 1.

106. National Association of Social Workers, *Proceedings of NASW's National Social Action Workshop on the Urban Crisis* (Washington, DC, 1968), 50–51.

107. "Social Education Asks," *Social Education* 33, no. 1 (January 1969): 24.

108. King to Kerner, telegram, March 7, 1968, "Kerner Commission: Individuals" folder, box 7, Kerner Family Papers, ALPL. I assume King sent it to each commissioner, since Wilkins received the same one. See Wilkins, *Standing Fast*, 327–328.

109. "4000 Hear Dr. King at Cathedral," *WP*, April 1, 1968, A1.

110. Thomas Johnson, "12 Arrested Here," *NYT*, April 5, 1968, 1; "Negro Violence Hits US Cities," *Chicago Tribune*, April 5, 1968, 2.

111. "Youths Roam South Side," *Chicago Tribune*, April 7, 1968, 1. On Daley's order to shoot to maim looters (arsonists were to be killed), see Adam Cohen and Elizabeth Taylor, *American Pharaoh: Mayor Richard J. Daley; His Battle for Chicago and the Nation* (Boston: Little, Brown, 2000), 455.

112. "Riot Task Force Restores Order," *Chicago Tribune*, April 8, 1968, 2.

113. "400 Whites Hold March to 'Confess' Racism," *NYT*, April 13, 1968, 13.

CHAPTER SIX

1. Waggoner, "Hughes Observes Looting of Stores," *NYT*, July 15, 1967, 11; "Jersey Governor Gives President Riot Report," *NYT*, July 15, 1967, 11; Carroll, "Curfew Imposed on City; Sniper Slays Policeman," *NYT*, July 15, 1967, 1; Warshaw and James McHugh, "Hughes: 'A City in Open Rebellion,'" *SL*, July 15, 1967, 1; Quotation of the Day, *NYT*, July 15, 1967, 20.

2. Shabazian, "Hughes Denies Riots Started by Communists," *NEN*, July 16, 1967, 11; Bigart, "Newark Riot Deaths at 21," *NYT*, July 16, 1967, 1.

3. Peter Carter, "Driscoll, Meyner Join Riot Probers," *NEN*, July 20, 1967, 1; Abbie Ziffren and Connie Cedrone, "Hughes Committee to Prove Unrest," *SL*, July 20, 1967, 1.

4. Carter, "Driscoll, Meyner Join Riot Probers."

5. "Members of State Commission," *NEN*, February 11, 1968, 21. On Lilley, "Rutgers Sets Business Forum," *NYT*, December 25, 1966, 40. On Driscoll and Meyner, see Paul A. Stellhorn and Michael J. Birkner, eds., *The Governors of New Jersey: 1664–1974* (Trenton: New Jersey Historical Society, 1982), 214–222; Maxine N. Lurie and Marc Mappen, eds., *Encyclopedia of New Jersey* (New Brunswick, NJ: Rutgers University Press, 2004), 218–219, 518. On Taylor, "Methodists' Leader," *NYT*, April 23, 1965, 14; "Convention Schedule," *NYT*, August 24, 1964, 17; "Theologians Ask End to Draft," *NYT*, March 10, 1965, 15. On Dougherty, "Hose Halts Protest at Seton Hall," *NYT*, February 28, 1964, 1; "Fight with Russia Declared Satanic," *NYT*, March 6, 1955, 52.

6. "Address of Governor Richard J. Hughes before the 75th Anniversary Convention of the International Longshoremen's Association," July 20, 1967, box 12, GSCCD.

7. Sanford Jaffe, interview by author, May 18, 2006.

8. Lofton, head of the Newark Legal Services Project, was Governor Hughes's special community liaison during the riots. Ray Brown was an officer in the National Guard and had been deployed to Newark during the riot. He set up several of Hughes's meetings with community representatives. Jaffe was born and raised in the South Ward, was a graduate of Rutgers-Newark, and had worked in the county prosecutor's and US attorney's offices in Newark. Gibbons practiced law in town, had helped arrange lawyers for riot arrestees, and had visited with residents to gather complaints about law enforcement misconduct. Lilley ran a corporation whose ties to Newark stretched back nearly a half century, and Bishop Dougherty ran a college campus that directly abuts the city. "Members of State Commission," *NEN*, February 11, 1968, 21; Jaffe, interview by author, May 18, 2006; Gibbons, interview by author, April 21, 2006; Larry Bilder, interview by author, February 23, 2012.

9. "Statement by Governor Richard J. Hughes to the Governor's Select Commission for the Study of Civil Disorder in New Jersey," August 8, 1967, exhibit C58, box 13, GSCCD.

10. Douglas Robinson, "'Brutality' Is Laid to Newark Police," *NYT*, July 15, 1967, 10.

11. Heckel speech transcript, November 9, 1967, folder 1, box 59, Mason Gross Papers, RUA.

12. Quoted in Bigart, "Newark Rioting Is Declared Over," *NYT*, July 18, 1967, 1.

13. Olson, Lofton interview notes, June 18, 1968, 2, folder 6, box 4, LOP; GSCCD hearing transcript, October 2, 1967, 78–81; Lofton remarks at Newark History Society, May 5, 2014. King had married Lofton and his wife and was godfather to their child.

14. "Statement of Governor Richard J. Hughes on Newark Radio Station WNJR at 6:30pm, Sunday Evening," folder 1, box 12, GSCCD; Bigart, "House-to-House Search for Snipers," *NYT*, July 17, 1967, 1.

15. Bigart, "House-to-House Search for Snipers."

16. Hughes, GSCCD hearing transcript, October 2, 1967, 85–87; Curvin, GSCCD hearing transcript, October 17, 1967, 42–45; Curvin, interview by author, January 31, 2006; Hayden, *Reunion*, 157–161.

17. "Statement of Governor Richard J. Hughes at Newark Armory, Monday Morning, July 17, 1967, at Noon," box 285, Hughes Records, NJSA; Bigart, "Newark Rioting Is Declared Over"; "Governor Told to Rest," *NYT*, July 19, 1967, 42. A handwritten note on the last page of this copy of Hughes's statement says that the governor also read aloud the telegram from Roy Wilkins mentioned above.

18. "Wants Help for Urban Renewal," *TET*, January 16, 1962, 1; Winters, "Richard J. Hughes," in Stellhorn and Birkner, *The Governors of New Jersey*, 224.

19. GSCCD hearing transcript, August 16, 1967, 3–6.

20. Ylvisaker in ibid., 5–9, 23–24.

21. Ibid., September 7, 1967, 131–135, 146; September 26, 1967, 27.

22. Ibid., September 26, 1967, 18, 30–31, 51.

23. Ibid., 54–58, 63, 85.

24. Ibid., 94–98.

25. Jaffe interview, May 18, 2006.

26. GSCCD hearing transcript, November 13, 1967, 10–19, 26–31.

27. Ibid., 39–45.

28. Ibid., November 20, 1967, 111–114; November 17, 1967, 4–6.

29. Ibid., November 17, 1967, 29–32.

30. Ibid., October 3, 1967, 103–105, 78–87; NLSP, "Preliminary Analysis of Statements

Concerning Law Enforcement during Newark Riots," folder 4, box 3, Eldridge Papers, NPL.

31. GSCCD hearing transcript, October 3, 1967, 94–95.
32. Ibid., September 29, 1967, 3–11, 15–22.
33. Ibid., 41–45.
34. Ibid., 46–49, 61, 74–81, 98–101.
35. Ibid., October 30, 1967, 1–10.
36. Ibid., 136–137, 71–72; November 6, 1967, 41.
37. Ibid., November 6, 1967, 47–48.
38. Ibid., 109.
39. Ibid., 55–60, 85–86.
40. Ibid., 69–73, 101, 104.
41. Ibid., October 30, 1967, 34–39, 48–51, 54–55.
42. Ibid., November 17, 1967, 165, 178–179.
43. Jaffe and Gibbons interviews by author.
44. Jaffe interview, May 18, 2006; Sullivan, "Hughes Asks Action," *NEN*, February 12, 1968, 1.
45. Draft of Lilley's opening remarks, folder 3, box 3, Eldridge Papers, NPL; Leo Standora, "Jersey Riot Panel Report," *SL*, February 11, 1968, 1, 34; "Lilley Sees Fast Action," *NEN*, February 11, 1968, 24; Jaffe interview, May 18, 2006.
46. GSCCD, *Report for Action* (Trenton, 1968), 7–8, 16.
47. Ibid., 143.
48. Ibid., 88–89.
49. Ibid., 22, 32, 143.
50. Ibid., 143–144.
51. Ibid., 163–164.
52. Ibid., x–xi.
53. Ibid., 104–106.
54. Ibid., 141–142.
55. Ibid., 21, 143.
56. "Riot Study Seen as 'Alarm Clock,'" *SL*, February 11, 1968, 29. See also "Addonizio for Probe," *NEN*, February 11, 1968, 18; Higgins, "Lordi Studies Panel Call for Inquiry," *NEN*, February 12, 1968, 1; Martin Gansberg, "Top Newark Aides Score Riot Report," *NYT*, February 12, 1968, 1.
57. Eldridge, "Redden to Head Gambling Drive," *NEN*, February 13, 1968, 1.
58. Ibid.
59. Sullivan, "Hughes Asks Action."
60. Hughes to Lofton, February 14, 1968, "Newark Disorders—Summer 1967—Post Mortems & Related Subsequent Events" folder, box 2, Dickinson Debevoise personal papers; Jaffe interview, May 18, 2006.
61. Hughes, untitled statement, April 5, 1968, box 285, Hughes Records, NJSA; John Wefing, *The Life and Times of Richard J. Hughes: The Politics of Civility* (New Brunswick, NJ: Rutgers University Press, 2009), 192.
62. Hughes, untitled statement, April 8, 1968, box 285, Hughes Records, NJSA.
63. Hughes, Special Message to the Legislature, April 8, 1968, box 285, Hughes Records, NJSA; Dick Gale, "Hughes Puts Hard Questions to State," *TET*, April 9, 1968, 5.
64. "Bells, Chimes Ring in Area's Eulogy," *TET*, April 9, 1969, 1; Hughes, untitled statement, April 8, 1968, box 285, Hughes Records, NJSA.

65. Peter Millones, "Racial Clashes in Suburbs Shut Many Schools and Some Bars," *NYT*, April 6, 1968, 27; Ronald Sullivan, "Negro Is Killed in Trenton," *NYT*, April 10, 1968, 1.
66. James Goodman and Lee Pasternack, "City Wary after Night of Terror," *TET*, April 10, 1968, 1; Pasternack, "8 Injured in City Violence," *TET*, April 9, 1968, 2; Herb Wolfe, "Flames, Gunshots, Taunting Laughter," *TET*, April 10, 1968, 1; Sullivan, "Negro Is Killed in Trenton."
67. Thomas H. Greer, "Dead Youth Was in Social Work," *TET*, April 10, 1968, 1; "Hughes, Armenti Visit Youth's Kin," *TET*, April 11, 1968, 1; Sullivan, "Negro Is Killed in Trenton"; Sullivan, "Trenton Is Calm; Guard Stands By," *NYT*, April 11, 1968, 1.
68. Ted Partlow and James Goodman, "'A Tragedy,' Hughes Tells Mother," *TET*, April 12, 1968, 1; Sullivan, "Trenton Relaxes Period of Curfew," *NYT*, April 12, 1968, 18.
69. Partlow and Goodman, "'A Tragedy,' Hughes Tells Mother."
70. "Daley's Order Irks Hughes," *TET*, April 17, 1968, 1.
71. State of New Jersey, *Senate Journal: 1968* (Trenton, 1968), 741, 761; Dick Gale, "Governor Presents Blueprint," *TET*, April 25, 1968, 1.
72. Hughes, "Special Message to the Legislature on Emergent State Problems," June 20, 1969, folder 7, box 111, Robert Meyner Papers, Lafayette College.

CHAPTER SEVEN

1. NACCD, *Report*, 69–84; GSCCD, *Report for Action*, 145–160.
2. "Whelan Warning," *NEN*, July 17, 1967, 5.
3. Michael Flamm, *Law and Order: Street Crime, Civil Unrest, and the Crisis of Liberalism in the 1960s* (New York: Columbia University Press, 2005), especially 1–3, where Flamm credits Goldwater with moving the issue "from the margins to the mainstream." Also, Rick Perlstein, *Nixonland: The Rise of a President and the Fracturing of America* (New York: Scribner, 2008), 363–365.
4. Novellino, "Cops Losing All Rights: PBA Chief," *SL*, September 27, 1967, 7.
5. Hy Kuperstein, "Sills Cites Public 'Debt,'" *NEN*, September 27, 1967, 35.
6. Hayden, "The Occupation of Newark," *New York Review of Books* 9, no. 3 (August 24, 1967): 18–19, 22 (and see chapter 9 for more). On the Governor's Commission and the NLSP, see chapter 6.
7. "PBA Sets Riot Probe," *NEN*, September 27, 1967, 35. The complete resolution can be found in NJSPBA, *The Road to Anarchy: Findings of the Riot Study Commission of the New Jersey State Patrolmen's Benevolent Association, Inc.* (Jersey City, 1968), 33.
8. Kuperstein, "Police Urge Jury Probe," *NEN*, January 25, 1968, 20; Anthony Giuliano, Newark PBA press release, undated [February 1968], folder 3, box 3, Eldridge Papers, NPL.
9. NJSPBA, *Road to Anarchy*, ix.
10. NJSPBA, *Road to Anarchy*, 32. I contacted the NJSPBA main office in Woodbridge several times and was told several times that material on the Newark riot could be found at various repositories across the state. The staff member who corresponded with me never answered my question about whether the NJSPBA still had the commission records, let alone whether they would let me see them. In my tally, of the 294 notes that refer to hearing transcripts, 111 clearly referred to 27 identifiable law enforcement personnel (of whom 8, including 1 informant, were Newark witnesses), and 49 referred to 16 identifiable civilians (only 3 of whom were Newark witnesses), including mayors and councilmen, county and city prosecutors, a couple of business owners, and a couple of newspaper reporters.

11. NJSPBA, *Road to Anarchy*, 30; "PBA Sets Riot Probe," *NEN*, September 27, 1967, 35. The chairmanship must have changed over the course of the investigation. The final report lists William Connelly of Newark as chairman.
12. "PBA Carries On Own Riot Probe," *SL*, November 8, 1967, 16.
13. Jeffrey Stoll, "Kept from Rioting Area," *NEN*, November 10, 1967, 23; Stoll, "Riot Cause Questioned," *NEN*, November 14, 1967, 21.
14. "State PBA Opens City Riots Probe," *NEN*, January 18, 1968, 26.
15. Kuperstein, "Police Urge Jury Probe of Newark Riot 'Plotters,'" *NEN*, January 25, 1968, 20.
16. "Newark Police Back PBA Probe," *SL*, February 25, 1968, 12; "PBA Says Reds Fanned Riot Fires," *SL*, March 3, 1968, 6.
17. PBA Local no. 3 press release, February 12, 1968, folder 3, box 3, Eldridge Papers, NPL; Sullivan, "Lordi Studies Panel Call for Inquiry," *NEN*, February 12, 1968, 1.
18. "Two Police Groups Hit Review Board Plan," *NEN*, February 13, 1968, 14. See also the statements of the Essex County chapter of the New Jersey Retired Police and Firemen's Association and of the New Jersey Narcotic Enforcement Officers Association in Novellino, "Newark Council Assails the Report," *SL*, February 16, 1968, 1.
19. "Statement of the Committee of Concern," February 21, 1968, folder 2, box 3, Eldridge Papers, NPL.
20. Giuliano, Newark PBA press release, undated [February 1968], folder 3, box 3, Eldridge Papers, NPL.
21. Bob Dubill, "Riot Panel Asked Why Hughes' Role Left Out," *SL*, February 26, 1968, 1; Novellino, "Newark Council Assails the Report"; "Newark PBA Praises Jury's Report on Riot," *SL*, May 1, 1968, 13.
22. NJSPBA press release, February 19, 1968, folder 3, box 3, Eldridge Papers, NPL.
23. Sullivan, "Lordi Studies Panel Call for Inquiry."
24. Roger Harris, "PBA Sees a Conspiracy in Last Year's Jersey Riots"; "Cabbie Smith Gets Two Years"; both *SL*, May 16, 1968, 10.
25. Robert Tedder, "We'll Follow Letter of Law, Jersey PBA Chief Says," *SL*, May 17, 1968, 1.
26. NJSPBA, *Road to Anarchy*, ix, 13.
27. Ibid., 87–89. Copies of the Molotov cocktail flyer can be found in exhibit C42, box 13, GSCCD.
28. NJSPBA, *Road to Anarchy*, 91–97.
29. Ibid., 53–54. This is actually the number of *out-of-state* arrestees; the number of non-Newark *New Jersey* residents arrested during the uprising was actually 109. See US Attorney, District of New Jersey, "Newark Riots—July 12–17, 1967: Analysis of Arrest Reports," exhibit C66, box 13, GSCCD.
30. NJSPBA, *Road to Anarchy*, 88, 127–128.
31. Ibid., 129–130.
32. Ibid., 67.
33. Ibid., 12–14, 92, 124–126.
34. "Target of Snipers," *NEN*, July 14, 1967, 3.
35. Farrell, Novellino, and Leo Standora, "Police Battle Snipers," *SL*, July 15, 1967, 1.
36. David Berliner, "7 More Slain in Riots," *NEN*, July 15, 1967, 1.
37. Carroll, "Curfew Imposed on City; Sniper Slays Policeman," *NYT*, July 15, 1967, 1.
38. Ibid.; "Visits Prohibited by City Hospital," *NYT*, July 16, 1967, 54.
39. John Caufield, GSCCD hearing transcript, October 24, 1967, 65–66; Michael Hayes, "Snipers Besiege Three Firehouses," *NEN*, July 15, 1967, 4; Bigart, "Newark Riot Deaths at 21."

40. Charles McLean, GSCCD hearing transcript, November 28, 1967, 44–46.

41. William Doolittle, "Bullets Fly during Fire," *NEN*, July 15, 1967, 4.

42. See photos in *SL*, July 16, 1967, 1–3; *NEN*, July 15, 1967, 2, 5; *Life*, July 28, 1967, 24–25; *Time*, July 21, 1967, 18–19.

43. "7 More Deaths Raise Riot Toll," *NEN*, July 16, 1967, 1.

44. GSCCD hearing transcript, November 29, 1967, 12, 19–20.

45. Russell Sacket, "A Secret Meeting with the Snipers," *Life*, July 28, 1967, 27–28. On the fabrication, see Porambo, *No Cause for Indictment*, 130–131; GSCCD hearing transcript, October 2, 1967, 85–86.

46. David Kelly, GSCCD hearing transcript, September 26, 1967, 54–55; Planning and Research Office, Newark Police Department, "Chronological Summary of Newark Riots," page marked "Weapons Confiscated during Riots," folder 4, box 12, GSCCD; US Attorney, District of New Jersey, "Newark Riots—July 12–17, 1967: Analysis of Arrest Reports," exhibit C66, box 13, GSCCD.

47. State of New Jersey, Department of Defense, Operational Report, August 22, 1967, 6, exhibit C20, box 1, GSCCD; Newark Police Department, Planning and Research Office, "Chronological Summary of Newark Riots," 8, folder 4, box 12, GSCCD.

48. Hoover, "Violence in American Society," *George Washington Law Review* 36, no. 2 (December 1967), 417.

49. Berliner, "7 More Slain in Riots."

50. Farrell, Novellino, and Standora, "Police Battle Snipers"; Charles Finley, "Hospital Tends Wounded," *SL*, July 16, 1967, 19.

51. Shabazian, "Exhausted Mayor Sad at Inspection," *NEN*, July 15, 1967, 4. One policeman equated the violence with his experiences in Korea. Bruce Buck, "Riot Victims Jam into City Hospital," *NEN*, July 14, 1967, 5. An *Evening News* correspondent compared it to World War II. Warren Kennet, "Patrol Is like WWII's," *NEN*, July 16, 1967, 13.

52. See, for example, Newark Police Department, Planning and Research Office, "Chronological Summary of Newark Riots," 19.

53. Warshaw and Standora, "Guard, Troopers Pull Out," *SL*, July 18, 1967, 1.

54. Kelly, GSCCD hearing transcript, September 26, 1967, 77.

55. GSCCD hearing transcript, November 29, 1967, 62. Earlier in his testimony that same day, however, Spina provided a very different accounting of sniper activity: "There was no pattern, really. The sniping that went on made no sense at all." Ibid, 14.

56. Cantwell to Jaffe, November 9, 1967, exhibit C109; Major Olaff to Colonel Kelly, December 29, 1967, exhibit C119; both box 2, GSCCD.

57. Bigart, "Newark Riot Deaths at 21."

58. Thomas Henry, GSCCD hearing transcript, November 28, 1967, 19–20; Deputy Police Chief Redden, GSCCD hearing transcript, November 3, 1967, 89–90. Henry testified that, though forbidden by department regulations, police officials tacitly approved the use of personal firearms during the riot.

59. Novellino et al., "More Sniping, Looting," *SL*, July 16, 1967, 1.

60. These were only *some* of the deaths caused by massive retaliatory fire. See GSCCD, *Report for Action*, 138–39; Porambo, *No Cause for Indictment*, 18–23.

61. This number excludes those reportedly killed by National Guardsmen and those seemingly individually targeted by police. It is based on the reports of riot deaths in GSCCD, *Report for Action*, 138–141; Porambo, *No Cause for Indictment*, 216–219, 224–230, 239; Tom Hayden, *Rebellion in Newark: Official Violence and Ghetto Re-*

sponse (New York: Vintage Books, 1967), 74–84. The victims were Rose Abraham, Rebecca Brown, Isaac Harrison, Hattie Gainer, Rufus Hawk, Robert Martin, Cornelius Murray, and Eloise Spellman.

62. GSCCD hearing transcript, November 29, 1967, 8–12, 43–44; Arnold Kotz, Harold Hair, and John K. Scales, *Firearms, Violence, and Civil Disorders* (Menlo Park, CA: Stanford Research Institute, 1968), 9, 42; Hayden, *Rebellion in Newark*, 76.

63. NJSPBA, *Road to Anarchy*, 4–5, 40–41; emphasis in the original.

64. Ibid., 19, 138–139.

65. Ibid., 141. Donald Malafronte, the mayor's chief assistant, said that police officers were under the impression that they weren't to fire because of a long-standing administration policy of police restraint, but no formal order had ever been given. He invoked the shooting of Lester Long to explain some of this apprehension. GSCCD hearing transcript, October 27, 1967, 93–97.

66. NJSPBA, *Road to Anarchy*, 152–54.

67. Ibid., ix; emphasis in original.

68. GSCCD hearing transcript, October 30, 1967, 20–21, 95–96. Also Kuperstein, "3 Cops Resign, Brings Total to 22," *NEN*, September 10, 1967, C5. Spina kept up these themes for a while: "Spina Alarmed by Dwindling Police Force," *SL*, January 9, 1968, 13; "Spina Warns His Men: 'Shape Up,'" *SL*, January 10, 1968, 10; "Spina Concerned by Loss of Cops," *SL*, March 18, 1968, 8; Novellino, "It's a Tough Life, Spina Advises Police Graduates," *SL*, April 20, 1968, 3.

69. GSCCD hearing transcript, October 30, 1967, 22–23. For local reaction, Edward Anderson, "Police Say Curbs Make Job Harder," *NEN*, June 14, 1966, 1. The head of Newark's Fraternal Order of Police said, "They might as well take away our guns."

70. Arthur Sills, GSCCD hearing transcript, October 2, 1967, 61.

71. GSCCD hearing transcript, October 30, 1967, 23. It's not clear if Spina was including assaults made on officers during the riot or not.

72. "D'Ambola Rips Riot Commission Report," *Italian Tribune*, March 22, 1968, 1.

73. NJSPBA, *Road to Anarchy*, 34.

74. "Jersey PBA Forming Permanent Riot Panel," *SL*, May 19, 1968, 21. On the nationwide phenomenon of "arming for Armageddon," see Garry Wills, *The Second Civil War: Arming for Armageddon* (New York: New American Library, 1968).

75. Addonizio, GSCCD hearing transcript, September 29, 1967, 27; Spina deposition, January 2, 1968, 93, "Depositions Newark" folder, box 4, series 32, NACCD.

76. Young Americans for Freedom flier, folder 2, box 3, Eldridge Papers, NPL.

77. Hooper, "Gun Applications Increase," *NEN*, August 3, 1967, 6.

78. Robert Semple, "Nixon Scores Panel for 'Undue' Stress on White Racism," *NYT*, March 7, 1968, 1, quoted in NJSPBA, *Road to Anarchy*, 34–35; Martin Gershen, "Hughes Rips Nixon's 'Platitudes,'" *SL*, March 8, 1968, 1.

79. Richard Shafer, "Nixon Plays Symphony Hall," *SL*, May 18, 1968, 1.

80. Shabazian, "Police Riot Costs May Hit $800,000," *NEN*, August 10, 1967, 1; "Anti-riot Equipment Planned," *NYT*, August 11, 1967, 34.

81. GSCCD hearing transcript, November 29, 1967, 40.

82. Ibid., November 17, 1967, 159. The NPD eventually decided against the armored personnel carriers for fear of sparking resentment and because the costs of maintaining the vehicles and their crews would be too exorbitant. Shabazian, "Study Warns on Overkill," *NEN*, March 1, 1968, 1.

CHAPTER EIGHT

1. Shabazian, "Go-Ahead Given for Police Dogs," *NEN*, September 21, 1967, 1. In 1966, Calvin West became the first black person elected to a citywide office and joined Irvine Turner on the city council.

2. Leaflets, folder 10, box 8, Malcolm Talbott Papers, RUA; leaflets, exhibit C54, box 13, GSCCD.

3. Eldridge, "Shape Up or Lose Funds," *NEN*, September 22, 1967, 20; Waggoner, "Group Assails Use of Dogs," *NYT*, September 23, 1967, 14.

4. William J. Bopp, *The Police Rebellion: A Quest for Blue Power* (Springfield, IL: Thomas Books, 1971); William C. Kronholm, "Blue Power: The Threat of the Militant Policeman," *Journal of Criminal Law, Criminology, and Police Science* 63, no. 2 (1972): 294–299.

5. US Senate, Committee on the Judiciary, *Antiriot Bill—1967: Hearings, Ninetieth Congress, First Session, Part I* (Washington, DC: GPO, 1967), 267, 273. The bill was later appended to the civil rights legislation President Johnson signed the following spring.

6. Ibid., 354.

7. Kowalewski to Addonizio, June 18, 1967, reprinted in US Senate, *Antiriot Bill*, 361–362.

8. GSCCD hearing transcript, October 27, 1967, 22–24.

9. US Senate, *Antiriot Bill*, 357–358.

10. Ibid., 368.

11. Ibid., 368–369.

12. John Herbers, "McClellan Group Chosen to Make Study," *NYT*, August 2, 1967, 1.

13. Jean White, "Probers Focus on Militants," *WP*, November 2, 1967, A2; "Houston Poverty Aides Accused of Riot Role," *WP*, November 3, 1967, A2.

14. US Senate, Permanent Subcommittee on Investigations, *Riots, Civil and Criminal Disorders: Hearings before the Permanent Subcommittee on Investigations, Part VIII* (Washington, DC: GPO, 1968), 1609, 1611–1612.

15. Ibid., 1591.

16. Ibid., 1674; Kinney to Robert Donnelly, "Investigation into Possible Criminal Conspiracy during Riots of July 1967," undated [April or May 1968], 1–2, Newark Documents file, Newark Police Department Misc., NPL. Kinney provided very similar testimony to the House Un-American Activities Committee. See Peter Bernstein, "Militants Sparked Riot in Newark, Cop Testifies," *SL*, April 24, 1968, 7.

17. US Senate, *Riots, Civil and Criminal Disorders*, 1610–1623. A week later, the clerk-typist confirmed the investigators' story and said that she based the handbill's contents on the posters several people in the area board office were already making when Kennedy called. See 1719–1721.

18. Another, Harry Wheeler, schoolteacher and UCC trustee, was not invited, but was allowed to testify after he read news reports of Kinney's appearance, phoned one of the subcommittee members, and demanded to be heard. See US Senate, *Riots, Civil and Criminal Disorders*, 1763.

19. Ibid., 1722–1723, 1736.

20. For a good overview of the Chicago investigations, see David Sanford, "South Side Story," *New Republic*, July 6, 1968, 13–14.

21. "PAL in Newark Ends Poverty Tie," *NYT*, August 21, 1967, 1; C. B. Patrick and Joe Argrett to Edgar May, September 1, 1967, "Newark, NJ—Evaluation 1967" folder, box 42, Subject Files 1965–1969, Records of the Director, CAP Office, OEOR.

22. Eldridge, "Mayor Rejects Request on Precinct Command," *NEN*, January 17, 1968, 13; Eldridge, "Name in the News," *NEN*, January 21, 1968, 40.
23. "2 Police Groups Hit Review Board Plan," *NEN*, February 13, 1968, 14; "Cops Want Zizza Back," *SL*, February 20, 1968, 9; Waggoner, "Negro in Newark in Key Police Job," *NYT*, February 14, 1968, 1.
24. Addonizio to Lilley, folder 3, box 3, Eldridge Papers, NPL; "Capt. Williams Takes Command," *SL*, March 2, 1968, 1; Bigart, "Negro in Newark Police Post," *NYT*, March 2, 1968, 31; Edward D. Williams, *The First Black Captain* (New York: Vantage, 1974), 95–97.
25. Malcolm Feeley and Austin Sarat, *The Policy Dilemma: Federal Crime Policy and the Law Enforcement Assistance Administration* (Minneapolis: University of Minnesota Press, 1980); Stuart Scheingold, *The Politics of Law and Order: Street Crime and Public Policy* (New York: Longman, 1984), 83–86; Flamm, *Law and Order*.
26. Spina to Daniel L. Skoler, August 1, 1967, New Jersey folder 2 of 2, box 4, General Correspondence, 1965–1968, LEAA.
27. Frank Addonizio et al. to Johnson, telegram, April 18, 1968; Courtney Evans to Addonizio et al., May 29, 1968; both New Jersey folder 1 of 2, box 4, General Correspondence, 1965–1968, LEAA.
28. B. Douglas Harman, "The Bloc Grant: Readings from a First Experiment," *Public Administration Review* 30, no. 2 (March–April 1970): 141–153; Murakawa, *The First Civil Right*, 86–87.
29. See rankings in US House of Representatives Subcommittee No. 5, *Law Enforcement Assistance Amendments* (Washington, DC: GPO, 1970), 5.
30. Hughes, speech at regional SLEPA conference, November 13, 1968, reprinted in SLEPA, *A Plan for Law Enforcement and the Administration of Justice in New Jersey* (Trenton, June 23, 1969), 28–29, NJSL.
31. Harman, "The Bloc Grant," 142.
32. Flamm, *Law and Order*, 132–134. See also William Cahill (Hughes's successor), in US House of Representatives Subcommittee No. 5, *Law Enforcement Assistance Amendments* (Washington, DC: GPO, 1970), 230–231.
33. List of advisory council members in US Senate, Subcommittee on Criminal Laws and Procedures, *Federal Assistance to Law Enforcement* (Washington, DC: GPO, 1970), 700.
34. SLEPA, *A Plan for Law Enforcement*, 71–73.
35. US Senate, Subcommittee on Criminal Laws and Procedures, *Federal Assistance to Law Enforcement* (Washington, DC: GPO, 1970), 699–700; "1969 Local Action Grant Awards," *Justice* (SLEPA newsletter) 2, no. 1 (January 1970), 3, NJSL.
36. SLEPA, *1970 Guide for Action Grants* (May 15, 1970), 3–4, NJSL.
37. Charles Unkovic, foreword to Bopp, *The Police Rebellion*, vii.
38. Seymour Martin Lipset, "Why Cops Hate Liberals—and Vice Versa," in Bopp, *The Police Rebellion*, 23–39; Hans Toch, "Cops and Blacks: Warring Minorities," *Nation*, April 21, 1969, 491; Dennis Deslippe, "'Do Whites Have Rights?': White Detroit Policemen and 'Reverse Discrimination' Protests in the 1970s," *Journal of American History* 91, no. 3 (December 2004): 932–960.
39. A. James Reichley, "The Way to Cool the Police Rebellion," *Fortune* 78 (December 1968): 113; Unkovic, foreword to Bopp, *The Police Rebellion*, 30–32.
40. See "City of Newark—Riot Area" map, exhibit C32, box 13, GSCCD; Redden, GSCCD hearing transcript, October 31, 1967, 88.
41. Paul Goldberger, "Tony Imperiale Stands Vigilant for Law and Order," *NYT Maga-*

zine, September 29, 1968, 30–31, 117–122; Ronald Gasparinetti, interview by author, March 17, 2006. One local journalist claimed that, according to his federal dossier, Imperiale had applied to be a policeman thirteen times. Porambo, *No Cause for Indictment*, 198.

42. Walter Afflitto, interview by author, August 30, 2005; Vincent Testa, interview by author, August 4, 2005; Arleen Sachs, "Law and Order Axis," *NEN*, October 9, 1968, 38.

43. Detective Junious T. Hedgespeth to Lieutenant Rocco Ferrante, Newark Police Department memo, July 17, 1967, exhibit C72, box 14, GSCCD.

44. Detective Rothlein to Chief Kelly, NPD memo, undated [August 1967], exhibit C72, box 14, GSCCD.

45. Police trainees to Director Spina, NPD administrative submission, September 11, 1967, exhibit C72, box 14, GSCCD.

46. Shabazian, "Police Funds Voted at Stormy Meeting," *NEN*, September 7, 1967, 9; "15 in Protest at City Hall," *NEN*, September 10, 1967, 21.

47. Typescript, exhibit C72, box 14, GSCCD. The officer's name is not given in the typescript. But I believe, based on the content of the speech and a mention of testifying before a government panel, that it was once again Kowalewski.

48. Ibid.

49. Shabazian, "Go-Ahead Given for Police Dogs," *NEN*, September 21, 1967, 1. Mayor Addonizio later told the Governor's Commission that this meeting was the first time he had ever seen so many white citizens come to city hall. GSCCD hearing transcript, September 29, 1967, 126–127.

50. Shabazian, "Council Reverses, Rejects K-9 Plan." For more on the response to the clergy, see GSCCD hearing transcript, November 20, 1967, 42–43; LALO leaflet, exhibit C72, box 14, GSCCD, which reads, in part, "The clergy of Newark are asking us to turn thy cheek to the other side and love thy enemy. Would you like your policeman to turn his head the other way while your wife and daughter are being raped?"

51. LALO, Petition for Canine Corps, exhibit C26, box 13, GSCCD. The issue dragged on into the spring of 1968, when the city council finally put an end to it by decisively rejecting a canine unit, with only Frank Addonizio and Lee Bernstein dissenting. The decision was booed by a crowd of NWCC members, led by Imperiale. Ladley Pearson, "City Says No to K-9 Corps," *NEN*, April 4, 1968, 15.

52. "Imperiale Raps Report on Riot," *NEN*, February 14, 1968, 17; Porambo, *No Cause for Indictment*, 199; photo, *SL*, April 25, 1968, 18.

53. ACLU flier, "Newark Disorders—Summer 1967 & Immediate Aftermath" folder, box 2, Debevoise personal papers. The NLSP took a lot of heat over this flier, but, it turned out, the ACLU had referred to NLSP without the organization's consent. See New Jersey Bar Association, Committee on Law and Poverty, "Report on Investigation of Allegations of Participation by Legal Service Systems in the Newark and Plainfield Riots," *New Jersey Law Journal* 40, no. 51 (December 21, 1967): 10; Eldridge, "Lawyers Absolved of Riot Charges," *NEN*, December 8, 1967, 11.

54. Complaint, "Drafts & Data RE Kidd v. Addonizio," folder, box 2, Debevoise personal papers; Thomas Johnson, "Suit Bids US Run Police in Newark," *NYT*, August 25, 1967, 1. The suit was dismissed in 1972. Mary Jo Patterson, *On the Frontlines of Freedom: A Chronicle of the First 50 Years of the American Civil Liberties Union of New Jersey* (Newark: ACLU of New Jersey, 2012), 30–31.

55. "WORLD Honor Spina and Imperiale," *Italian Tribune*, May 30, 1969, 6; "WORLD to Honor Imperiale and Spina," *Italian Tribune*, May 16, 1969, 16.

56. Gerald Somerville, "Picket Charges Assault against ACLU Head," *NEN*, April 21, 1968, 21; "ACLU Aide Seized in Newark," *NYT*, April 21, 1968, 78; Goldberger, "Tony Imperiale Stands Vigilant," 123; John de J. Pemberton to ACLU Leadership, April 25, 1968, "Paramilitary" folder, box 2, Debevoise personal papers. Di Suvero was acquitted of all charges in November 1968. See ACLU of New Jersey, *Civil Liberties Reporter* 4, no. 9 (December 1968): 1; "Acquittal Won by di Suvero," *NEN*, November 26, 1968, 1.
57. Sidney Zion, "Newark Police Accused in Suit," *NYT*, April 27, 1968, 25; Pemberton to ACLU leadership, April 25, 1968. Not coincidentally, the Grand Dragon of the New Jersey Klan claimed he had inducted Imperiale into the order in April 1967. Imperiale repeatedly denied it, saying he had met with the Grand Dragon only to discuss giving the Klan karate lessons. Though he offered them a special group rate, the deal fell through. See Sullivan, "Newark's White Citizen Patrol," *NYT*, June 24, 1968, 23.
58. Waggoner, "Hughes Asks Ban on Vigilantes," *NYT*, May 16, 1968, 43; "Bill Aims at Imperiale Organization," *NEN*, May 21, 1968, 16; "Senate Approves Anti-Vigilante Bill," *NEN*, June 25, 1968, 16.
59. Novellino, "Extremist Groups Ruled Out for Cops," *SL*, May 18, 1968, 3; "PBA Defies Spina," *SL*, May 28, 1968, 11.
60. "Law Asked to Combat Vigilantes," *NEN*, June 23, 1968, 25.
61. "Senate Approves Anti-Vigilante Bill," *NEN*, June 25, 1968, 16; ACLU of NJ, *Civil Liberties Reporter* 5, no. 9 (December 1970): 9.
62. Shabazian, "Imperiale Will End Patrols," *NEN*, June 24, 1968, 1.
63. "Petitions Ask a Return to Newark's Old Charter," *SL*, May 16, 1968, 11.
64. "Richardson Calls Charter Change a 'Racist Attempt,'" *SL*, May 17, 1968, 13.
65. "3,825 Names Cut from Petitions," *SL*, May 21, 1968, 11; "6,104 Signatures Cut from Petition," *SL*, May 23, 1968, 17.
66. See results in *SL*, August 14, 1968, 16.
67. "Newark's Moderate Message," *NYT*, August 17, 1968, 26.
68. Robert Ruth, "Bombings Probed," *NEN*, August 26, 1968, 1.
69. "Petition Filed by Imperiale," *NEN*, August 27, 1968, 17.
70. Carroll, "Imperiale Files Petitions for Newark City Council," *NYT*, August 27, 1968, 18.
71. Shabazian, "Imperiale, Giuliano Victors," *NEN*, November 6, 1968, 1.
72. "Imperiale Praises Negro Moderates," *NEN*, November 11, 1968, 29; "Imperiale Invites Ties with Negroes," *NYT*, November 11, 1968, 23.
73. Higgins, "Citizen Patrols Set to Keep City Peace," *NEN*, May 20, 1969, 1; Higgins, "Peace Patrol Calms City," *NEN*, May 21, 1969, 1.
74. Waggoner, "Curfew in Newark Lifted by Mayor," *NYT*, May 22, 1969, 40.

CHAPTER NINE

1. Sample charges against Wright: NACCD hearing transcript, August 9, 1967, 232. Against Hayden: GSCCD hearing transcript, October 23, 1967, 23–25.
2. "Negro Spokesman," *NYT*, July 22, 1967, 11; John Winslow, "Riot in Their Hearts," *Suburban Life*, September 1967, 38, 44, 60–61; GSCCD hearing transcript, October 24, 1967, 4–5. Wright sometimes traced his thinking back to Booker T. Washington very explicitly. Wright, "Thinking Prosperity," "Writings Unpublished—Semi-Monthly Summaries, Legislative Alert, Black Empowerment, Other, 1981–82" folder; Wright "The Dignity of Work," "Writings—Published *Monitor* Articles" folder; both box 3, NWP.

3. Wright interview footage in *You Don't Have to Ride Jim Crow*, DVD, directed by Robin Washington (1995; Wombat Media home video, 2007); Bayard Rustin, "We Challenged Jim Crow," in *Time on Two Crosses: The Collected Writings of Bayard Rustin*, ed. Devon W. Carbado and Donald Weise (San Francisco: Cleis, 2003), 20–21.

4. Untitled booklet; Boston Committee on Racial Equality, "A Note About Discrimination in Greater Boston Hotels," undated [November 1949]; untitled, undated typescript detailing hotel visits; *CORE Newsletter*, October 1949, 1, and March 1950, 1; all series 3, reel 8, folder 9, CORE Papers (microfilm edition).

5. Handwritten statement attached to letter, Wright to Farrakhan, March 11, 1999, "Family/Personal" folder, box 1, NWP; Robin Washington, "Rights Pioneer's Life Spanned Freedom Ride, Black Power," *Duluth News Tribune*, March 12, 2005, accessed December 4, 2008, http://www.robinwashington.com/jimcrow/articlegroup.html.

6. For some early examples of his developing thinking on black empowerment, see Wright, *The Riddle of Life and Other Sermons* (Boston: Bruce Humphries, 1952), preface and 17; Wright, *The Song of Mary* (Boston: Bruce Humphries, 1958), 38, 45, 48.

7. On liturgical renewal, see especially Wright, *One Bread, One Body* (Greenwich, CT: Seabury Press, 1962).

8. Wright, "An Approach to an Urban Ministry," *Christianity Today* 7, no. 18 (June 7, 1963): 26–28.

9. "Three-Alarm Fire Damages Church in Newark," *NYT*, December 21, 1964, 39; Leslie Laughlin, phone interview by author, September 16, 2008. Reverend Laughlin was dean at Trinity at the time.

10. Wright, "A Proposal to Develop a Coordinated Community Organization for Development," undated [November 1966], box 2R604, James and Lula Peterson Farmer Papers, Center for American History, Austin, Texas.

11. Wright, "Black Power: Are Negroes Ready, Willing, and Able?," printed in *Baptist* 3, no. 3 (1967), copy in Writing—Publications 2 of 2 folder, box 4, NWP; "Black Power Seen in Two Shadings," *NYT*, July 23, 1966, 9.

12. Wright, *Black Power and Urban Unrest: Creative Possibilities* (New York: Hawthorn Books, 1967), 1, 3, 24, 59, 30, 174.

13. See the slightly differing versions and pieces of this story in Dr. Calvin Rolark to Chairperson, Committee on Nominations for Distinguished Professorship, December 8, 1971, "Autobiographical" folder, box 1, NWP; clipping, *Bergen Sunday Record*, June 12, 1983, "About Nathan Wright" folder, box 1, NWP; Eldridge, "Stark, Spina Give OK to Black Power Conference," *NEN*, July 13, 1967, 7; Wright, GSCCD hearing transcript, October 24, 1967, 25.

14. Robert S. Browne to Jewell Mazique, May 20, 1967; Mazique to Wright, May 8, 1967; Bill of Particulars, undated [Spring 1967]; all "National Conference on Black Power, 1966, April–May 1967" folder, box 18, Robert S. Browne Papers, SCNYPL.

15. Wright, "The Specific Expression of Black Power," "Writings Published Re Black Power" folder; Wright, "A Better Way," undated [May or June 1967], "Writings, Speeches, Addresses, and Papers (3 of 4)" folder; both box 3, NWP.

16. Minutes, Black Power Continuations Committee, April 1, 1967, "National Conference on Black Power, 1966, April–May 1967" folder, box 18, Browne Papers, SCNYPL.

17. Albert Camus, *The Plague* (New York: Knopf, 1948), 5. For Camus's influence on Hayden, see Hayden, *Reunion*, 76–77, 95.

18. Hayden, *Reunion*, 9–19. Such personal alienation—from family, from politics, from

work, from power—would become a major motivation and intellectual theme for the New Left more broadly. In this, their intellectual forbears were many, but one could do worse than begin with C. Wright Mills and Herbert Marcuse, both of whom held deep meaning for Hayden. See Hayden, *Reunion*, 14, 77–81.

19. Ibid., 39–40.
20. Ibid., 66; Tim Findley, "Tom Hayden: The Rolling Stone Interview," *Rolling Stone*, October 26, 1972, 42.
21. Hayden, *Reunion*, 73.
22. Hayden, *The Port Huron Statement*, 51.
23. Hayden, *The Port Huron Statement*, 53; on Mills and SDS, Miller, *Democracy Is In the Streets*, 78–91.
24. Hayden in Frost, *"An Interracial Movement of the Poor,"* 8.
25. Hayden, *Reunion*, 123.
26. Wright, *Ready to Riot*, 1–4, 25, 42–43.
27. Ibid., 3–4.
28. Hayden, *Reunion*, 151–152. The lawyer was Leonard Weinglass, who would later represent Hayden during the Chicago Eight conspiracy trial.
29. Hayden, *Reunion*, 157; Findley, "Tom Hayden," 46.
30. GSCCD hearing transcript, October 17, 1967, 42–45; Hayden, *Reunion*, 157–159; Miller, *Democracy Is in the Streets*, 407n35.
31. Hayden, "The Occupation of Newark," *New York Review of Books* 9, no. 3 (August 24, 1967): 18–19, 22; Miller, *Democracy Is In the Streets*, 276. Citing this issue's cover, Tom Wolfe later called the journal "the chief theoretical organ of Radical Chic." Wolfe, *Radical Chic and Mau-Mauing the Flak Catchers* (New York: Farrar, Strauss and Giroux, 1970), 74.
32. "Black Power Meetings Will Be Held," *SL*, July 18, 1967, 5; Eldridge, "Riots Top Agenda of Negro Parley," *NEN*, July 19, 1967, 4; Leland Stark to members of the Newark diocese, July 28, 1967, folder 6, box 8, Trinity Cathedral Records, NJHS.
33. Eldridge, "Riots Top Agenda"; Leland Stark, letter, July 28, 1967.
34. Chuck Stone, "The National Conference on Black Power," in *The Black Power Revolt: A Collection of Essays*, ed. Floyd Barbour (Boston: P. Sargent, 1968), 189–190; "400 Due at Parley," *NEN*, July 20, 1967, 1. Others, however, were not so enthusiastic. See the letters to Bishop Leland Stark, who supported the conference, folders 6 through 8, box 8, Trinity Cathedral Records, NJHS.
35. Carroll, "Threats Change Meeting's Plans," *NYT*, July 20, 1967, 28.
36. Registration form, folder 10, box 8, Trinity Cathedral Records, NJHS; Wright, GSCCD hearing transcript, October 24, 1967, 26.
37. "Conference on Black Power Opens," *NEN*, July 21, 1967, 1.
38. Stone, "The National Conference on Black Power," 191–192.
39. Quoted in Alfred Duckett, "Special Black Power Report," 6, folder 11, box 8, Trinity Cathedral Records, NJHS.
40. "Conference on Black Power Opens," *NEN*, July 21, 1967, 1; Stone, "The National Conference on Black Power," 193; GSCCD hearing transcript, October 24, 1967, 27; workshop schedule attached to "A Better Way," folder 9, box 8, Trinity Cathedral Records, NJHS.
41. Press release, July 13, 1967, 2, folder 10, box 8, Trinity Cathedral Records, NJHS.
42. "Still Much More to Be Done," *NYT*, July 23, 1967, 131.
43. "Black Phoenix," *NYT*, July 22, 1967, 24.
44. "Conference on Black Power Opens," *NEN*, July 21, 1967, 1.

45. "Picket Injured," *NEN*, July 22, 1967, 2; Thomas Johnson, "McKissick Holds End of Violence Up to Whites," *NYT*, July 22, 1967, 11.

46. Johnson, "Negroes Disrupt Newark Parley," *NYT*, July 23, 1967, 18; "Black Power Delegates Chase White Newsmen," *SL*, July 23, 1967, 1; "Melee Ends Press Parley," *NEN*, July 23, 1967, 1; "Black Power Leaders Call for a 'Separate Nationhood,'" *NJAA*, July 29, 1967, 2. Another version of Kenyatta's "confession" can be found in Library of Congress, Legislative Reference Service, vol. 3, *Subversive, Extremist and Black Nationalist Organizations*, 1, "Exhibit #3" folder, box 1, series 2, NACCD.

47. L. H. Stanton to *NJAA*, August 5, 1967, 4. The delegates officially passed only one resolution, a two-page "Black Power Manifesto," which recognized the colonized status of black people throughout the world and called on delegates to organize regional conferences on black power, with an eye toward the eventual establishment of an International Black Congress. "Black Power Manifesto and Resolutions," folder 14, box 8, Trinity Cathedral Records, NJHS; Wright to conference participants, undated [July–August 1967], 2, folder 11, box 8, Trinity Cathedral Records, NJHS; Stone, "The National Conference on Black Power," 193, 195.

48. "Black Power Manifesto and Resolutions," 25.

49. "Black Power Leaders Call for a 'Separate Nationhood,'" *NJAA*, July 29, 1967, 1; Rudy Johnson, "Separate Negro State Asked," *NEN*, July 24, 1967, 1; Richard Prince, "Black Power Delegates May Seek Separate State," *SL*, July 24, 1967, 1.

50. "Solves Nothing," *NEN*, July 25, 1967, 18; Ralph Matthews, "The Black Power Conf. Adults Playing Kids Games," *NJAA*, August 5, 1967, 20.

51. "Black Racism," *NYT*, July 24, 1967, 25.

52. "Rule of Law," *NYT*, July 25, 1967, 34.

53. Wright to conference participants, undated, folder 11, box 8, Trinity Cathedral Records, NJHS; GSCCD hearing transcript, October 24, 1967, 28.

54. "Book Editors Finish Summer," *NYT*, December 21, 1967, 34.

55. Wright, *Ready to Riot*, 13.

56. Quote from ibid., 4. In a review of the book for the *New York Times*, J. Anthony Lukas remarked on the shock value of the front image, especially when compared with the book's contents, which he deemed "pallid and harmless." Lukas, "Intended to Shock," *NYT Book Review*, June 16, 1968, 10.

57. Hayden, *Rebellion in Newark*, 4.

58. Ibid., 3–4.

59. Hayden, *Reunion*, 175–176; Betty Moss, interview by author, February 2, 2006; Carol Glassman, interview by author, September 21, 2005; Eric Mann, interview by author, March 7, 2006; Mary Hershberger, *Traveling to Vietnam: American Peace Activists and the War* (Syracuse, NY: Syracuse University Press, 1998), 37.

60. Fred P. Graham, "3 on Hanoi Mission Could Face Court," *NYT*, December 29, 1965, 3; John Corry, "Yale Professor Is Visiting Hanoi," *NYT*, December 28, 1965, 1; Staughton Lynd and Tom Hayden, *The Other Side* (New York: Signet, 1966), 56–58.

61. Lynd and Hayden, *The Other Side*, 191–192, 199–204.

62. Ibid., 16–18, 59–62, 65, 72–74.

63. Aptheker, *Mission to Hanoi* (New York: International, 1966).

64. Lynd and Hayden, *The Other Side*, 150–153.

65. Flier, "Newark Ex. N" folder, box 2, series 33, NACCD; Findley, "Tom Hayden," 46; "Hayden's Report on Vietnam Trip," *National Guardian*, January 29, 1966, 6–7; "A Visit to Hanoi," *National Guardian*, February 5, 1966, 7; Hayden, "Report from the North," *New Left Notes* 1, no. 1 (January 21, 1966): 1.

66. Hayden, preface to Aptheker, *Mission to Hanoi*, 8–9.

67. Lynd and Hayden, *The Other Side*, 168–170. James Miller places this conundrum at the center of his analysis of Hayden ("a moralist in search of power") in *Democracy Is in the Streets*, 260–313.

68. Hayden, *Rebellion*, 4.

69. "Negro Spokesman," *NYT*, July 22, 1967, 11; "Racial Ties Urged by Black Militant," *NYT*, February 9, 1969, 63; "Urban Affairs Expert Named to Professorship," *NYT*, April 25, 1969, 93; Wright, *Let's Work Together* (New York: Hawthorn Books, 1968), 166, 208.

70. The Johnson administration quickly regrouped, however, and offered its own housing bill, which included Percy's key tenet of subsidizing mortgages for lower-income buyers. Percy voted for the administration's bill in May 1968, and Johnson signed the Housing and Urban Development Act that August. See John Finney, "$5 Billion on Housing Voted by Senate," *NYT*, May 29, 1968, 1; Zelizer, *The Fierce Urgency of Now*, 296–297.

71. John McClaughry, "Selling Opportunity," *Reason*, March 1999, copy in "Biographical" folder, box 1, NWP; McClaughry to Wright, July 8, 1997; Paul Fargis to Wright, May 27, 1969; both "Publishing—Publications Correspondence" folder, box 3, NWP.

72. *Congressional Record* 114, no. 199 (December 6, 1967), S18016–S18018, copy in "Senate Investigation" folder, box 2, NWP. On similarities in Great Society and conservative discourse, see Gareth Davies, *From Opportunity to Entitlement: The Transformation and Decline of Great Society Liberalism* (Lawrence: University Press of Kansas, 2006), 10–16.

73. "Nixon Would Use Force in the Cities," *NYT*, March 8, 1968, 23.

74. Scholarship on Nixon often assigns to him a pragmatic attempt to balance two main goals: the creation of equal opportunity for self-advancement and the attempt to keep both moderates and conservatives in the Republican Party. See Paul Frymer and John David Skrentny, "Coalition-Building and the Politics of Electoral Capture during the Nixon Administration: African Americans, Labor, Latinos," *Studies in American Political Development* 12, no. 1 (1998): 138–139; Dean J. Kotlowski, *Nixon's Civil Rights: Politics, Principle, and Policy* (Cambridge, MA: Harvard University Press, 2001); A. James Reichley, *Conservatives in an Age of Change: The Nixon and Ford Administrations* (Washington, DC: Brookings Institution, 1981), 53–54.

75. "Nixon Urges Black Ownership," *NYT*, April 26, 1968, 27. See also Robert E. Weems Jr. and Lewis A. Randolph, "The Ideological Origins of Richard M. Nixon's 'Black Capitalism' Initiative," *Review of Black Political Economy* 29, no. 1 (2001): 53–57; Dean Kotlowski, "Black Power—Nixon Style: The Nixon Administration and Minority Business Enterprise," *Business History Review* 72, no. 3 (Autumn 1998): 409–445.

76. Robert Semple, "Nixon Is Reported to Pledge Gains in Negro Benefits," *NYT*, January 14, 1969, 1.

77. Wright, "The Ethics of Power in the Black Revolution," in *The Black Man in America: Integration and Separation*, ed. James Allen Moss (New York: Dell, 1971), 18; Wright, *Let's Work Together*, 54.

78. Bahrenburg, "Controversial Hayden Would Aid in Release of More GI Captives," *NEN*, November 21, 1967, 12; Eldridge, "New Book on Riots Contends White Hate Stirred Negroes," *NEN*, September 21, 1967, 24.

79. "Foe Hands 3 GIs to Antiwar Group," *NYT*, November 11, 1967, 6; Neil Sheehan, "No Brainwashing of 3 POWs Seen," *NYT*, November 18, 1967, 1; Hayden, *Reunion*, 206–239.

80. Miller, *Democracy Is In the Streets*, 283–299; Hayden, *Reunion*, 165–166; Hoffmann, "The New Left Turns to Mood of Violence in Place of Protest," *NYT*, May 7, 1967, 1; Jerry Flint, "Students Debate New Left Tactics," *NYT*, July 3, 1967.

81. GSCCD hearing transcript, December 8, 1967, 46–47.

82. Jack Newfield, *Robert Kennedy: A Memoir* (New York: Dutton, 1969), 134–135; Hayden, *Reunion*, 166–167.

83. Findley, "Tom Hayden," 48.

84. Hayden, *Reunion*, 271, 64–69.

85. Hayden, *Rebellion in Newark*, 70–71; Hayden, *Reunion*, 165–166.

86. Findley, "Tom Hayden," 42.

87. Bahrenburg, "Hayden Quits City," *NEN*, May 21, 1968, 1.

88. Wright, "Why the Party of Lincoln?," *Fact Sheet* 1, no. 1 (June 1979), "Writings—Publications 1 of 2" folder, box 4; newspaper clipping, Reagan, "Sound Investment in Life of the Nation," *Columbia Missourian*, August 13 or 15, 1979, "Autobiographical" folder, box 1; letters and telegram, Reagan to Wright, February 6, 1981, March 13, 1981, May 22, 1981, "Correspondence" folder, Box 1; all NWP; Lee A. Daniels, "The New Black Conservatives," *NYT Magazine*, October 4, 1981. Christopher Alan Bracey uses "modern black conservatism" to distinguish this new generation from "traditional black conservatism." See Bracey, *Saviors or Sellouts: The Promise and Peril of Black Conservatism, from Booker T. Washington to Condoleezza Rice* (Boston: Beacon, 2008).

CHAPTER TEN

1. Joe Argrett to Edgar May, July 13, 1967, "Civil Rights—Newark—UCC 1967" folder, box 37, Subject Files 1965–1969, Records of the Director, CAP Office, OEOR.

2. Ron Thomson to Shirley Jones, July 20, 1967, "Civil Rights—Newark—UCC 1967" folder, box 37, Subject Files 1965–1969, Records of the Director, CAP Office, OEOR.

3. Gregory Farrell to Shriver, telegram, July 19, 1967, "Civil Rights—Newark—Riot 1967, 1 of 2" folder, box 36, Subject Files 1965–1969, Records of the Director, CAP Office, OEOR; "LSPs Play Crucial Role in Riots," *Law in Action* 2, no. 5 (August 1967), in OEO folder, box 31, General Correspondence 1965–1968, Office of Law Enforcement Assistance, LEAA; "Play It Cool!" flier, folder 2, box 3, Eldridge Papers, NPL; Dickinson Debevoise, "Report to the GSCCD," October 3, 1967, exhibit 138, box 9, series 2, NACCD.

4. Thomson to Jones.

5. Argrett to May, cover sheet.

6. Spina to Johnson et al., telegram, May 25, 1967, exhibit CC, series 33, NACCD.

7. Senate Subcommittee on Employment, Manpower, and Poverty, *Examination of the War on Poverty*, part 10 (Washington, D.C.: GPO, 1967), 3270–3272; "Newark Warning to OEO Cited," *WP*, July 19, 1967, A3.

8. UPI dispatches, July 18, 1967, "Congressional Relations—folder 2," box 20, subject file, 1964–1972, Office of Planning, Research, and Evaluations, OEOR.

9. Guy Savino, "Links Riots to Aid," *NEN*, July 20, 1967, 6; James Cusick, "N. Carolina Congressman Tours City," *NEN*, July 21, 1967, 5.

10. House Committee on Education and Labor, *Economic Opportunity Act Amendments of 1967*, part 4 (Washington, D.C.: GPO, 1967), 3419–3421, 3477–3481.

11. Marjorie Hunter, "House GOP Bloc Offers a Substitute Poverty Plan," *NYT*, April 11, 1967, 1; House Committee on Education and Labor, *Economic Opportunity Act Amendments of 1967*, 3467, 3561.

12. House Committee on Education and Labor, *Economic Opportunity Act Amendments of 1967*, 3560; Cohen and Taylor, *American Pharaoh*, 318–320. The director of Chicago's machine-controlled poverty program had cochaired Pucinski's reelection campaign.

13. House Committee on Education and Labor, *Economic Opportunity Act Amendments of 1967*, 3569, 3577–3578; Gerald Grant, "Oregon's Rep. Green—Pivotal Democrat," *WP*, June 15, 1967, F6.

14. Jean White, "Marking Up of Poverty Bill Is a Rare Public Spectacle," *WP*, October 30, 1967, A1; Joseph Loftus, "Antipoverty Bill Derided in House," *NYT*, November 8, 1967, 20; John Farmer, "Poverty Bill Passes Test," *NEN*, November 15, 1967, 1.

15. Loftus, "2-Year Extension of Poverty Drive Gains in Congress," *NYT*, December 6, 1967, 1; Sar Levitan, "Is OEO Here to Stay?," *Poverty and Human Resources Abstracts* 3, no. 2 (March–April 1968).

16. Ron Thomson to Shirley Jones, July 20, 1967; Walter Waggoner, "Shriver Will Act in Newark Crisis," *NYT*, July 21, 1967, 1.

17. Still to Shriver, telegram, July 21, 1967, "Civil Rights—Newark—UCC 1967" folder, box 37, Subject Files 1965–1969, Records of the Director, CAP Office, OEOR.

18. Everett Crawford to Theodore Berry, August 25, 1967, "Newark, NJ—Evaluation 1967" folder, box 42, Subject Files 1965–1969, Records of the Director, CAP Office, OEOR. See similar findings in "Report of A. Donald Bourgeois re On-Site Visit to Newark, NJ," undated, "Newark, NJ—Evaluation 1967" folder; C. B. Patrick et al. to Edgar May, October 6, 1967, "Newark, NJ—Miscellaneous 1967" folder; both box 42, Subject Files 1965–1969, Records of the Director, CAP Office, OEOR.

19. Crawford to Berry, August 25, 1967.

20. "Little Headway Seen in Antipoverty Rifts," *NEN*, August 17, 1967, 25; memorandum to Berry, September 5, 1967, "Newark, NJ—Consultant Team Reports 1967" folder, box 42, Subject Files 1965–1969, Records of the Director, CAP Office, OEOR.

21. Eldridge, "UCC Starts Major Reorganization Plan," *NEN*, September 10, 1967, 2; minutes of the Committee on Reorganization, September 12, 1967, "Newark, NJ—Consultant Team Reports 1967" folder, box 42, Subject Files 1965–1969, Records of the Director, CAP Office, OEOR.

22. Eldridge, "Shape Up or Lose Funds," *NEN*, September 22, 1967, 20; Waggoner, "Group Assails Use of Dogs," *NYT*, September 23, 1967, 14.

23. "$1.9 Million for UCC, Must Still Revamp," *SL*, September 29, 1967, 4. See also Report of OEO Team, September 30, 1967; Larrie Stalks to Theodore Berry, October 16, 1967; report of Subcommittee on UCC Finances, October 17, 1967; all "Newark, NJ—Consultant Team Reports 1967" folder, box 42, Subject Files 1965–1969, Records of the Director, CAP Office, OEOR.

24. Eldridge, "UCC Trustees Vote Top Post to Odom," *NEN*, October 20, 1967, 4.

25. Malafronte, GSCCD hearing transcript, October 27, 1967, 73–74.

26. Sale, *SDS*, 223; John McMillian, *Smoking Typewriters: The Sixties Underground Press and the Rise of Alternative Media in America* (New York: Oxford University Press, 2011), 13–30; James Sullivan, *On the Walls and in the Streets: American Poetry Broadsides from the 1960s* (Champaign: University of Illinois Press, 1997).

27. OEO, *Workbook: Community Action*, 42.

28. Detective Junious T. Hedgespeth to Captain Rocco Ferrante, August 16, 1967, exhibit C54, box 13, GSCCD. On the social significance of this White Castle restaurant, Bob Curvin, interview by author, August 17, 2005.

29. "Black Survival" fliers, exhibit C54, box 13, GSCCD.

30. Grand jury presentment, NLSP response, and sworn statement of Junius Williams, June 4, 1968, all in "Reply to Presentment, Master Copies—Supporting Data" folder, box 3, Debevoise personal papers; GSCCD hearing transcript, November 17, 1967, 18; Williams, *Unfinished Agenda*,156–158.
31. "Investigation into Possible Criminal Conspiracy During Riots," 46–54, NPD Miscellaneous folder, Newark Documents Collection, NPL; House Committee on Education and Labor, *Economic Opportunity Act Amendments of 1967*, part 4, 3561.
32. AP news release, "Newark Patrol," August 1, 1967, "Civil Rights—Riots 1967 Folder 2 of 2," box 37, Subject Files 1965–1969, Records of the Director, CAP Office, OEOR.
33. OEO press release, August 1, 1967, "Riots—July Aug. 1967" folder, box 5, General Records Relating to Public Reaction to OEO Programs, 1965–71, Office of Public Affairs, OEOR.
34. Threat reported: Argrett, minutes of UCC executive committee, August 3, 1967, "Civil Rights—Riots 1967 Folder 2 of 2," box 37, Subject Files 1965–1969, Records of the Director, CAP Office, OEOR. Threat denied: Sullivan, "Poverty Aid Fight in Newark Wanes," *NYT*, August 18, 1967, 19. James H. Heller to Shriver, August 10, 1967, "Civil Rights—Newark—United Community Corporation 1967" folder, box 37, Subject Files 1965–1969, Records of the Director, CAP Office, OEOR.
35. UCC statement, attached to Argrett, meeting minutes of UCC executive committee, August 3, 1967.
36. Rudy Johnson, "Wright Retained on UCC's Board," *NEN*, August 4, 1967, 6. The dispute went one more round before being resolved. Eldridge, "OEO Is Pressing UCC Suspensions," *NEN*, August 10, 1967, 6; *UCC News* 1, no. 4 (August 11, 1967): 2, "Newark Ex. V," box 3, series 33, NACCD; "UCC Seeks Shriver's Aid," *NEN*, August 11, 1967, 5.
37. UAAA handbills, exhibit C54, box 13, GSCCD.
38. Argrett, memorandum, August 18, 1967, "Newark, NJ—Evaluation 1967" folder, box 42, Subject Files 1965–1969, Records of the Director, CAP Office, OEOR; Eldridge, "UCC Splits in Asking Riot Amnesty," *NEN*, August 18, 1967, 19.
39. Ronald Sullivan, "Poverty Aid Fight Wanes," *NYT*, August 18, 1967, 19.
40. Richard Prince, "UCC Refuses to Suspend Wright," *SL*, August 18, 1967, 1.
41. Louis Lomax, "Newark Called a Hub for Black Revolutionaries," *SL*, August 27, 1967, 1; Haywood Perry to Milan Miskovsky, November 21, 1967; IRS assistant commissioner to Miskovsky, January 10, 1968; both "Weapons" folder, series 20, NACCD.
42. Eldridge, "New Book on Riots," *NEN*, September 21, 1967, 24; Guy Savino, "Freed Prisoners Hailed by Pacifists," *NEN*, November 14, 1967, 6.
43. "Quiet Halloween Cited by Wright," *NEN*, November 2, 1967, 13.
44. Johnston, "UCC to Deal with Discontent," *SL*, February 14, 1968, 16.
45. Eldridge, "UCC Splits in Asking Riot Amnesty," *NEN*, August 18, 1967, 19.
46. "NJ Tour Triumphal," *NEN*, April 5, 1968, 4; Waggoner, "Shift in Position Is Hinted by King," *NYT*, March 28, 1968, 40; Komozi Woodard, *A Nation within a Nation: Amiri Baraka (LeRoi Jones) and Black Power Politics* (Chapel Hill: University of North Carolina Press, 1999), 94.
47. Shabazian, "Addonizio Hails Lack of Friction," *NEN*, April 6, 1968, 1.
48. Gerald Somerville, "Mayor Lauds Teenagers," *NEN*, April 7, 1968, 19.
49. Somerville, "Teen Aid Keeping City Calm," *NEN*, April 6, 1968, 3.
50. Eldridge, "Negroes, Whites in Tribute," *NEN*, April 8, 1968, 1; emphasis added.

51. Michael Hayes, "Tributes Planned for King," *NEN*, April 8, 1968, 5; "UCC and City Pursue Peace," *NEN*, April 9, 1968, 4

52. See Fred J. Cook, "Newark's 'Responsible Militants' Say: 'It's Our City, Don't Destroy It,'" *NYT Magazine*, June 30, 1968, 11.

53. Ladley Pearson, "Arsonists Strike in Central Ward"; Baglivo, "Addonizio's Long Night"; both *NEN*, April 10, 1968, 1.

54. Shabazian, "Group Lauds Mayor," *NEN*, April 12, 1968, 1.

55. Baglivo, "Addonizio's Long Night"; Pearson, "Arsonists Strike in Central Ward."

56. "UCC Youth Patrols Try to Cool Crisis," *NEN*, April 10, 1968, 6; Baglivo, "Addonizio's Long Night."

57. Somerville, "Central Ward Asks: Why Our Homes?," *NEN*, April 10, 1968, 8; Berliner, "195 Fires Hit City, Most Seen Arson," *NEN*, April 10, 1968, 10; Somerville, "Agencies Providing Shelter, Food," *NEN*, April 11, 1968, 12; "Relief Agencies Assist Homeless," *NEN*, April 12, 1968, 4; Cook, "Newark's 'Responsible Militants,'" 11.

58. Shabazian, "Community Efforts Lessen City Trouble," *NEN*, April 11, 1968, 1.

59. Cook, "Newark's 'Responsible Militants,'" 11.

60. "Avenging What's-His-Name," *Time*, April 19, 1968, 16.

61. On the formation of HUD and Model Cities: John B. Willmann, *The Department of Housing and Urban Development* (New York: Praeger, 1967), 21–40, 108–109; Charles M. Haar, *Between the Idea and the Reality: A Study in the Origin, Fate and Legacy of the Model Cities Program* (Boston: Little, Brown, 1975), 3–56; Frieden and Kaplan, *The Politics of Neglect*, 35–66; Wendell E. Pritchett, *Robert Clifton Weaver and the American City: The Life and Times of an Urban Reformer* (Chicago: University of Chicago Press, 2008), 262–286.

62. US Senate, Committee on Government Operations, Subcommittee on Executive Reorganization, *Federal Role in Urban Affairs* (Washington, DC: Government Printing Office, 1966–1968), Part II, 392–395, Part I, 34–39, Part III, 577, 636; Lichtenstein, *Walter Reuther*, 402–403.

63. NACCD hearing transcript, August 22, 1967, 616–617; Malafronte interview by author, June 6, 2006.

64. "Med School Plan Pushed," *NEN*, November 22, 1967, 8.

65. "Negroes in Newark Protest Renewal," *NYT*, November 28, 1967, 35; "Medical College in Newark Fought," *NYT*, December 21, 1967, 44; Williams, *Unfinished Agenda*, 163–179.

66. Waggoner, "College Cuts Size of Site in Newark," *NYT*, December 24, 1967, 39.

67. Robert C. Wood and Wilbur Cohen to Hughes, January 10, 1968, folder 4, box 4, Malcolm Talbott Papers, RUA; Waggoner, "Hughes Disputed on Newark Plan," *NYT*, January 16, 1968, 44.

68. Hearing on Medical School Site transcript, February 17, 1968, 83, 91–92, George F. Smith Library of the Health Sciences, Rutgers Biomedical and Health Sciences, Newark.

69. "Agreements Reached between Community and Government Negotiators Regarding New Jersey College of Medicine and Dentistry and Related Matters," April 30, 1968, 1–9, NPL. The American Medical Association reportedly derided such public interference in health care matters. See Luther Carter, "Negroes Demand and Get Voice in Medical School Plans," *Science* 160, no. 3825 (April 19, 1968): 292.

70. "Agreements Reached between Community and Government Negotiators," 9.

71. See results in *SL*, August 14, 1968, 16. On Matos, see Business and Industrial Coordinating Council, *Skill Escalation and Employment Development* (Newark, 1968), 72.

72. Jean Joyce, "Medical School Contracts Delayed," *NEN*, May 8, 1968, 19; New Jersey College of Medicine and Dentistry, *Progress since the Community-State Agreement* (Jersey City, 1968), 5–7, NJSL; Eldridge, "State Hit for Failing to Abide by Med School Hiring Accord," *NEN*, January 11, 1969, 5.

73. OEO press release, "Summary of Yankelovich, Inc., Study on Effects of Sections 210 and 211 of 1967 Amendments to the Economic Opportunity Act," March 27, 1969, Green Amendment folder, box 2, Office of Public Affairs, General Records Relating to Public Reaction to OEO Programs, 1965–71, OEOR. See also David Rosenbaum, "Poverty Report Allays '67 Fears," *NYT*, March 28, 1969, 30.

74. Berry oral history transcript, March 15, 1969, 7–8, LBJL.

75. "UCC, Addonizio Agree Agency Will Keep Reins," *SL*, February 20, 1968, 9; "Poverty Reins Stay Loose in Newark," *SL*, April 18, 1968, 14.

76. Robert Ruth, "UCC Finishes Reorganization," *NEN*, June 21, 1968, 20.

77. "Timothy Still Dies at 48," *SL*, July 15, 1968, 1.

78. Ernest Johnston, "The People, the Leaders Pay Final Respects to Still," *SL*, July 19, 1968, 1.

79. "Militants Find Power in System," *NJAA*, May 4, 1968, 12.

80. "Hutchings Reveals SNCC Link with Black Panthers," *NEN*, June 24, 1968, 8; Clayborne Carson, *In Struggle: SNCC and the Black Awakening of the 1960s* (Cambridge, MA: Harvard University Press, 1981), 290–291.

81. Amiri Baraka, *The Autobiography of LeRoi Jones / Amiri Baraka* (New York: Freundlich Books, 1984), 267–268, 272; Woodard, *A Nation within a Nation*, 88–89.

82. Kenneth Gibson, remarks to the Newark History Society, May 5, 2014. On Pinckney, "City Hospital Employees Fear Loss of Rights," *NEN*, June 28, 1968, 31; Somerville, "Blacks Name Slate," *NEN*, June 24, 1968, 1. On Tucker, Eldridge, "Blacks Vow to Control City Hall," *NEN*, November 17, 1969, 1. On Harris, GSCCD hearing transcript, December 8, 1967, 133; "Report of A. Donald Bourgeois re On-Site Visit to Newark, NJ," undated, "Newark, NJ—Evaluation 1967" folder, box 42, Subject Files 1965–1969, Records of the Director, CAP Office, OEOR. On Wheeler, House Committee on Education and Labor, *Economic Opportunity Act Amendments of 1967*, part 4, 3541–3546. On Ward, Tyson, *2 Years before the Riot*, 66. On Williams, *Unfinished Agenda*, 114–119.

83. Woodard, *A Nation within a Nation*, 64–5.

84. Alphonso Pinckney and Roger Woock, *Poverty and Politics in Harlem: Report on Project Uplift 1965* (New Haven, CT: College and University Press, 1970), 93, 108–110; Baraka, *The Autobiography of LeRoi Jones / Amiri Baraka*, 211–213.

85. Emanuel Perlmutter, "Separatists Get HARYOU-ACT Jobs," *NYT*, September 14, 1965, 26.

86. OEO press release, undated, quoting Shriver's statement of September 15, 1965, and various letters of complaint, "New York City (HARYOU-ACT), New York" folder, box 20, Records Relating to the Administration of the Civil Rights Program in the Regions, 1965–66, Region 1—New York, Records of the Office of the Director, OEOR.

87. Quoted in Levitan, *The Great Society's Poor Law*, 87.

88. "Shriver Prodded by Fino," *NYT*, December 29, 1965, 15; Alfred Friendly, "Powell Says His Study Clears Antipoverty Program," *NYT*, February 28, 1966, 11.

89. OEO press release, undated, "Black Arts Theater" folder, box 1, General Records Relating to Public Reaction to OEO Programs, 1965–71, Office of Public Affairs, OEOR.

90. House Subcommittee on the War on Poverty Program, *1966 Amendments to the Economic Opportunity Act of 1964* (Washington, DC: GPO, 1966), 148.

91. Baraka, *The Autobiography of LeRoi Jones / Amiri Baraka*, 214–15, 232.

92. Ibid., 253–254; Woodard, *A Nation within a Nation*, 70.

93. Baraka, *The Autobiography of LeRoi Jones / Amiri Baraka*, 243–244.

94. Ibid., 262; Porambo, *No Cause for Indictment*, 34–35.

95. Edgar May to Sargent Shriver, August 31, 1967, "Civil Rights, 1967" folder, box 18, Office of Planning, Research and Evaluation, Subject File, 1964–1972, OEOR.

96. Frank Ferro to Still, telegram, July 31, 1967, "Civil Rights—Riots 1967 Folder 2 of 2," box 37, Subject Files 1965–1969, Records of the Director, CAP Office, OEOR; *UCC News* 1, no. 4 (August 11, 1967), "Newark Ex. V" folder, box 3, series 33, NACCD; minutes, UCC board of trustees, August 18, 1967, 4, "Newark, NJ— Evaluation 1967" folder, box 42, Subject Files 1965–1969, Records of the Director, CAP Office, OEOR.

97. Exhibit C50, box 13, GSCCD; Odom, "Incident Concerning Reproduction of an Unauthorized Flier," November 8, 1967, "Newark, NJ—Evaluation 1967" folder, box 42, Subject Files 1965–1969, Records of the Director, CAP Office, OEOR.

98. GSCCD hearing transcript, November 27, 1967, 129–131; "Addonizio Asks Report on Jones' School Job," *SL*, February 7, 1968, 23.

99. Ernest Johnston, "LeRoi Named to Panel Working for Med School," *SL*, February 29, 1968, 15; Johnston, "Record Turnout in Model Cities Vote," *SL*, August 14, 1968, 1.

100. Attendance lists, Committee on Community Tensions, April 30, 1968, folder 1, box 1, Talbott Papers, RUA; Michael Kaufman, "Jones Asks Votes, Not Rioting," *NYT*, April 14, 1968, 60.

101. GSCCD hearing transcript, November 27, 1967, 123–25.

102. Ruth, "Blacks Open Parley," *NEN*, June 22, 1968, 3; Gerald Fraser, "Newark Negroes Meet on Election," *NYT*, June 22, 1968, 28.

103. See Curvin, "The Persistent Minority," 68–69; Woodard, *A Nation within a Nation*, 112.

104. The pledge was printed in *NEN*, November 14, 1969, 10.

105. Eldridge, "Negroes, Puerto Ricans Applaud Political Unity," *NEN*, November 13, 1969, 3.

106. There were some limits to this black unity, however, and not everyone chose to attend the convention. Willie Wright had launched his own, very similar, attempt to empower the community to choose its own candidates. See "To Take Hand in City Race," *NEN*, November 13, 1968, 1. Two other potential mayoral candidates, George Richardson and Harry Wheeler, both announced their intent to skip the convention and run for mayor without its backing. See Eldridge, "Convention Expected to Nominate Gibson," *NEN*, November 14, 1969, 10; Woodard, *A Nation within a Nation*, 140–141.

107. Eldridge, "Negroes, Puerto Ricans Applaud Political Unity."

108. Eldridge, "Blacks Vow to Control City Hall," *NEN*, November 17, 1969, 1. The one candidate without any ties to the UCC was Rev. Dennis Westbrooks (Central Ward), who had moved to Newark in June 1967, the month before the riot. Alvin Oliver (East Ward) was the director of community development for the UCC. Sharpe James (South Ward) was former chairman of Area Board 9. In addition to Pinckney (who had, since the previous convention, been elected a UCC trustee; see Eldridge, "Militants Take Over Chaotic UCC Session," *NEN*, June 20, 1969) and Tucker, the at-large council candidates were Earl Harris, a coordinator for the UCC, and Ra-

mon Añeses, chairman of the Field Orientation Center for Underprivileged Spanish (FOCUS), a UCC delegate agency.

CONCLUSION

1. Eldridge, "Gibson's Triumph Years in the Making," *NEN*, June 17, 1970, 1.

2. For good overviews, see George Amick, "The Mayor and the Mob," *New Jersey: Magazine of Public Issues*, February 1976, 13–19; "Sketches of Others Indicted in Newark," *NYT*, December 18, 1969, 54.

3. Waggoner, "Newark Votes Tomorrow," *NYT*, June 15, 1970, 1.

4. James J. Vanecko, *Community Organization Efforts, Political and Institutional Change, and the Diffusion of Change Produced by Community Action Programs* (Chicago: National Opinion Research Center, University of Chicago, 1970), 227–230.

5. Levitan, *The Great Society's Poor Law*, 88.

6. Moynihan, *Maximum Feasible Misunderstanding*, 129.

7. One notable exception was the attention paid by the Governor's Commission on Civil Disorder, which heard testimony from two Puerto Rican Newarkers and included in its report a special section on the "growth and problems of the Spanish-speaking community." It concluded that "the rising needs of Spanish-speaking people are being neglected as we grapple with the more massive pressures from the Negro population." GSCCD, *Report for Action*, 100–101. In this, the Governor's Commission acted with more thoughtfulness and foresight than its presidential counterpart, which included only two mentions of "Spanish-surname" groups. NACCD, *Report*, 2, 33.

8. "Report Outlining the Special Requirements of the Spanish-American Community," folder 19, box 2, Eldridge Papers, NPL; Eldridge, "Funds Sought for Agency to Help Spanish-Speaking," *NEN*, July 5, 1966, 25.

9. "Little Headway Seen in Antipoverty Rifts," *NEN*, August 17, 1967, 25; *Información* news clipping, April 1973, Antipoverty Programs—UCC vertical file, NPL; *Crusader*, January 1968, folder 14, box 2, Eldridge Papers, NPL; "Poverty Cuts Worry Newark Spanish Unit," *SL*, March 24, 1968, 25.

10. Louis Turco, press release, and "Demands of the Spanish Speaking Community of Newark to the UCC," both folder 9, box 1, Eldridge Papers, NPL; Eldridge, "Militants Take Over Chaotic UCC Session," *NEN*, June 20, 1969; Eldridge, "UCC Pledge Ends Sit-In," *NEN*, July 18, 1969, 1.

11. Eldridge, "Militants Take Over"; Eldridge, "West Wins UCC Vote," *NEN*, August 22, 1969.

12. Hilda Hidalgo, *The Puerto Ricans in Newark, NJ* (Newark: Aspira, 1971), 26–28.

13. For early manifestations of those tensions, see Pedro Linares, "Latin Americans in Newark Seek More Public Aid," *SL*, November 8, 1970, 34; Linares, "Añeses Backs Complaint on City Hall Language Gap," *SL*, June 22, 1971, 13; "Newark Rights Chief Urges Hiring More Puerto Ricans," *SL*, July 23, 1972.

14. Fox Butterfield, "Newark's New Minority, the Italians, Demands Equity," *NYT*, August 28, 1971, 27; David Shipler, "The White Niggers of Newark," *Harper's*, August 1972, 77–83.

15. David Halbfinger, "Anthony Imperiale Dies," *NYT*, December 28, 1999, B9; Sullivan, "Gibson Wins Reelection," *NYT*, May 15, 1971, 1.

16. Butterfield, "Newark's New Minority"; Butterfield, "Gibson Is Widely Regarded as Successful in Restoring Integrity," *NYT*, October 3, 1971, 73; Brian Hohmann, "Adubato Agonistes: Stephen Adubato, White Ethnicity, and the Reconstruction of Public

Selfhood" (MA thesis, Rutgers University–Newark, 2010). At the national level, allegations of white exclusion from OEO programs were voiced most stridently by the Ethnic Foundation in Washington, DC. See "Ethnic Foundation" folder, box 3, Office of Research and Evaluation, Office Files of Thomas Glennan, OEOR.

17. "Imperiale Takes Issue," *Italian Tribune*, August 27, 1971.

18. H. Paul Friesema, "Black Control of Central Cities: A Hollow Prize," *Journal of the American Institute of Planners* 35, no. 2 (1969): 75–79.

19. See, for example, Fred Cook, "Mayor Kenneth Gibson Says . . . ," *NYT Magazine*, July 25, 1971, 7; Arthur M. Louis, "The Worst American City," *Harper's*, January 1975, 67–71.

20. "Newark May Be First in Bankruptcy," *NJAA*, September 12, 1970, 1; Ronald Sullivan, "Gibson Goes to Assembly Floor to Plead for Bill on Newark Aid," *NYT*, December 8, 1970, 53; Sullivan, "Cahill Criticizes US Fiscal Goals," *NYT*, December 24, 1970, 41.

21. "LeRoi Jones, Part I," *Guardian*, March 23, 1968, 3.

22. Eldridge, "UCC Post to Barrett," *NEN*, July 17, 1970, 1. See also Sullivan, "Gain in Power by LeRoi Jones Shown in Newark Poverty Vote," *NYT*, June 19, 1971, 1; Lawrence Hall, "UCC Chief Promises to Build a Pioneering Image," *SL*, June 21, 1970, 31; Woodard, *A Nation within a Nation*, 223–24.

23. Baraka, "Newark Seven Years Later: ¡Unidad y Lucha!" *Monthly Review* 26, no. 8 (January 1975): 17.

24. Alan Brinkley, *Liberalism and Its Discontents* (Cambridge, MA: Harvard University Press, 1998), x; David L. Chappell, "The Triumph of Conservatives in a Liberal Age," in *A Companion to Post-1945 America*, ed. Jean-Christophe Agnew and Roy Rosenzweig (Oxford: Blackwell, 2002), 303–304.

25. Lily Geismer, *Don't Blame Us: Suburban Liberals and the Transformation of the Democratic Party* (Princeton, NJ: Princeton University Press, 2015).

26. On Model Cities under Gibson, who appointed Junius Williams to head the program, see Williams, *Unfinished Agenda*, 245–270.

27. Nixon, "Special Message to the Congress on the Nation's Antipoverty Programs," February 19, 1969, 112–116; "Statement on Proposals Concerning the Office of Economic Opportunity," June 2, 1969, 424–425; "Statement on the Office of Economic Opportunity," August 11, 1969, 654–658; all in *Public Papers of the Presidents: Richard Nixon, 1969* (Washington, DC: GPO, 1971).

28. Rowland Evans and Robert Novak, *Nixon in the White House: The Frustration of Power* (New York: Random House, 1971), 115–120; Bradley Graham, *By His Own Rules: The Ambitions, Successes, and Ultimate Failures of Donald Rumsfeld* (New York: Public Affairs, 2009), 76–78; John Osborne, "The President and the Poor," *New Republic* 160, no. 21 (May 24, 1969): 16–18.

29. Google yields innumerable blog posts and essays on Nixon as a liberal. See also John C. Whitaker, "Nixon's Domestic Policy: Both Liberal and Bold in Retrospect," *Presidential Studies Quarterly* 26, no. 1 (Winter 1996): 131–153.

30. Rumsfeld, *Known and Unknown: A Memoir* (New York: Sentinel, 2011), 119–120.

31. David Shribman, "Death Comes to a Federal Agency," *NYT*, September 19, 1981, 7.

32. A useful history is Marcia Bok, "The Current Status of Community Action Agencies in Connecticut," *Social Service Review* 62, no. 3 (September 1988): 396–398.

33. Timothy Conlan, *From New Federalism to Devolution: Twenty-Five Years of Intergovernmental Reform* (Washington, DC: Brookings Institution, 1998), 153–160. Of course, Newark and other cities have also received federal funds through Community De-

velopment Block Grants (CDBGs), which were created in 1974. On CDBGs, see Michael T. Rich, "Targeting Federal Grants: The Community Development Experience, 1950–1986," *Publius* 21, no. 1 (1991): 29–49. CDBGs and other more recent development policies, like HUD's Empowerment Zone / Enterprise Community program, indeed have participatory mandates, but citizens are restricted to an advisory role. See: HUD, *Citizen Participation in the CDBG: A Guidebook* (Washington, DC: 1978), 1–3; City of Newark, *2010–2015 HUD Consolidated Plan* (Newark, 2010), 3.9–3.10; Daniel Schulgasser, "Making Something Out of Almost Nothing: Social Capital Development in Newark, New Jersey's, Enterprise Community," *National Civic Review* 88, no. 4 (1999): 342.

34. Lawrence Hall, "Speakers Praise and Damn the Great Society," *SL*, October 5, 1981.
35. Community Economic Opportunity Act of 2014, HR 3854, section 672(2)(f).
36. For examples, Gary Thomas, "Antipoverty Group Probed," *SL*, August 14, 1977, 21; Robert Rudolph, "Ex-Poverty Chief Gets Six-Year Prison Term," *SL*, December 13, 1978; Stanley Terrell, "Antipoverty Group Will Lose Funding," *SL*, February 4, 1979, 38.
37. "US to Aid 8 Cities in Fight on Crime," *NYT*, January 14, 1972, 21; Richard Johnston, "Newark Crime Foe Quits," *NYT*, November 22, 1972, NJ74.
38. Woodard, *A Nation within a Nation*, 230–43; "Baraka and Gibson at Odds over Newark Foes," *Jet*, September 6, 1973, 31; Curvin, *Inside Newark*, 170–175.
39. Baraka, "Newark Seven Years Later"; Baraka, *The Autobiography of LeRoi Jones / Amiri Baraka*, 304–305.
40. "Police review board" vertical file, NPL; Paul von Zeilbauer, "Newark Strategist Moves to Checkmate Crime," *NYT*, September 21, 2008, NJ1; Curvin, *Inside Newark*, 242–250.
41. Kathe Newman, "Newark, Decline and Avoidance, Renaissance and Desire: From Disinvestment to Reinvestment," *Annals of the American Academy of Political and Social Science* 594 (July 2004): 34–48; Newman and Robert W. Lake, "Democracy, Bureaucracy, and Difference in US Community Development Politics since 1968," *Progress in Human Geography* 30, no. 1 (2006): 44–61.
42. James Barron, "A Livable City? Newark. Yes, Newark," *NYT*, June 18, 1991, B1; Curvin, *Inside Newark*, 186–208; Dan O'Flaherty, "Newark's Non-Renaissance and Beyond," jagiellonia.econ.columbia.edu/~b02/newark/newark.pdf.
43. Tara Nurin, "Assembly Supports Conditional Veto of Economic Opportunity Act," njspotlight.com, September 10, 2013; Matt Friedman, "Christie Signs Bill to Expand Corporate Tax Breaks in NJ," *SL*, September 18, 2013; Jon Whiten, *New Jersey's Surge in Business Tax Subsidies Reaches New Heights* (Trenton: New Jersey Policy Perspective, 2014), 7–9.
44. Castells, *The City and the Grassroots: A Cross-Cultural Theory of Urban Social Movements* (Berkeley: University of California Press, 1983), 71–72. For a thoughtful case study of the limitations and possibilities of community development strategies, see Guian McKee's account of the Philadelphia Industrial Development Corporation in *The Problem of Jobs: Liberalism, Race, and Deindustrialization in Philadelphia* (Chicago: University of Chicago Press, 2008).
45. Johnston, "Hughes, Other Dignitaries to Attend Still Rites," *SL*, July 17, 1968, 12.
46. Rabig, "Broken Deal: Devolution, Development, and Civil Society in Newark, 1960–1990" (PhD diss., University of Pennsylvania, 2007), 302–342.
47. William Linder, "An Urban Community Development Model" (PhD diss., Fordham University, 1988), 118, 110; Linder, interview by author, October 14, 2009; "Poverty War Assailed by Man Who Helps Run It," *SL*, March 24, 1968, 30.

48. Rabig, "Broken Deal," 328–330; Tyson, *2 Years before the Riot*, 73, 100, 106. On the NCC's subsequent decades of work, see Community Development Studio, *Building Community: The Work of the New Community Corporation* (New Brunswick, NJ: Edward J. Bloustein School of Planning and Public Policy, 2002).

49. Rabig, "Broken Deal," 257–276; Rebecca (Andrade) Doggett interview by author, January 19, 2010; Doggett, correspondence with author, June 27, 2015; Ernest Thompson and Mindy Thompson, *Homeboy Came to Orange: A Story of People's Power* (New York: Author's Choice, 2008), 167–175; Tyson, *2 Years before the Riot*, 73.

50. Glassman interview, September 21, 2005.

51. David Gerwin, transcript of interview with Winans, September 24, 1995, 13–24, Derek Winans Papers, folder 11, box 1, NJHS; Nancy Zak, interview by author, January 28, 2010; Bob Cartwright, correspondence with author, March 25, 2015.

52. Ernest Johnson, "'We the People Ticket Gains Board 9 Control," March 15, 1968, 8; Sharpe James, *Political Prisoner: You Can Be Indicted, Arrested, Convicted and Sent to Prison without Committing a Crime; A Memoir* (Newark: Nutany, 2013), 113–114; Curvin, *Inside Newark*, 186–208; O'Flaherty, "Newark's Non-Renaissance and Beyond."

53. Dan Ivers, "Newark Police Unions Say Civilian Review Board Plans Would Violate State Law," *SL*, January 21, 2015; Ivers, "With Stroke of a Pen, Long-Awaited Civilian Review Board Becomes Reality in Newark," *SL*, April 20, 2015; City of Newark, *State of the City 2015 Report* (March 2015), 4, 9. Executive order available at http://www.ci.newark.nj.us/government/mayor/newark-civilian-complaint-review-board/.

INDEX

Commission, 127–31, 14–43, 148–49, 325n15, 327n55
Jones, LeRoi. *See* Baraka, Amiri
Joseph, Harlan, 176–77
Junior Crime Fighters, 103, 168
juvenile delinquency, 18–19

Karenga, Ron, *233*, 274
Kelly, David, 160–62, 190
Kennedy, Eunice, 18
Kennedy, James, 204–5
Kennedy, John F., 1, 15–16, 27
Kennedy, Robert, 17–19, 22–24, 26–27, 99, 244, 265
Kenyatta, Charles, 235
Kerner Commission. *See* National Advisory Commission on Civil Disorders
Kerner, Otto, 130, 131, 148, 149
Keyserling, Leon, 15
Kidd, Marion, 74–76, 217, *248*
Kidd v. Addonizio, 217
Killingsworth, Mary, 176–77
King, Enez, 162–64
King, Martin Luther, Jr., 150–51, 158, 332n13; assassination of, 175, 261; visit to Newark, 260–61
Kinney, Charles, 183, 203–4
Knowles, John, 17
Kowalewski, Leonard, 201–2, 214–15
Ku Klux Klan, 54, 341n57

Labor-Negro Vanguard Conference, 40
last-hurrah thesis, 46
Law Enforcement Assistance Act, 111
Law Enforcement Assistance Administration, 287
Leuchter, Ben, 155
Levitan, Sar, 280
liberalism, 6–9, 25, 90, 160, 285; and black power, 304n21. *See also* growth liberalism
Lilley Commission. *See* Governor's Select Commission on Civil Disorder
Lilley, Robert, 155, 169, 332n8
Linder, William, 289
Lindsay, John, 131, 265; and King assassination, 151; and Kerner Commission, 130, 144–46, 148–49; visit to Newark, 136–38, 326n30

Lofton, Oliver, 134, 267, 290; and GSCCD, 155, 162, 166, 332n8, 332n13; and Newark riots, 121, 158
Long, Lester, 80–82, 105–6, 337n65
Lowenstein, Alan, 5, 38, 94
Lowenstein, Roger, 4, 38
Loyal Americans for Law and Order (LALO), 213–16, 340n50
Lynd, Staughton, 238–39

Malafronte, Donald, 113, 165–66, 265–66
Malcolm X, 225
March on Washington (1963), 30
Marshall, Burke, 229
Martinez, Henry, 80–82
Matos, Zain, 268, 281
maximum feasible participation, 29, 37–38, 287, 317n50; creation of, 26; dismantling of, 51–52, 59–62, 269; in Newark, 44, 62, 80, 89–90
Mayor's Commission on Group Relations, 6, 53, 96, 98–99
McCarthy, William, 181
McClain, Wyla, 74, 75, 79
McClellan, John, 201–5
McCollum, Betty, 287
McCray, Charles, 274, 326n42
McCulloch, William, 130, 141, 145
Means, Fred, 79, 81, 82, 84, 86–87
medical school fight, 63–64, 84–90, 166, 266–68
Melchior, Kenneth, 118–23, 183
Mennonite Board of Missions and Charities, 149
Meyner, Robert, 155
Millard, William, 201
Mills, C. Wright, 229, 342n18
mimeography, 32, 187, 204, 215, 255–58, 259, 274
Miranda v. Arizona, 113, 194
Mississippi Freedom Democratic Party, 42
Mobilization for Youth (MFY), 20–21, 29–34, 36
Mobilization of Mothers (MOM), 30–31, 33, 308n62, 309n74
Model Cities Program, 139, 160, 221, 265–68
Model Neighborhood Council, 221, 268, 275

Wright, Willie, 289, 326n42, 351n106; and King assassination, 261, 262–63; and medical school fight, 89; and UCC, 57–58, 60, 258–60

Wynn, Barry, 274

Xerox Corporation, 149

Yarmolinsky, Adam, 26, 33, 132, 307n44, 307n46

Ylvisaker, Paul, 208; accusations against, 182–83; and GSCCD, 160–61; and Kerner Commission, 132, 133–35, 329n78

Young Americans for Freedom, 195–96

Young, Whitney, 150

Zizza, Charles, 206, 260

HISTORICAL STUDIES OF URBAN AMERICA

Edited by Lilia Fernández, Timothy J. Gilfoyle, Becky M. Nicolaides,
and Amanda Seligman

James R. Grossman, editor emeritus

Series titles, continued from frontmatter:

Crucibles of Black Empowerment: Chicago's Neighborhood Politics from the New Deal to
Harold Washington
by Jeffrey Helgeson

The Streets of San Francisco: Policing and the Creation of a Cosmopolitan Liberal Politics,
1950–1972
by Christopher Lowen Agee

Harlem: The Unmaking of a Ghetto
by Camilo José Vergara

Planning the Home Front: Building Bombers and Communities at Willow Run
by Sarah Jo Peterson

Purging the Poorest: Public Housing and the Design Politics of Twice-Cleared Communities
by Lawrence J. Vale

Brown in the Windy City: Mexicans and Puerto Ricans in Postwar Chicago
by Lilia Fernández

Building a Market: The Rise of the Home Improvement Industry, 1914–1960
by Richard Harris

Segregation: A Global History of Divided Cities
by Carl H. Nightingale

Sundays at Sinai: A Jewish Congregation in Chicago
by Tobias Brinkmann

In the Watches of the Night: Life in the Nocturnal City, 1820–1930
by Peter C. Baldwin

Miss Cutler and the Case of the Resurrected Horse: Social Work and the Story of Poverty in
America, Australia, and Britain
by Mark Peel

The Transatlantic Collapse of Urban Renewal: Postwar Urbanism from New York to Berlin
by Christopher Klemek

I've Got to Make My Livin': Black Women's Sex Work in Turn-of-the-Century Chicago
by Cynthia M. Blair

Puerto Rican Citizen: History and Political Identity in Twentieth-Century New York City
by Lorrin Thomas

Staying Italian: Urban Change and Ethnic Life in Postwar Toronto and Philadelphia
by Jordan Stanger-Ross

New York Undercover: Private Surveillance in the Progressive Era
by Jennifer Fronc

African American Urban History since World War II
edited by Kenneth L. Kusmer and Joe W. Trotter

Blueprint for Disaster: The Unraveling of Chicago Public Housing
by D. Bradford Hunt

Alien Neighbors, Foreign Friends: Asian Americans, Housing, and the Transformation of Urban California
by Charlotte Brooks

The Problem of Jobs: Liberalism, Race, and Deindustrialization in Philadelphia
by Guian A. McKee

Chicago Made: Factory Networks in the Industrial Metropolis
by Robert Lewis

The Flash Press: Sporting Male Weeklies in 1840s New York
by Patricia Cline Cohen, Timothy J. Gilfoyle, and Helen Lefkowitz Horowitz
in association with the American Antiquarian Society

Slumming: Sexual and Racial Encounters in American Nightlife, 1885–1940
by Chad Heap

Colored Property: State Policy and White Racial Politics in Suburban America
by David M. P. Freund

Selling the Race: Culture, Community, and Black Chicago, 1940–1955
by Adam Green

The New Suburban History
edited by Kevin M. Kruse and Thomas J. Sugrue

Millennium Park: Creating a Chicago Landmark
by Timothy J. Gilfoyle

City of American Dreams: A History of Home Ownership and Housing Reform in Chicago, 1871–1919
by Margaret Garb

Chicagoland: City and Suburbs in the Railroad Age
by Ann Durkin Keating

The Elusive Ideal: Equal Educational Opportunity and the Federal Role in Boston's Public Schools, 1950–1985
by Adam R. Nelson

Block by Block: Neighborhoods and Public Policy on Chicago's West Side
by Amanda I. Seligman

Downtown America: A History of the Place and the People Who Made It
by Alison Isenberg

Places of Their Own: African American Suburbanization in the Twentieth Century
by Andrew Wiese

Building the South Side: Urban Space and Civic Culture in Chicago, 1890–1919
by Robin F. Bachin

In the Shadow of Slavery: African Americans in New York City, 1626–1863
by Leslie M. Harris

My Blue Heaven: Life and Politics in the Working-Class Suburbs of Los Angeles, 1920–1965
by Becky M. Nicolaides

Brownsville, Brooklyn: Blacks, Jews, and the Changing Face of the Ghetto
by Wendell Pritchett

The Creative Destruction of Manhattan, 1900–1940
by Max Page

Streets, Railroads, and the Great Strike of 1877
by David O. Stowell

Faces along the Bar: Lore and Order in the Workingman's Saloon, 1870–1920
by Madelon Powers

Making the Second Ghetto: Race and Housing in Chicago, 1940–1960
by Arnold R. Hirsch

Smoldering City: Chicagoans and the Great Fire, 1871–1874
by Karen Sawislak

Modern Housing for America: Policy Struggles in the New Deal Era
by Gail Radford

Parish Boundaries: The Catholic Encounter with Race in the Twentieth-Century Urban North
by John T. McGreevy